DOUBLE

02

**AYAKO
NODA**

TABLE OF CONTENTS

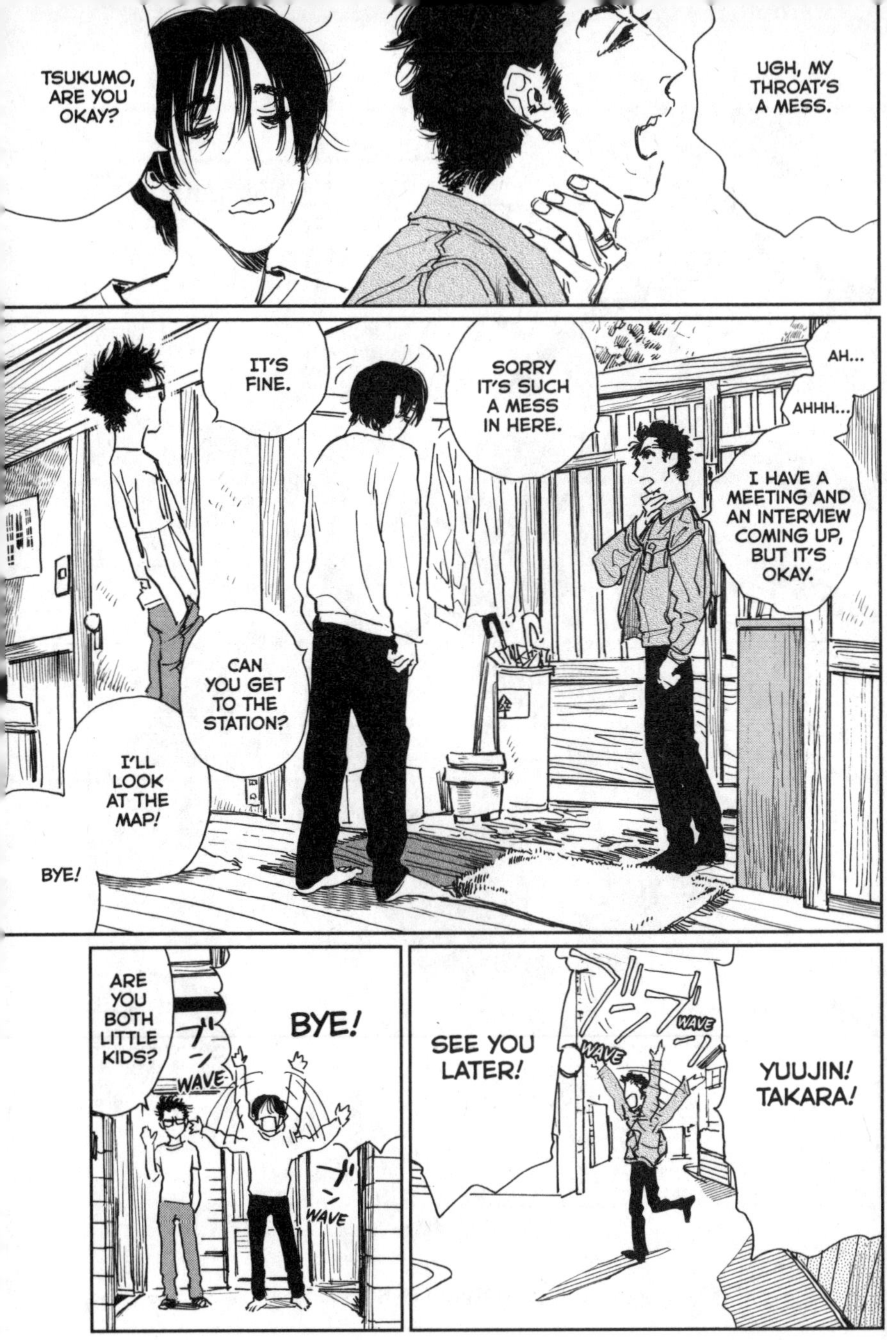
UGH, MY THROAT'S A MESS.
TSUKUMO, ARE YOU OKAY?
AH...
AHHH...
I HAVE A MEETING AND AN INTERVIEW COMING UP, BUT IT'S OKAY.
SORRY IT'S SUCH A MESS IN HERE.
IT'S FINE.
CAN YOU GET TO THE STATION?
I'LL LOOK AT THE MAP!
BYE!
YUUJIN! TAKARA!
WAVE
WAVE
SEE YOU LATER!
BYE!
ARE YOU BOTH LITTLE KIDS?
WAVE
WAVE

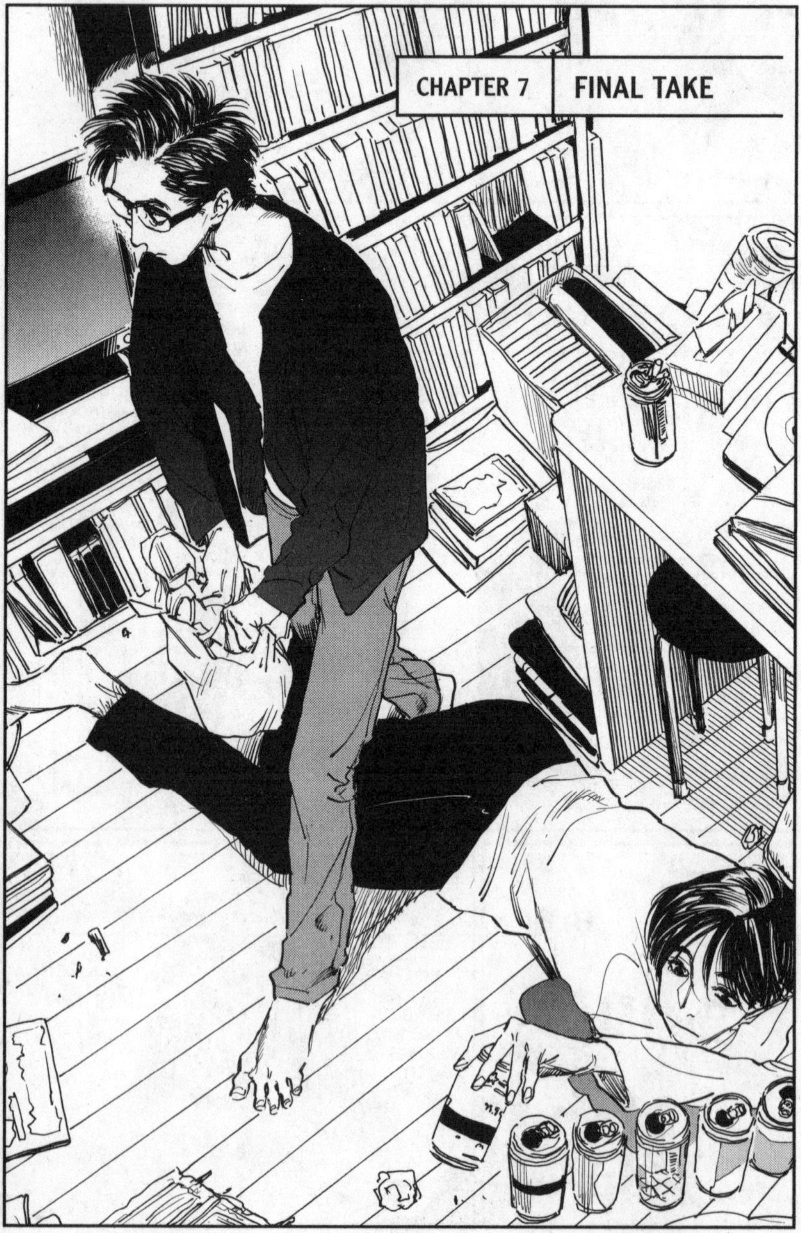
CHAPTER 7
FINAL TAKE

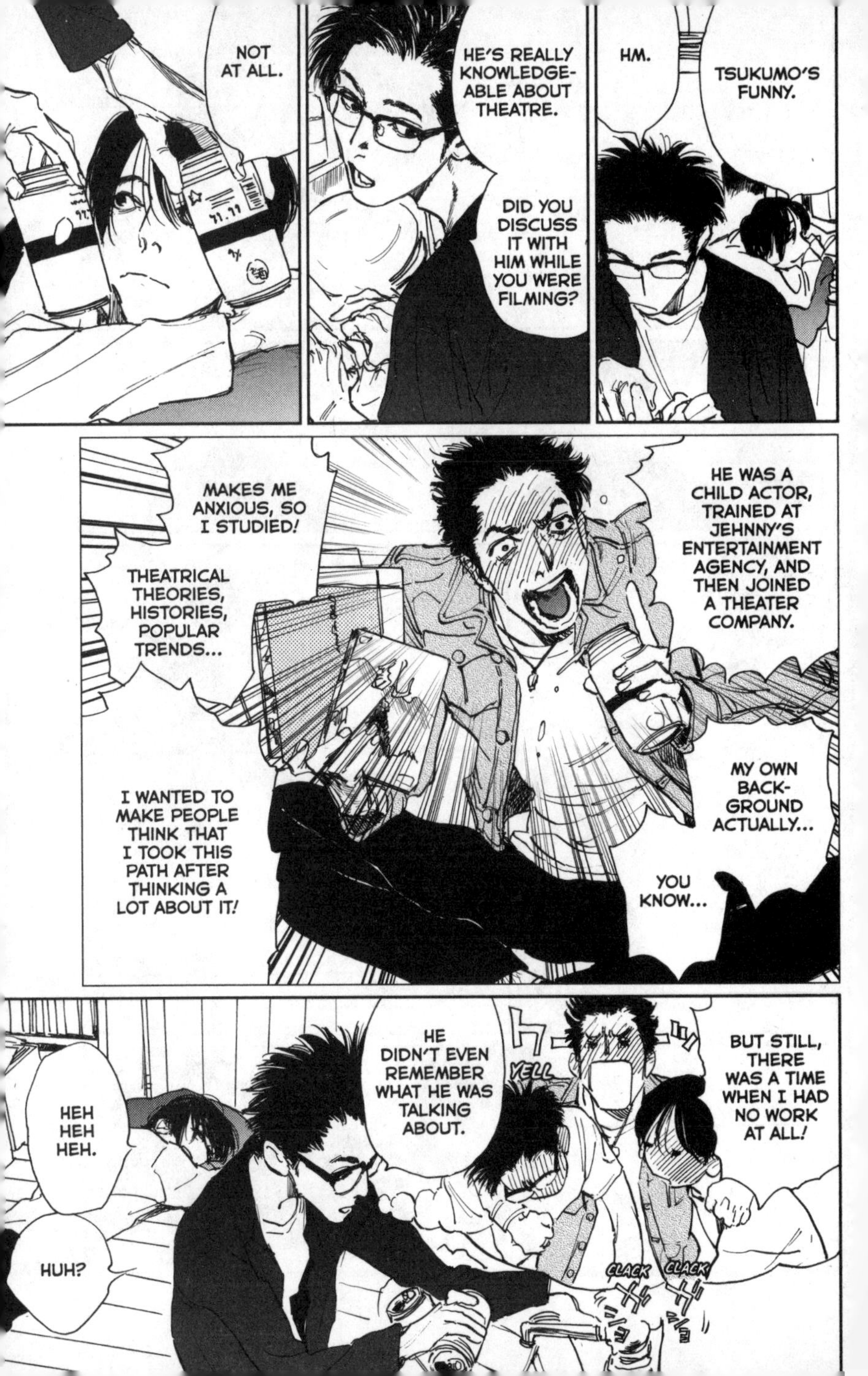

TSUKUMO'S FUNNY.
HM.
HE'S REALLY KNOWLEDGE-ABLE ABOUT THEATRE.
DID YOU DISCUSS IT WITH HIM WHILE YOU WERE FILMING?
NOT AT ALL.
HE WAS A CHILD ACTOR, TRAINED AT JEHNNY'S ENTERTAINMENT AGENCY, AND THEN JOINED A THEATER COMPANY.
MY OWN BACK-GROUND ACTUALLY...
YOU KNOW...
MAKES ME ANXIOUS, SO I STUDIED!
THEATRICAL THEORIES, HISTORIES, POPULAR TRENDS...
I WANTED TO MAKE PEOPLE THINK THAT I TOOK THIS PATH AFTER THINKING A LOT ABOUT IT!
BUT STILL, THERE WAS A TIME WHEN I HAD NO WORK AT ALL!
YELL
HE DIDN'T EVEN REMEMBER WHAT HE WAS TALKING ABOUT.
HEH HEH HEH.
HUH?
CLACK
CLACK

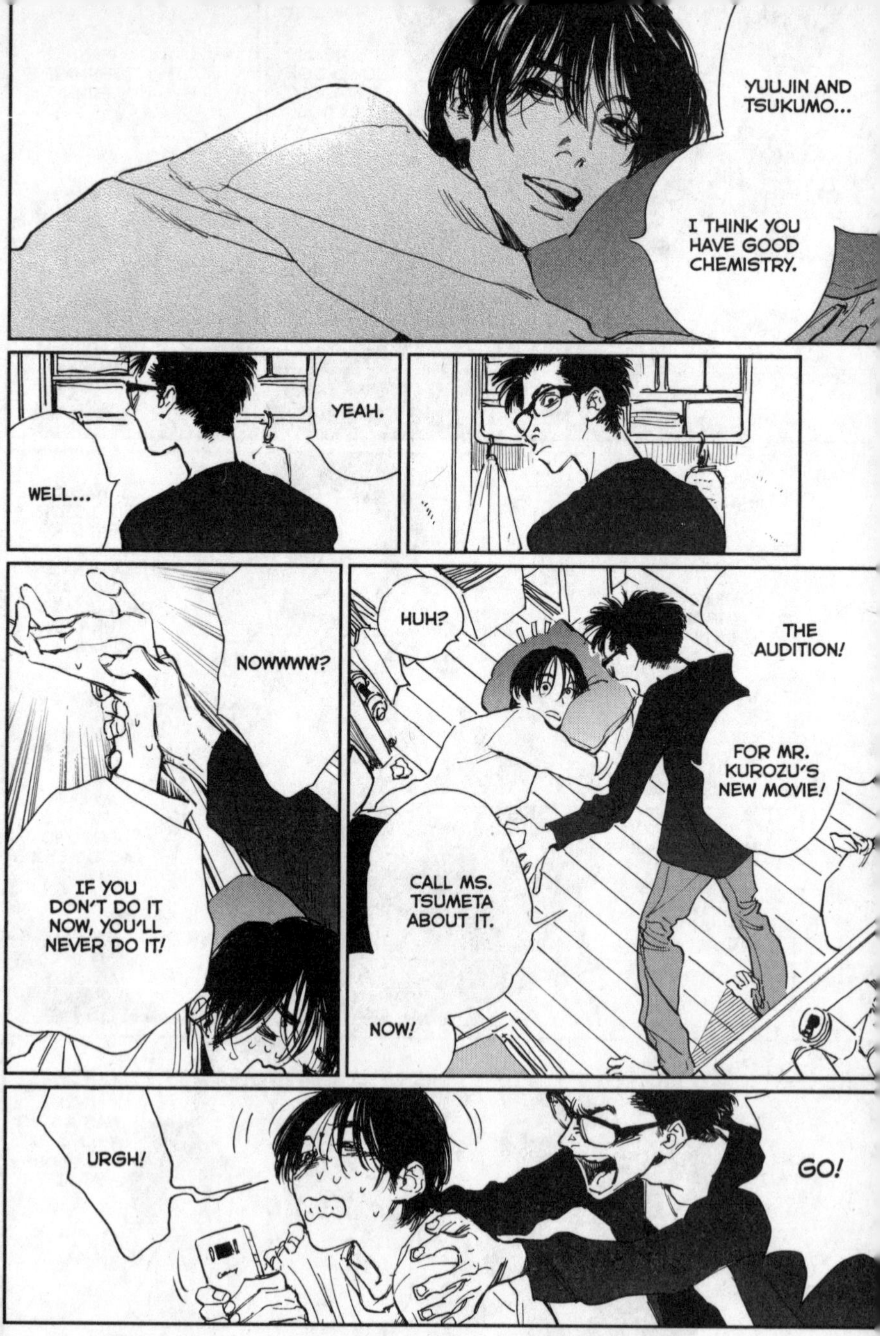
YUUJIN AND TSUKUMO...
I THINK YOU HAVE GOOD CHEMISTRY.
YEAH.
WELL...
HUH?
THE AUDITION!
FOR MR. KUROZU'S NEW MOVIE!
CALL MS. TSUMETA ABOUT IT.
NOW!
NOWWWW?
IF YOU DON'T DO IT NOW, YOU'LL NEVER DO IT!
GO!
URGH!

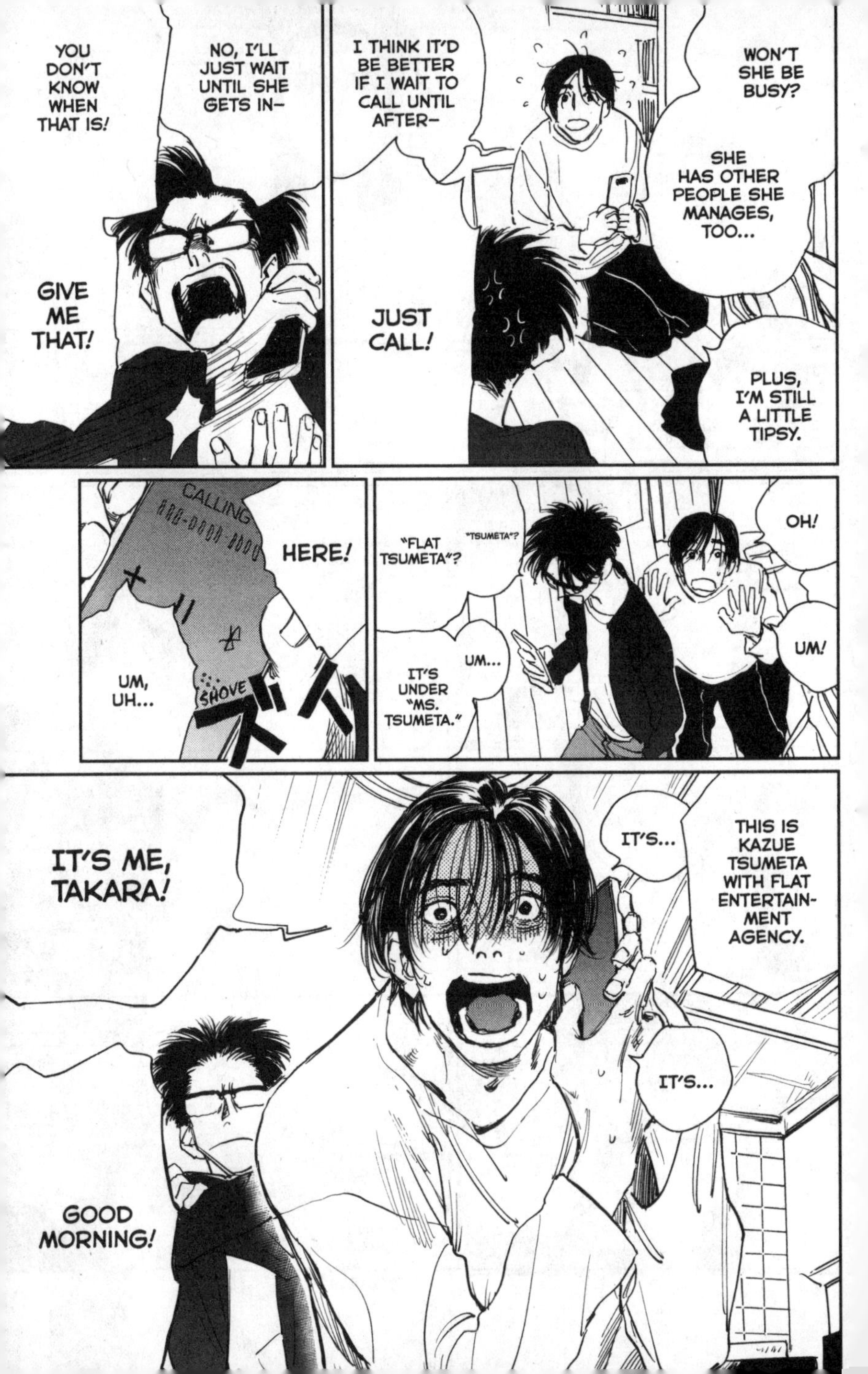
WON'T SHE BE BUSY?
SHE HAS OTHER PEOPLE SHE MANAGES, TOO...
I THINK IT'D BE BETTER IF I WAIT TO CALL UNTIL AFTER–
PLUS, I'M STILL A LITTLE TIPSY.
JUST CALL!
NO, I'LL JUST WAIT UNTIL SHE GETS IN–
YOU DON'T KNOW WHEN THAT IS!
GIVE ME THAT!
OH!
UM!
"TSUMETA"?
"FLAT TSUMETA"?
UM...
IT'S UNDER "MS. TSUMETA."
CALLING
HERE!
SHOVE
UM, UH...
THIS IS KAZUE TSUMETA WITH FLAT ENTERTAIN-MENT AGENCY.
IT'S...
IT'S...
IT'S ME, TAKARA!
GOOD MORNING!

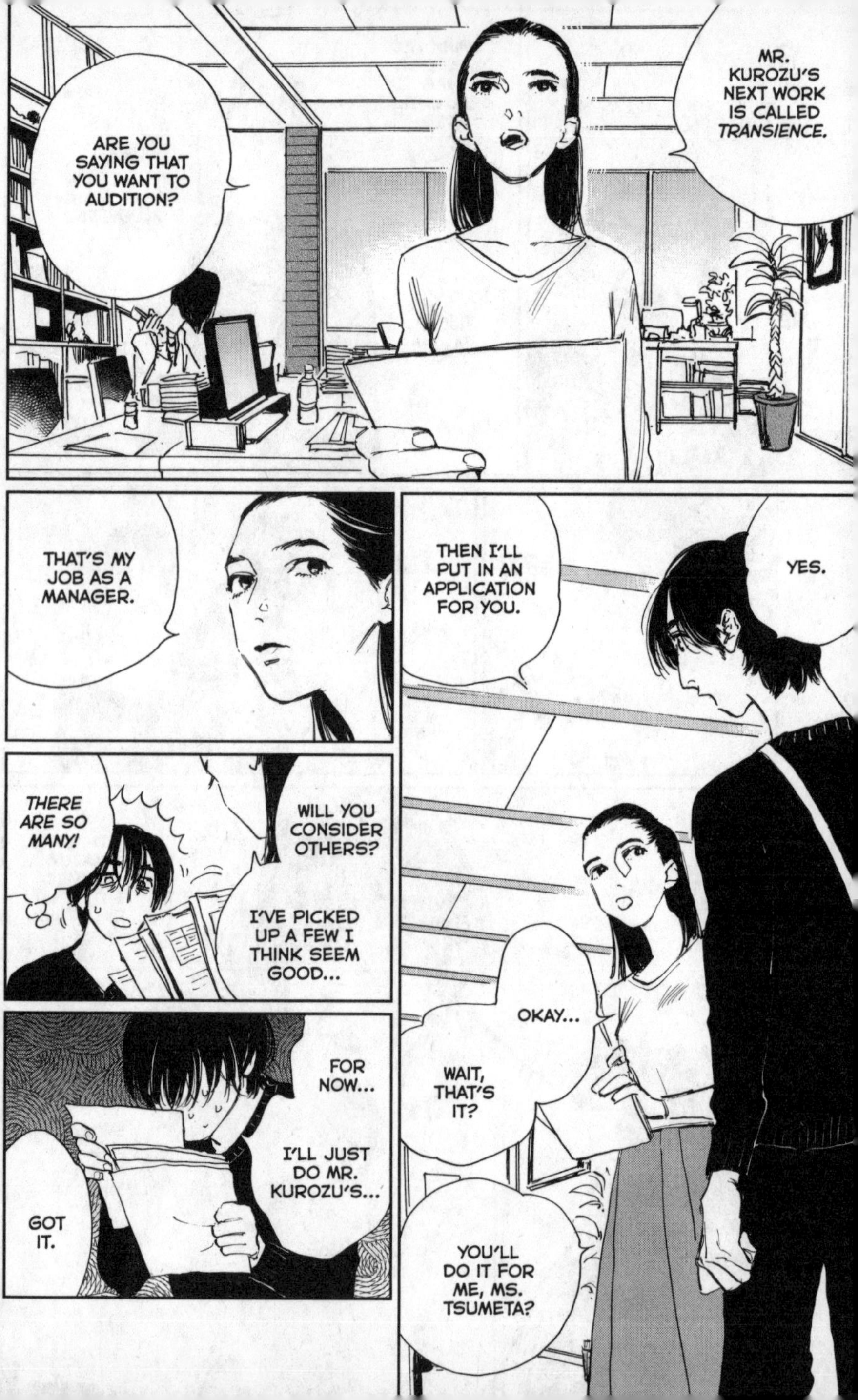
MR. KUROZU'S NEXT WORK IS CALLED *TRANSIENCE.*
ARE YOU SAYING THAT YOU WANT TO AUDITION?
YES.
THEN I'LL PUT IN AN APPLICATION FOR YOU.
OKAY...
WAIT, THAT'S IT?
YOU'LL DO IT FOR ME, MS. TSUMETA?
THAT'S MY JOB AS A MANAGER.
WILL YOU CONSIDER OTHERS?
I'VE PICKED UP A FEW I THINK SEEM GOOD...
THERE ARE SO MANY!
FOR NOW...
I'LL JUST DO MR. KUROZU'S...
GOT IT.

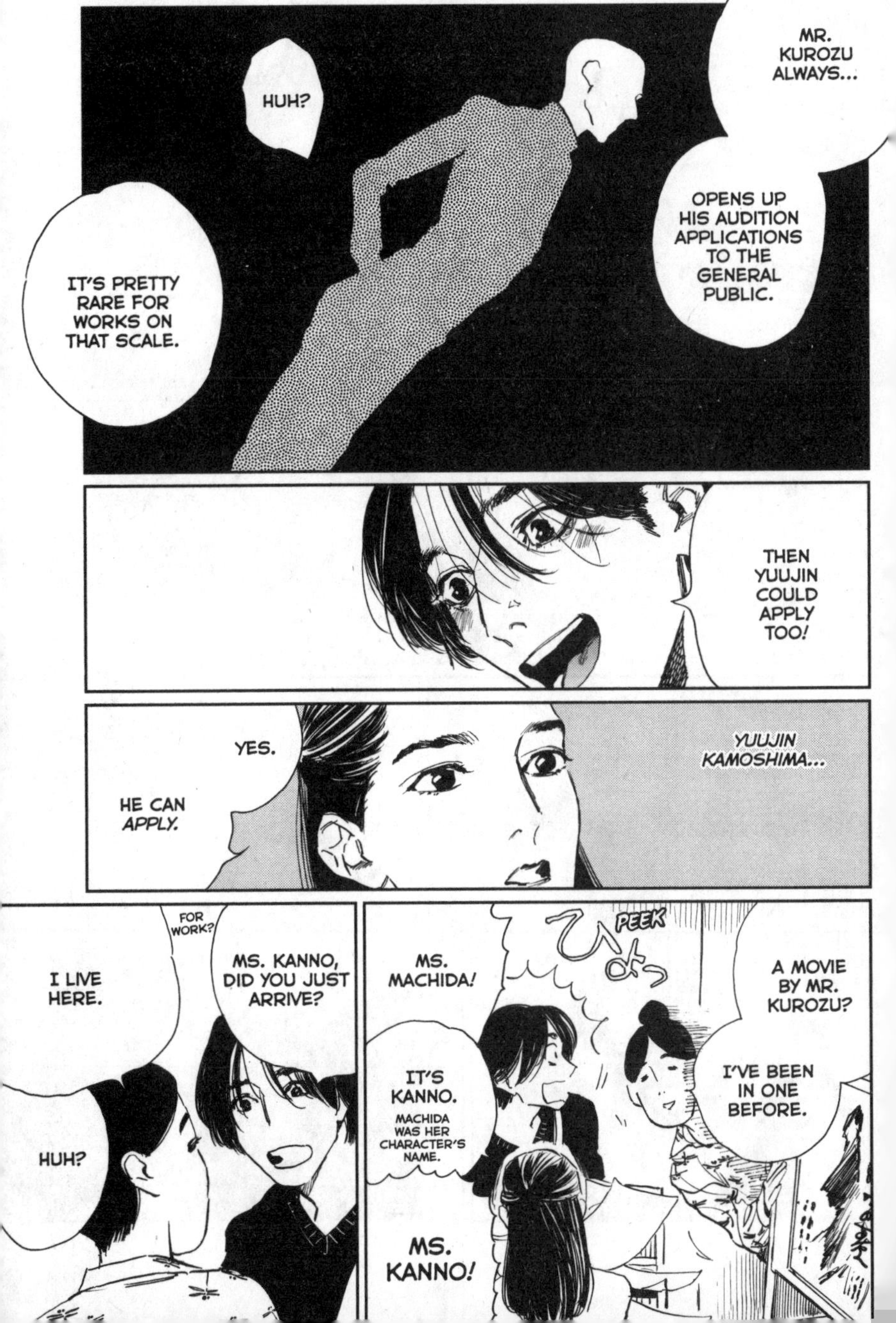
MR. KUROZU ALWAYS...
OPENS UP HIS AUDITION APPLICATIONS TO THE GENERAL PUBLIC.
HUH?
IT'S PRETTY RARE FOR WORKS ON THAT SCALE.
THEN YUUJIN COULD APPLY TOO!
YUUJIN KAMOSHIMA...
YES.
HE CAN APPLY.
A MOVIE BY MR. KUROZU?
I'VE BEEN IN ONE BEFORE.
PEEK
MS. MACHIDA!
IT'S KANNO.
MACHIDA WAS HER CHARACTER'S NAME.
MS. KANNO!
MS. KANNO, DID YOU JUST ARRIVE?
FOR WORK?
I LIVE HERE.
HUH?

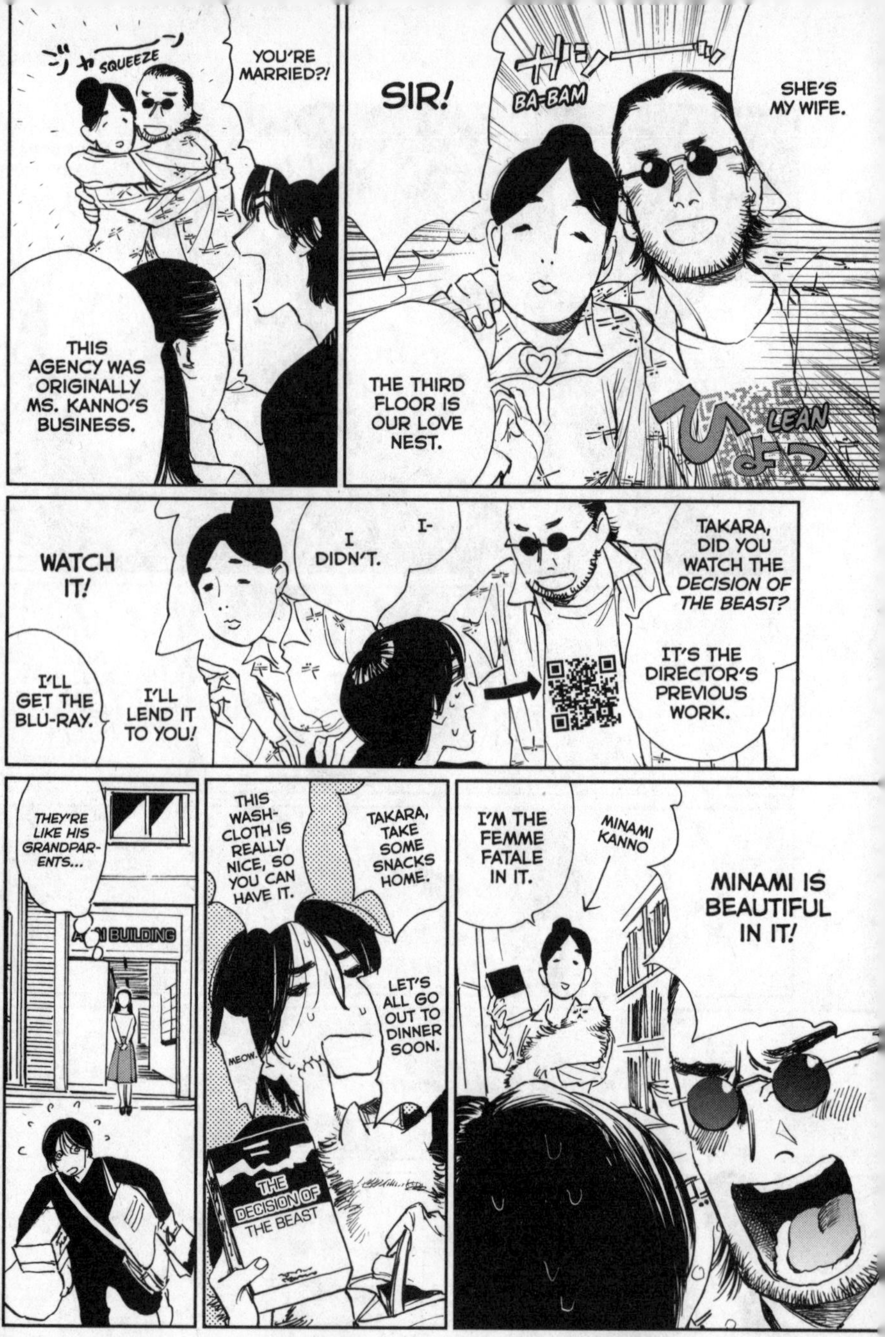
SHE'S MY WIFE.
BA-BAM
SIR!
LEAN
THE THIRD FLOOR IS OUR LOVE NEST.
YOU'RE MARRIED?!
SQUEEZE
THIS AGENCY WAS ORIGINALLY MS. KANNO'S BUSINESS.
TAKARA, DID YOU WATCH THE *DECISION OF THE BEAST?*
IT'S THE DIRECTOR'S PREVIOUS WORK.
I-
I DIDN'T.
WATCH IT!
I'LL LEND IT TO YOU!
I'LL GET THE BLU-RAY.
MINAMI IS BEAUTIFUL IN IT!
MINAMI KANNO
I'M THE FEMME FATALE IN IT.
TAKARA, TAKE SOME SNACKS HOME.
THIS WASH-CLOTH IS REALLY NICE, SO YOU CAN HAVE IT.
LET'S ALL GO OUT TO DINNER SOON.
MEOW.
THE DECISION OF THE BEAST
THEY'RE LIKE HIS GRANDPAR-ENTS...
BUILDING

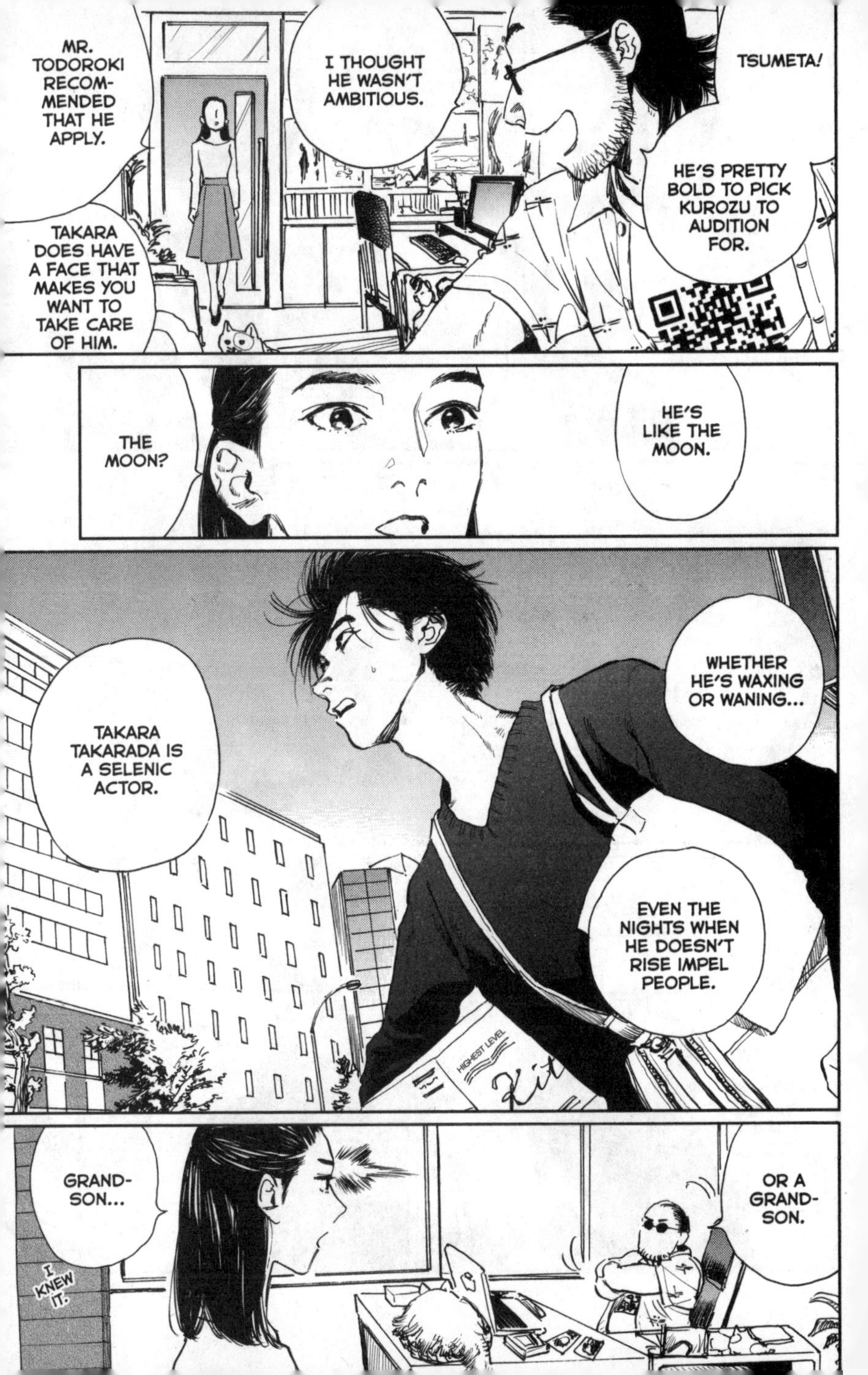
TSUMETA!
HE'S PRETTY BOLD TO PICK KUROZU TO AUDITION FOR.
I THOUGHT HE WASN'T AMBITIOUS.
MR. TODOROKI RECOM-MENDED THAT HE APPLY.
TAKARA DOES HAVE A FACE THAT MAKES YOU WANT TO TAKE CARE OF HIM.
HE'S LIKE THE MOON.
THE MOON?
WHETHER HE'S WAXING OR WANING...
EVEN THE NIGHTS WHEN HE DOESN'T RISE IMPEL PEOPLE.
TAKARA TAKARADA IS A SELENIC ACTOR.
HIGHEST LEVEL
OR A GRAND-SON.
GRAND-SON...
I KNEW IT.

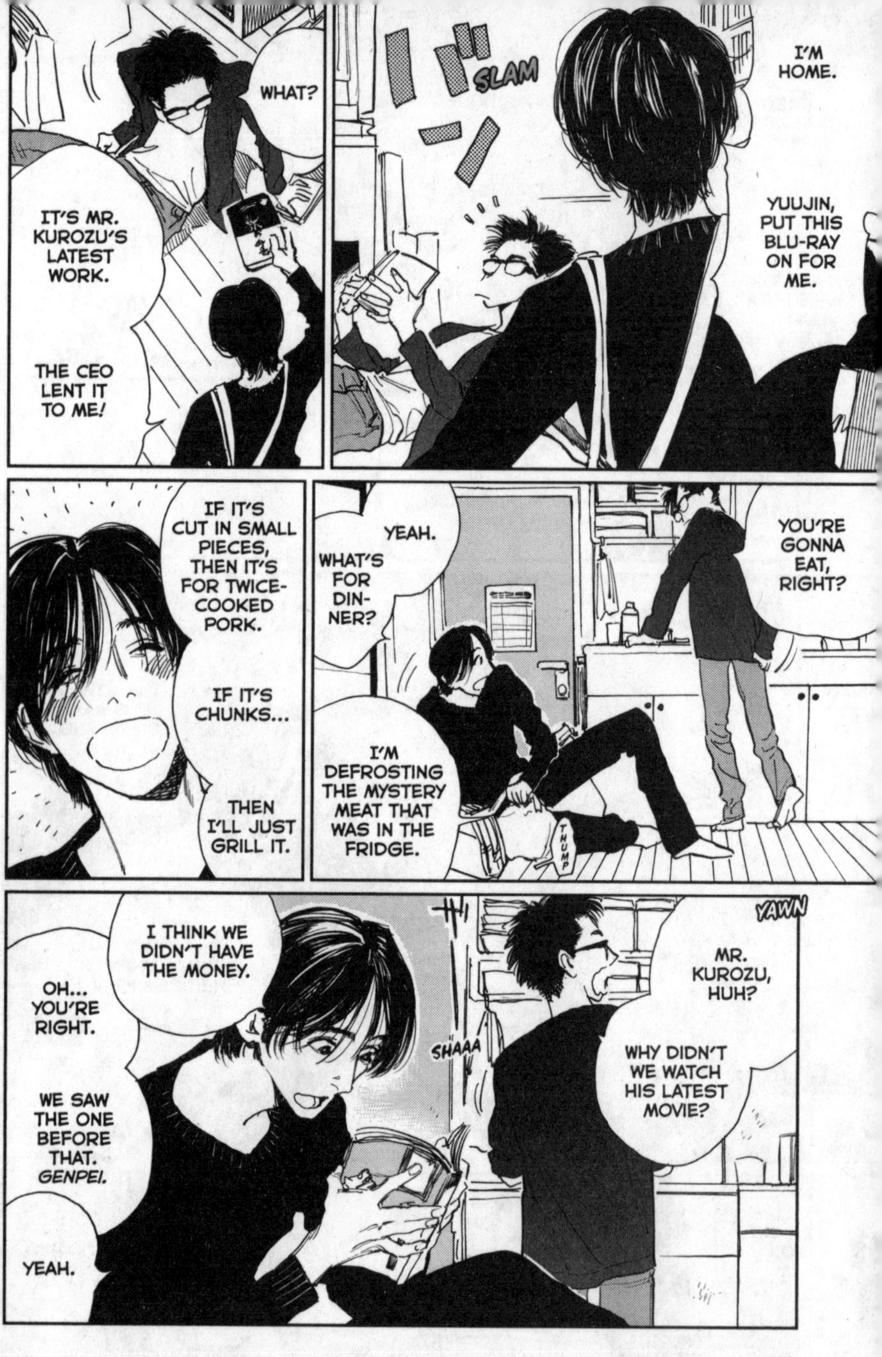
I'M HOME.
SLAM
YUUJIN, PUT THIS BLU-RAY ON FOR ME.
WHAT?
IT'S MR. KUROZU'S LATEST WORK.
THE CEO LENT IT TO ME!
YOU'RE GONNA EAT, RIGHT?
YEAH.
WHAT'S FOR DIN-NER?
I'M DEFROSTING THE MYSTERY MEAT THAT WAS IN THE FRIDGE.
THUMP
IF IT'S CUT IN SMALL PIECES, THEN IT'S FOR TWICE-COOKED PORK.
IF IT'S CHUNKS...
THEN I'LL JUST GRILL IT.
YAWN
MR. KUROZU, HUH?
WHY DIDN'T WE WATCH HIS LATEST MOVIE?
SHAAA
I THINK WE DIDN'T HAVE THE MONEY.
OH... YOU'RE RIGHT.
WE SAW THE ONE BEFORE THAT. *GENPEI.*
YEAH.

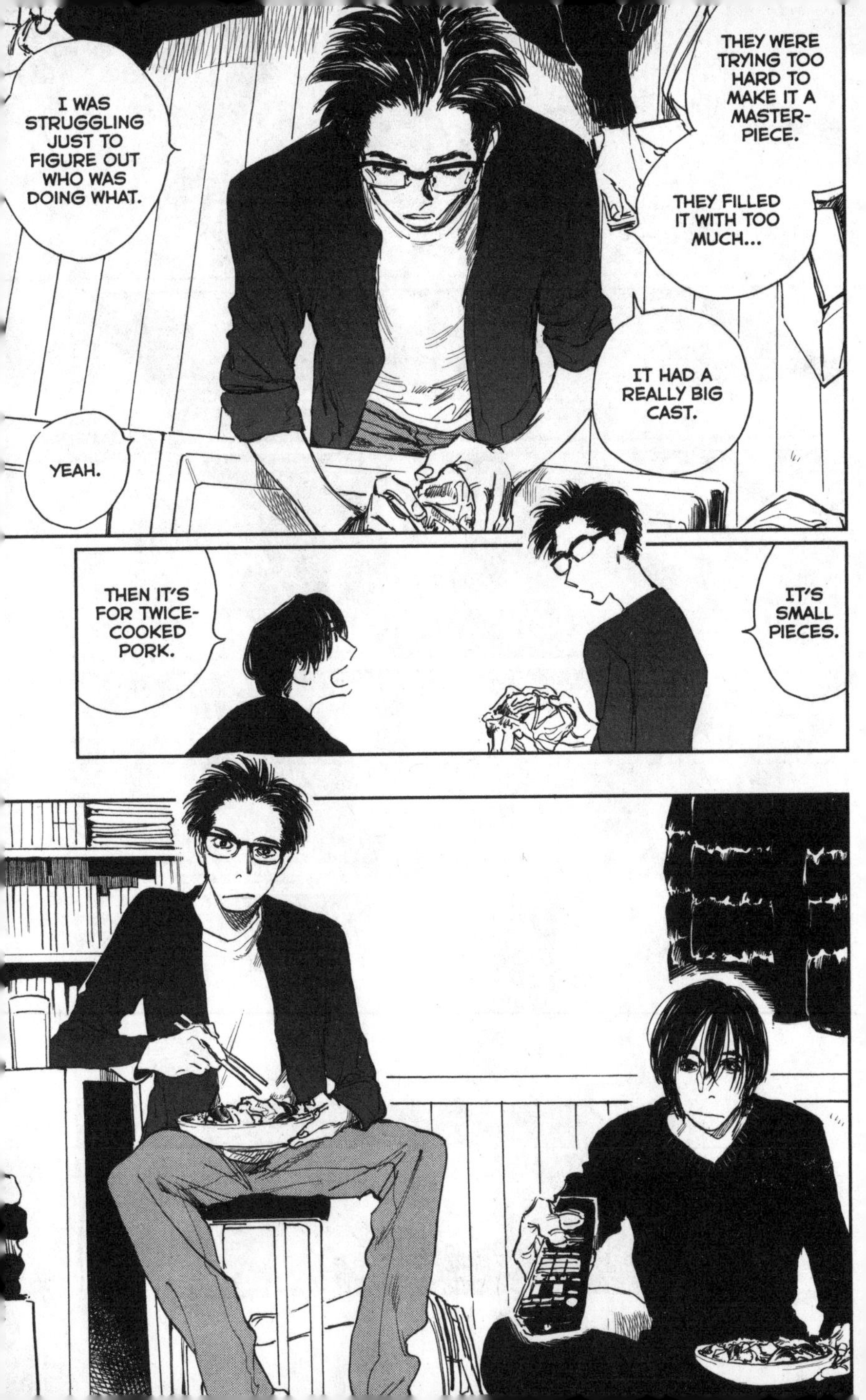
THEY WERE TRYING TOO HARD TO MAKE IT A MASTER-PIECE.
I WAS STRUGGLING JUST TO FIGURE OUT WHO WAS DOING WHAT.
THEY FILLED IT WITH TOO MUCH...
IT HAD A REALLY BIG CAST.
YEAH.
IT'S SMALL PIECES.
THEN IT'S FOR TWICE-COOKED PORK.

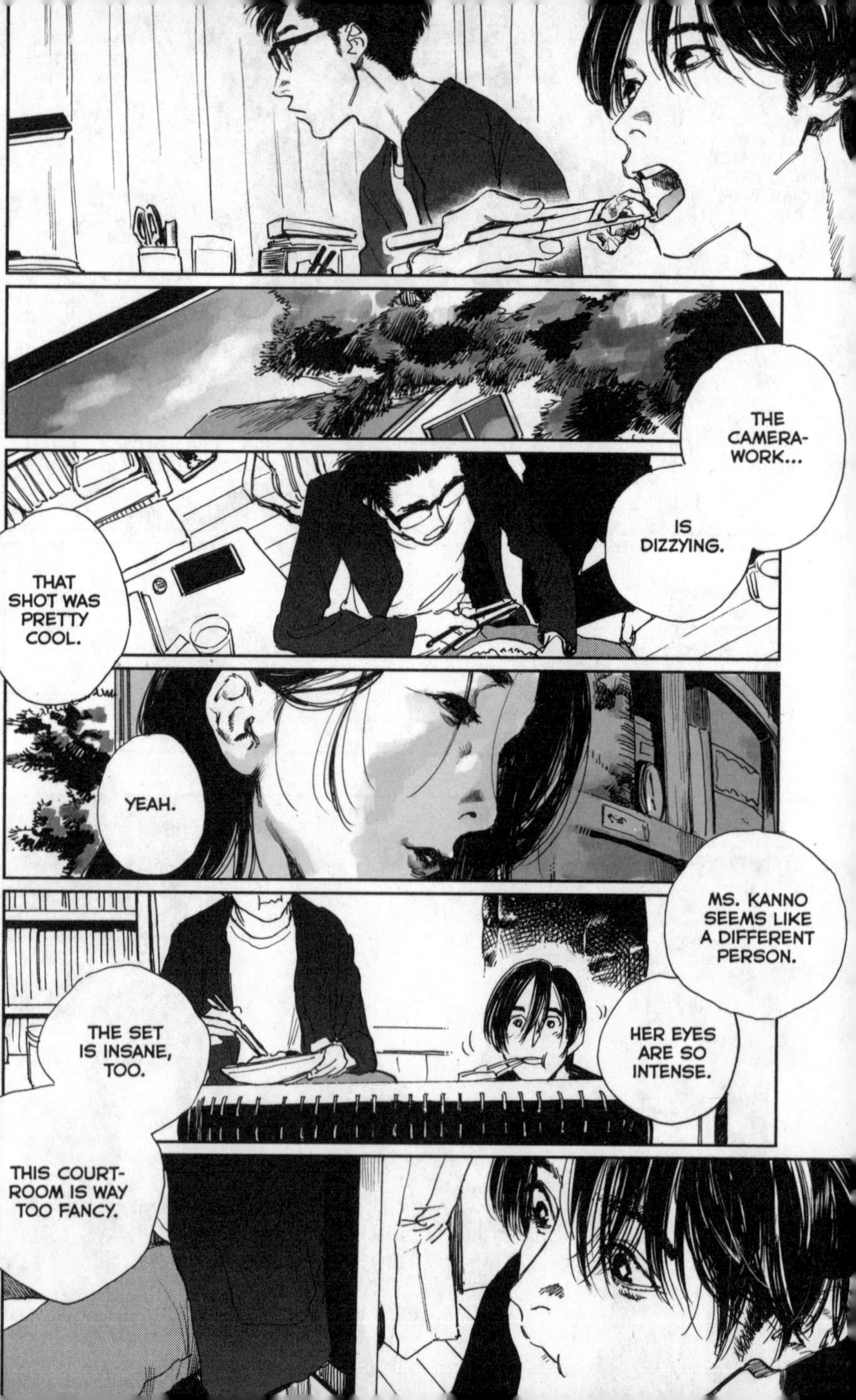
THE CAMERA-WORK...
IS DIZZYING.
THAT SHOT WAS PRETTY COOL.
YEAH.
MS. KANNO SEEMS LIKE A DIFFERENT PERSON.
HER EYES ARE SO INTENSE.
THE SET IS INSANE, TOO.
THIS COURTROOM IS WAY TOO FANCY.

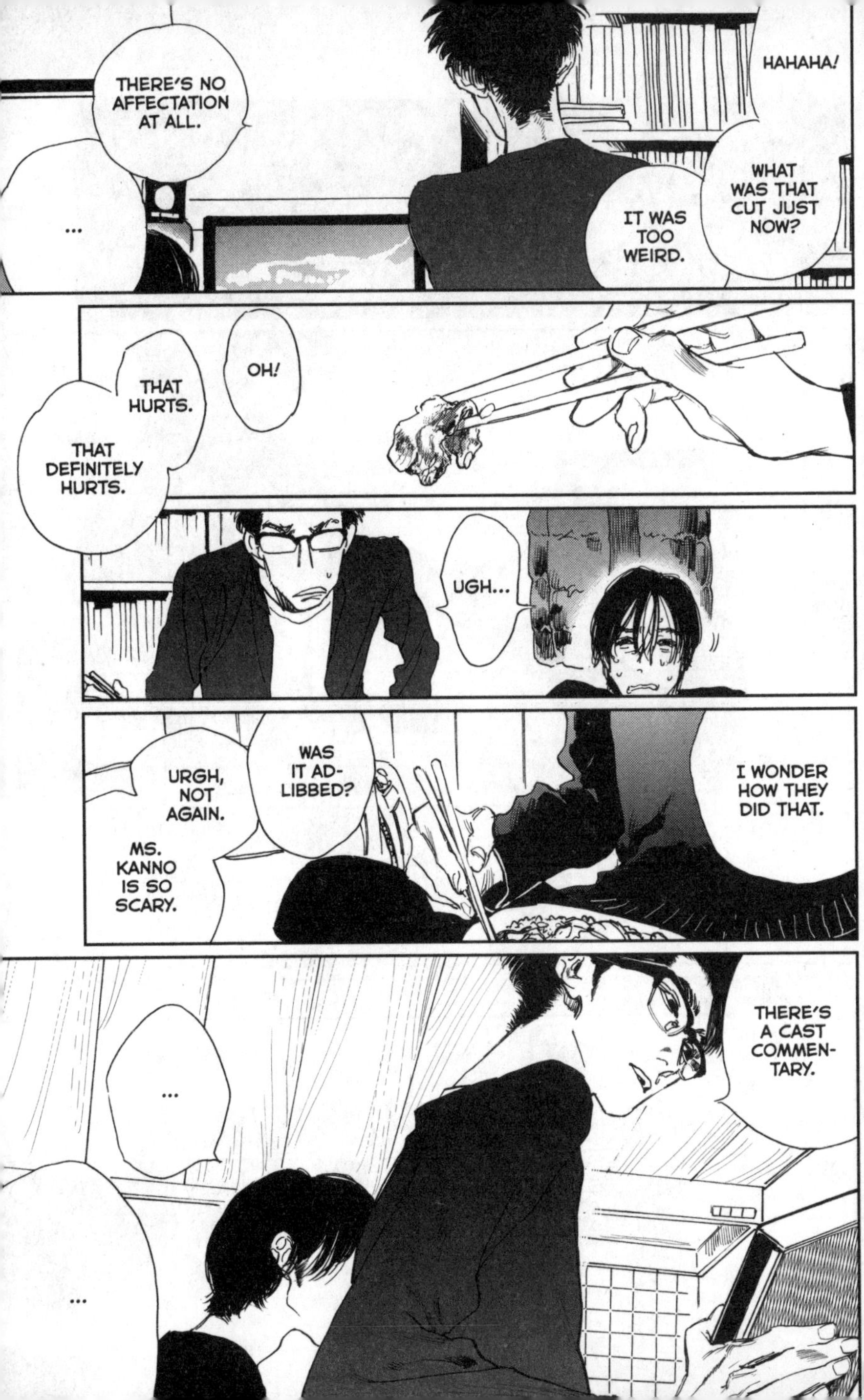
HAHAHA!
WHAT WAS THAT CUT JUST NOW?
IT WAS TOO WEIRD.
THERE'S NO AFFECTATION AT ALL.
...
OH!
THAT HURTS.
THAT DEFINITELY HURTS.
UGH...
I WONDER HOW THEY DID THAT.
WAS IT AD-LIBBED?
URGH, NOT AGAIN.
MS. KANNO IS SO SCARY.
THERE'S A CAST COMMENTARY.
...
...

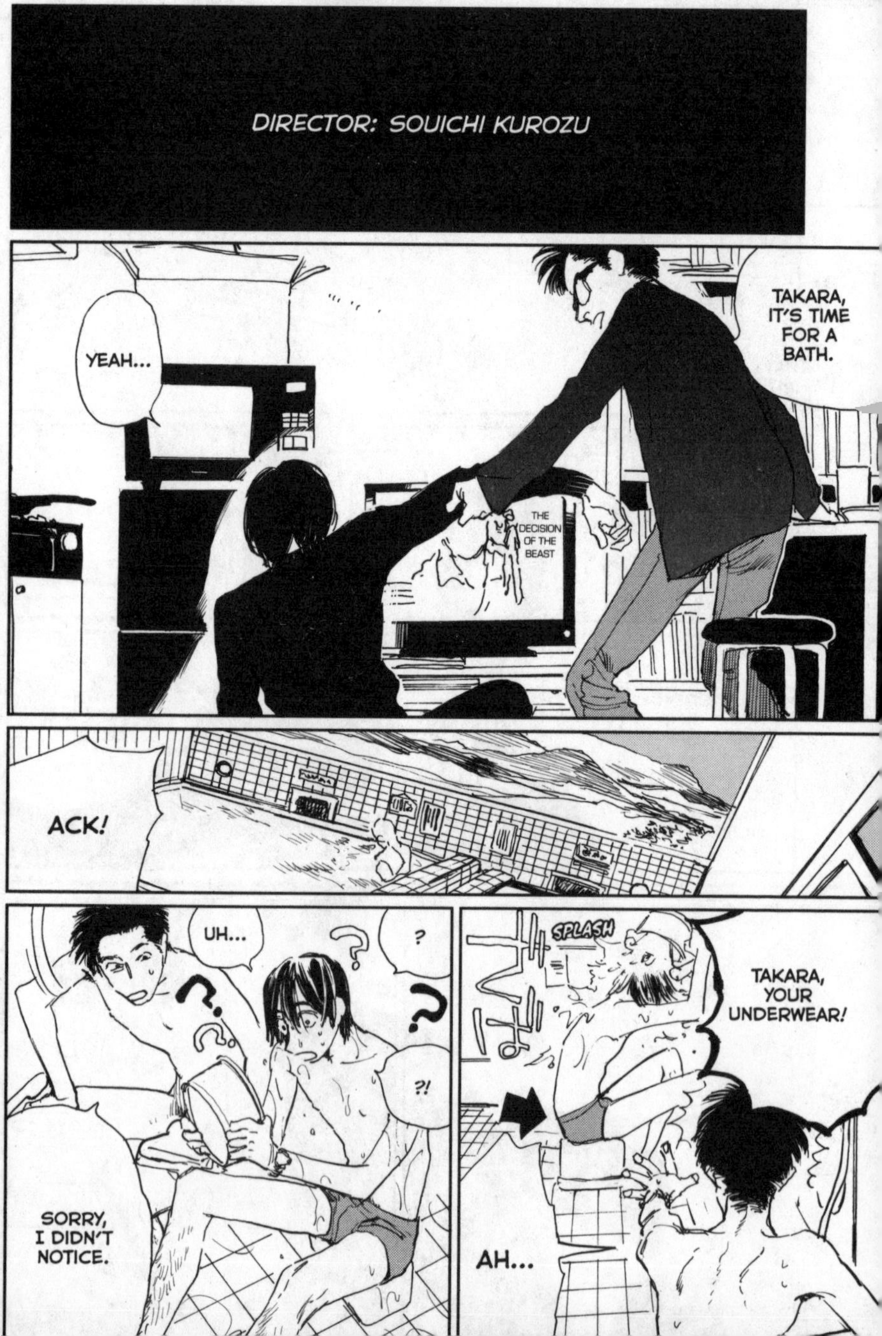
DIRECTOR: SOUICHI KUROZU
TAKARA, IT'S TIME FOR A BATH.
YEAH...
THE DECISION OF THE BEAST
ACK!
SPLASH
TAKARA, YOUR UNDERWEAR!
AH...
?
UH...
?!
SORRY, I DIDN'T NOTICE.

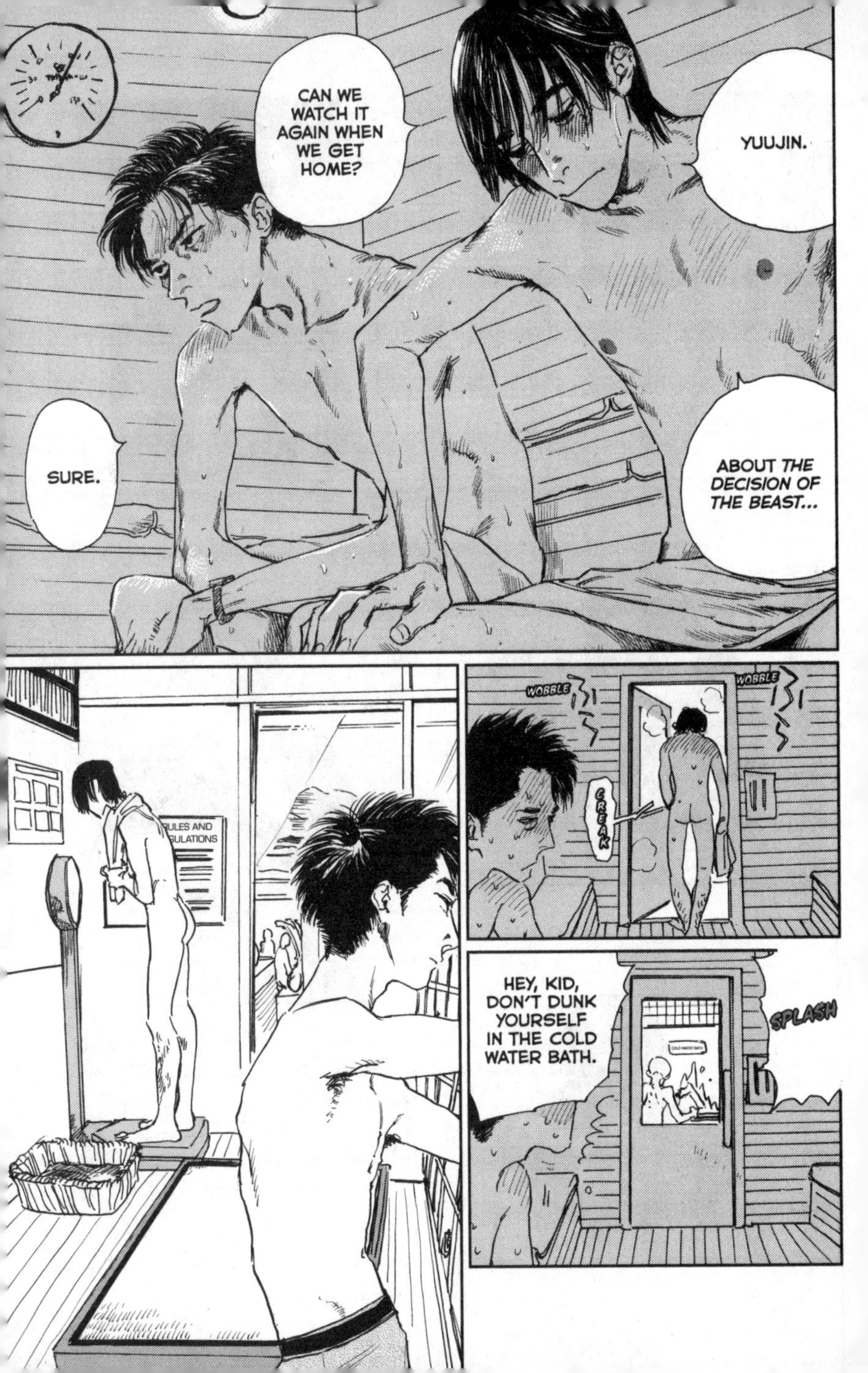
YUUJIN.
ABOUT THE DECISION OF THE BEAST...
CAN WE WATCH IT AGAIN WHEN WE GET HOME?
SURE.
WOBBLE
WOBBLE
CREAK
SPLASH
HEY, KID, DON'T DUNK YOURSELF IN THE COLD WATER BATH.
COLD WATER BATH
RULES AND

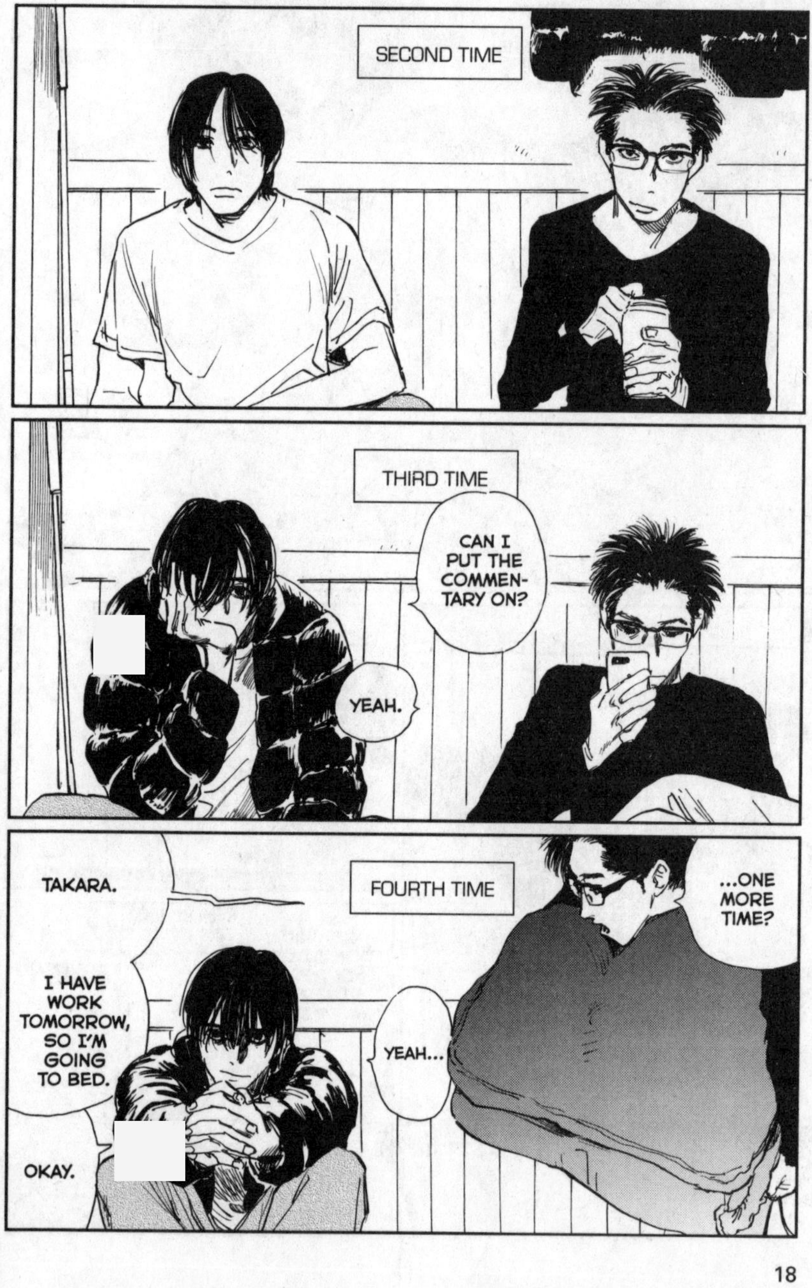
SECOND TIME
THIRD TIME
CAN I PUT THE COMMENTARY ON?
YEAH.
FOURTH TIME
...ONE MORE TIME?
YEAH...
TAKARA.
I HAVE WORK TOMORROW, SO I'M GOING TO BED.
OKAY.

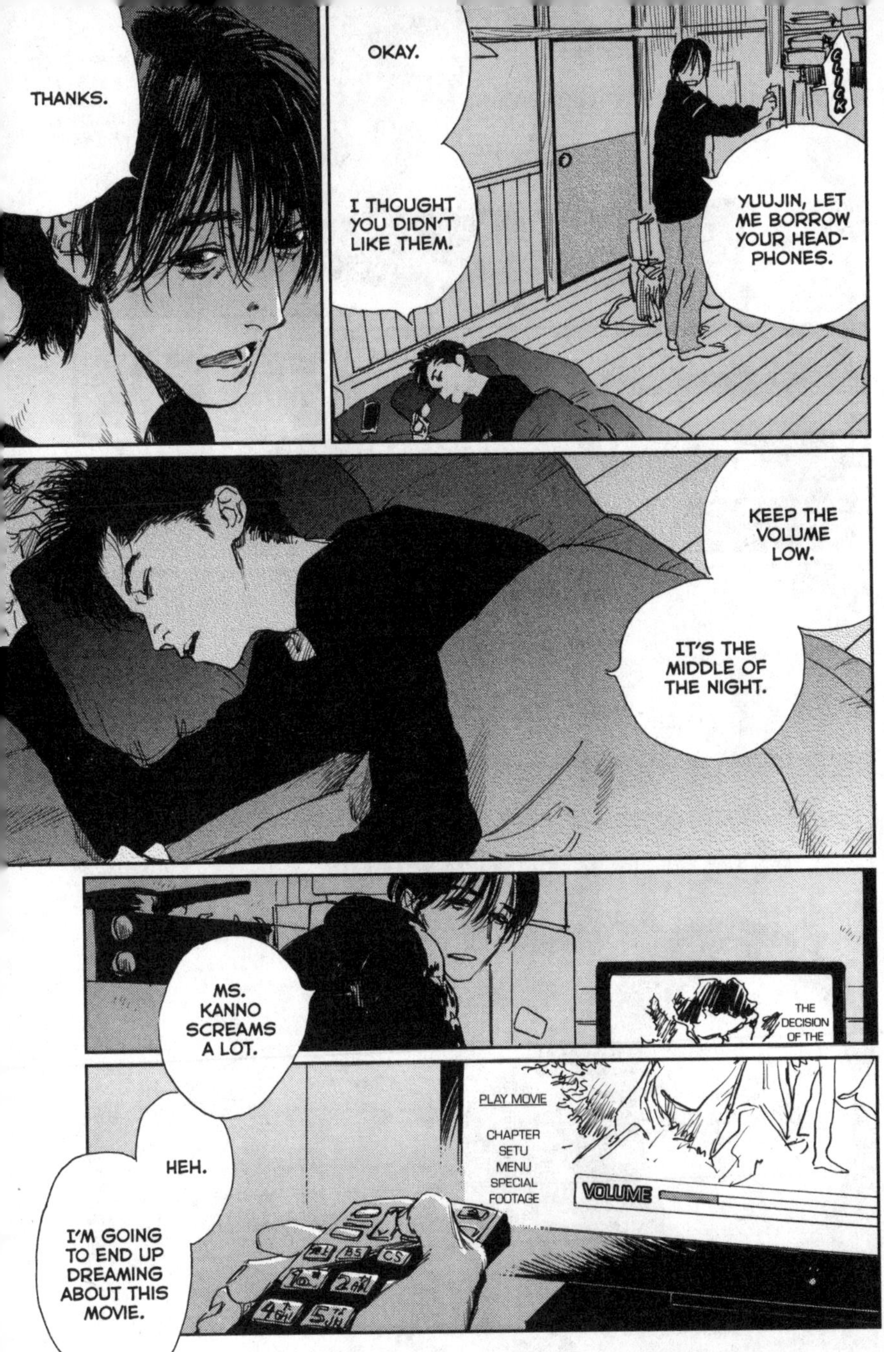
CLICK
YUUJIN, LET ME BORROW YOUR HEAD-PHONES.
OKAY.
I THOUGHT YOU DIDN'T LIKE THEM.
THANKS.
KEEP THE VOLUME LOW.
IT'S THE MIDDLE OF THE NIGHT.
THE DECISION OF THE
MS. KANNO SCREAMS A LOT.
VOLUME
PLAY MOVIE
CHAPTER
SETU
MENU
SPECIAL
FOOTAGE
HEH.
I'M GOING TO END UP DREAMING ABOUT THIS MOVIE.

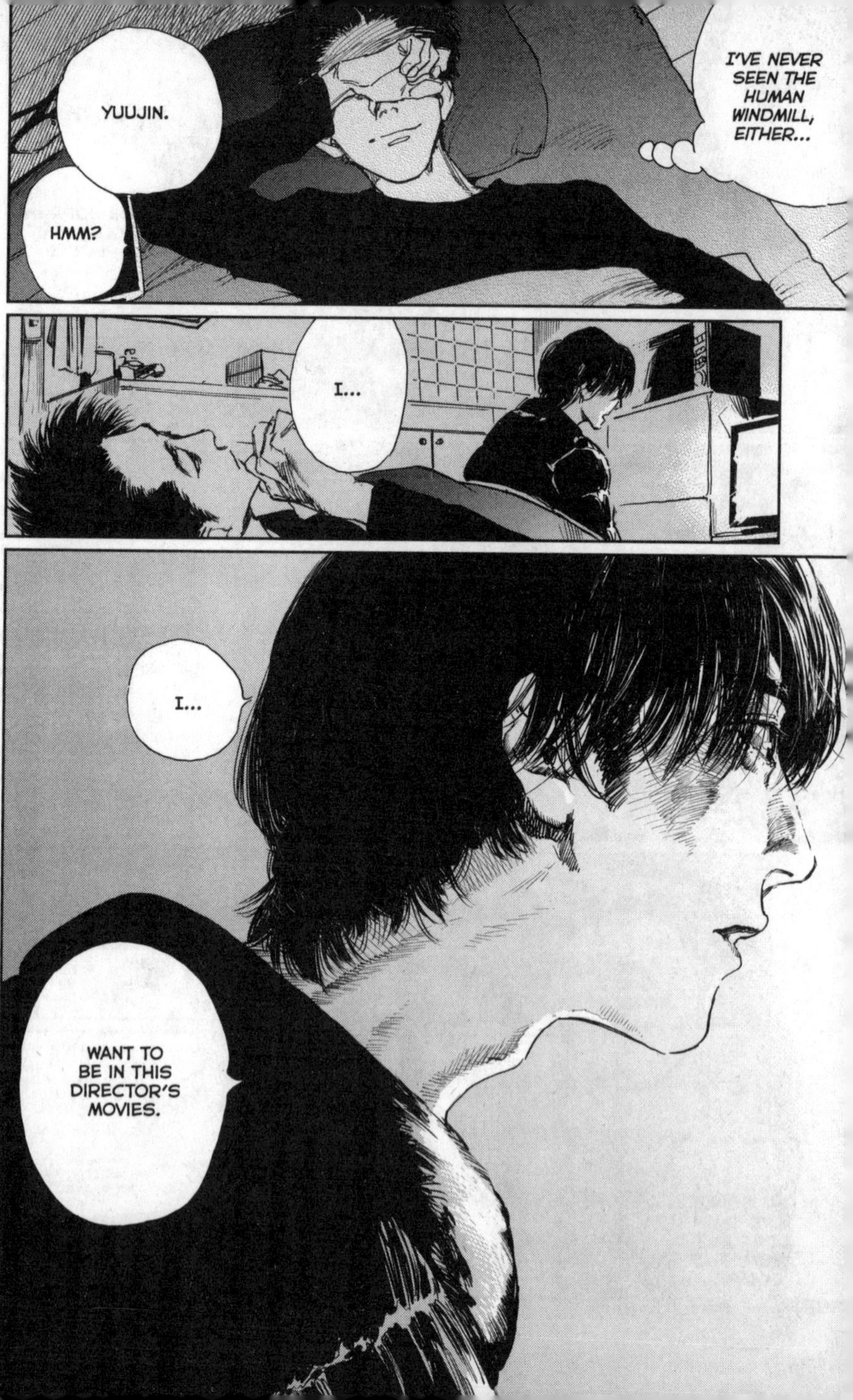
I'VE NEVER SEEN THE HUMAN WINDMILL, EITHER...
YUUJIN.
HMM?
I...
I...
WANT TO BE IN THIS DIRECTOR'S MOVIES.

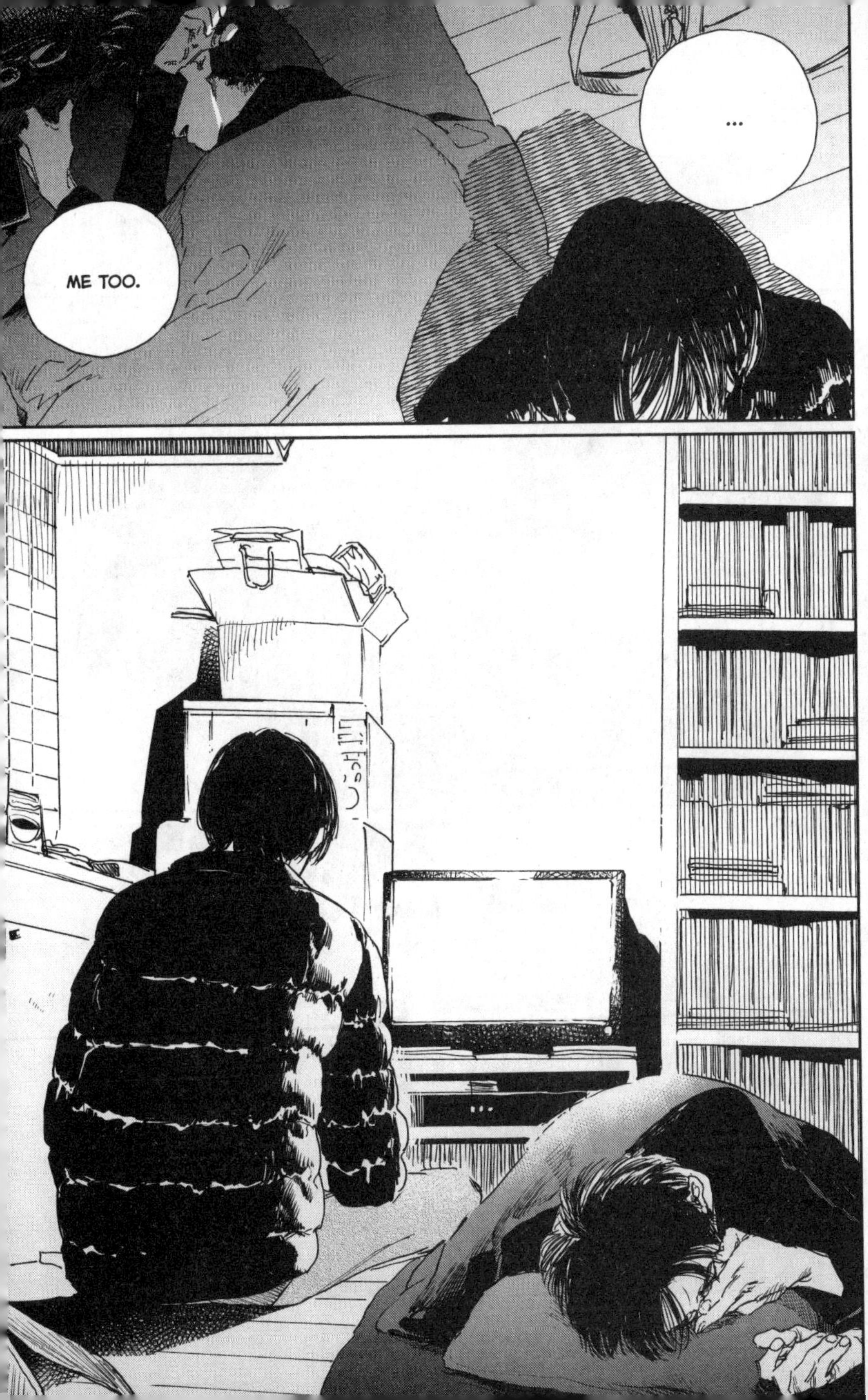
...
ME TOO.

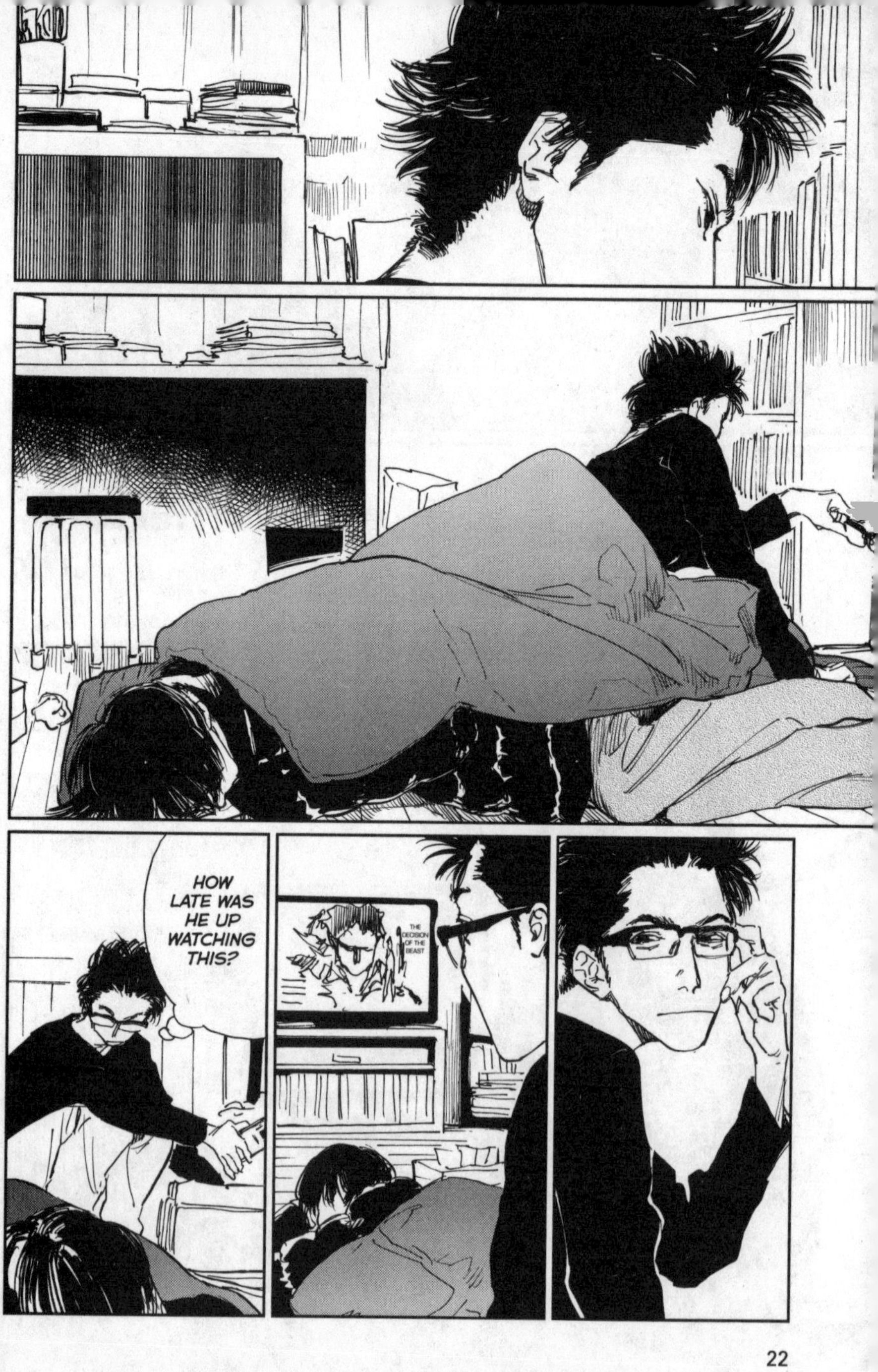
THE DECISION OF THE BEAST
HOW LATE WAS HE UP WATCHING THIS?

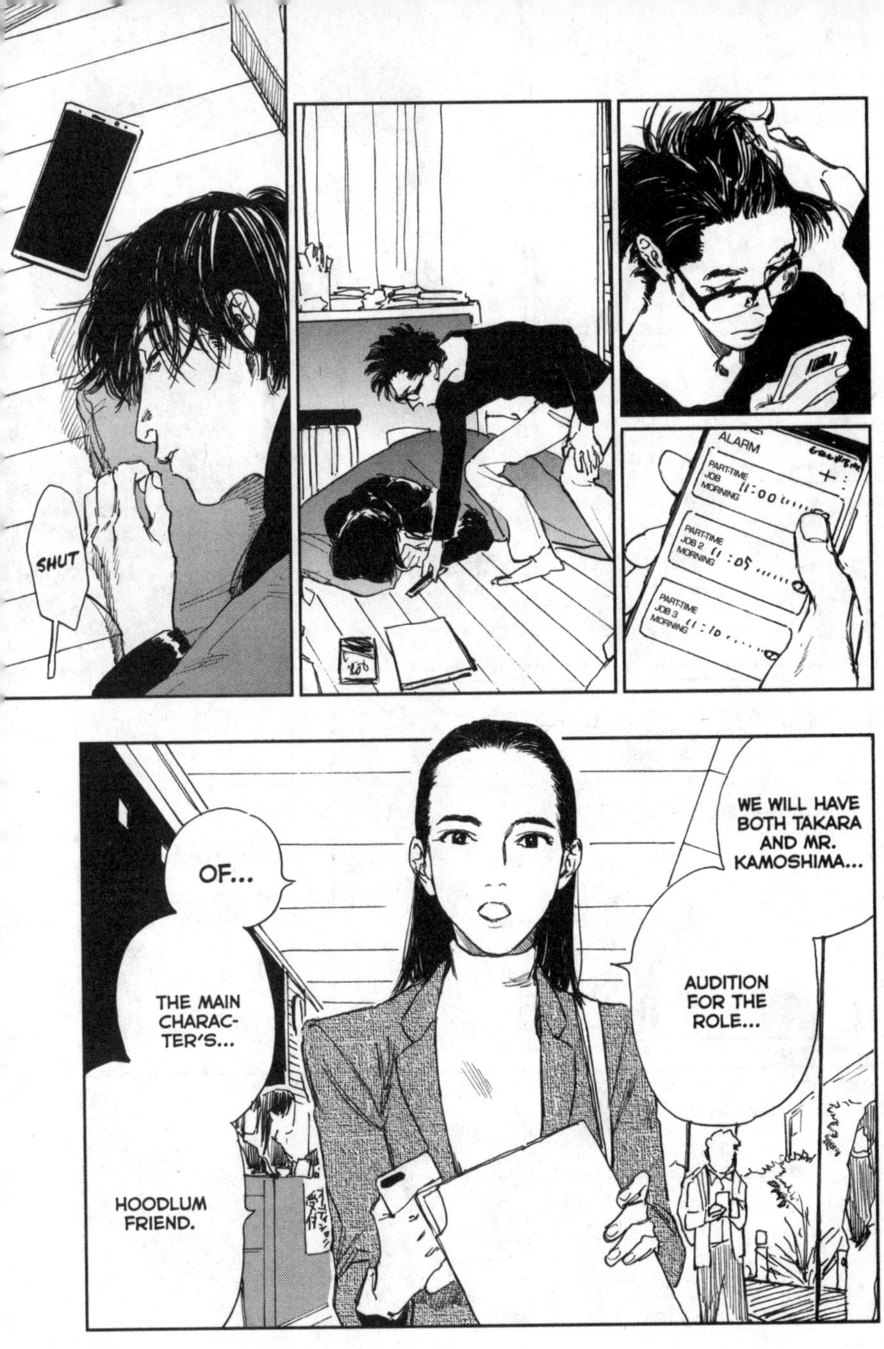
ALARM
PART-TIME JOB MORNING 11:00
PART-TIME JOB 2 MORNING 11:05
PART-TIME JOB 3 MORNING 11:10
SHUT
WE WILL HAVE BOTH TAKARA AND MR. KAMOSHIMA...
AUDITION FOR THE ROLE...
OF...
THE MAIN CHARAC-TER'S...
HOODLUM FRIEND.

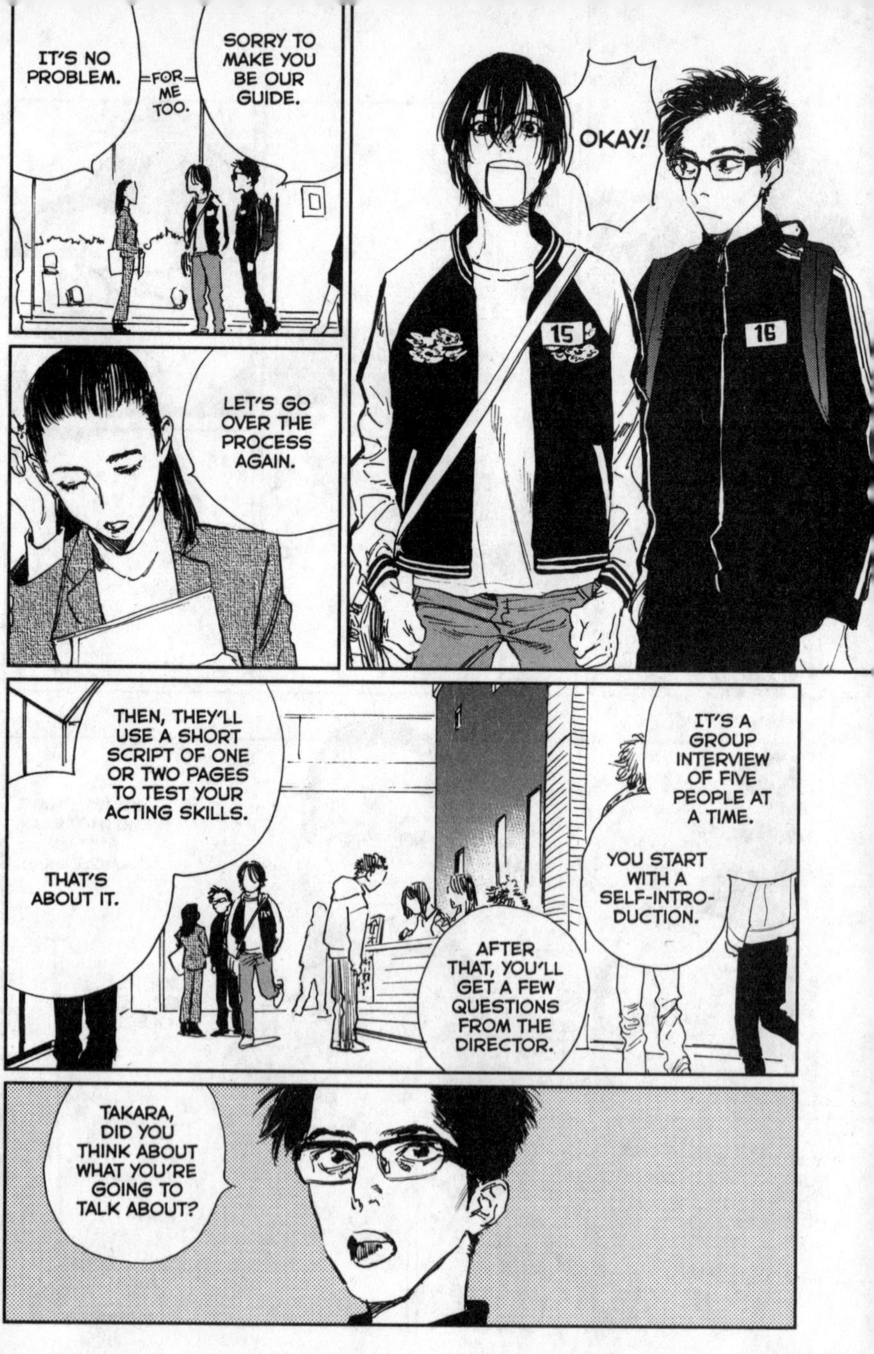
OKAY!
SORRY TO MAKE YOU BE OUR GUIDE.
IT'S NO PROBLEM.
FOR ME TOO.
LET'S GO OVER THE PROCESS AGAIN.
IT'S A GROUP INTERVIEW OF FIVE PEOPLE AT A TIME.
YOU START WITH A SELF-INTRO-DUCTION.
AFTER THAT, YOU'LL GET A FEW QUESTIONS FROM THE DIRECTOR.
THEN, THEY'LL USE A SHORT SCRIPT OF ONE OR TWO PAGES TO TEST YOUR ACTING SKILLS.
THAT'S ABOUT IT.
TAKARA, DID YOU THINK ABOUT WHAT YOU'RE GOING TO TALK ABOUT?

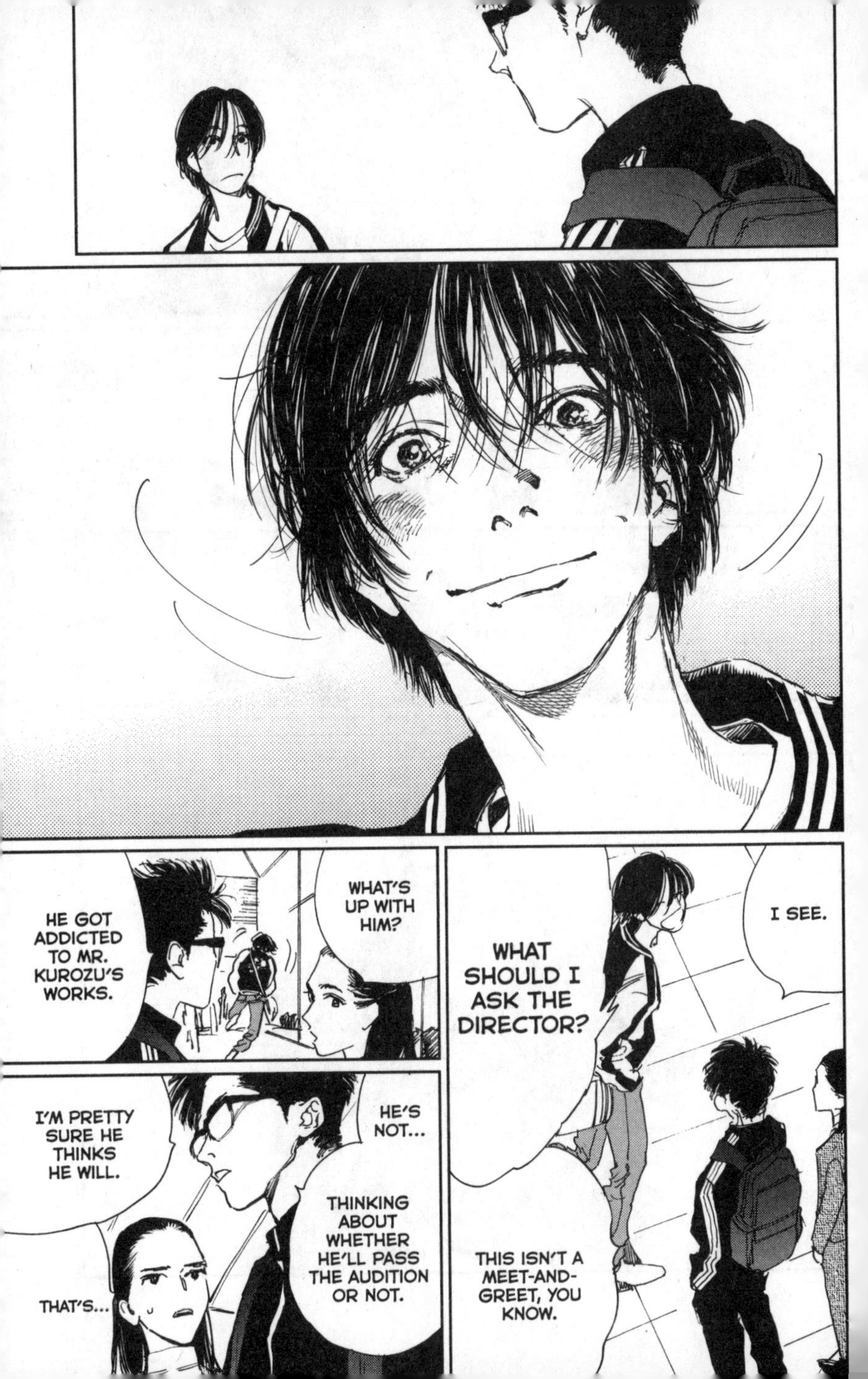
I SEE.
WHAT SHOULD I ASK THE DIRECTOR?
THIS ISN'T A MEET-AND-GREET, YOU KNOW.
WHAT'S UP WITH HIM?
HE GOT ADDICTED TO MR. KUROZU'S WORKS.
HE'S NOT...
THINKING ABOUT WHETHER HE'LL PASS THE AUDITION OR NOT.
THAT'S...
I'M PRETTY SURE HE THINKS HE WILL.

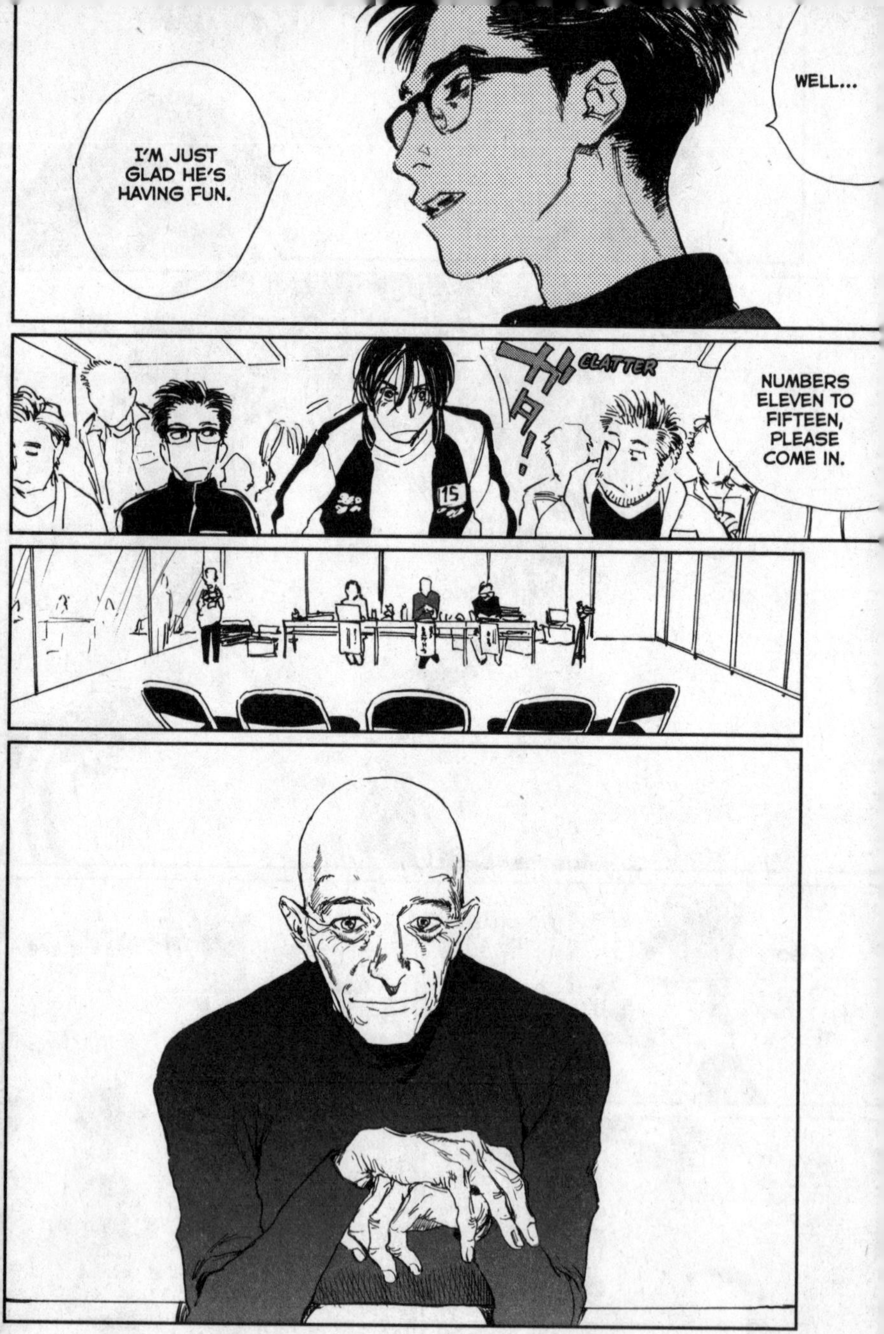
WELL...
I'M JUST GLAD HE'S HAVING FUN.
NUMBERS ELEVEN TO FIFTEEN, PLEASE COME IN.
CLATTER

DOUBLE

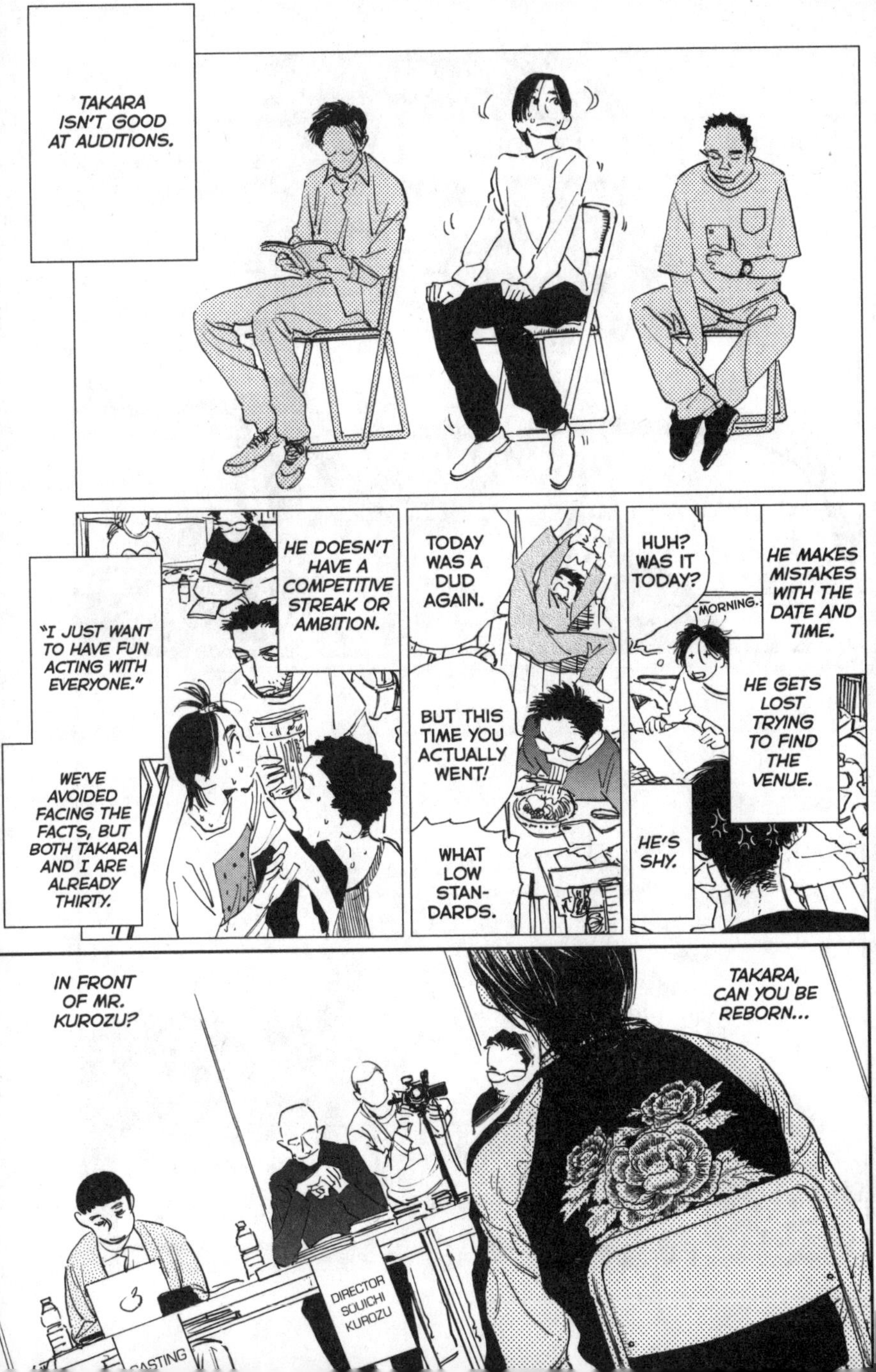
TAKARA ISN'T GOOD AT AUDITIONS.
HE MAKES MISTAKES WITH THE DATE AND TIME.
HUH? WAS IT TODAY?
MORNING.
HE GETS LOST TRYING TO FIND THE VENUE.
HE'S SHY.
TODAY WAS A DUD AGAIN.
BUT THIS TIME YOU ACTUALLY WENT!
WHAT LOW STANDARDS.
HE DOESN'T HAVE A COMPETITIVE STREAK OR AMBITION.
"I JUST WANT TO HAVE FUN ACTING WITH EVERYONE."
WE'VE AVOIDED FACING THE FACTS, BUT BOTH TAKARA AND I ARE ALREADY THIRTY.
TAKARA, CAN YOU BE REBORN...
IN FRONT OF MR. KUROZU?
DIRECTOR SŌUICHI KUROZU
CASTING

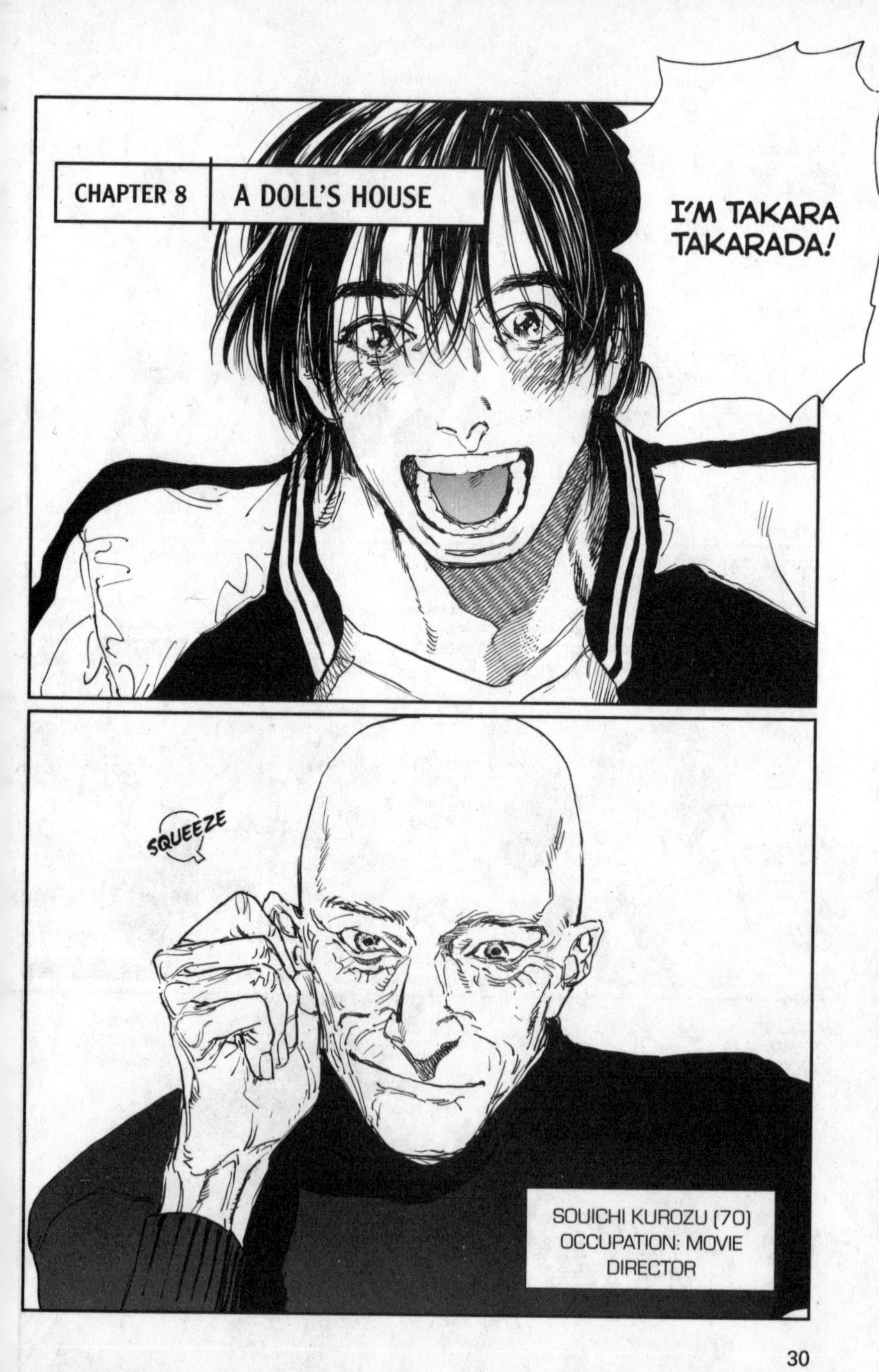
I'M TAKARA TAKARADA!
CHAPTER 8 A DOLL'S HOUSE
SQUEEZE
SOUICHI KUROZU (70) OCCUPATION: MOVIE DIRECTOR

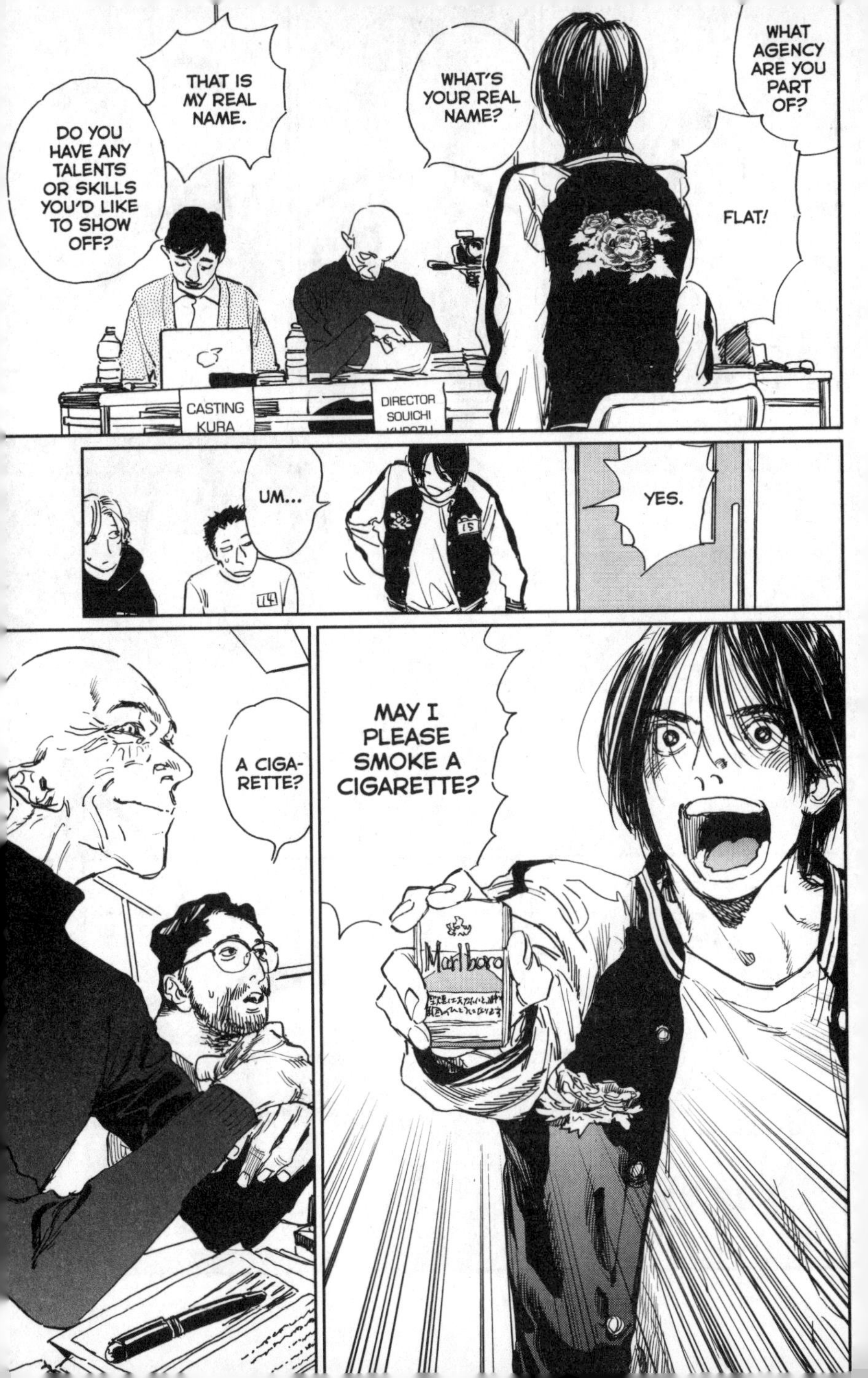
WHAT AGENCY ARE YOU PART OF?
FLAT!
WHAT'S YOUR REAL NAME?
THAT IS MY REAL NAME.
DO YOU HAVE ANY TALENTS OR SKILLS YOU'D LIKE TO SHOW OFF?
DIRECTOR SOUICHI
CASTING KURA
YES.
UM...
MAY I PLEASE SMOKE A CIGARETTE?
Marlboro
A CIGA-RETTE?

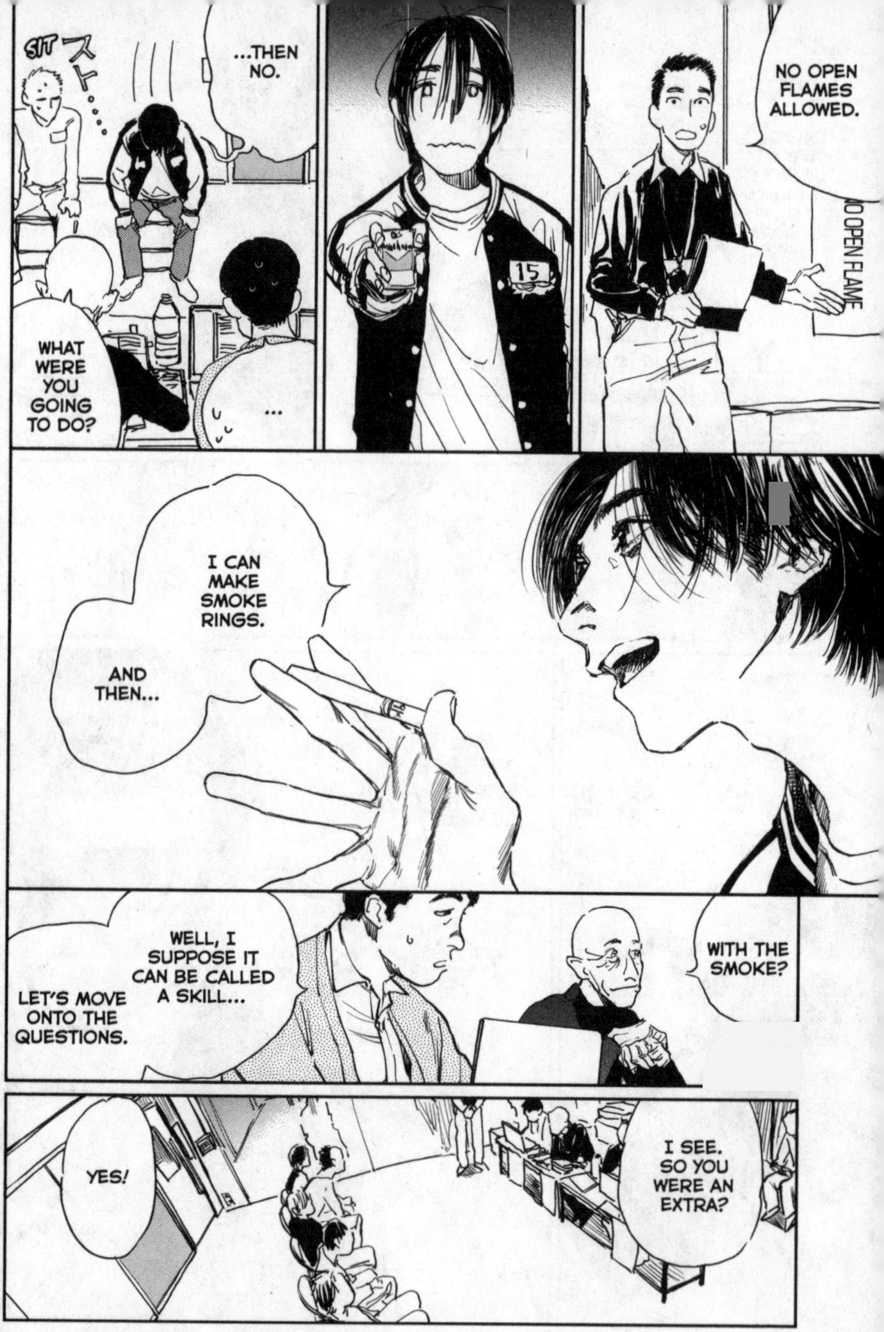
NO OPEN FLAMES ALLOWED.
OPEN FLAME
...THEN NO.
SIT スト
...
WHAT WERE YOU GOING TO DO?
I CAN MAKE SMOKE RINGS.
AND THEN...
WITH THE SMOKE?
WELL, I SUPPOSE IT CAN BE CALLED A SKILL...
LET'S MOVE ONTO THE QUESTIONS.
I SEE. SO YOU WERE AN EXTRA?
YES!

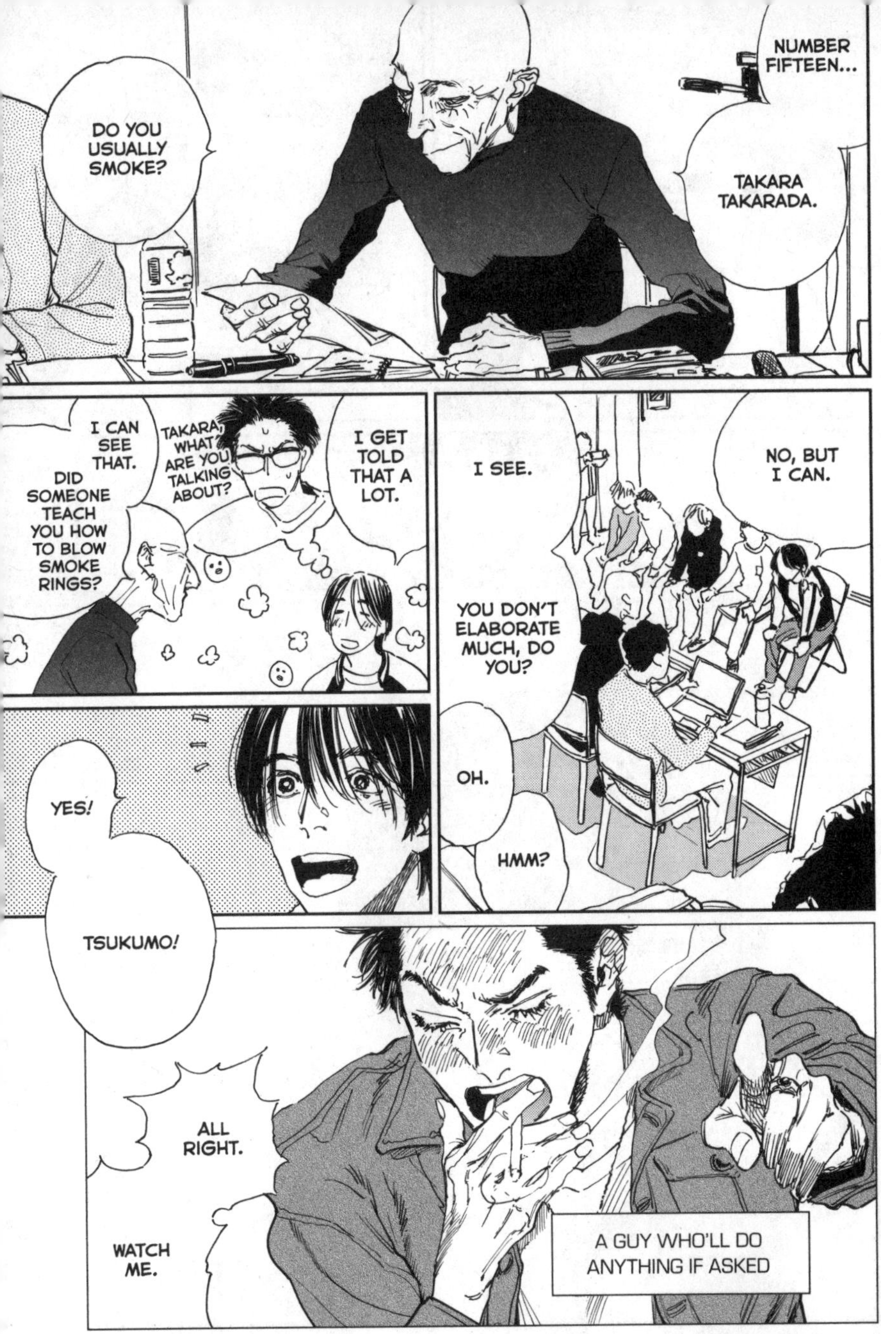
NUMBER FIFTEEN...
TAKARA TAKARADA.
DO YOU USUALLY SMOKE?
NO, BUT I CAN.
I SEE.
YOU DON'T ELABORATE MUCH, DO YOU?
OH.
HMM?
I GET TOLD THAT A LOT.
TAKARA, WHAT ARE YOU TALKING ABOUT?
I CAN SEE THAT.
DID SOMEONE TEACH YOU HOW TO BLOW SMOKE RINGS?
YES!
TSUKUMO!
ALL RIGHT.
WATCH ME.
A GUY WHO'LL DO ANYTHING IF ASKED

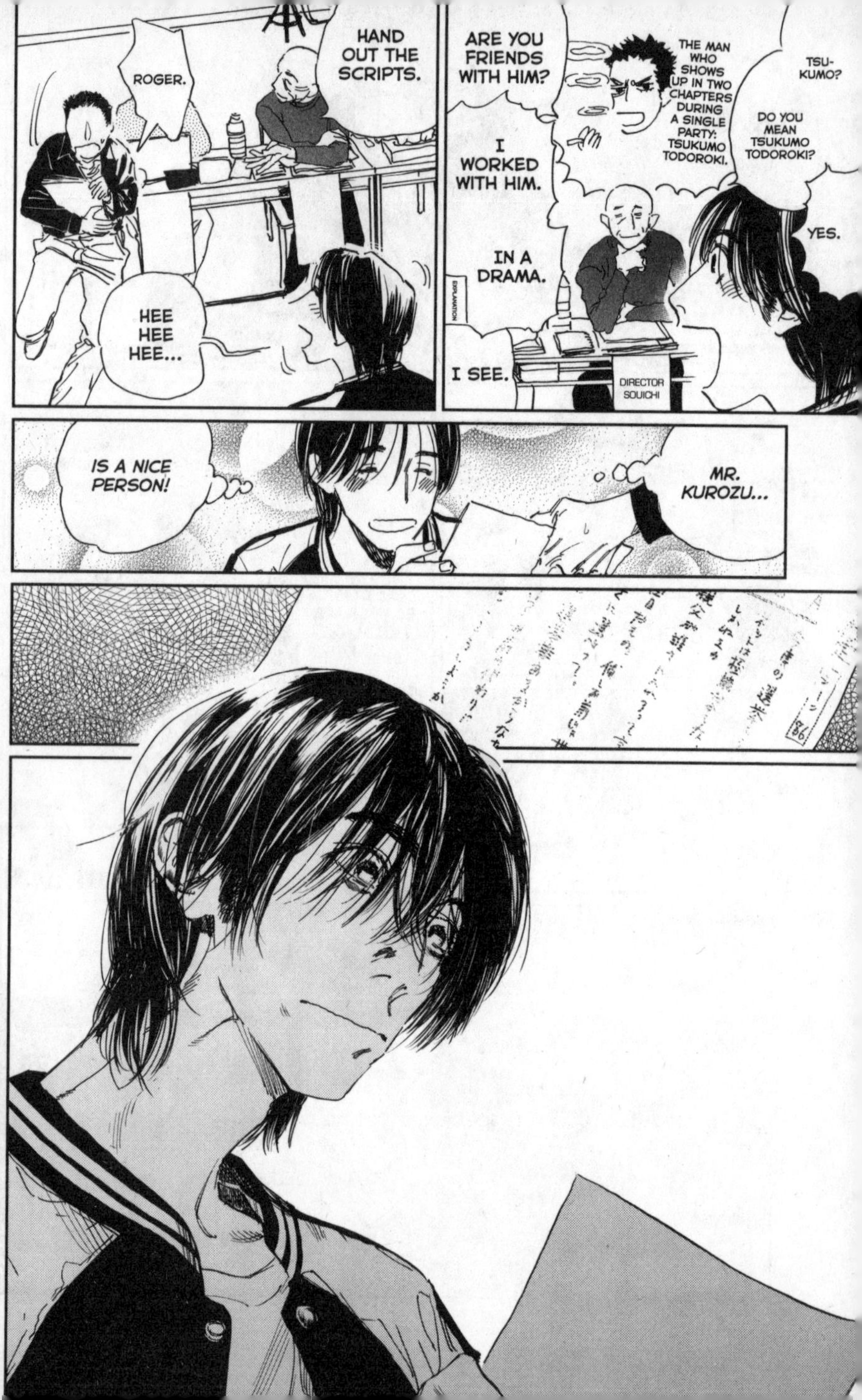
TSU-KUMO?
DO YOU MEAN TSUKUMO TODOROKI?
THE MAN WHO SHOWS UP IN TWO CHAPTERS DURING A SINGLE PARTY: TSUKUMO TODOROKI.
YES.
ARE YOU FRIENDS WITH HIM?
I WORKED WITH HIM.
IN A DRAMA.
EXPLANATION
DIRECTOR SOUICHI
I SEE.
HAND OUT THE SCRIPTS.
ROGER.
HEE HEE HEE...
MR. KUROZU...
IS A NICE PERSON!

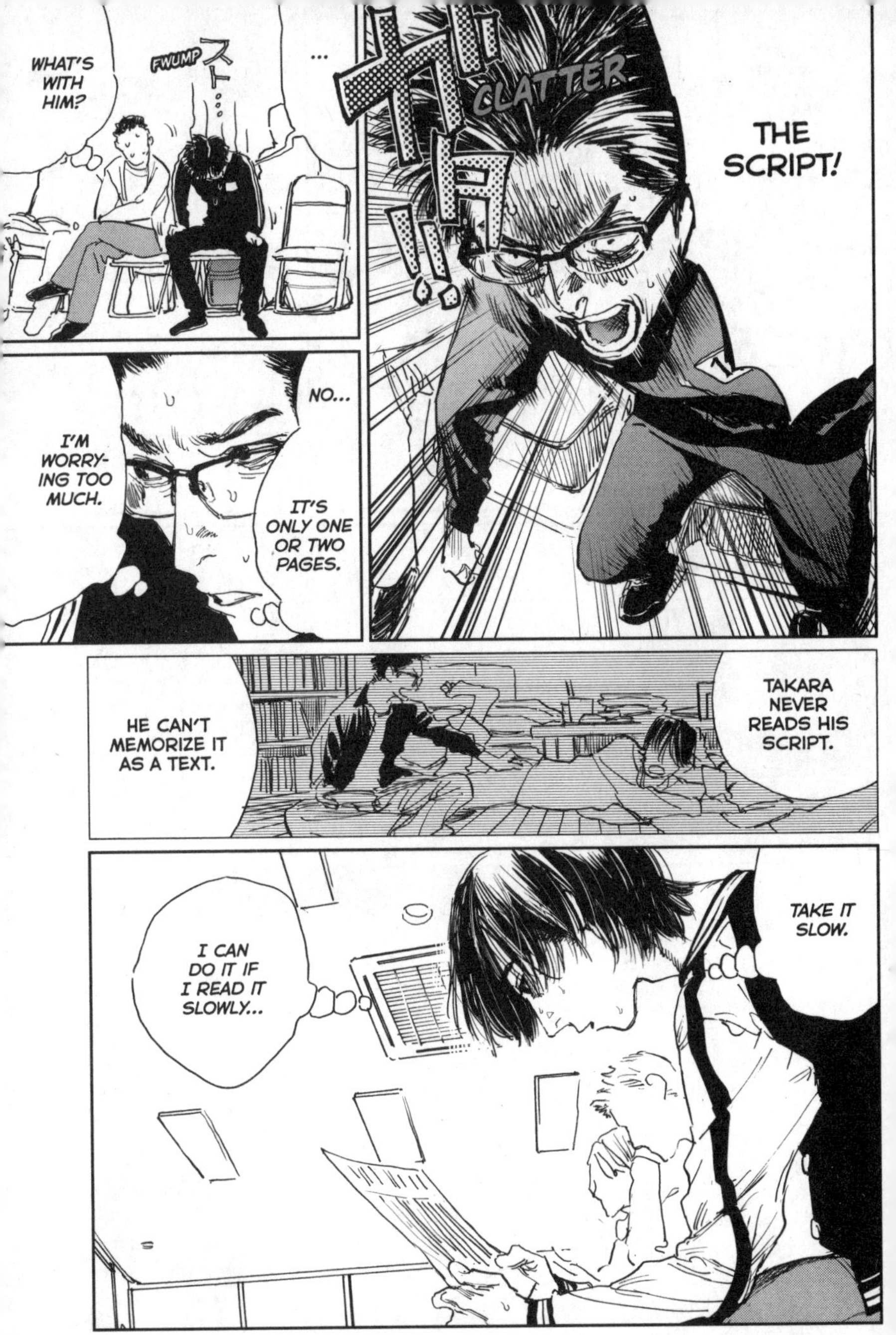
CLATTER
THE SCRIPT!
...
FWUMP
WHAT'S WITH HIM?
NO...
I'M WORRYING TOO MUCH.
IT'S ONLY ONE OR TWO PAGES.
TAKARA NEVER READS HIS SCRIPT.
HE CAN'T MEMORIZE IT AS A TEXT.
TAKE IT SLOW.
I CAN DO IT IF I READ IT SLOWLY...

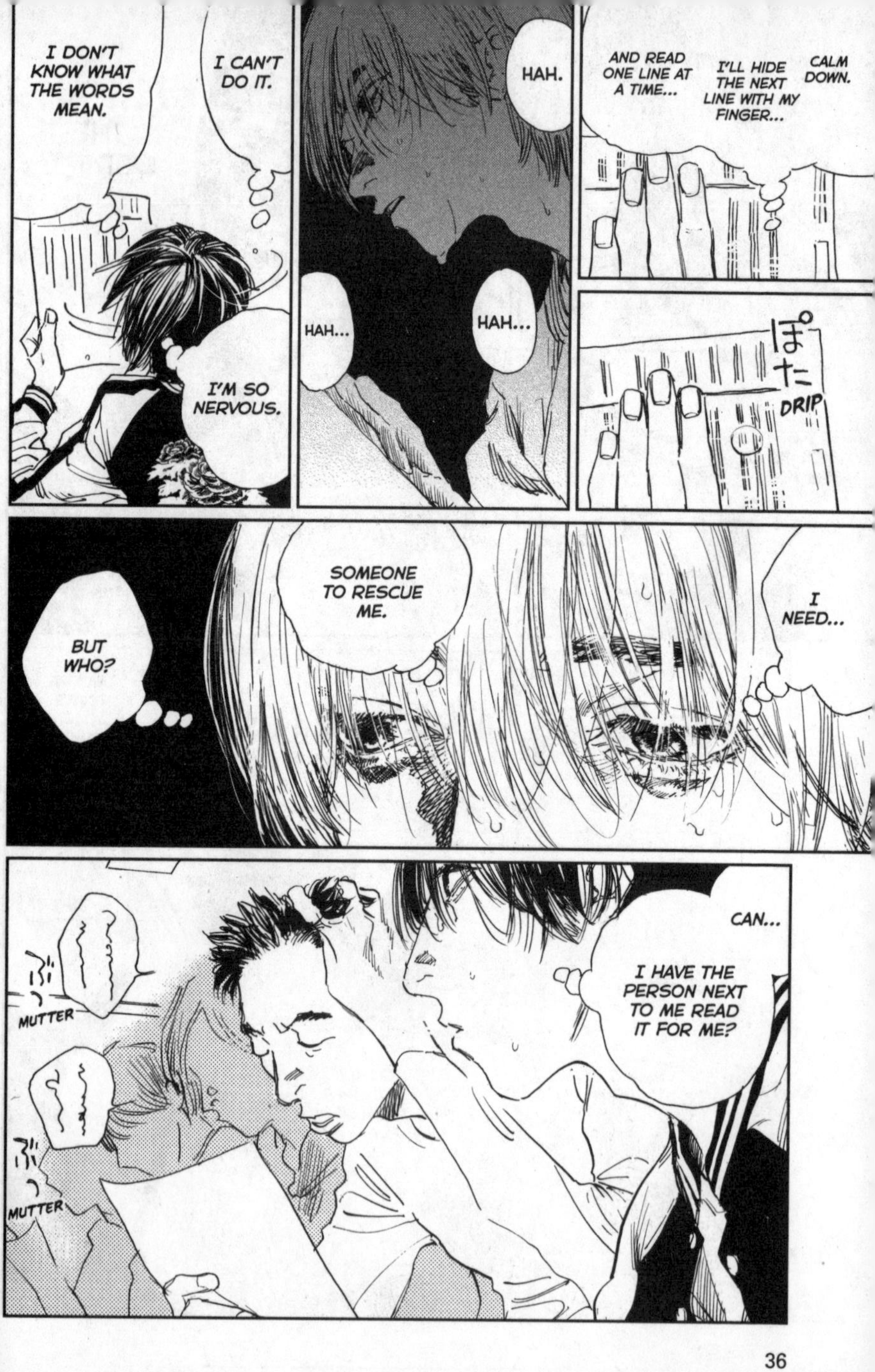
CALM DOWN.
I'LL HIDE THE NEXT LINE WITH MY FINGER...
AND READ ONE LINE AT A TIME...
ぽた
DRIP
HAH.
HAH...
HAH...
I CAN'T DO IT.
I DON'T KNOW WHAT THE WORDS MEAN.
I'M SO NERVOUS.
I NEED...
SOMEONE TO RESCUE ME.
BUT WHO?
CAN...
I HAVE THE PERSON NEXT TO ME READ IT FOR ME?
MUTTER
MUTTER

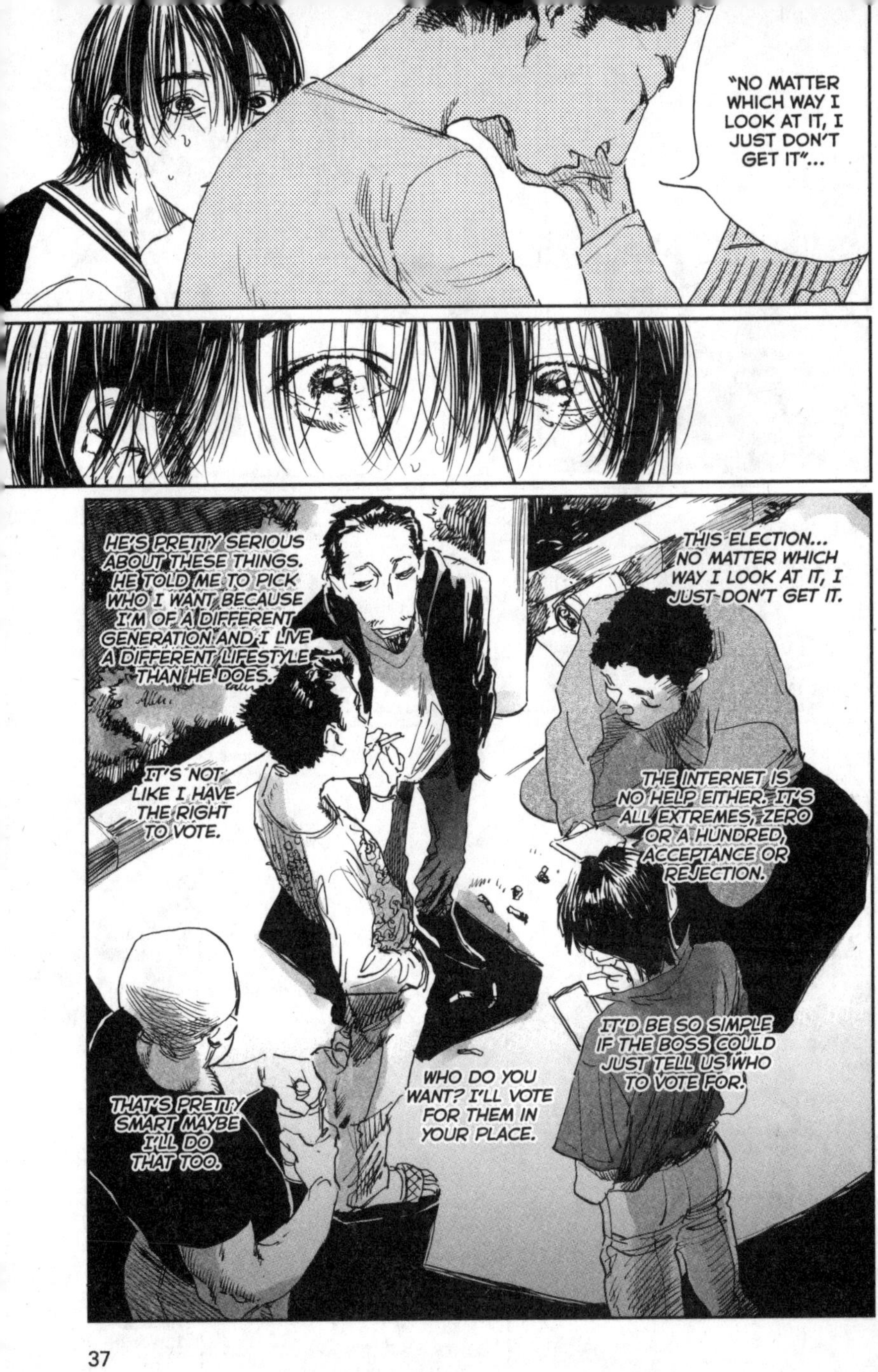
"NO MATTER WHICH WAY I LOOK AT IT, I JUST DON'T GET IT"...
THIS ELECTION... NO MATTER WHICH WAY I LOOK AT IT, I JUST DON'T GET IT.
HE'S PRETTY SERIOUS ABOUT THESE THINGS. HE TOLD ME TO PICK WHO I WANT BECAUSE I'M OF A DIFFERENT GENERATION AND I LIVE A DIFFERENT LIFESTYLE THAN HE DOES.
THE INTERNET IS NO HELP EITHER. IT'S ALL EXTREMES, ZERO OR A HUNDRED, ACCEPTANCE OR REJECTION.
IT'S NOT LIKE I HAVE THE RIGHT TO VOTE.
IT'D BE SO SIMPLE IF THE BOSS COULD JUST TELL US WHO TO VOTE FOR.
WHO DO YOU WANT? I'LL VOTE FOR THEM IN YOUR PLACE.
THAT'S PRETTY SMART MAYBE I'LL DO THAT TOO.

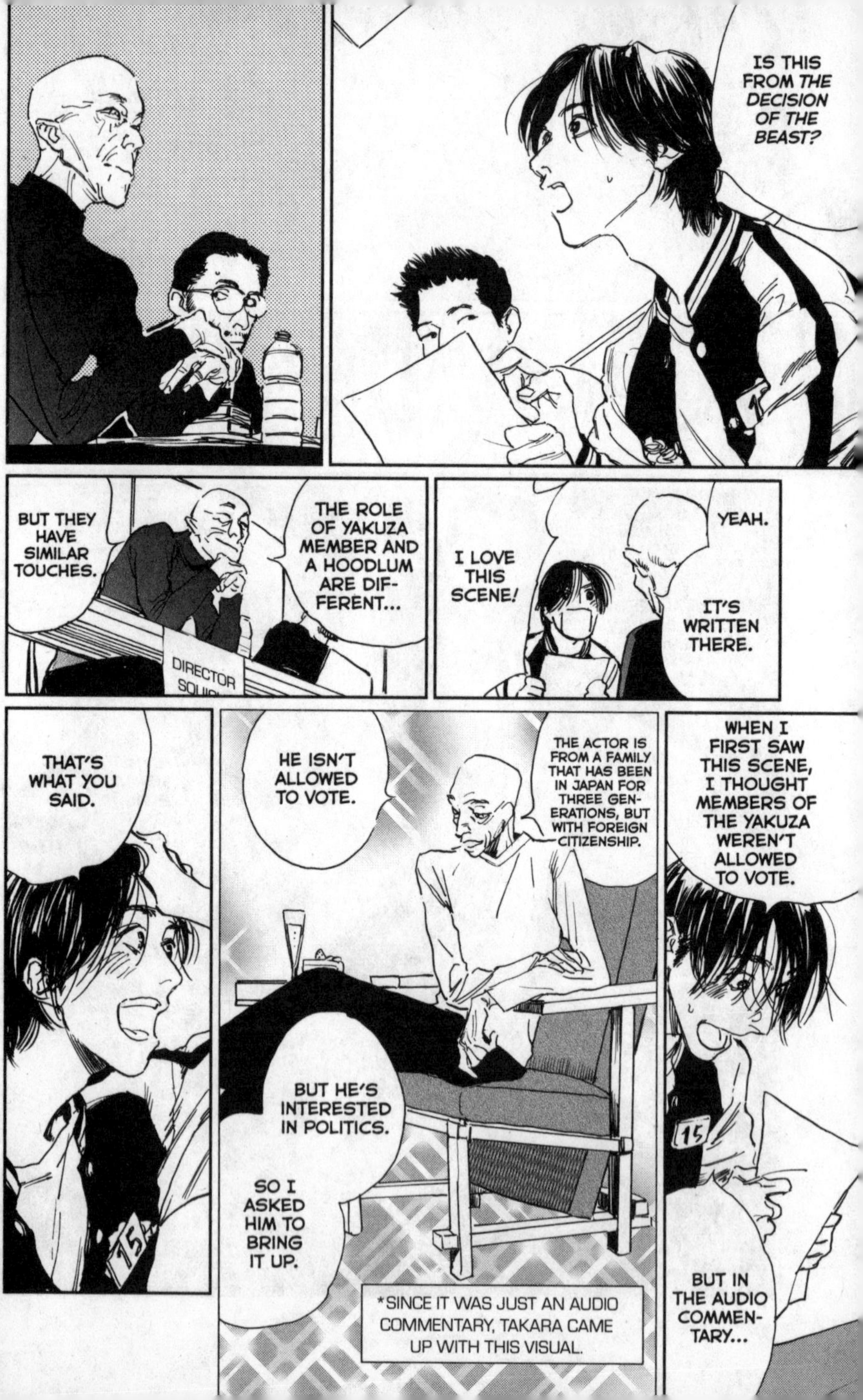
IS THIS FROM *THE DECISION OF THE BEAST?*
I LOVE THIS SCENE!
YEAH.
IT'S WRITTEN THERE.
THE ROLE OF YAKUZA MEMBER AND A HOODLUM ARE DIF-FERENT...
BUT THEY HAVE SIMILAR TOUCHES.
DIRECTOR
WHEN I FIRST SAW THIS SCENE, I THOUGHT MEMBERS OF THE YAKUZA WEREN'T ALLOWED TO VOTE.
15
BUT IN THE AUDIO COMMEN-TARY...
THE ACTOR IS FROM A FAMILY THAT HAS BEEN IN JAPAN FOR THREE GEN-ERATIONS, BUT WITH FOREIGN CITIZENSHIP.
HE ISN'T ALLOWED TO VOTE.
BUT HE'S INTERESTED IN POLITICS.
SO I ASKED HIM TO BRING IT UP.
*SINCE IT WAS JUST AN AUDIO COMMENTARY, TAKARA CAME UP WITH THIS VISUAL.
THAT'S WHAT YOU SAID.
15

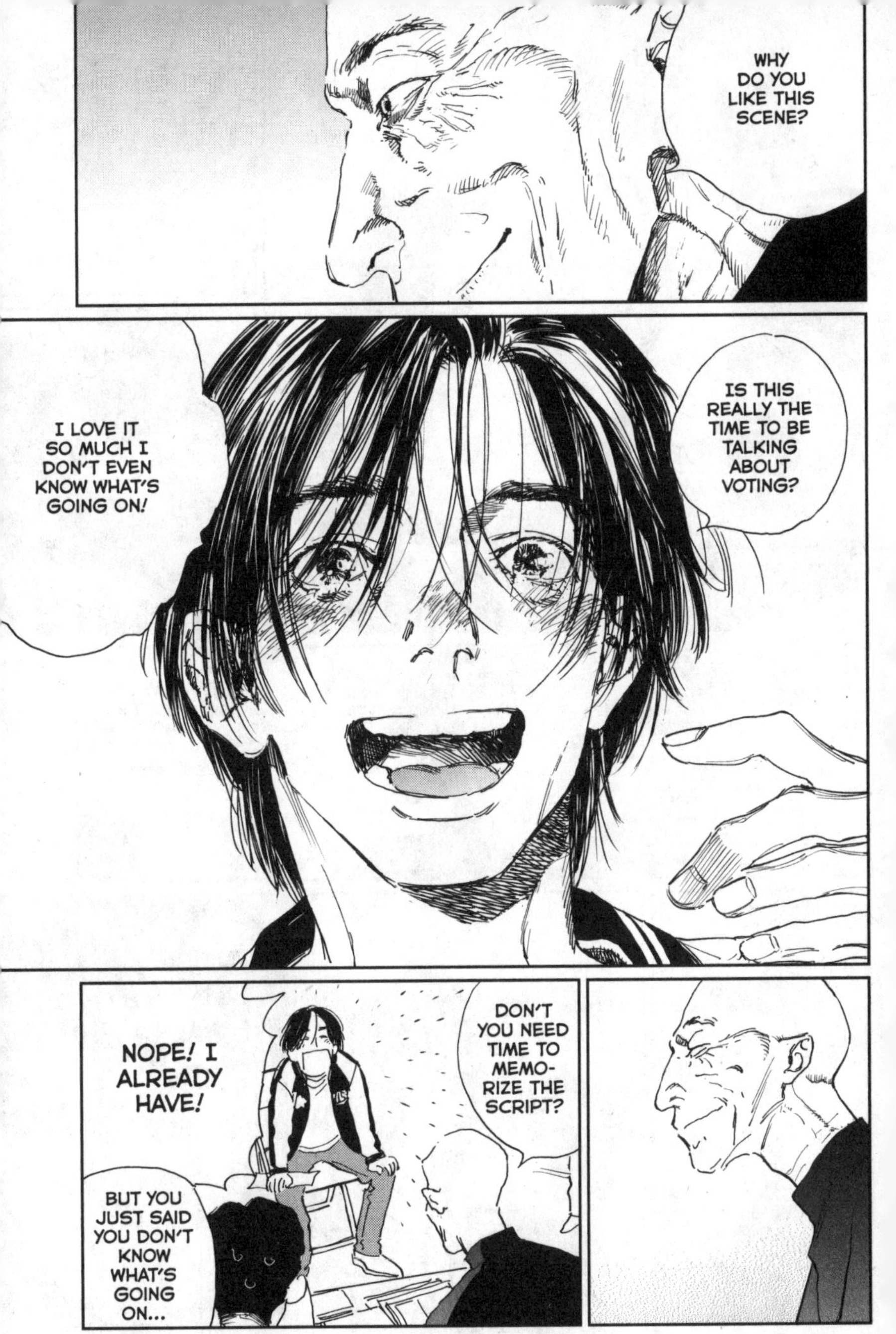
WHY DO YOU LIKE THIS SCENE?
IS THIS REALLY THE TIME TO BE TALKING ABOUT VOTING?
I LOVE IT SO MUCH I DON'T EVEN KNOW WHAT'S GOING ON!
DON'T YOU NEED TIME TO MEMO-RIZE THE SCRIPT?
NOPE! I ALREADY HAVE!
BUT YOU JUST SAID YOU DON'T KNOW WHAT'S GOING ON...

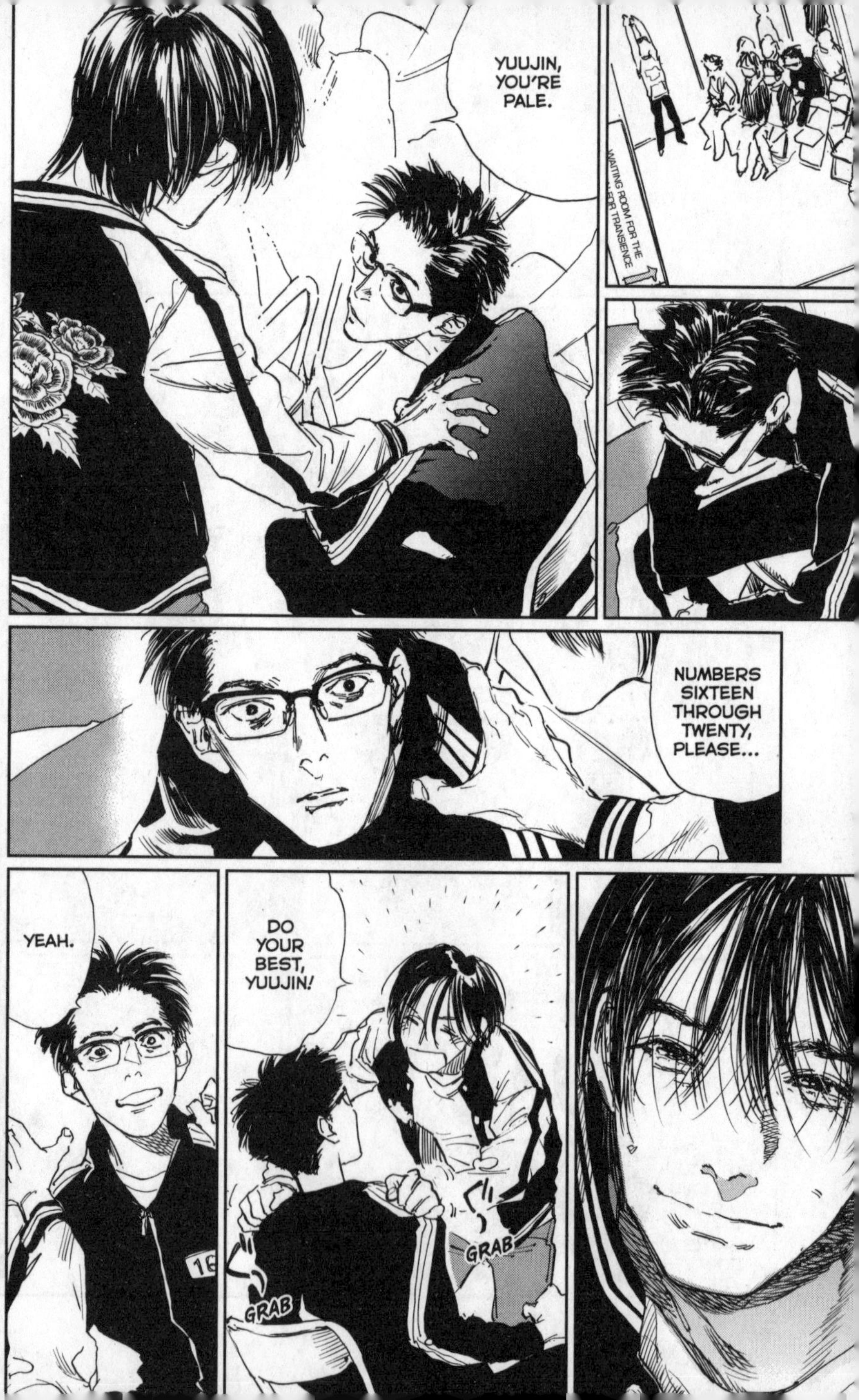
WAITING ROOM FOR THE
FOR TRANSIENCE
YUUJIN, YOU'RE PALE.
NUMBERS SIXTEEN THROUGH TWENTY, PLEASE...
DO YOUR BEST, YUUJIN!
GRAB
GRAB
YEAH.
16

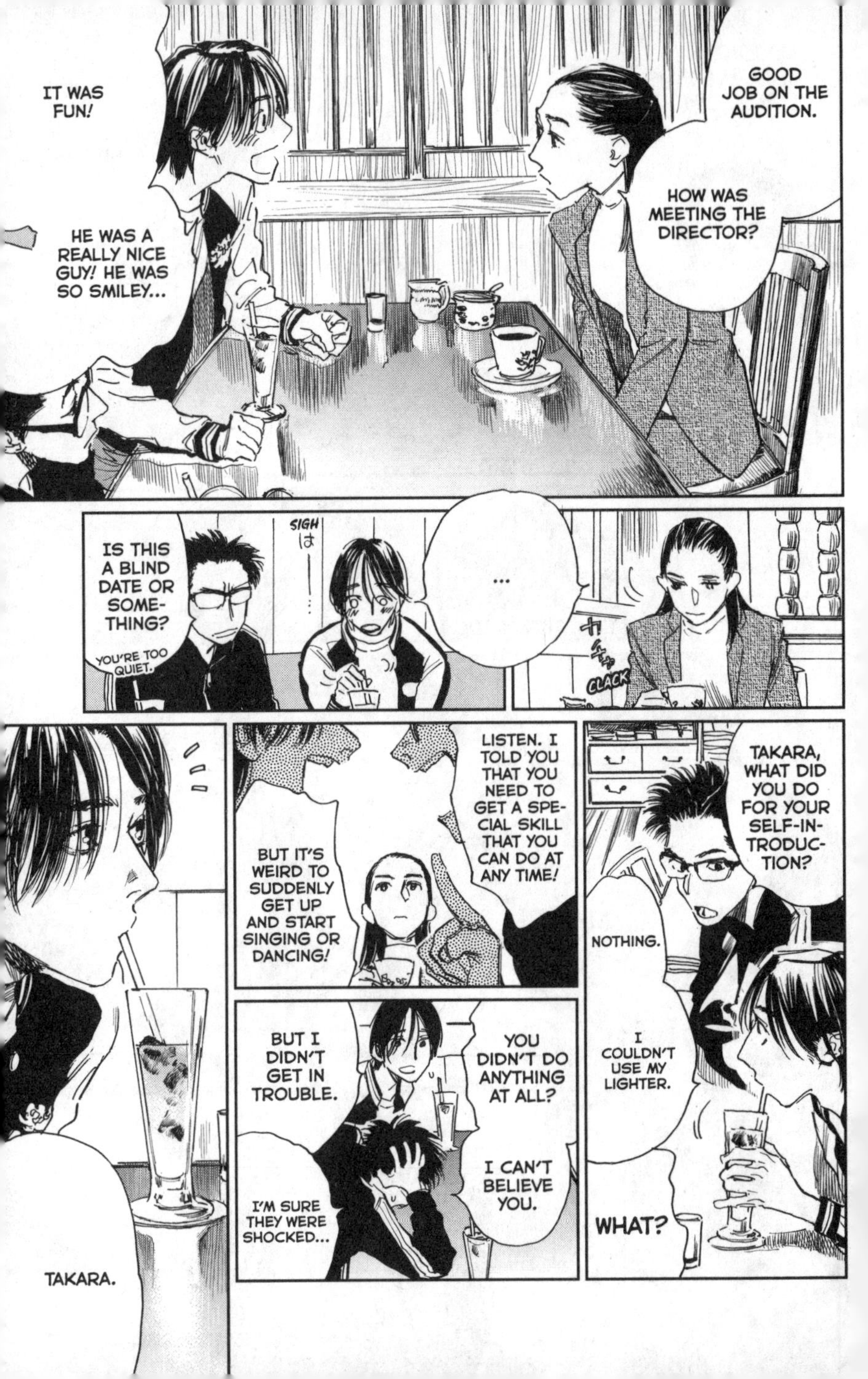
GOOD JOB ON THE AUDITION.
HOW WAS MEETING THE DIRECTOR?
IT WAS FUN!
HE WAS A REALLY NICE GUY! HE WAS SO SMILEY...
...
CLACK
SIGH
は
IS THIS A BLIND DATE OR SOME-THING?
YOU'RE TOO QUIET.
TAKARA, WHAT DID YOU DO FOR YOUR SELF-IN-TRODUC-TION?
NOTHING.
I COULDN'T USE MY LIGHTER.
WHAT?
LISTEN. I TOLD YOU THAT YOU NEED TO GET A SPE-CIAL SKILL THAT YOU CAN DO AT ANY TIME!
BUT IT'S WEIRD TO SUDDENLY GET UP AND START SINGING OR DANCING!
YOU DIDN'T DO ANYTHING AT ALL?
BUT I DIDN'T GET IN TROUBLE.
I CAN'T BELIEVE YOU.
I'M SURE THEY WERE SHOCKED...
TAKARA.

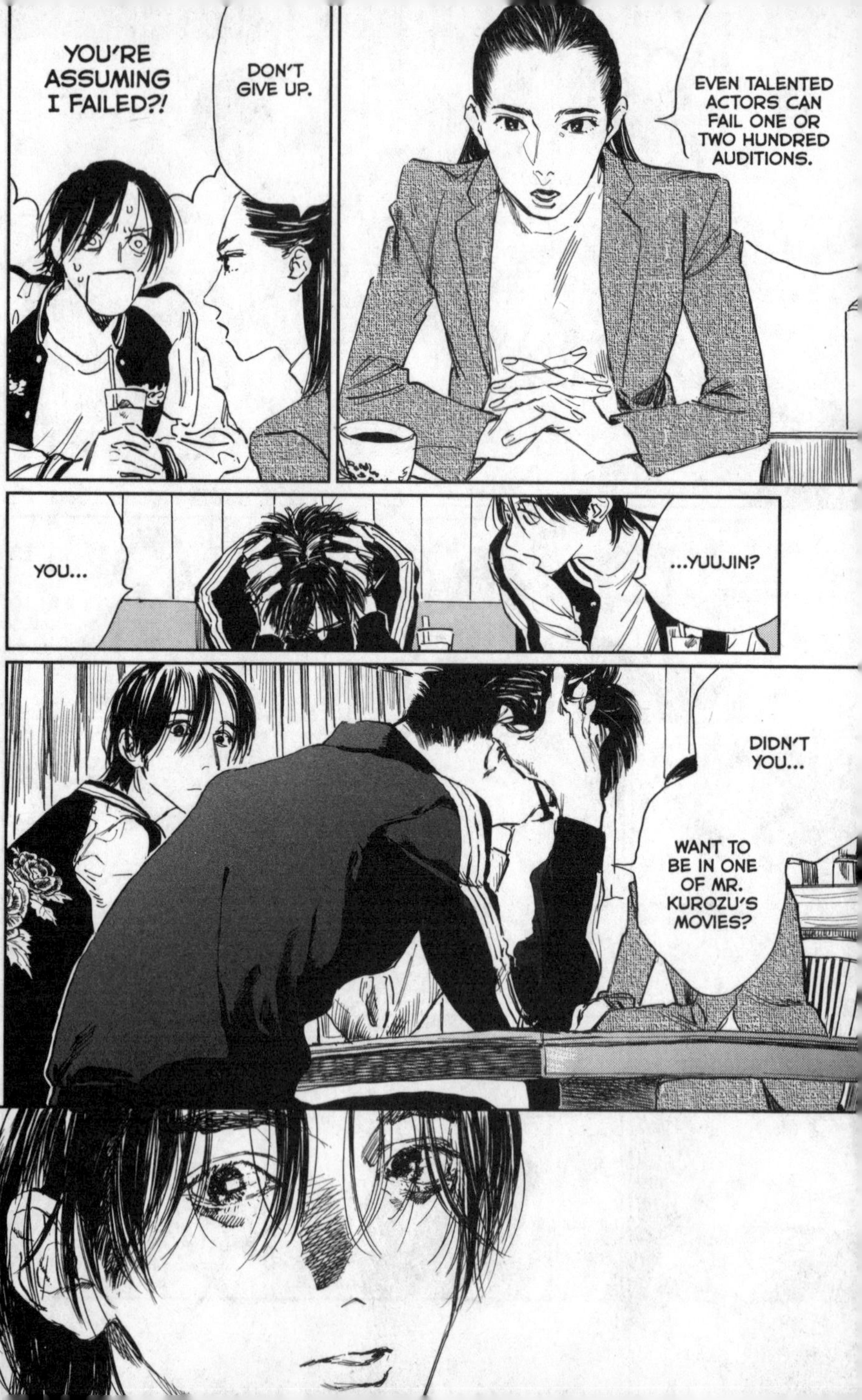
EVEN TALENTED ACTORS CAN FAIL ONE OR TWO HUNDRED AUDITIONS.
DON'T GIVE UP.
YOU'RE ASSUMING I FAILED?!
...YUUJIN?
YOU...
DIDN'T YOU...
WANT TO BE IN ONE OF MR. KUROZU'S MOVIES?

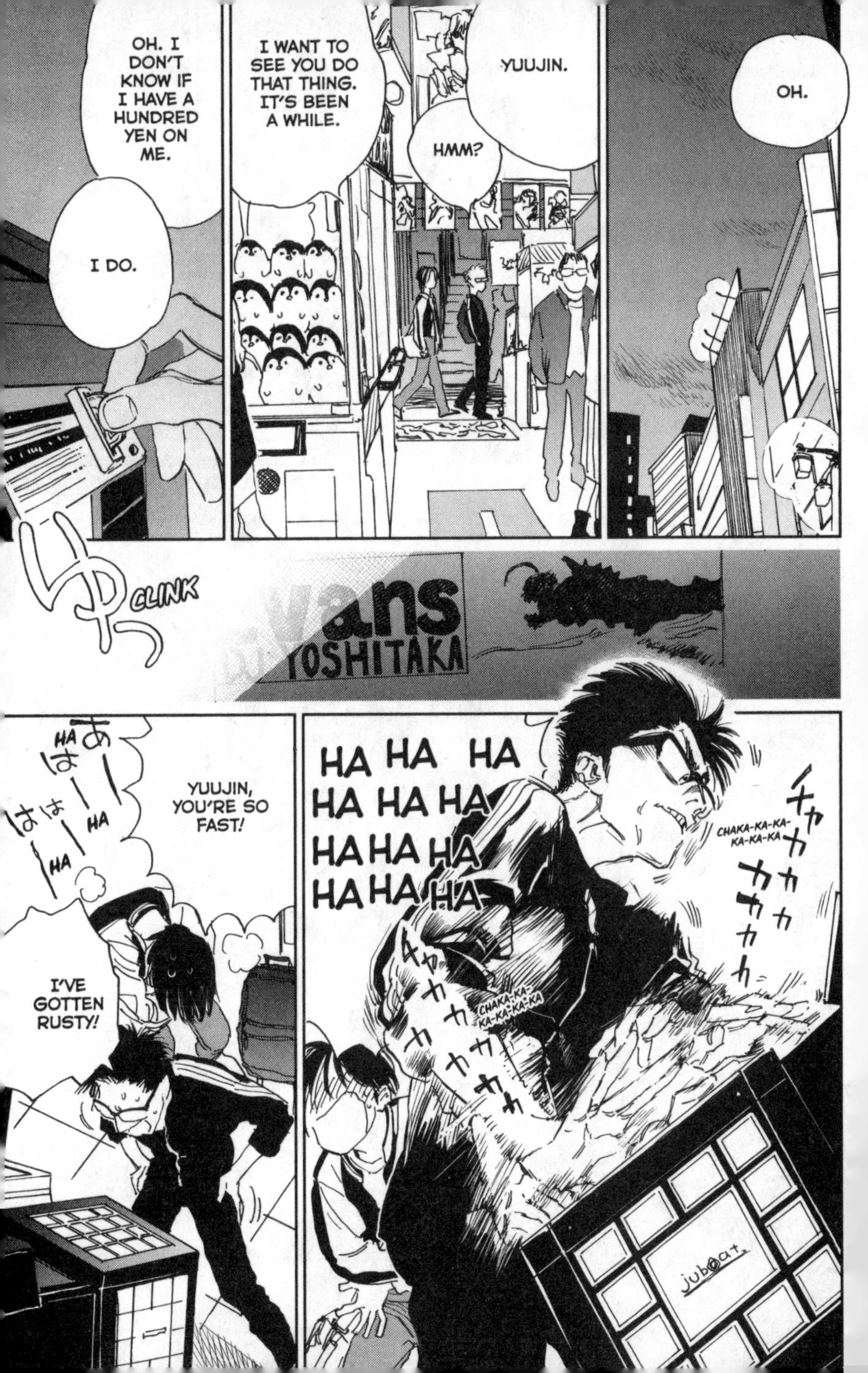
OH.
YUUJIN.
HMM?
I WANT TO SEE YOU DO THAT THING. IT'S BEEN A WHILE.
OH. I DON'T KNOW IF I HAVE A HUNDRED YEN ON ME.
I DO.
ゆっ
CLINK
YOSHITAKA
HA HA HA
HA HA HA
HA HA HA
HA HA HA
チャカカカカカカカ
CHAKA-KA-KA-KA-KA-KA
チャカカカカカカカ
CHAKA-KA-KA-KA-KA-KA
jubeat
あはーはー
HA HA HA HA
YUUJIN, YOU'RE SO FAST!
I'VE GOTTEN RUSTY!

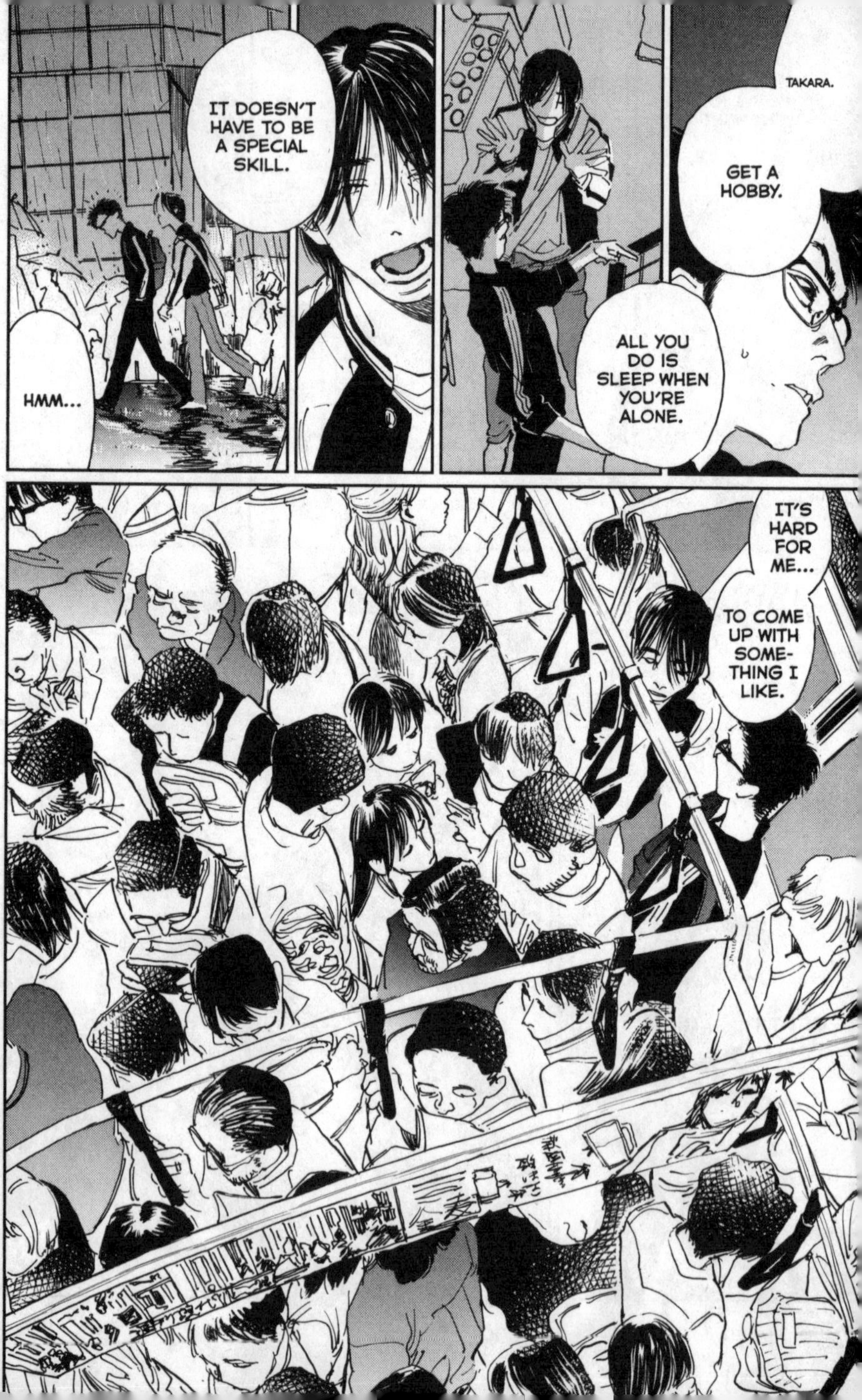
TAKARA.
GET A HOBBY.
ALL YOU DO IS SLEEP WHEN YOU'RE ALONE.
IT DOESN'T HAVE TO BE A SPECIAL SKILL.
HMM...
IT'S HARD FOR ME...
TO COME UP WITH SOME-THING I LIKE.

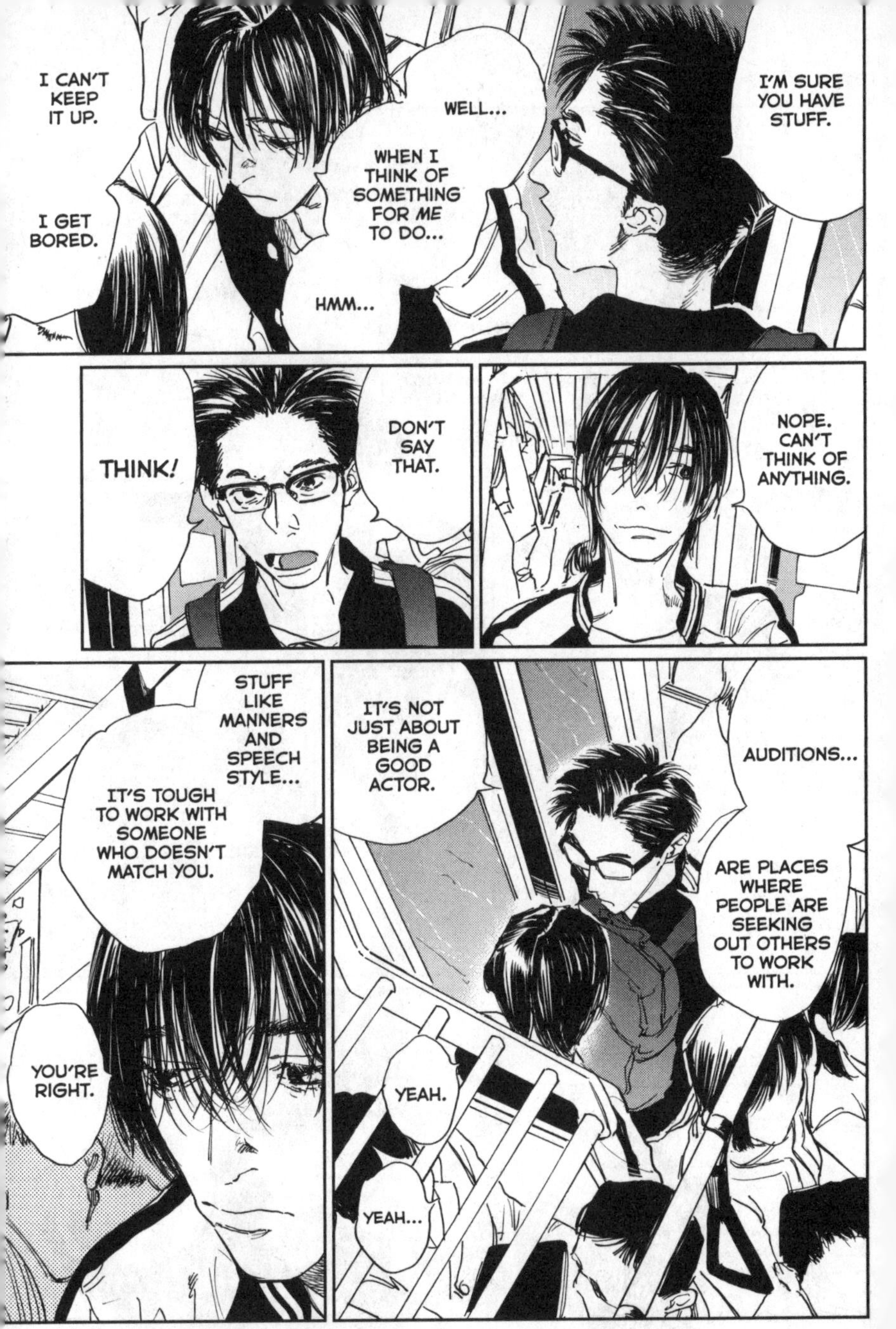
I'M SURE YOU HAVE STUFF.
WELL...
WHEN I THINK OF SOMETHING FOR *ME* TO DO...
HMM...
I CAN'T KEEP IT UP.
I GET BORED.
NOPE. CAN'T THINK OF ANYTHING.
DON'T SAY THAT.
THINK!
AUDITIONS...
ARE PLACES WHERE PEOPLE ARE SEEKING OUT OTHERS TO WORK WITH.
IT'S NOT JUST ABOUT BEING A GOOD ACTOR.
YEAH.
YEAH...
STUFF LIKE MANNERS AND SPEECH STYLE...
IT'S TOUGH TO WORK WITH SOMEONE WHO DOESN'T MATCH YOU.
YOU'RE RIGHT.

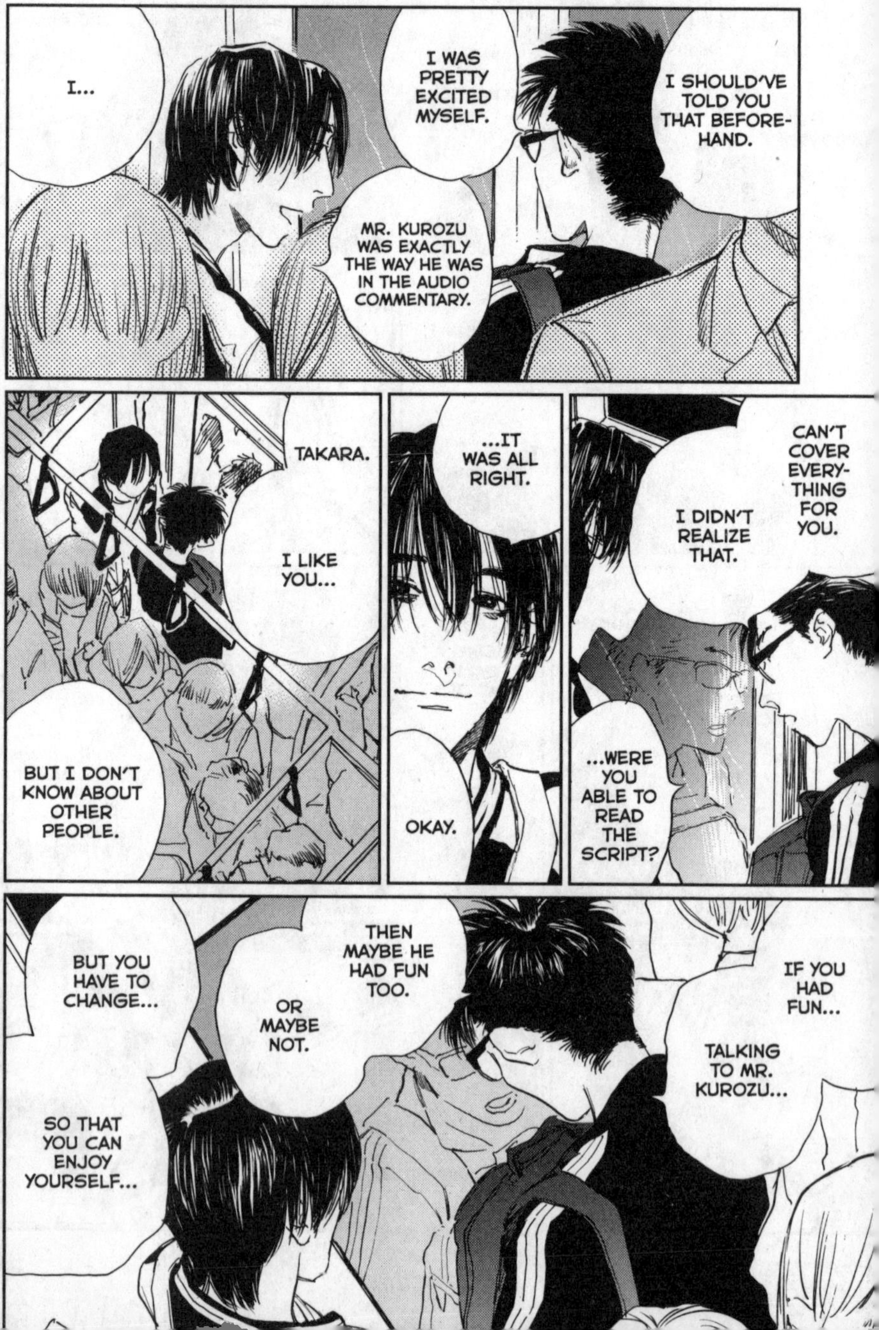
I SHOULD'VE TOLD YOU THAT BEFOREHAND.
I WAS PRETTY EXCITED MYSELF.
MR. KUROZU WAS EXACTLY THE WAY HE WAS IN THE AUDIO COMMENTARY.
I...
CAN'T COVER EVERYTHING FOR YOU.
I DIDN'T REALIZE THAT.
...WERE YOU ABLE TO READ THE SCRIPT?
...IT WAS ALL RIGHT.
OKAY.
TAKARA.
I LIKE YOU...
BUT I DON'T KNOW ABOUT OTHER PEOPLE.
IF YOU HAD FUN...
TALKING TO MR. KUROZU...
THEN MAYBE HE HAD FUN TOO.
OR MAYBE NOT.
BUT YOU HAVE TO CHANGE...
SO THAT YOU CAN ENJOY YOURSELF...

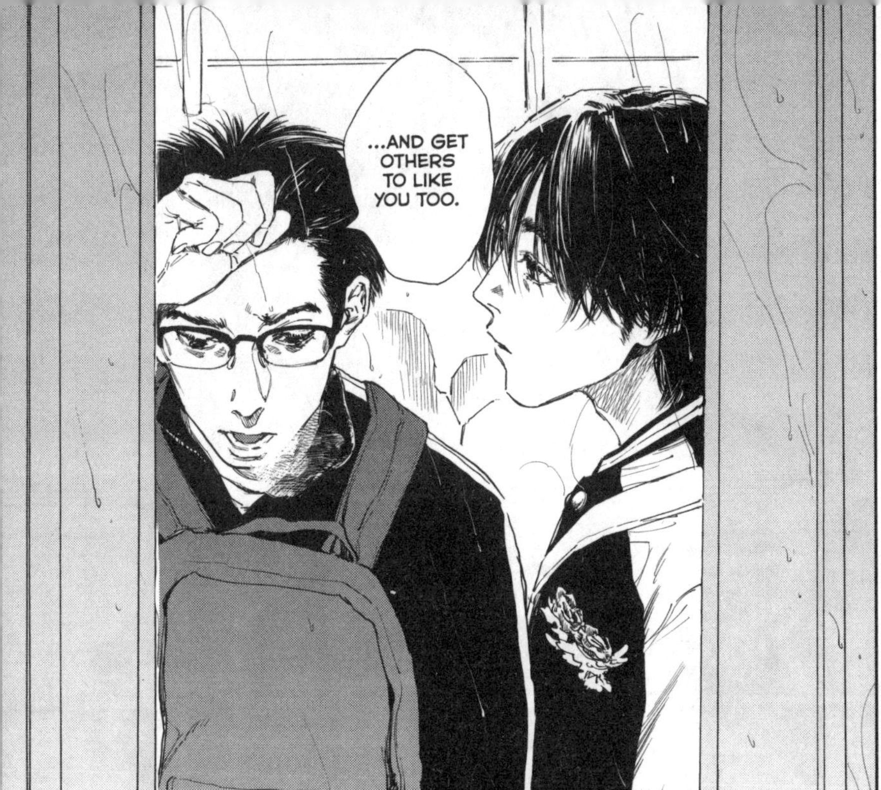
...AND GET OTHERS TO LIKE YOU TOO.
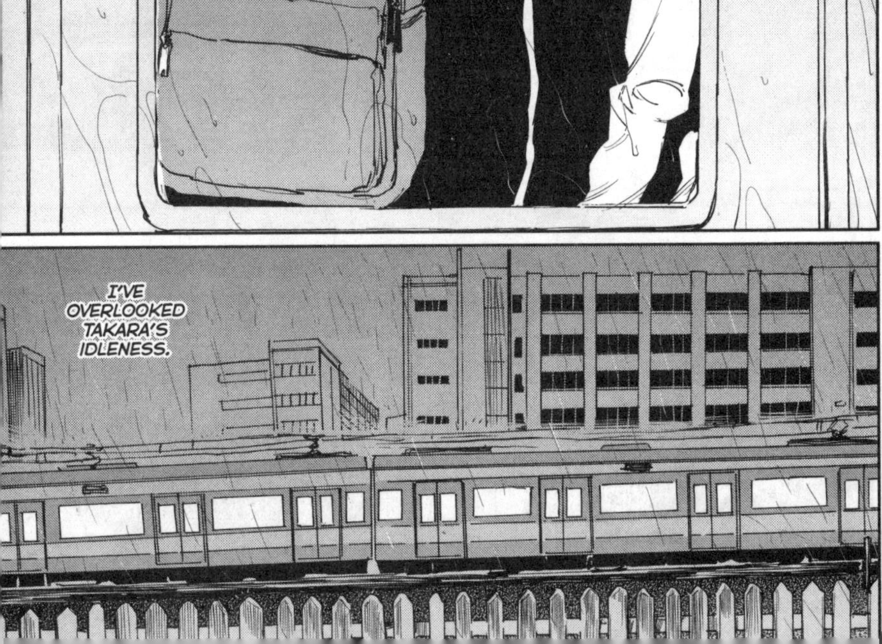
I'VE OVERLOOKED TAKARA'S IDLENESS.

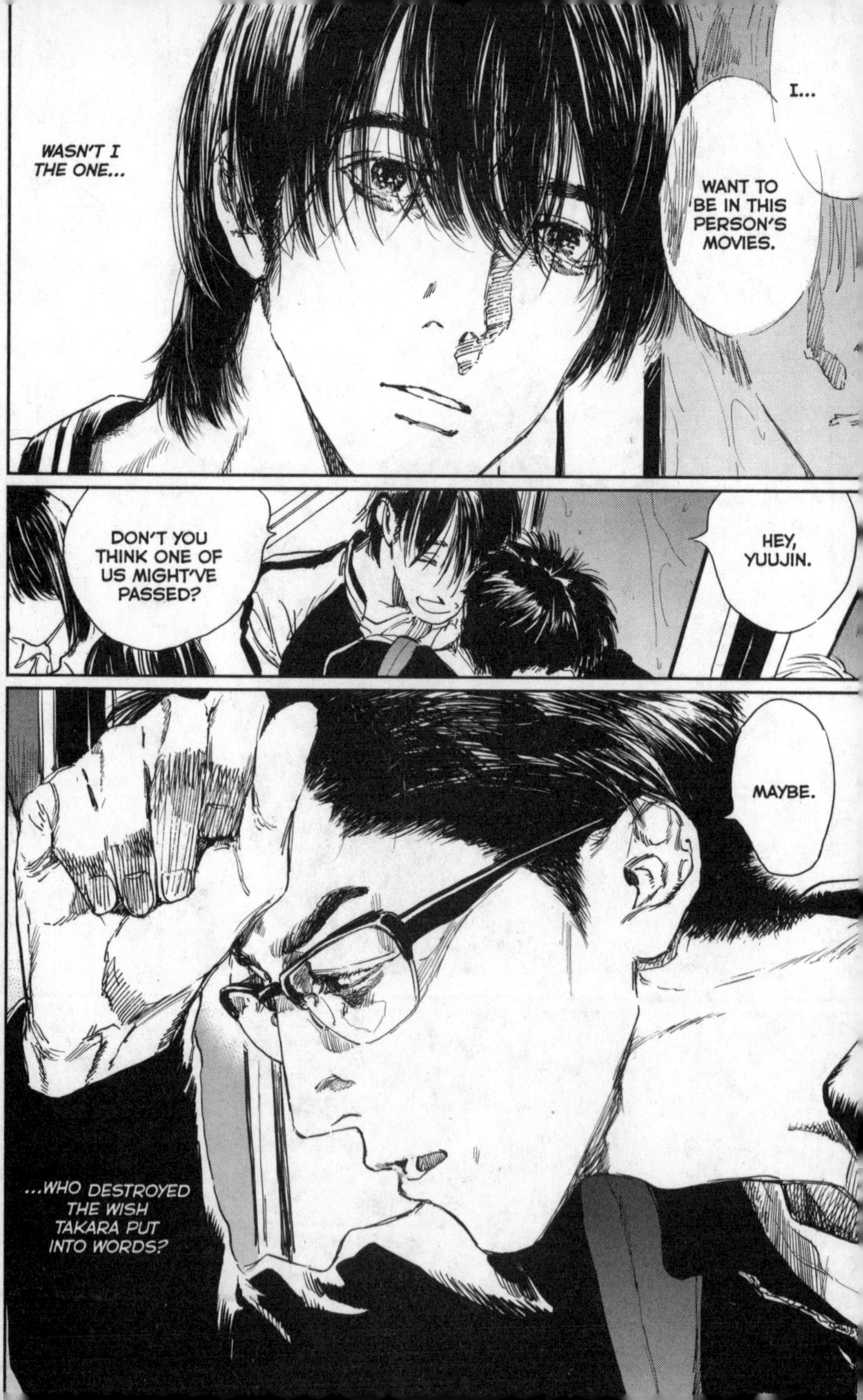
I...
WANT TO BE IN THIS PERSON'S MOVIES.
WASN'T I THE ONE...
HEY, YUUJIN.
DON'T YOU THINK ONE OF US MIGHT'VE PASSED?
MAYBE.
...WHO DESTROYED THE WISH TAKARA PUT INTO WORDS?

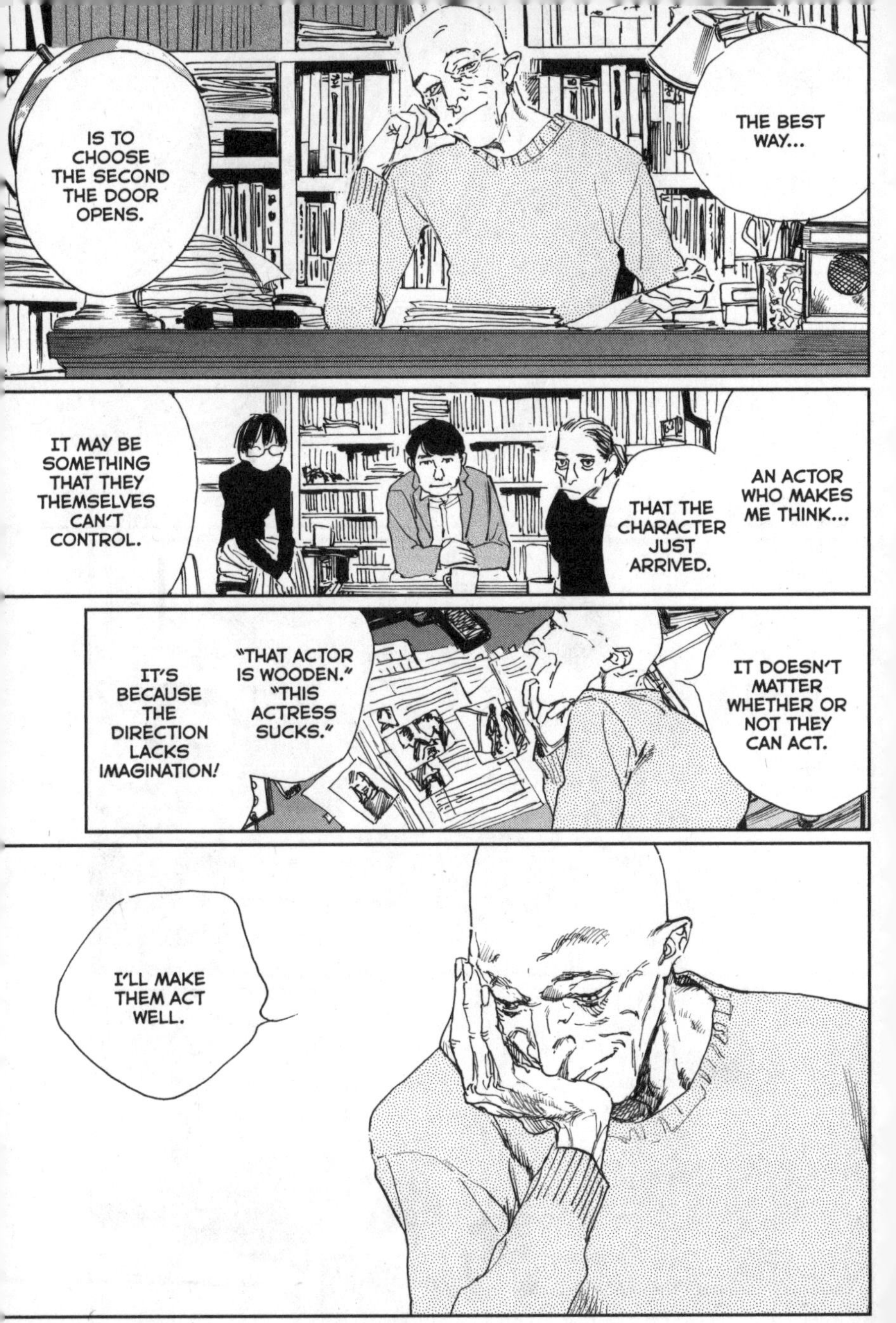
THE BEST WAY...
IS TO CHOOSE THE SECOND THE DOOR OPENS.
AN ACTOR WHO MAKES ME THINK...
THAT THE CHARACTER JUST ARRIVED.
IT MAY BE SOMETHING THAT THEY THEMSELVES CAN'T CONTROL.
IT DOESN'T MATTER WHETHER OR NOT THEY CAN ACT.
"THAT ACTOR IS WOODEN." "THIS ACTRESS SUCKS."
IT'S BECAUSE THE DIRECTION LACKS IMAGINATION!
I'LL MAKE THEM ACT WELL.

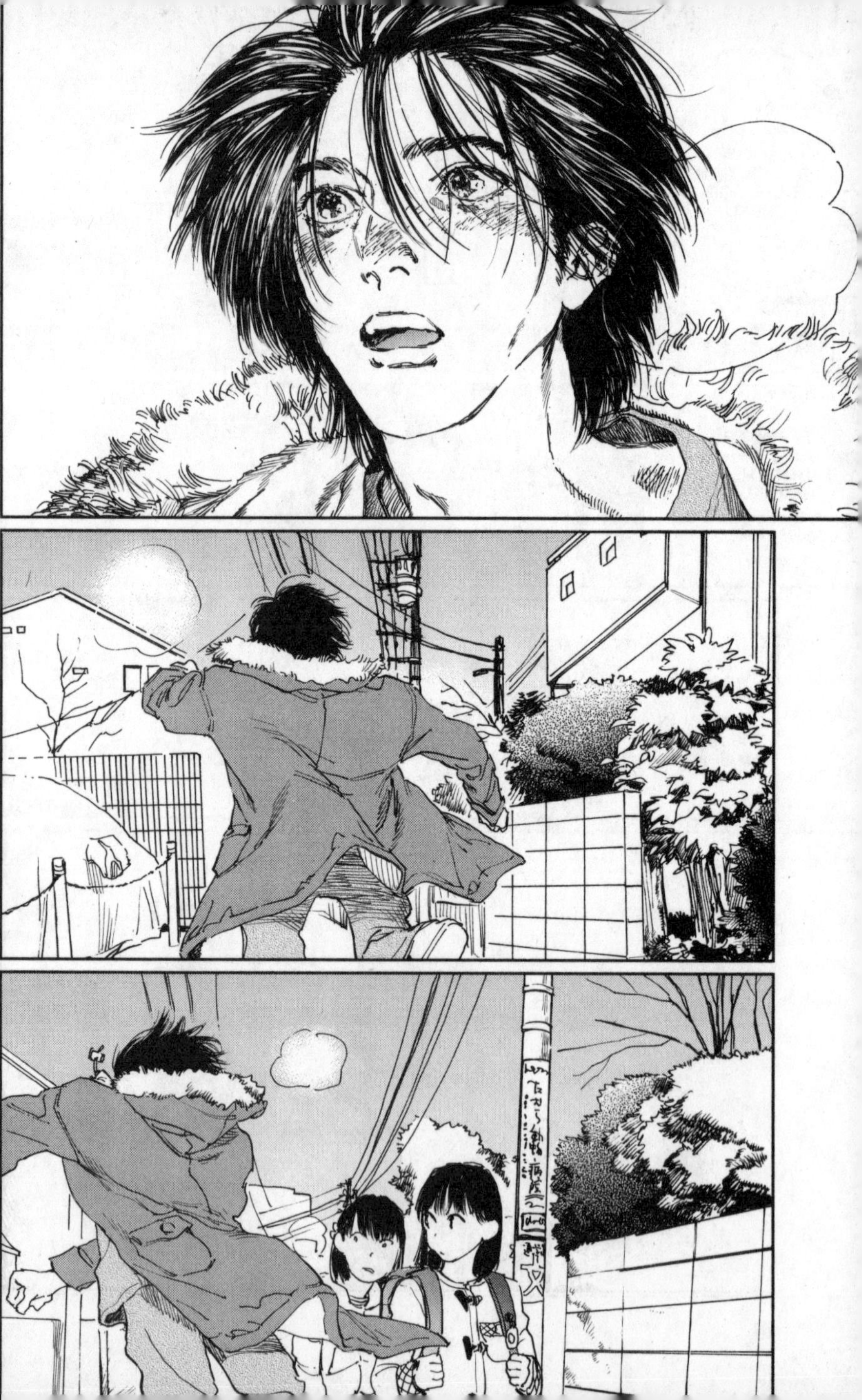

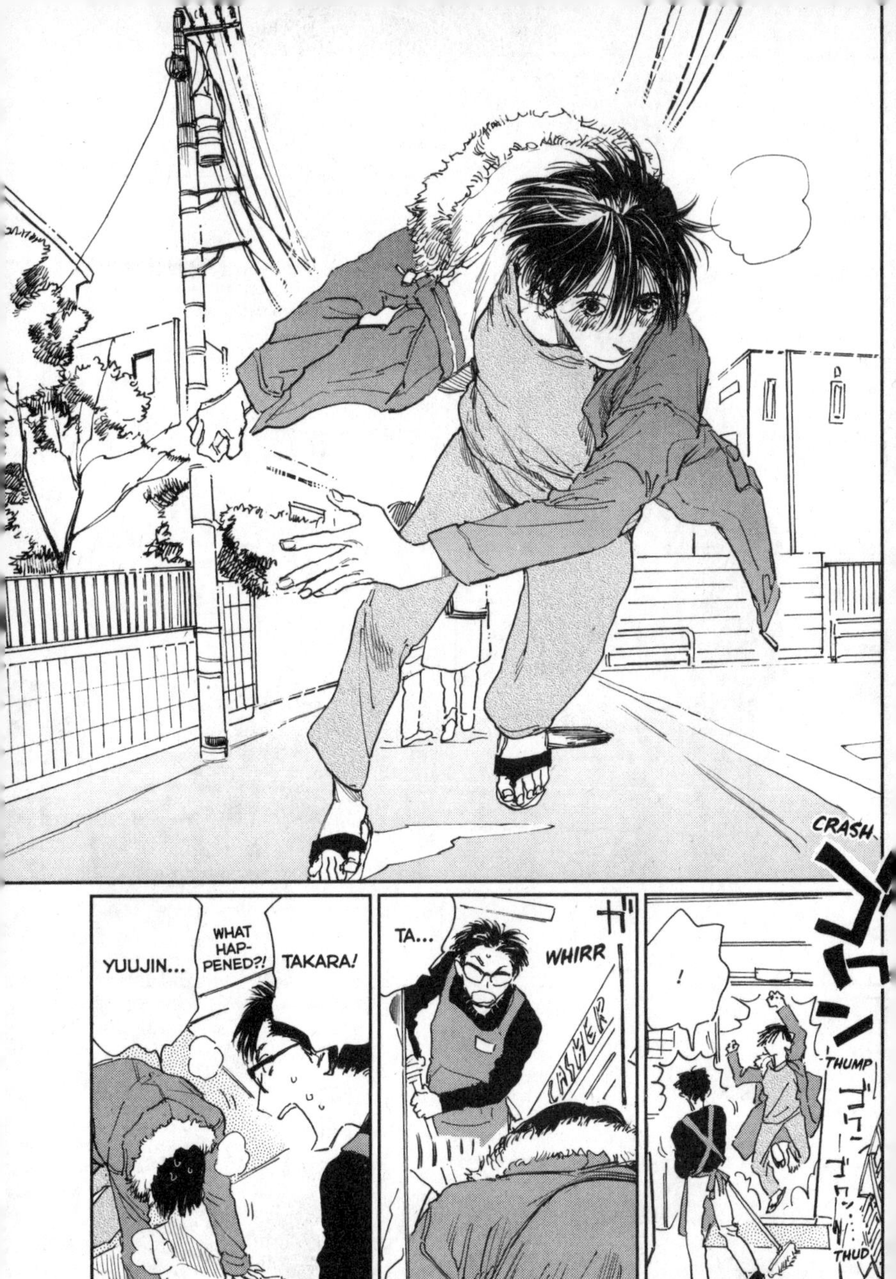
CRASH
!
THUMP
THUD
TA...
WHIRR
TAKARA!
WHAT HAP-PENED?!
YUUJIN...

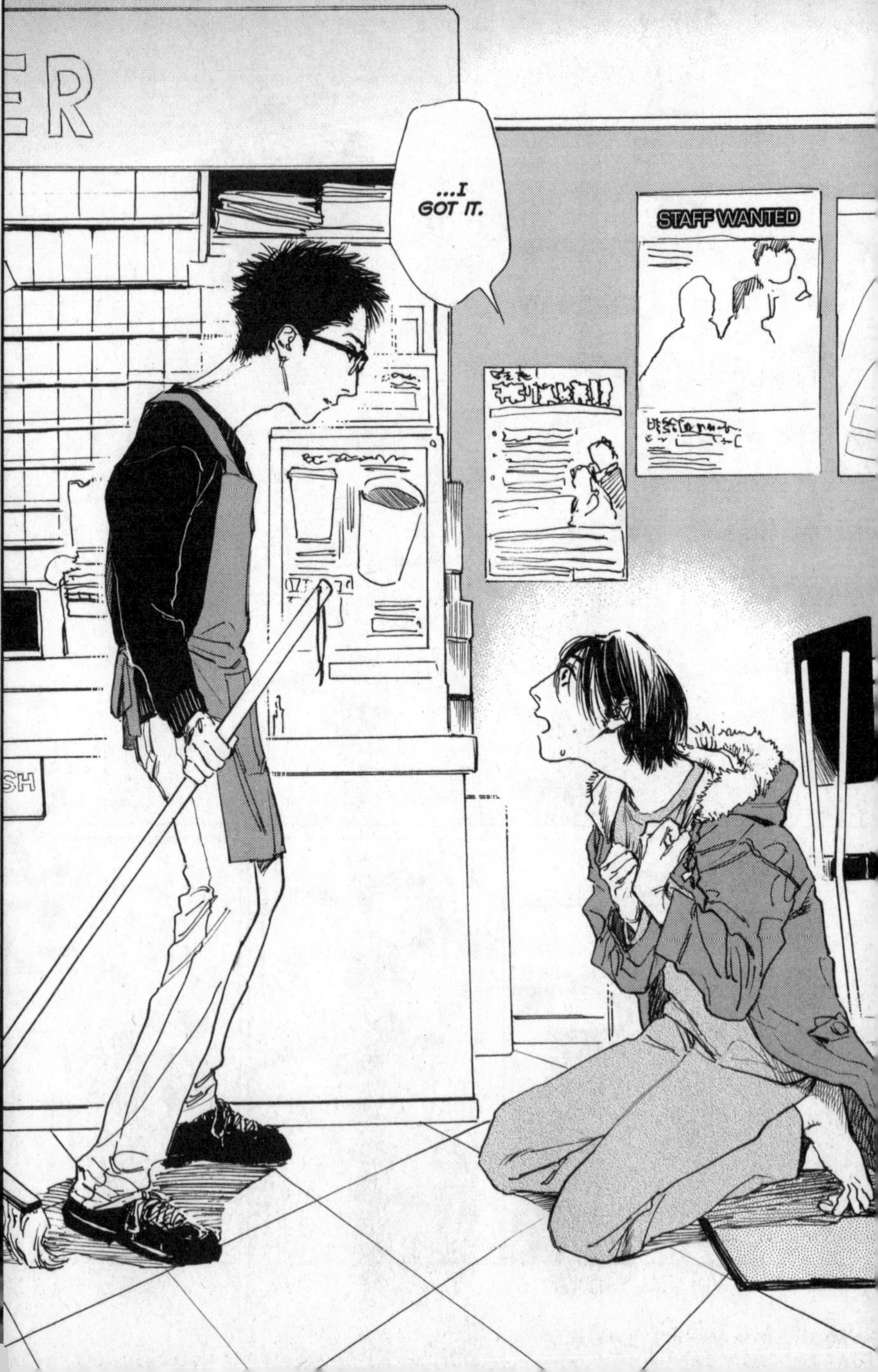
...I GOT IT.
STAFF WANTED

DOUBLE

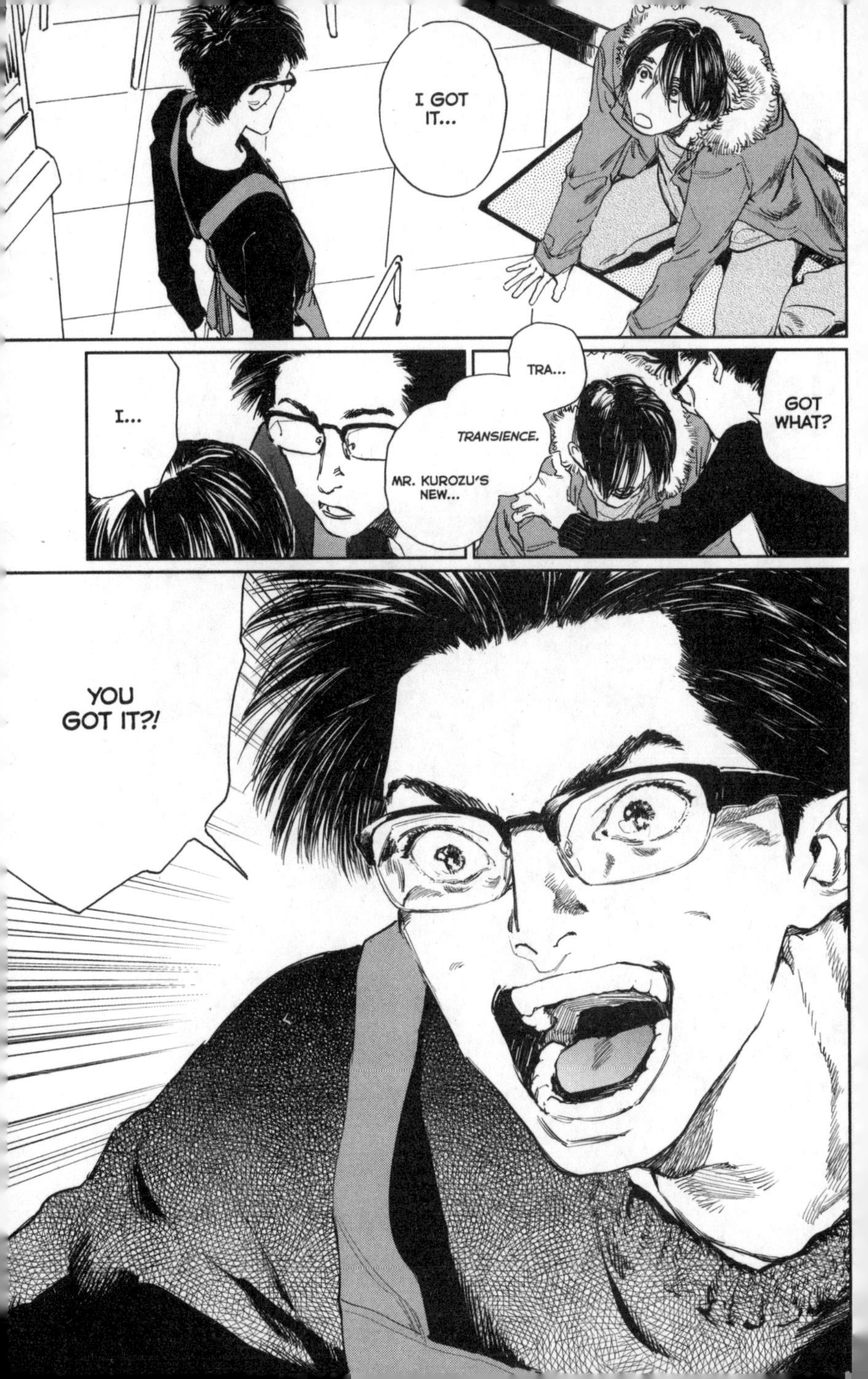

I GOT IT...
GOT WHAT?
TRA...
TRANSIENCE.
MR. KUROZU'S NEW...
I...
YOU GOT IT?!

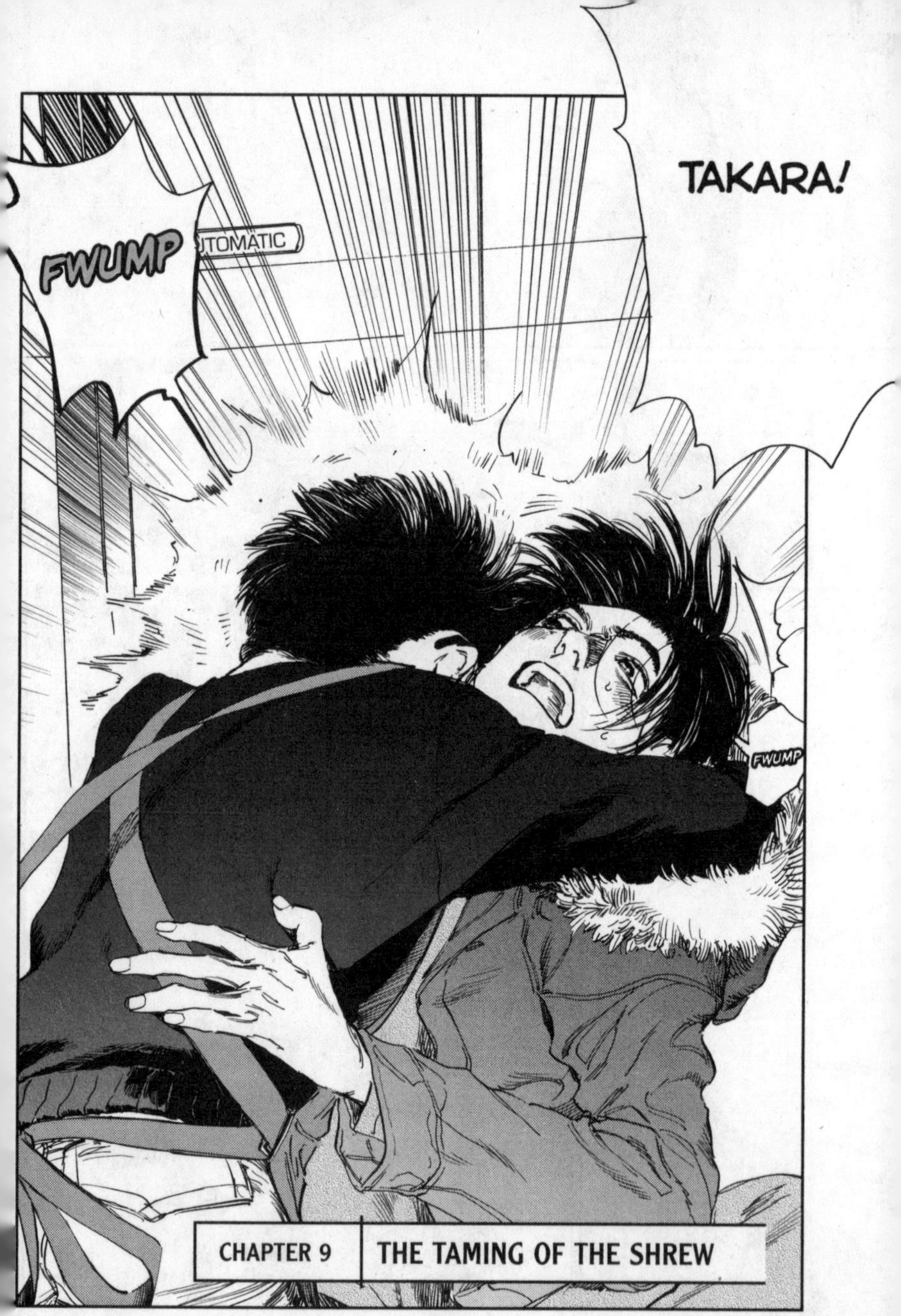
TAKARA!
FWUMP
UTOMATIC
FWUMP
CHAPTER 9
THE TAMING OF THE SHREW

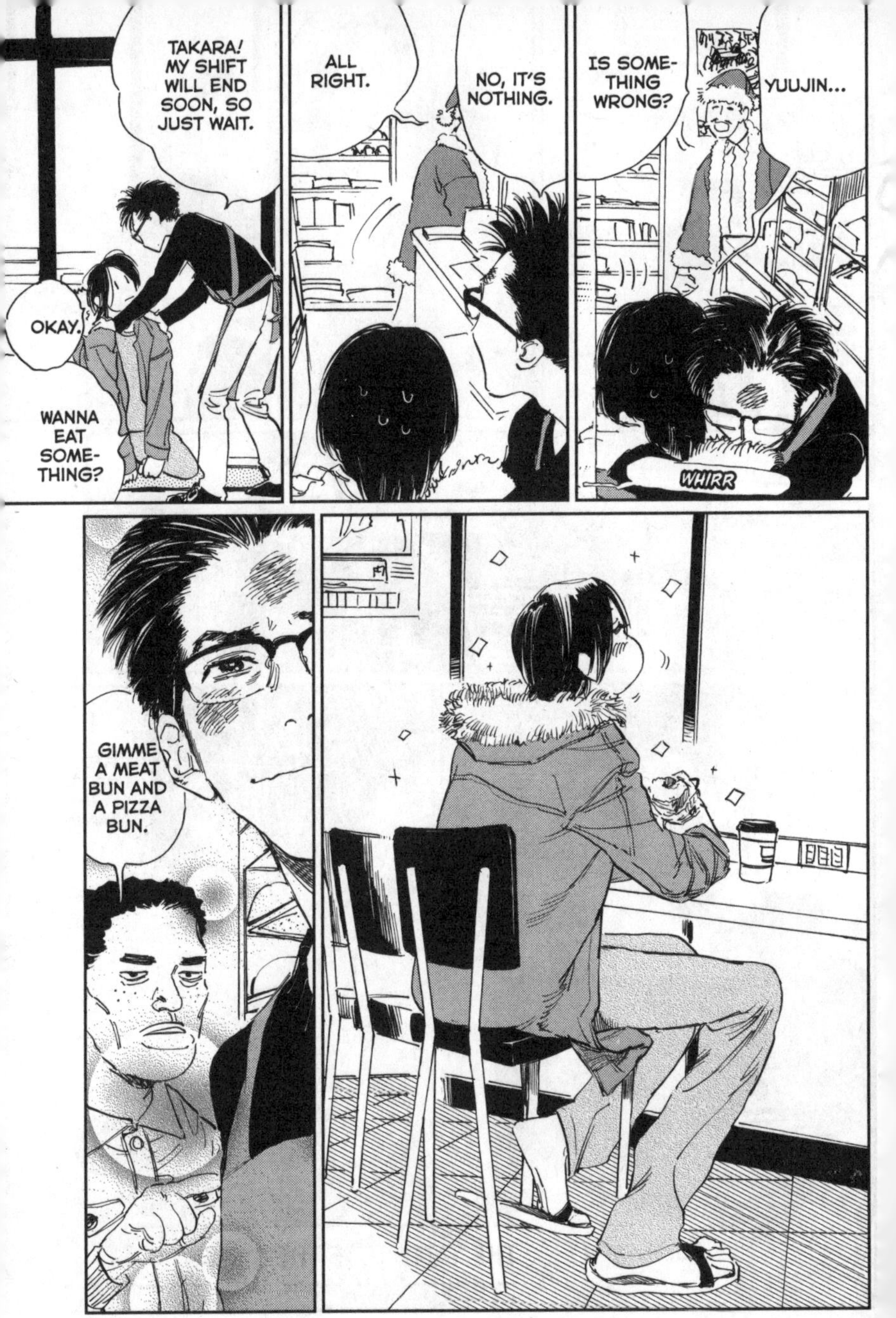
YUUJIN...
IS SOME-THING WRONG?
WHIRR
NO, IT'S NOTHING.
ALL RIGHT.
TAKARA! MY SHIFT WILL END SOON, SO JUST WAIT.
OKAY.
WANNA EAT SOME-THING?
GIMME A MEAT BUN AND A PIZZA BUN.

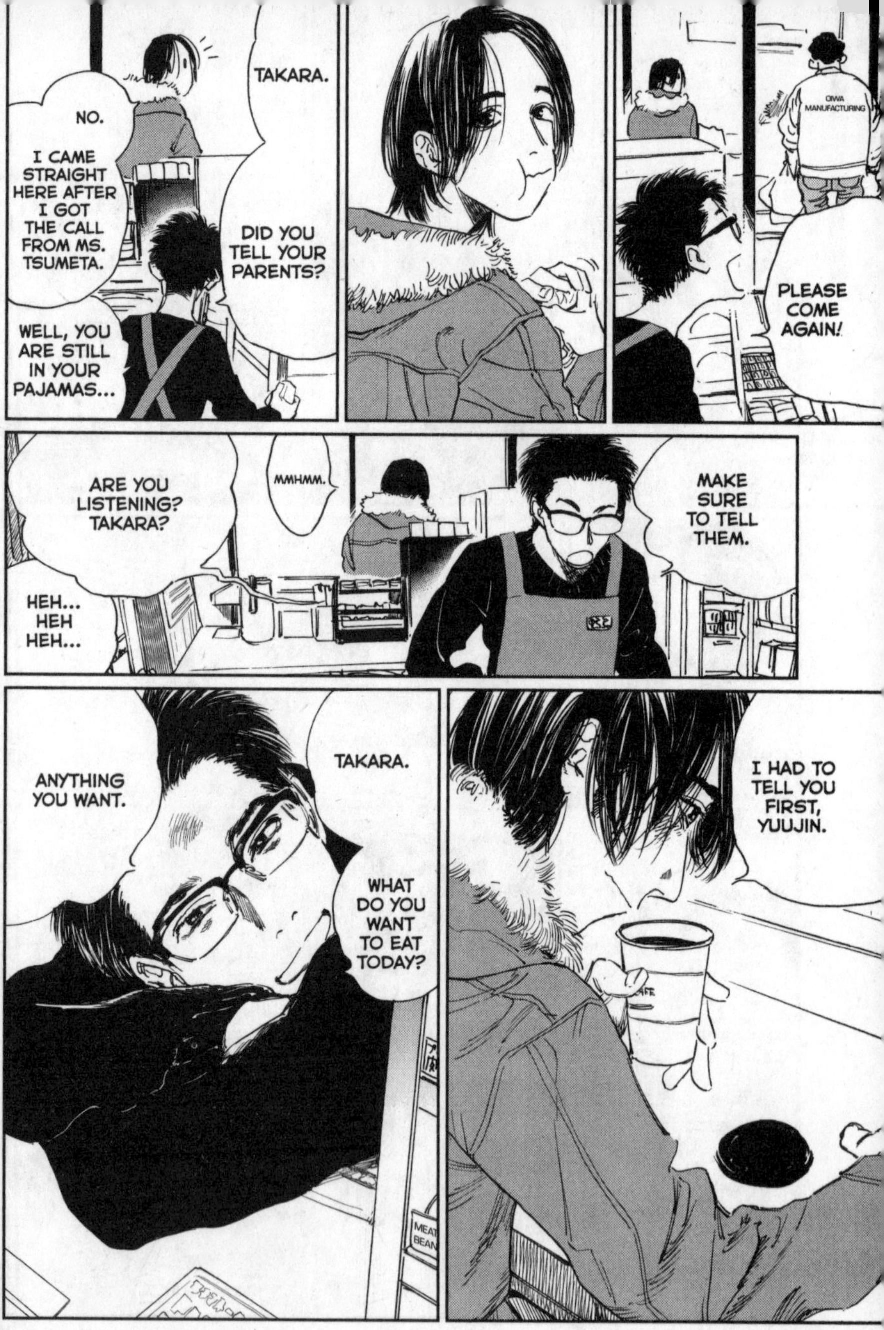
OIWA MANUFACTURING
PLEASE COME AGAIN!
TAKARA.
DID YOU TELL YOUR PARENTS?
NO.
I CAME STRAIGHT HERE AFTER I GOT THE CALL FROM MS. TSUMETA.
WELL, YOU ARE STILL IN YOUR PAJAMAS...
MAKE SURE TO TELL THEM.
MMHMM.
ARE YOU LISTENING? TAKARA?
HEH... HEH HEH...
I HAD TO TELL YOU FIRST, YUUJIN.
TAKARA.
WHAT DO YOU WANT TO EAT TODAY?
ANYTHING YOU WANT.

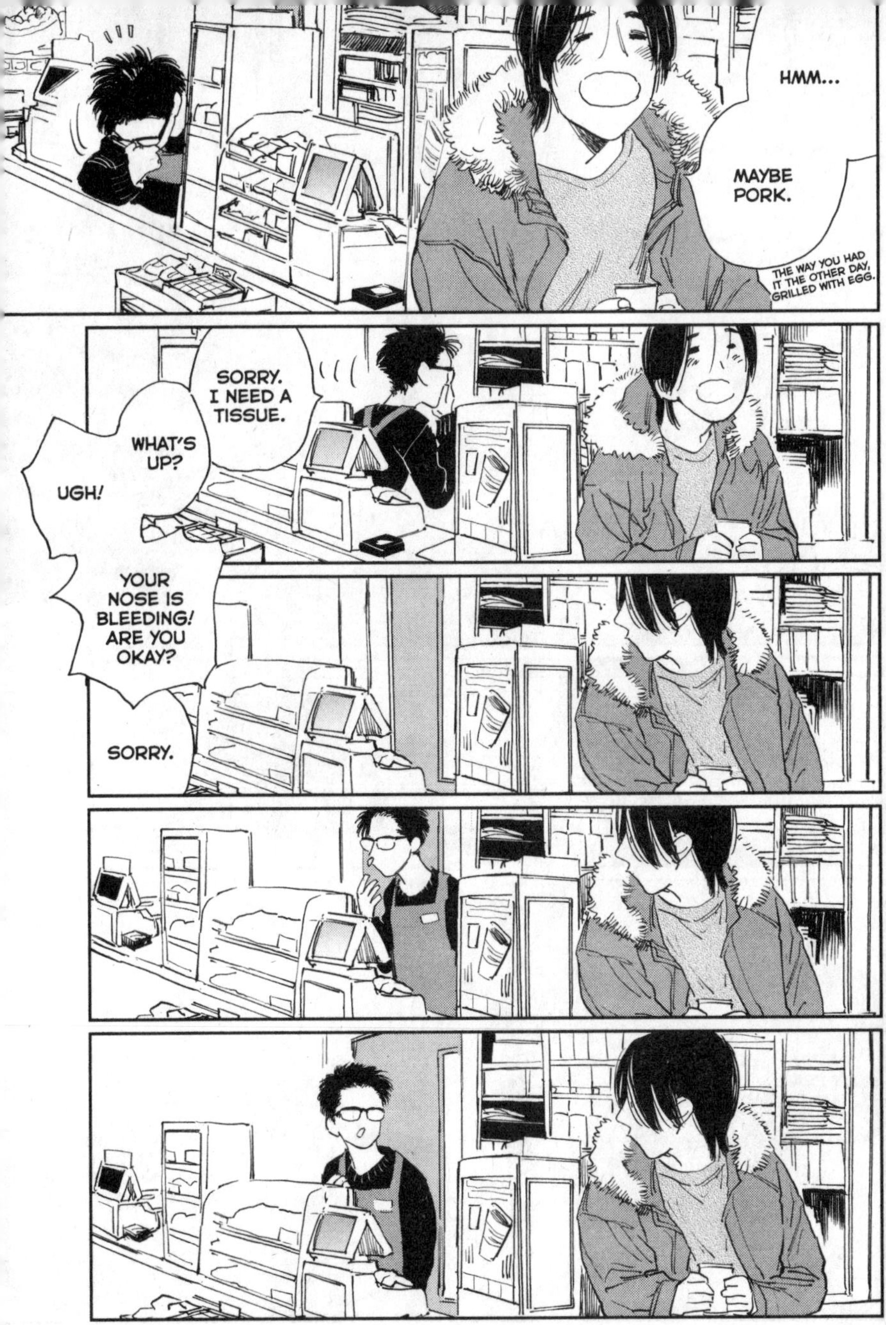
HMM...
MAYBE PORK.
THE WAY YOU HAD IT THE OTHER DAY, GRILLED WITH EGG.
SORRY. I NEED A TISSUE.
WHAT'S UP?
UGH!
YOUR NOSE IS BLEEDING! ARE YOU OKAY?
SORRY.

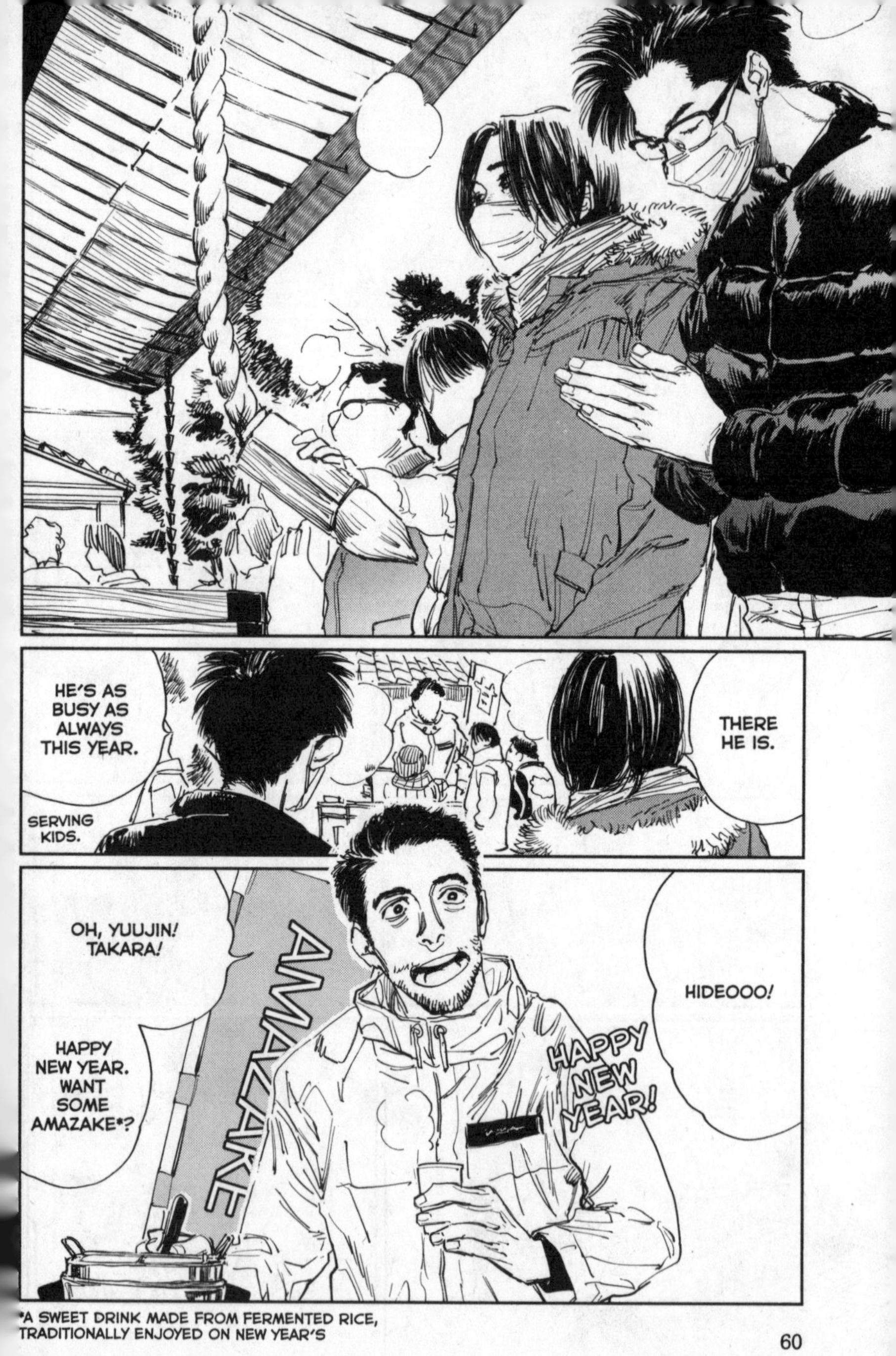
THERE HE IS.
HE'S AS BUSY AS ALWAYS THIS YEAR.
SERVING KIDS.
HIDEOOO!
HAPPY NEW YEAR!
OH, YUUJIN! TAKARA!
HAPPY NEW YEAR. WANT SOME AMAZAKE*?
AMAZAKE

*A SWEET DRINK MADE FROM FERMENTED RICE, TRADITIONALLY ENJOYED ON NEW YEAR'S

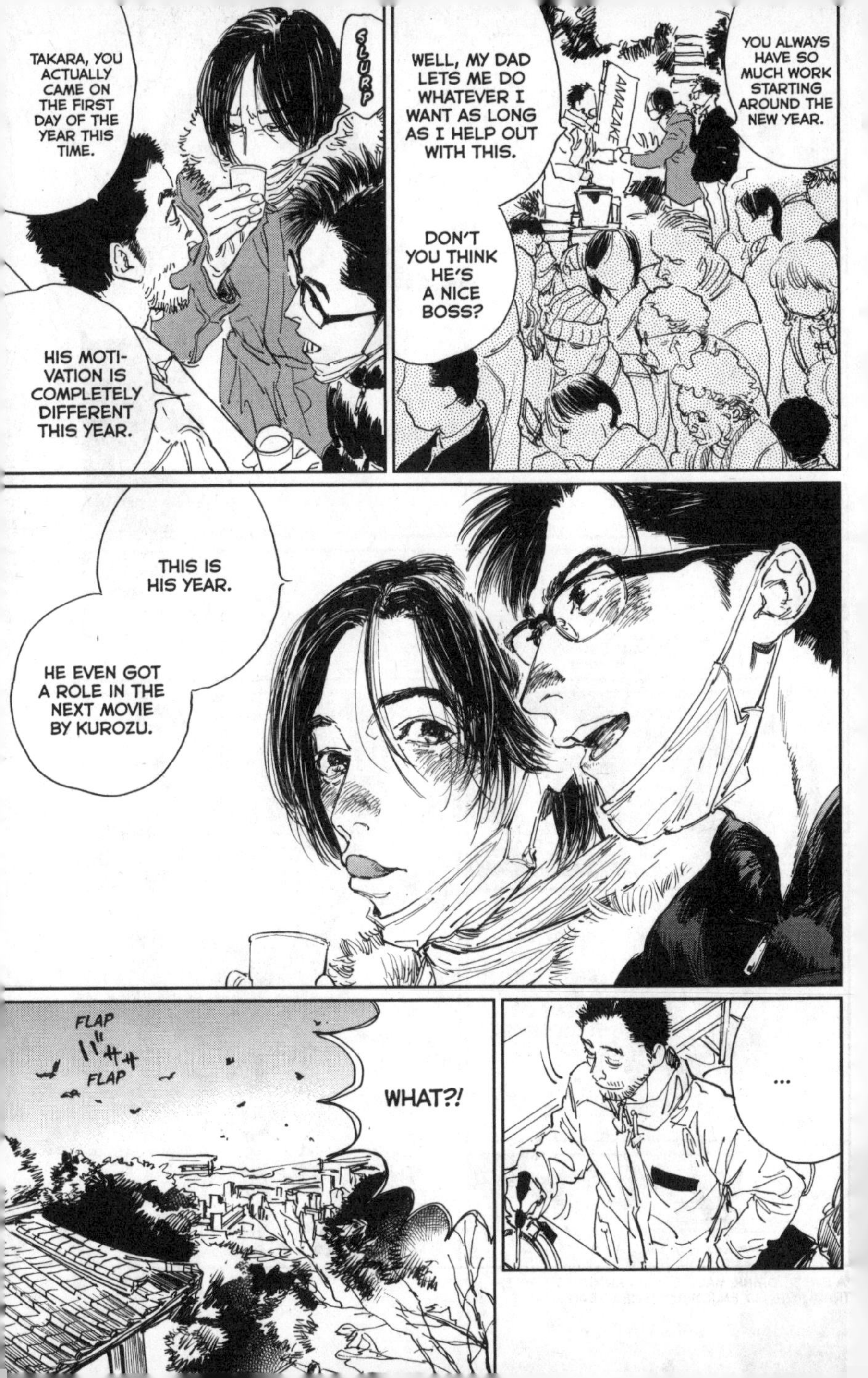
YOU ALWAYS HAVE SO MUCH WORK STARTING AROUND THE NEW YEAR.
WELL, MY DAD LETS ME DO WHATEVER I WANT AS LONG AS I HELP OUT WITH THIS.
AMAZAKE
DON'T YOU THINK HE'S A NICE BOSS?
SLURP
TAKARA, YOU ACTUALLY CAME ON THE FIRST DAY OF THE YEAR THIS TIME.
HIS MOTI-VATION IS COMPLETELY DIFFERENT THIS YEAR.
THIS IS HIS YEAR.
HE EVEN GOT A ROLE IN THE NEXT MOVIE BY KUROZU.
...
WHAT?!
FLAP FLAP

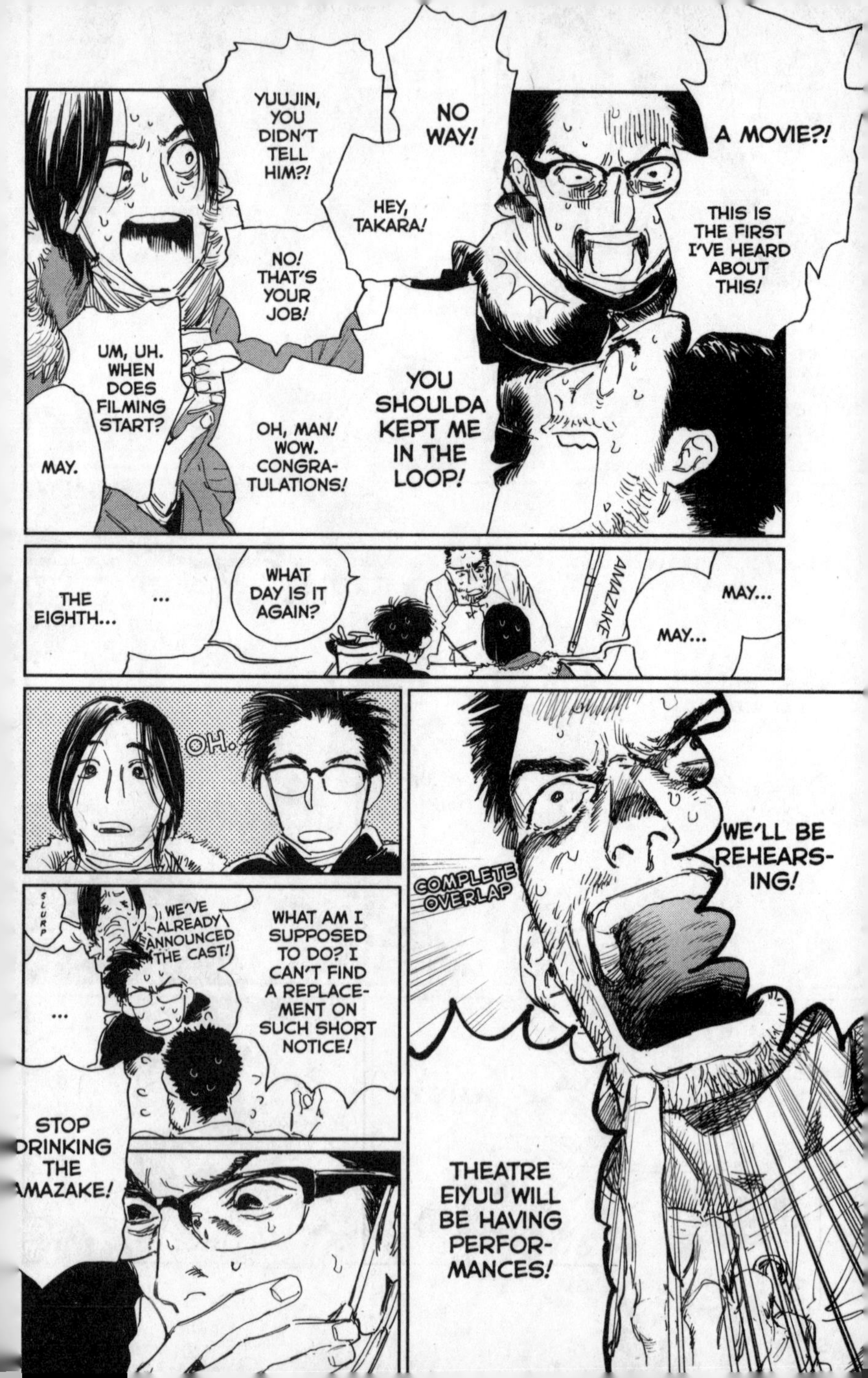
A MOVIE?!
THIS IS THE FIRST I'VE HEARD ABOUT THIS!
NO WAY!
HEY, TAKARA!
YUUJIN, YOU DIDN'T TELL HIM?!
NO! THAT'S YOUR JOB!
YOU SHOULDA KEPT ME IN THE LOOP!
OH, MAN! WOW. CONGRATULATIONS!
UM, UH. WHEN DOES FILMING START?
MAY.
MAY...
MAY...
AMAZAKE
WHAT DAY IS IT AGAIN?
...
THE EIGHTH...
WE'LL BE REHEARSING!
COMPLETE OVERLAP
THEATRE EIYUU WILL BE HAVING PERFORMANCES!
OH.
WHAT AM I SUPPOSED TO DO? I CAN'T FIND A REPLACEMENT ON SUCH SHORT NOTICE!
WE'VE ALREADY ANNOUNCED THE CAST!
SLURP
...
STOP DRINKING THE AMAZAKE!

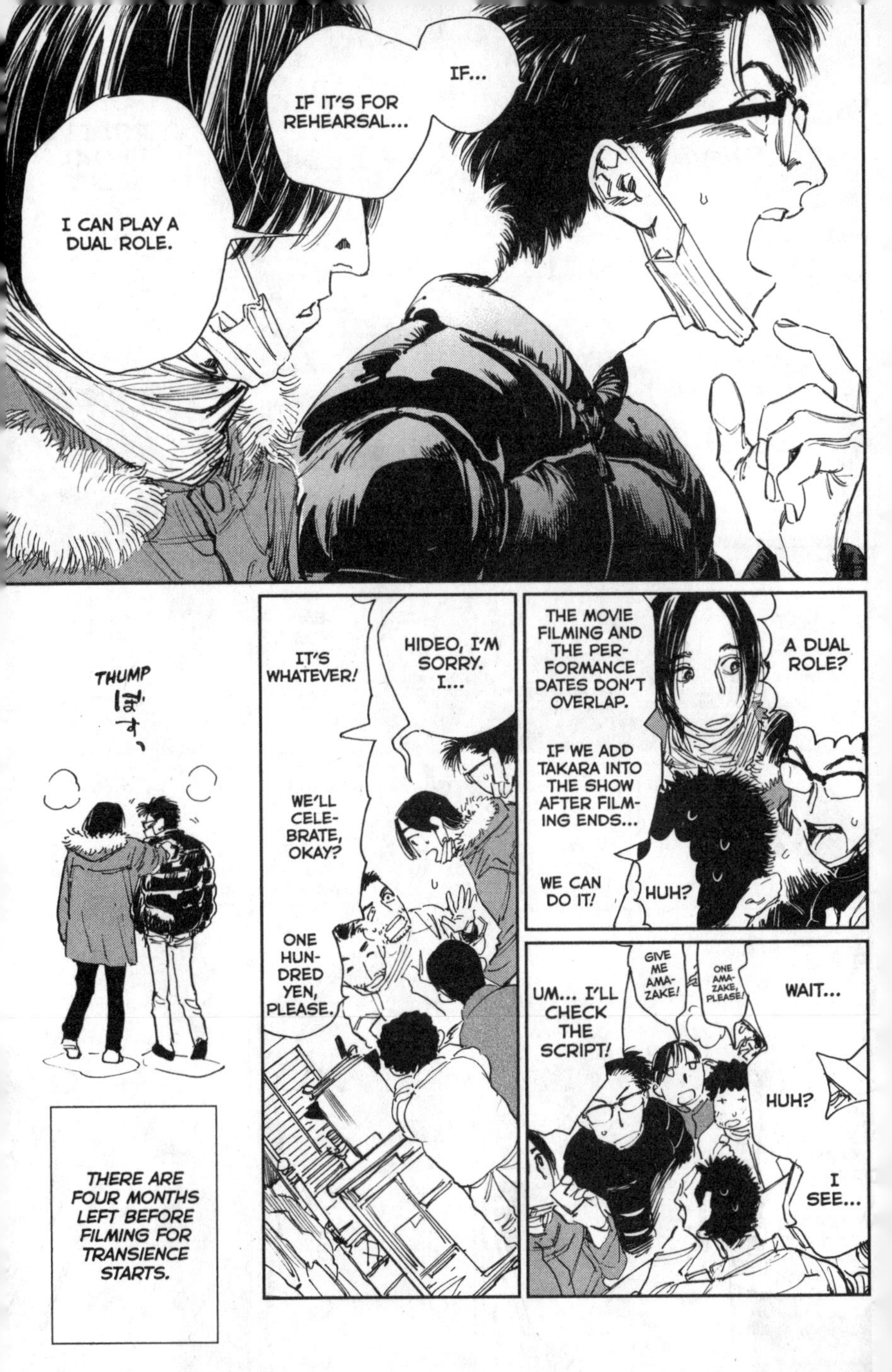
IF...
IF IT'S FOR REHEARSAL...
I CAN PLAY A DUAL ROLE.
A DUAL ROLE?
THE MOVIE FILMING AND THE PER-FORMANCE DATES DON'T OVERLAP.
IF WE ADD TAKARA INTO THE SHOW AFTER FILM-ING ENDS...
HUH?
WE CAN DO IT!
WAIT...
ONE AMA-ZAKE, PLEASE!
GIVE ME AMA-ZAKE!
UM... I'LL CHECK THE SCRIPT!
HUH?
I SEE...
HIDEO, I'M SORRY. I...
IT'S WHATEVER!
WE'LL CELE-BRATE, OKAY?
ONE HUN-DRED YEN, PLEASE.
THUMP
ぽす、
THERE ARE FOUR MONTHS LEFT BEFORE FILMING FOR TRANSIENCE STARTS.

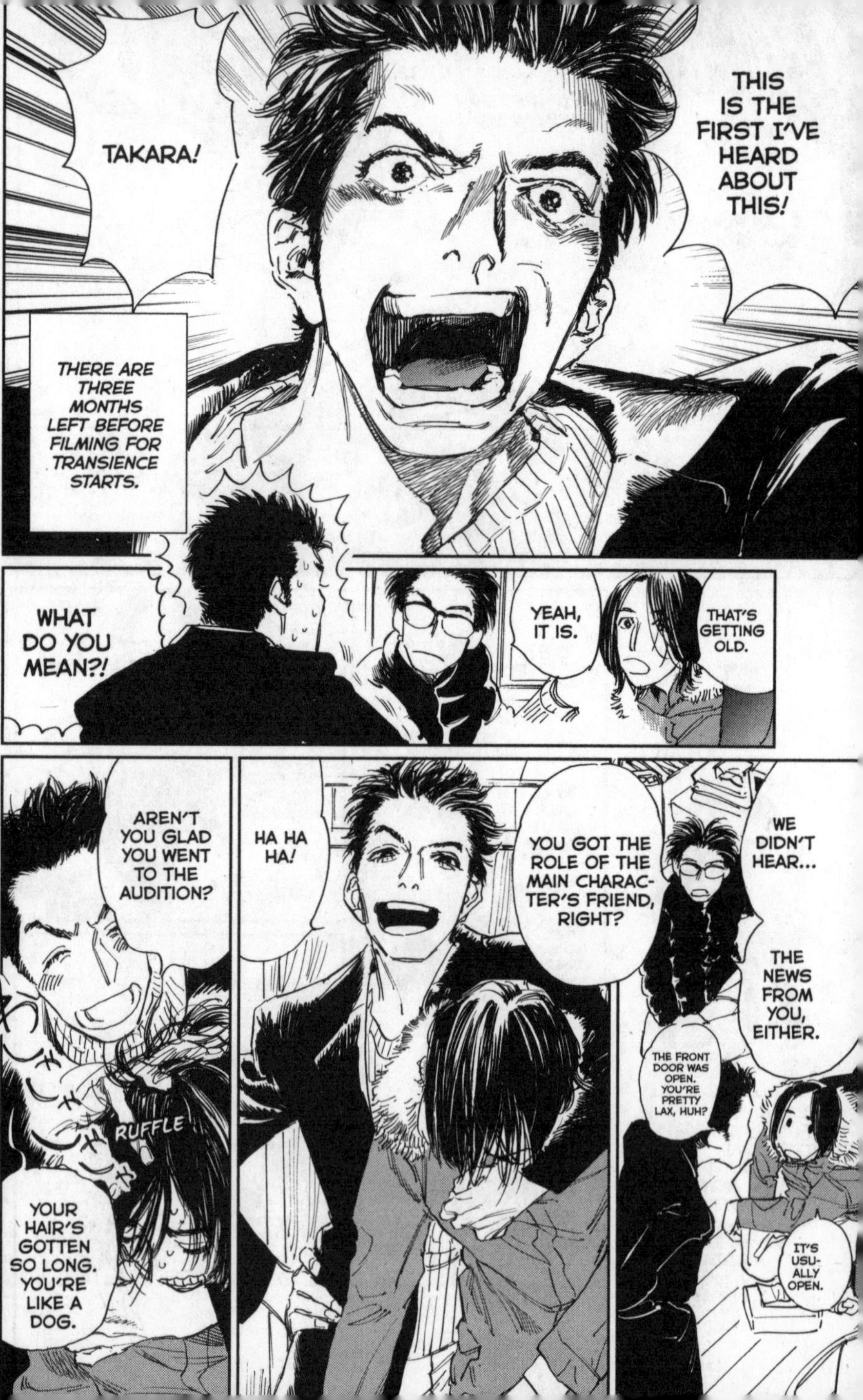
THIS IS THE FIRST I'VE HEARD ABOUT THIS!
TAKARA!
THERE ARE THREE MONTHS LEFT BEFORE FILMING FOR TRANSIENCE STARTS.
THAT'S GETTING OLD.
YEAH, IT IS.
WHAT DO YOU MEAN?!
WE DIDN'T HEAR...
THE NEWS FROM YOU, EITHER.
THE FRONT DOOR WAS OPEN. YOU'RE PRETTY LAX, HUH?
IT'S USUALLY OPEN.
YOU GOT THE ROLE OF THE MAIN CHARACTER'S FRIEND, RIGHT?
HA HA HA!
AREN'T YOU GLAD YOU WENT TO THE AUDITION?
RUFFLE
YOUR HAIR'S GOTTEN SO LONG. YOU'RE LIKE A DOG.

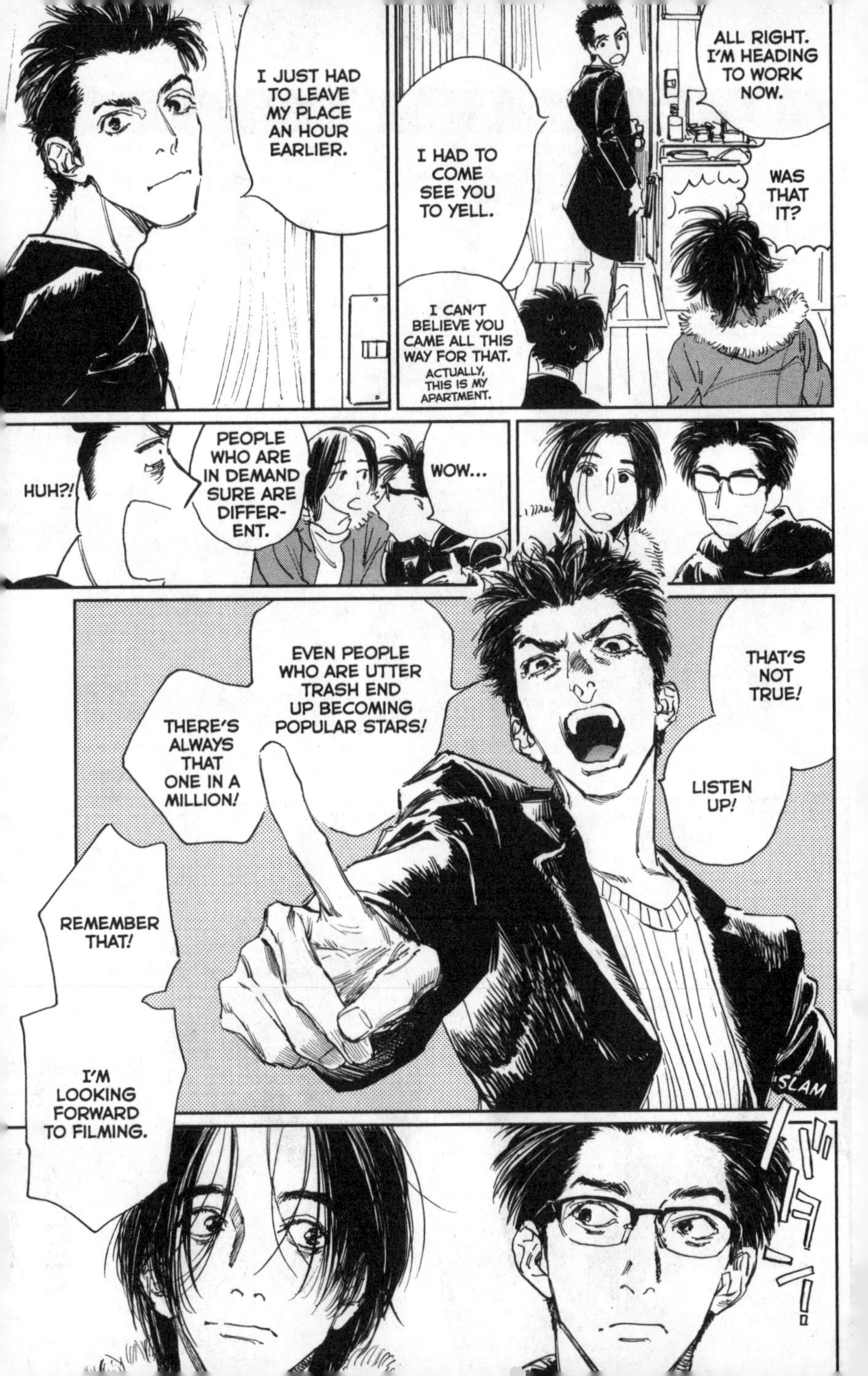
ALL RIGHT. I'M HEADING TO WORK NOW.
WAS THAT IT?
I HAD TO COME SEE YOU TO YELL.
I CAN'T BELIEVE YOU CAME ALL THIS WAY FOR THAT.
ACTUALLY, THIS IS MY APARTMENT.
I JUST HAD TO LEAVE MY PLACE AN HOUR EARLIER.
WOW...
PEOPLE WHO ARE IN DEMAND SURE ARE DIFFER-ENT.
HUH?!
THAT'S NOT TRUE!
LISTEN UP!
EVEN PEOPLE WHO ARE UTTER TRASH END UP BECOMING POPULAR STARS!
THERE'S ALWAYS THAT ONE IN A MILLION!
REMEMBER THAT!
SLAM
I'M LOOKING FORWARD TO FILMING.

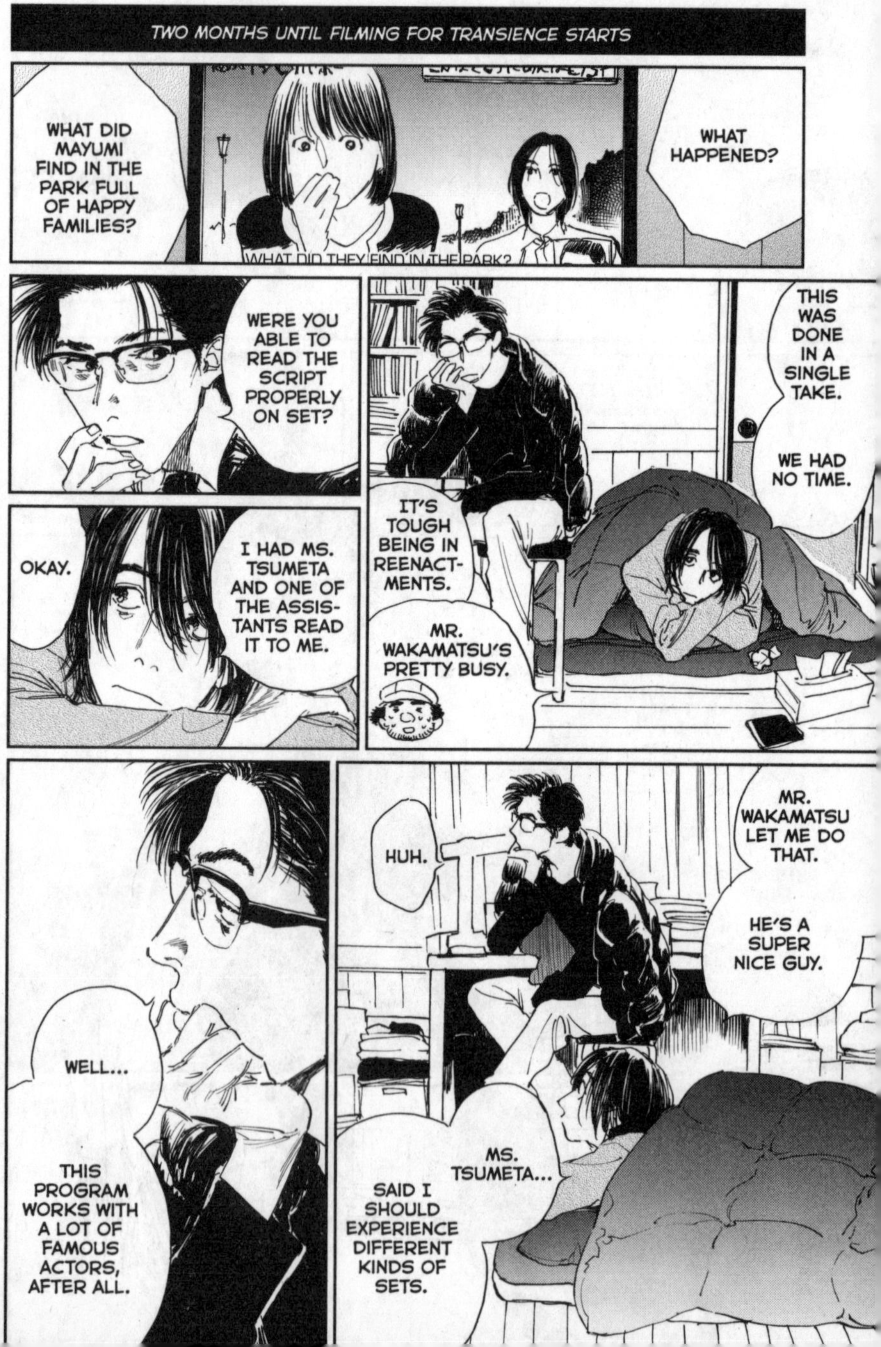
TWO MONTHS UNTIL FILMING FOR TRANSIENCE STARTS
WHAT HAPPENED?
WHAT DID THEY FIND IN THE PARK?
WHAT DID MAYUMI FIND IN THE PARK FULL OF HAPPY FAMILIES?
THIS WAS DONE IN A SINGLE TAKE.
WE HAD NO TIME.
IT'S TOUGH BEING IN REENACTMENTS.
MR. WAKAMATSU'S PRETTY BUSY.
WERE YOU ABLE TO READ THE SCRIPT PROPERLY ON SET?
I HAD MS. TSUMETA AND ONE OF THE ASSISTANTS READ IT TO ME.
OKAY.
MR. WAKAMATSU LET ME DO THAT.
HE'S A SUPER NICE GUY.
HUH.
MS. TSUMETA...
SAID I SHOULD EXPERIENCE DIFFERENT KINDS OF SETS.
WELL...
THIS PROGRAM WORKS WITH A LOT OF FAMOUS ACTORS, AFTER ALL.

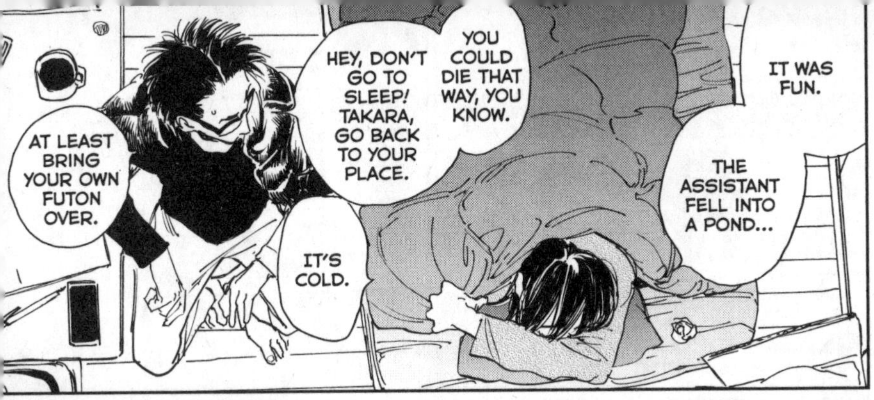
IT WAS FUN.
THE ASSISTANT FELL INTO A POND...
YOU COULD DIE THAT WAY, YOU KNOW.
HEY, DON'T GO TO SLEEP! TAKARA, GO BACK TO YOUR PLACE.
IT'S COLD.
AT LEAST BRING YOUR OWN FUTON OVER.

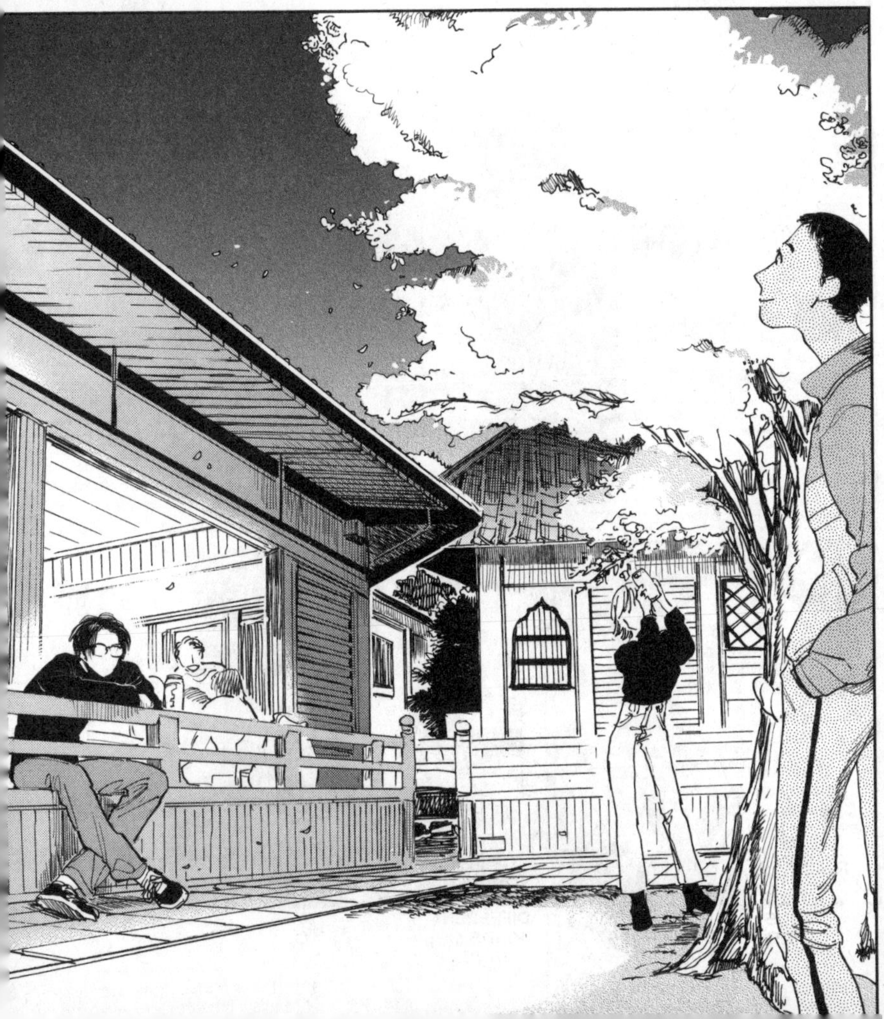

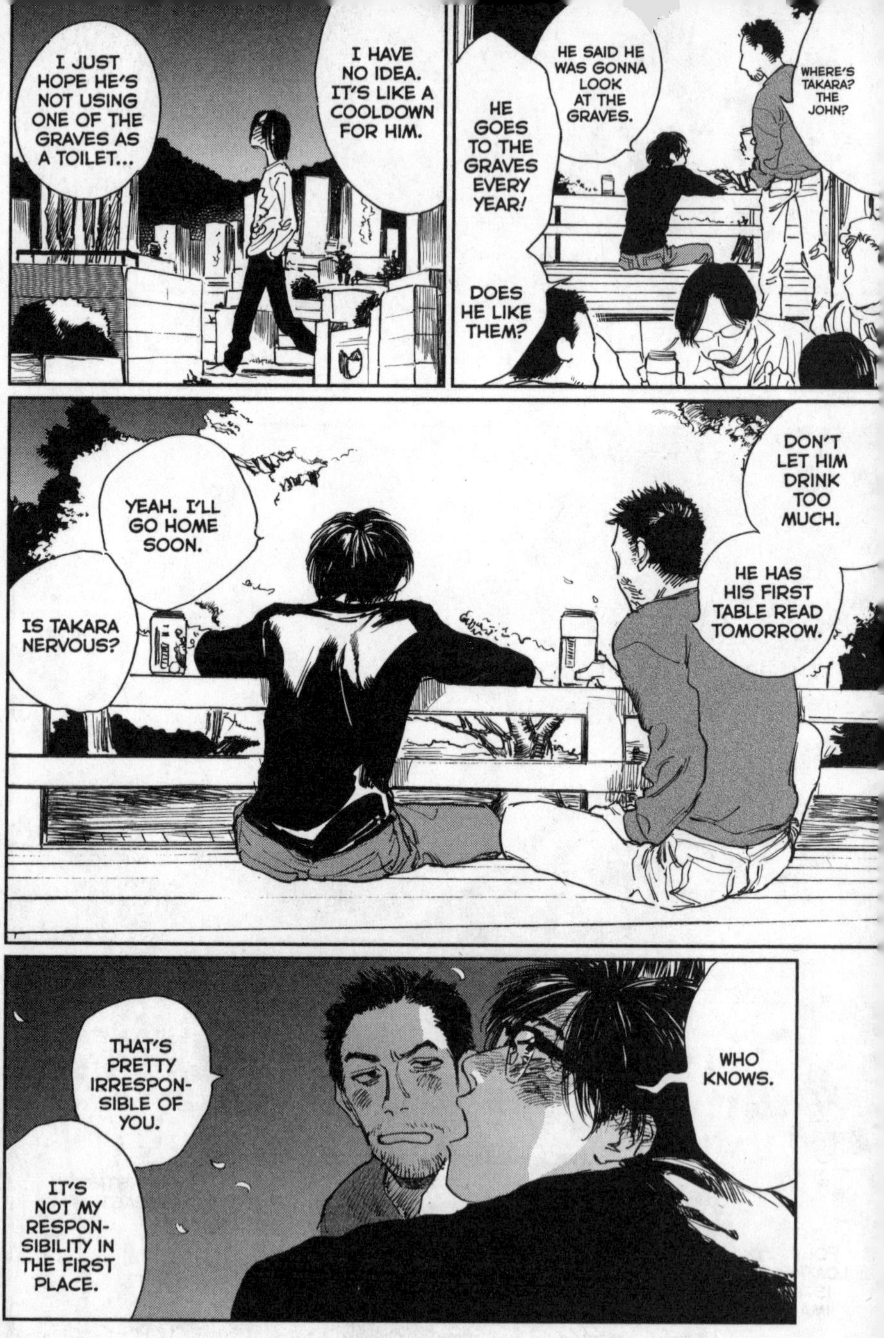
WHERE'S TAKARA? THE JOHN?
HE SAID HE WAS GONNA LOOK AT THE GRAVES.
HE GOES TO THE GRAVES EVERY YEAR!
DOES HE LIKE THEM?
I HAVE NO IDEA. IT'S LIKE A COOLDOWN FOR HIM.
I JUST HOPE HE'S NOT USING ONE OF THE GRAVES AS A TOILET...
DON'T LET HIM DRINK TOO MUCH.
HE HAS HIS FIRST TABLE READ TOMORROW.
YEAH. I'LL GO HOME SOON.
IS TAKARA NERVOUS?
WHO KNOWS.
THAT'S PRETTY IRRESPON-SIBLE OF YOU.
IT'S NOT MY RESPON-SIBILITY IN THE FIRST PLACE.

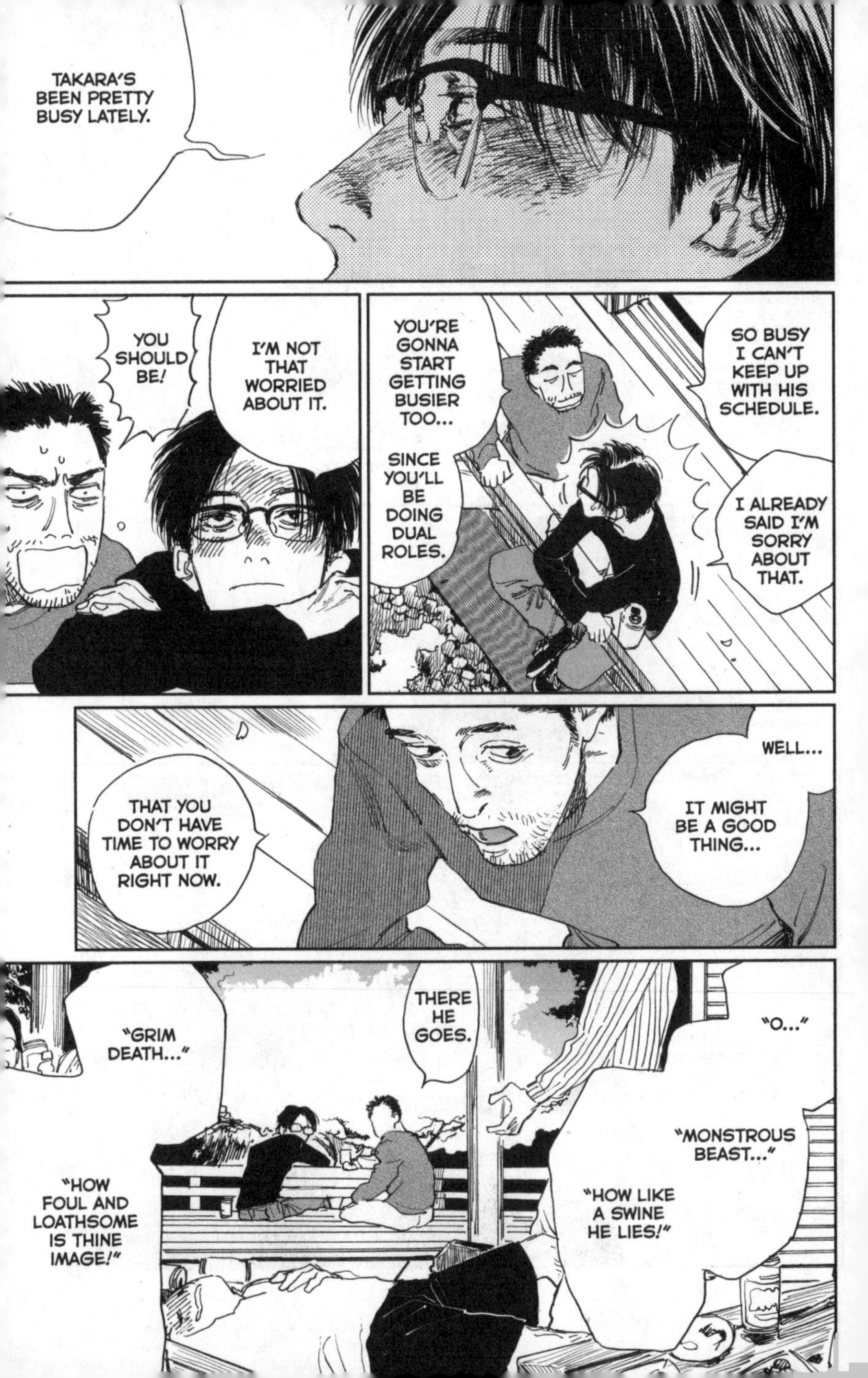
TAKARA'S BEEN PRETTY BUSY LATELY.
SO BUSY I CAN'T KEEP UP WITH HIS SCHEDULE.
I ALREADY SAID I'M SORRY ABOUT THAT.
YOU'RE GONNA START GETTING BUSIER TOO...
SINCE YOU'LL BE DOING DUAL ROLES.
I'M NOT THAT WORRIED ABOUT IT.
YOU SHOULD BE!
WELL...
IT MIGHT BE A GOOD THING...
THAT YOU DON'T HAVE TIME TO WORRY ABOUT IT RIGHT NOW.
"O..."
"MONSTROUS BEAST..."
"HOW LIKE A SWINE HE LIES!"
THERE HE GOES.
"GRIM DEATH..."
"HOW FOUL AND LOATHSOME IS THINE IMAGE!"

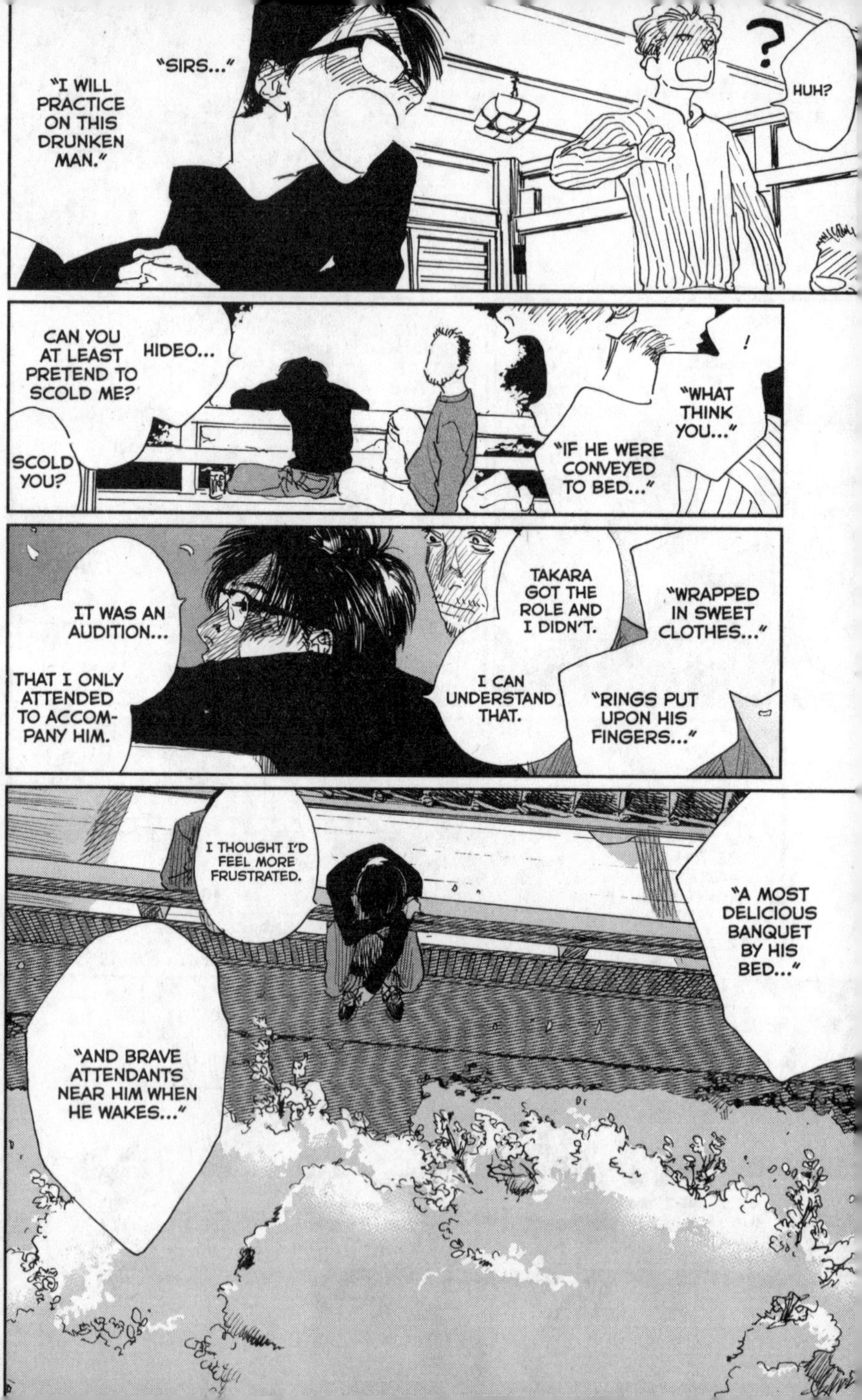
?
HUH?
"SIRS..."
"I WILL PRACTICE ON THIS DRUNKEN MAN."
!
"WHAT THINK YOU..."
"IF HE WERE CONVEYED TO BED..."
HIDEO...
CAN YOU AT LEAST PRETEND TO SCOLD ME?
SCOLD YOU?
"WRAPPED IN SWEET CLOTHES..."
"RINGS PUT UPON HIS FINGERS..."
TAKARA GOT THE ROLE AND I DIDN'T.
I CAN UNDERSTAND THAT.
IT WAS AN AUDITION...
THAT I ONLY ATTENDED TO ACCOMPANY HIM.
"A MOST DELICIOUS BANQUET BY HIS BED..."
I THOUGHT I'D FEEL MORE FRUSTRATED.
"AND BRAVE ATTENDANTS NEAR HIM WHEN HE WAKES..."

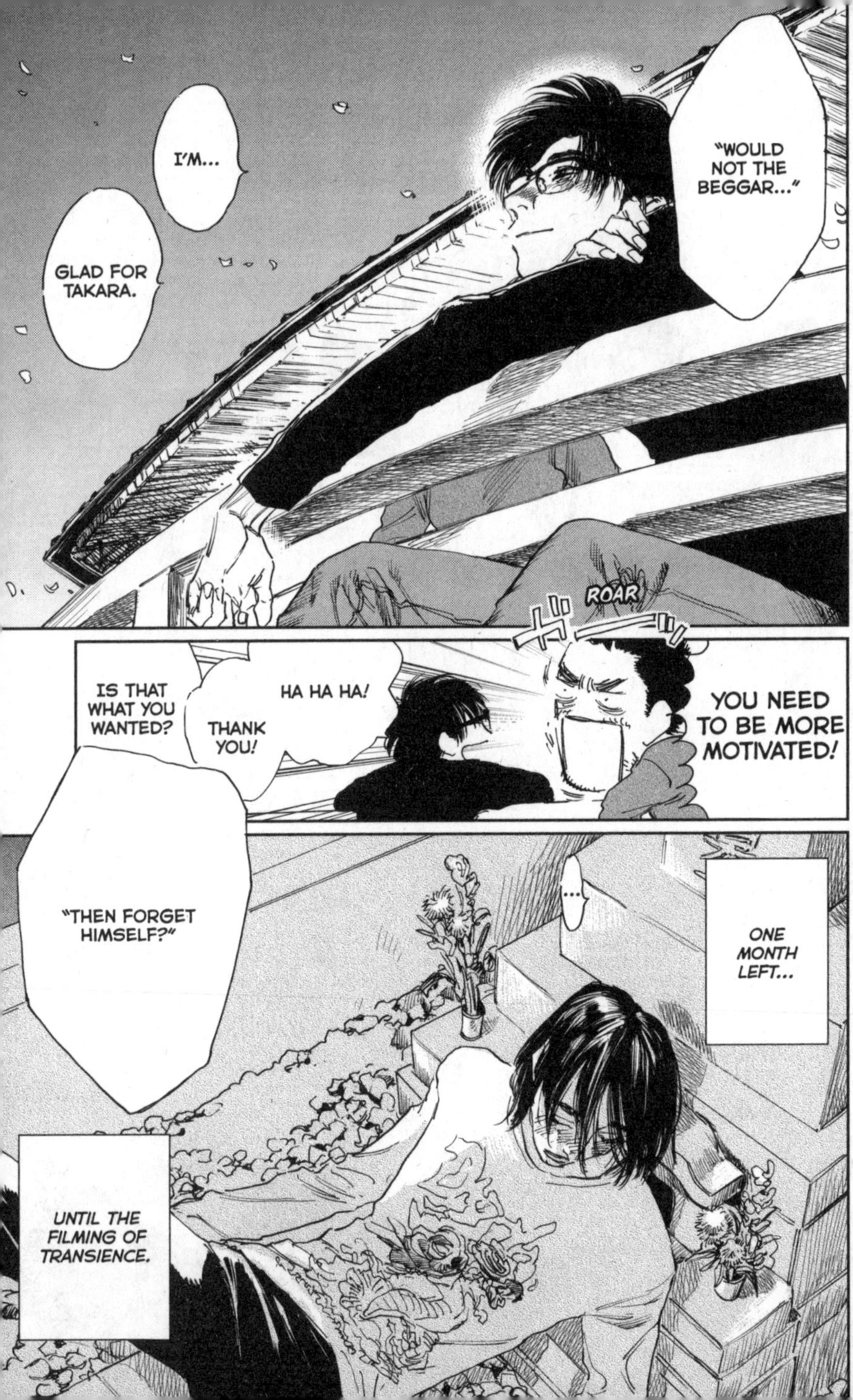
"WOULD NOT THE BEGGAR..."
I'M...
GLAD FOR TAKARA.
ROAR
YOU NEED TO BE MORE MOTIVATED!
HA HA HA!
THANK YOU!
IS THAT WHAT YOU WANTED?
ONE MONTH LEFT...
...
"THEN FORGET HIMSELF?"
UNTIL THE FILMING OF TRANSIENCE.

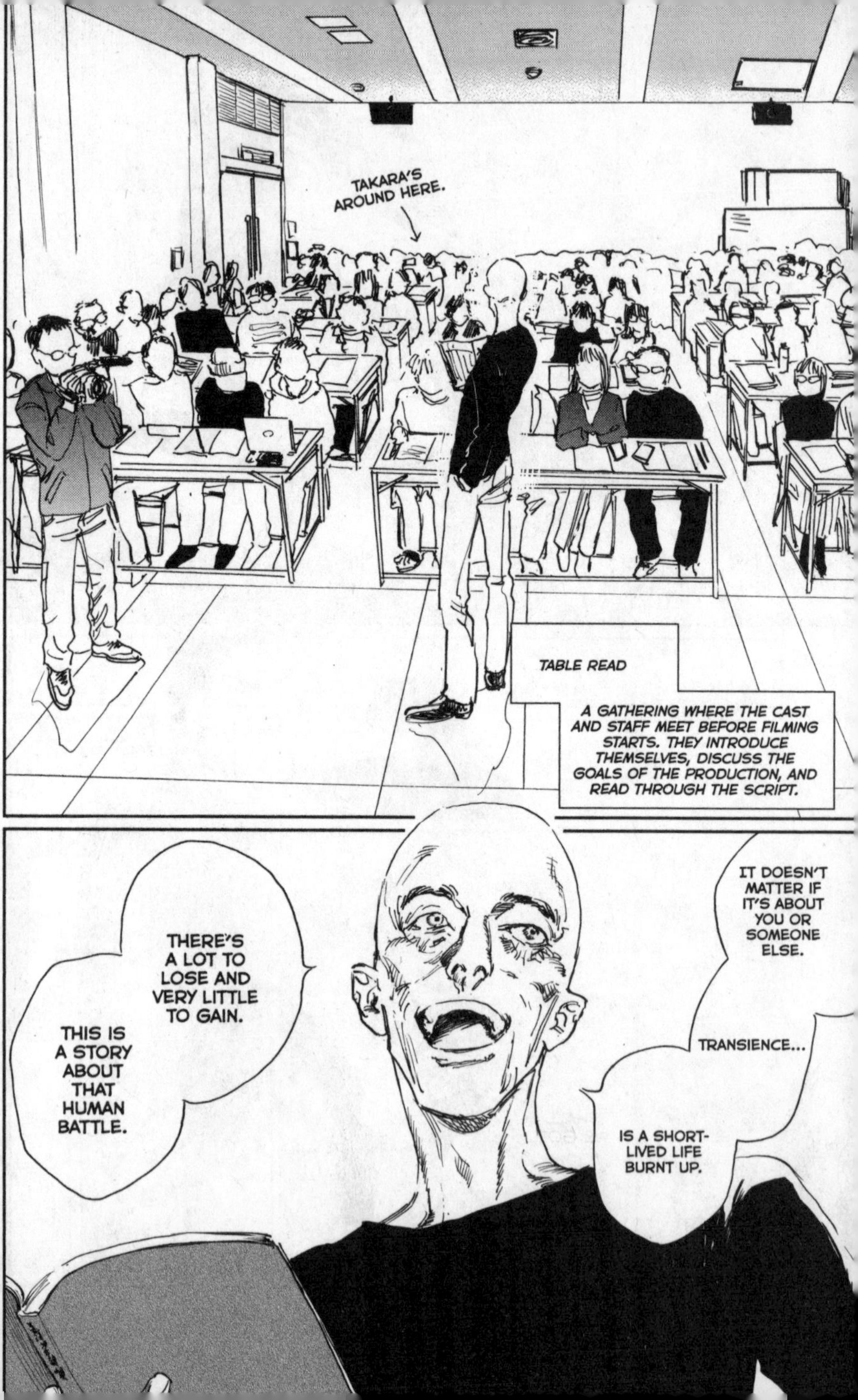
TAKARA'S AROUND HERE.
TABLE READ
A GATHERING WHERE THE CAST AND STAFF MEET BEFORE FILMING STARTS. THEY INTRODUCE THEMSELVES, DISCUSS THE GOALS OF THE PRODUCTION, AND READ THROUGH THE SCRIPT.
IT DOESN'T MATTER IF IT'S ABOUT YOU OR SOMEONE ELSE.
TRANSIENCE...
IS A SHORT-LIVED LIFE BURNT UP.
THERE'S A LOT TO LOSE AND VERY LITTLE TO GAIN.
THIS IS A STORY ABOUT THAT HUMAN BATTLE.

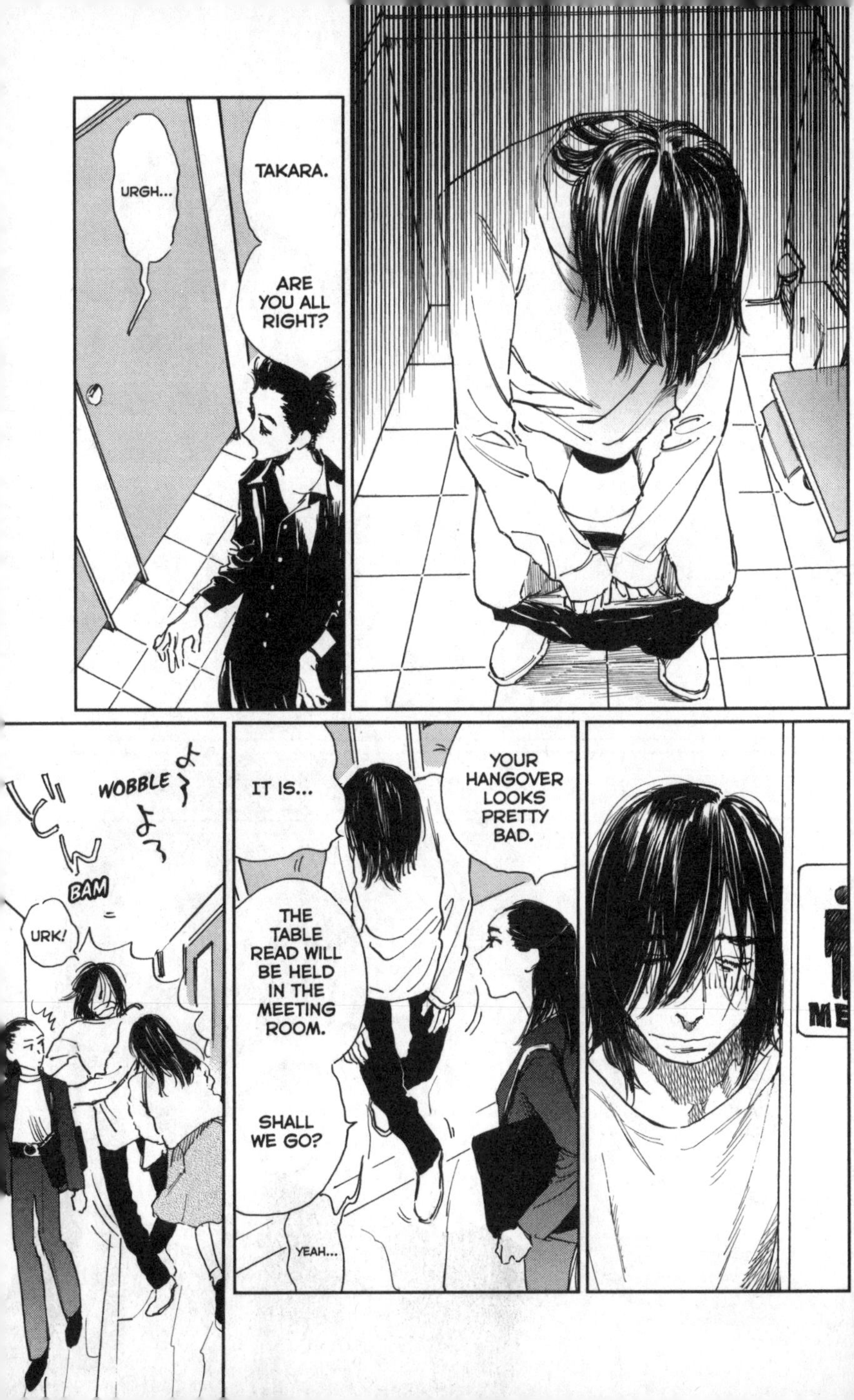
TAKARA.
ARE YOU ALL RIGHT?
URGH...
YOUR HANGOVER LOOKS PRETTY BAD.
IT IS...
THE TABLE READ WILL BE HELD IN THE MEETING ROOM.
SHALL WE GO?
YEAH...
WOBBLE
BAM
URK!

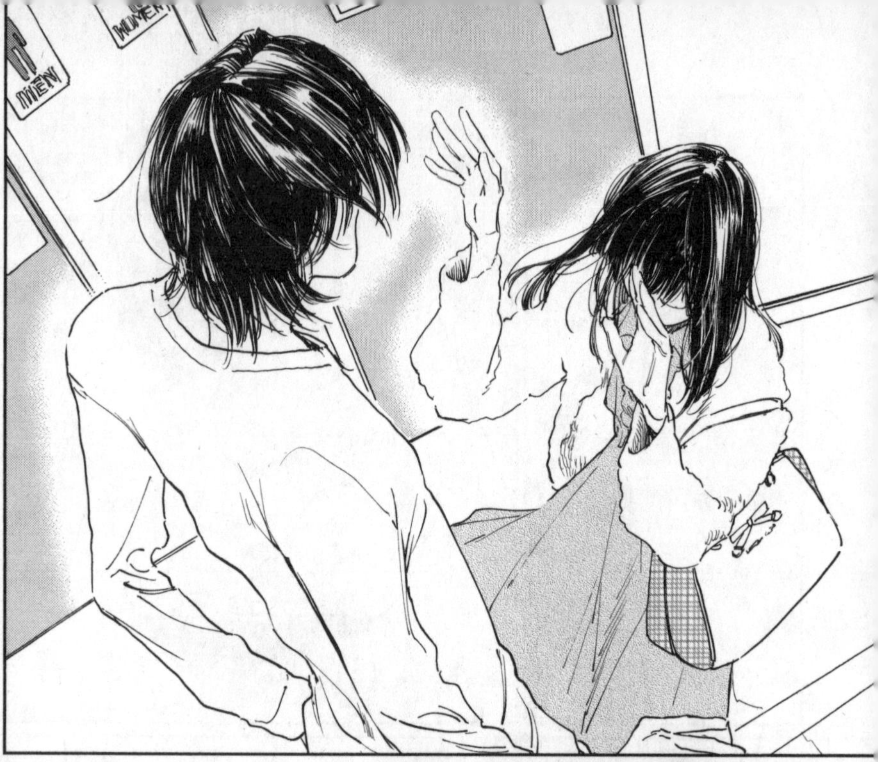
WOMEN
MEN
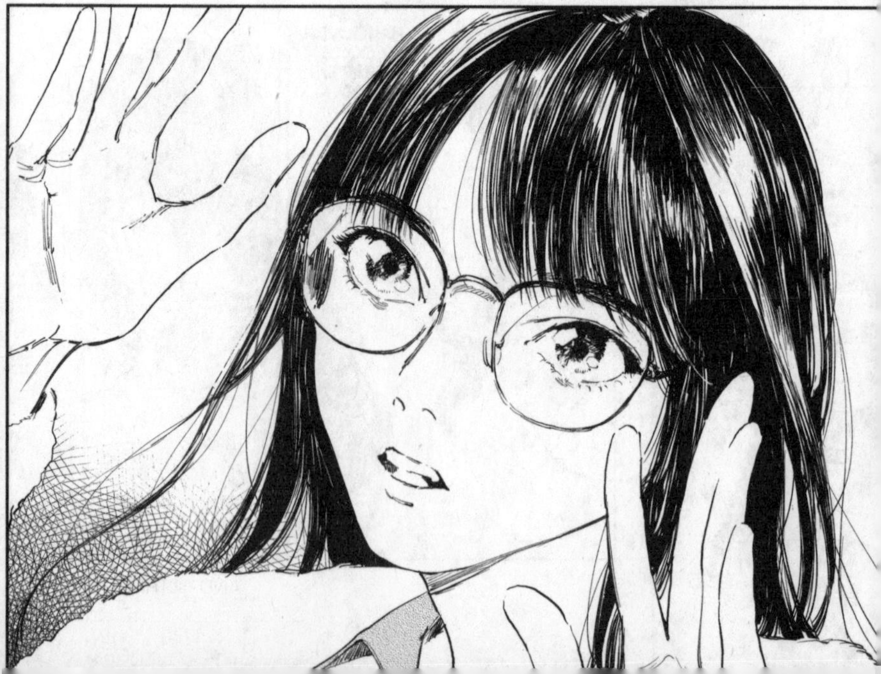

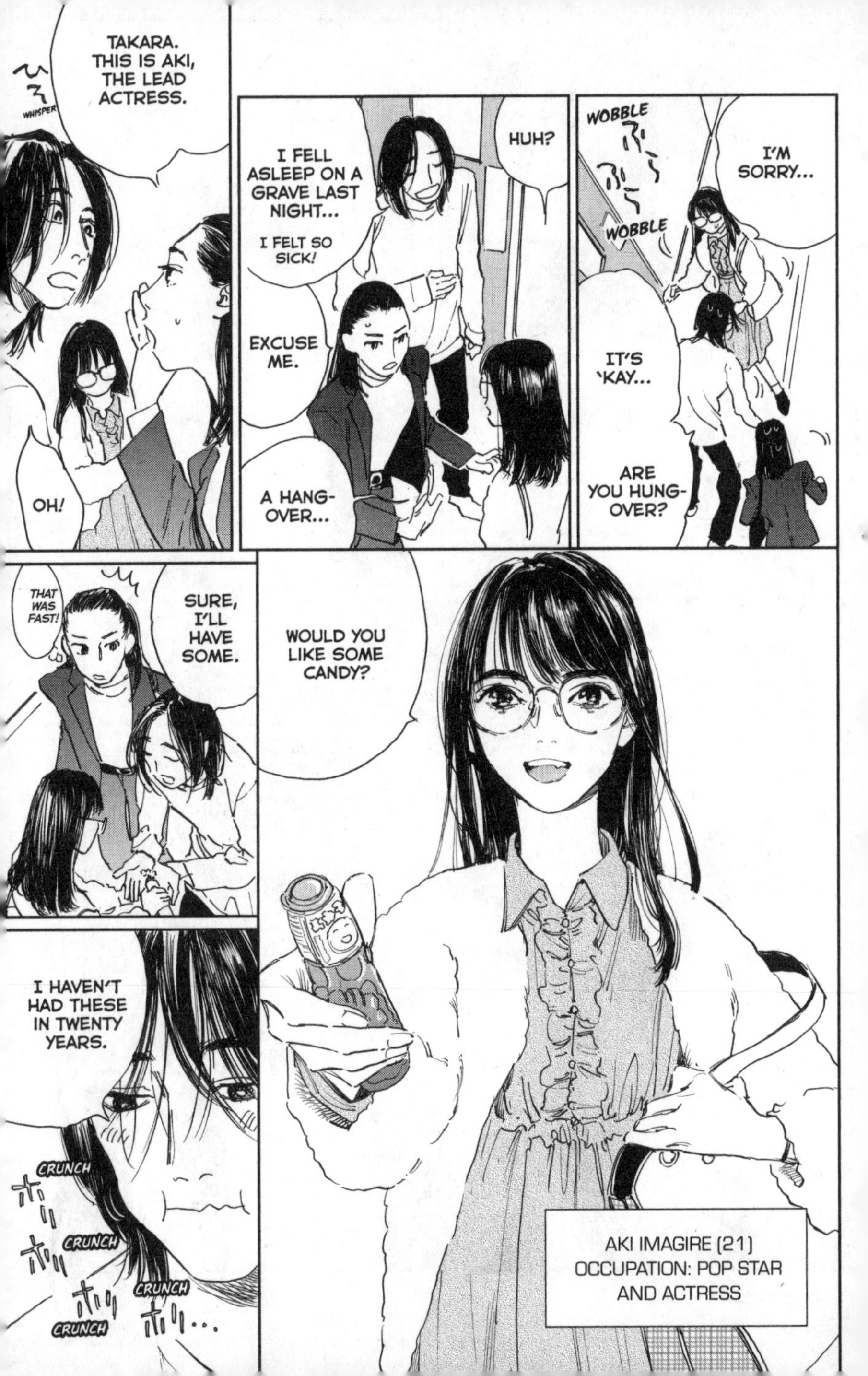
WOBBLE
I'M SORRY...
WOBBLE
IT'S 'KAY...
ARE YOU HUNG-OVER?
HUH?
I FELL ASLEEP ON A GRAVE LAST NIGHT...
I FELT SO SICK!
EXCUSE ME.
A HANG-OVER...
TAKARA. THIS IS AKI, THE LEAD ACTRESS.
WHISPER
OH!
WOULD YOU LIKE SOME CANDY?
AKI IMAGIRE (21)
OCCUPATION: POP STAR AND ACTRESS
SURE, I'LL HAVE SOME.
THAT WAS FAST!
I HAVEN'T HAD THESE IN TWENTY YEARS.
CRUNCH
CRUNCH
CRUNCH
CRUNCH

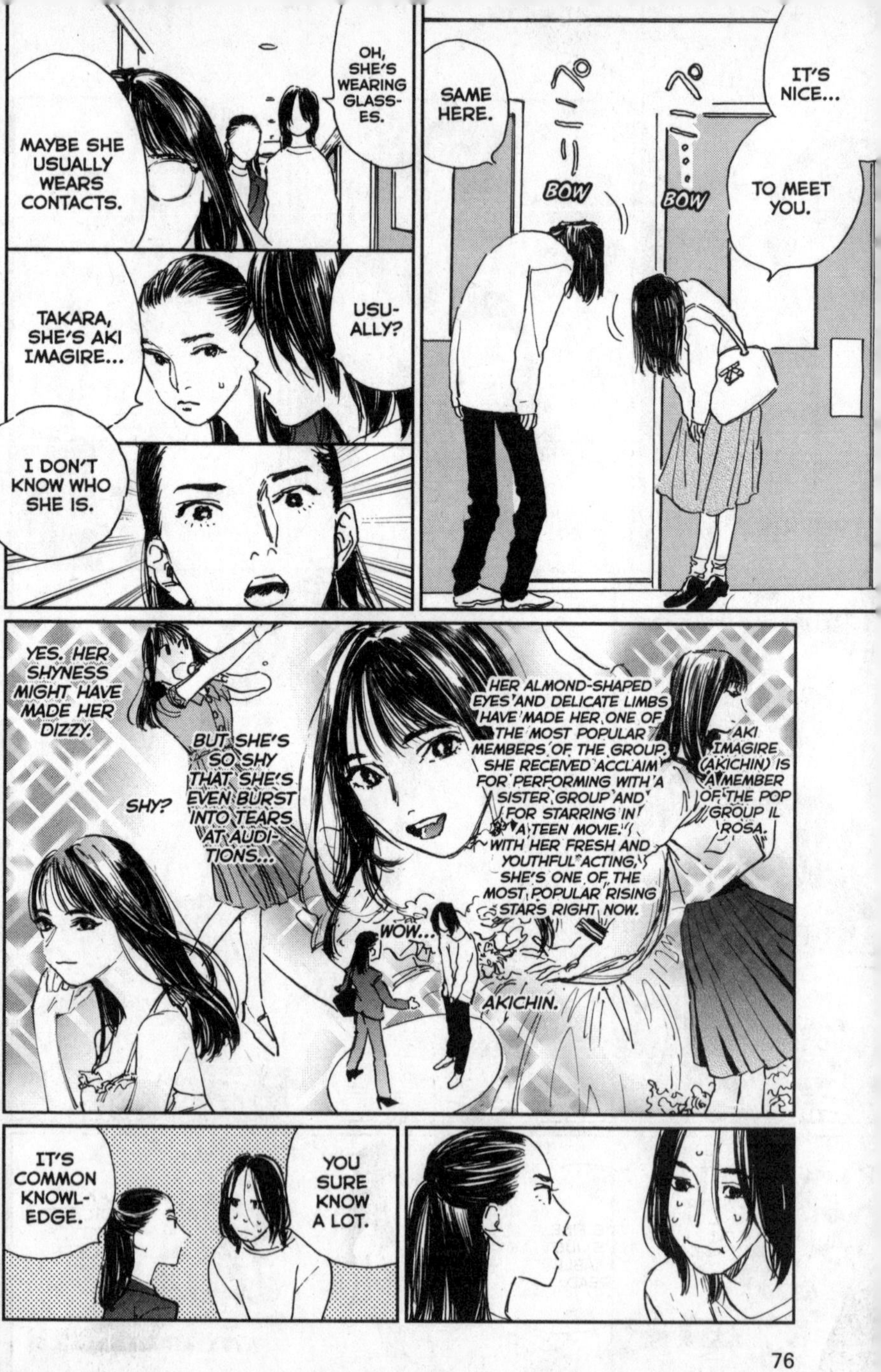
IT'S NICE...
TO MEET YOU.
BOW
SAME HERE.
BOW
OH, SHE'S WEARING GLASS-ES.
MAYBE SHE USUALLY WEARS CONTACTS.
USU-ALLY?
TAKARA, SHE'S AKI IMAGIRE...
I DON'T KNOW WHO SHE IS.
AKI IMAGIRE (AKICHIN) IS A MEMBER OF THE POP GROUP IL ROSA.
HER ALMOND-SHAPED EYES AND DELICATE LIMBS HAVE MADE HER ONE OF THE MOST POPULAR MEMBERS OF THE GROUP. SHE RECEIVED ACCLAIM FOR PERFORMING WITH A SISTER GROUP AND FOR STARRING IN A TEEN MOVIE. WITH HER FRESH AND YOUTHFUL ACTING, SHE'S ONE OF THE MOST POPULAR RISING STARS RIGHT NOW.
AKICHIN.
WOW...
BUT SHE'S SO SHY THAT SHE'S EVEN BURST INTO TEARS AT AUDI-TIONS...
SHY?
YES. HER SHYNESS MIGHT HAVE MADE HER DIZZY.
YOU SURE KNOW A LOT.
IT'S COMMON KNOWL-EDGE.

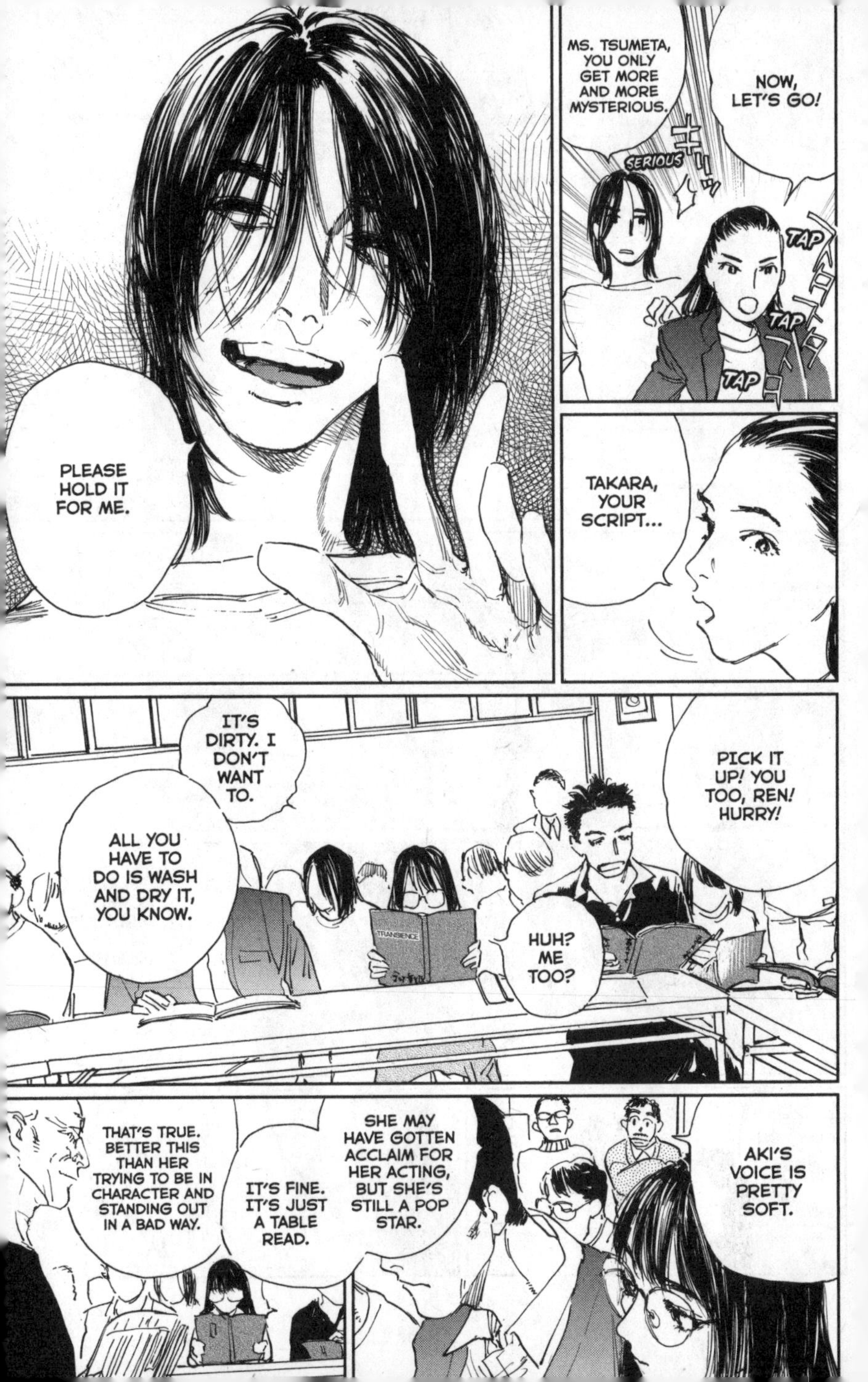
NOW, LET'S GO!
MS. TSUMETA, YOU ONLY GET MORE AND MORE MYSTERIOUS.
SERIOUS
TAP
TAP
TAP
TAKARA, YOUR SCRIPT...
PLEASE HOLD IT FOR ME.
PICK IT UP! YOU TOO, REN! HURRY!
HUH? ME TOO?
TRANSIENCE
IT'S DIRTY. I DON'T WANT TO.
ALL YOU HAVE TO DO IS WASH AND DRY IT, YOU KNOW.
AKI'S VOICE IS PRETTY SOFT.
SHE MAY HAVE GOTTEN ACCLAIM FOR HER ACTING, BUT SHE'S STILL A POP STAR.
IT'S FINE. IT'S JUST A TABLE READ.
THAT'S TRUE. BETTER THIS THAN HER TRYING TO BE IN CHARACTER AND STANDING OUT IN A BAD WAY.

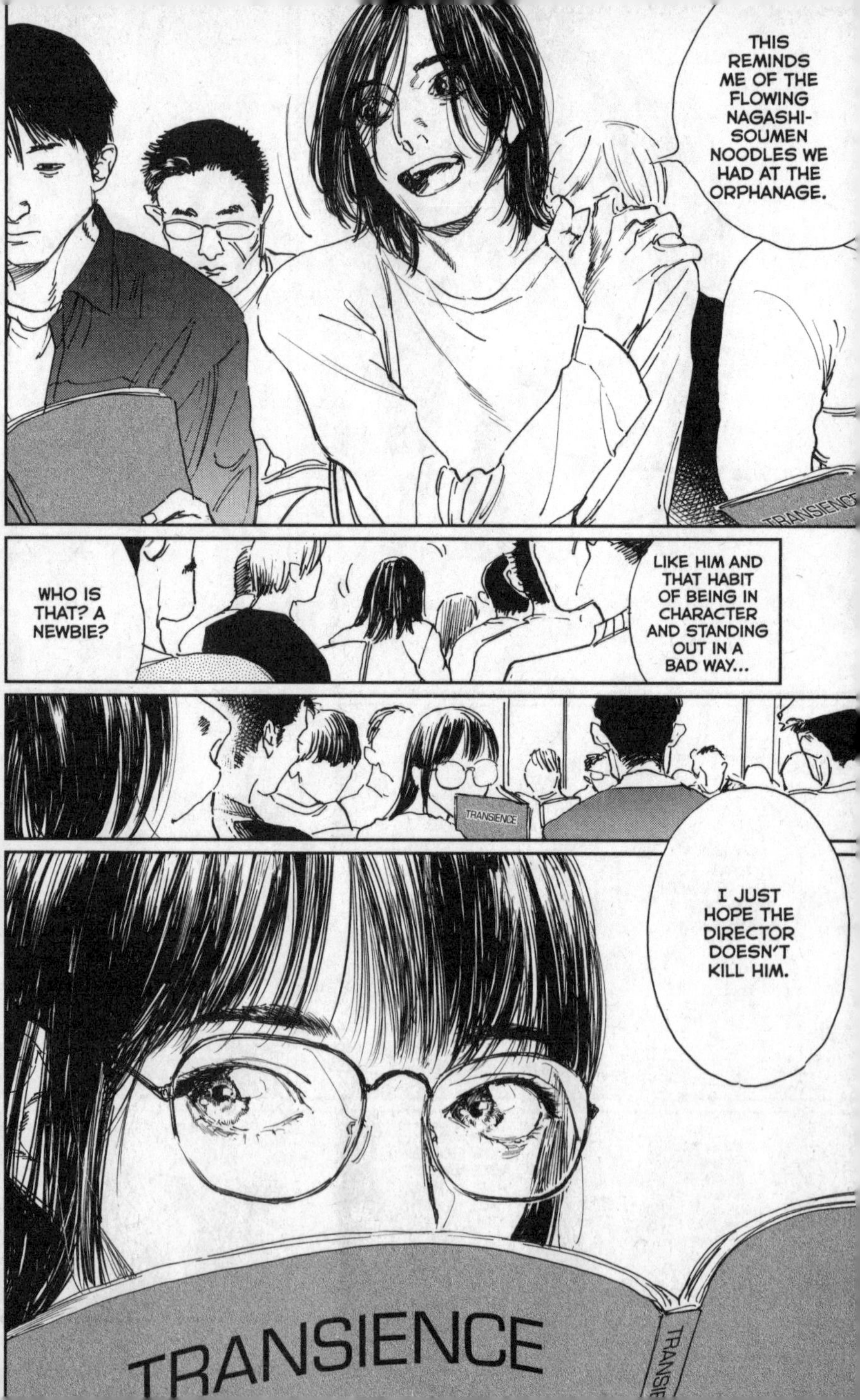
THIS REMINDS ME OF THE FLOWING NAGASHI-SOUMEN NOODLES WE HAD AT THE ORPHANAGE.
LIKE HIM AND THAT HABIT OF BEING IN CHARACTER AND STANDING OUT IN A BAD WAY...
WHO IS THAT? A NEWBIE?
TRANSIENCE
I JUST HOPE THE DIRECTOR DOESN'T KILL HIM.
TRANSIENCE

DOUBLE

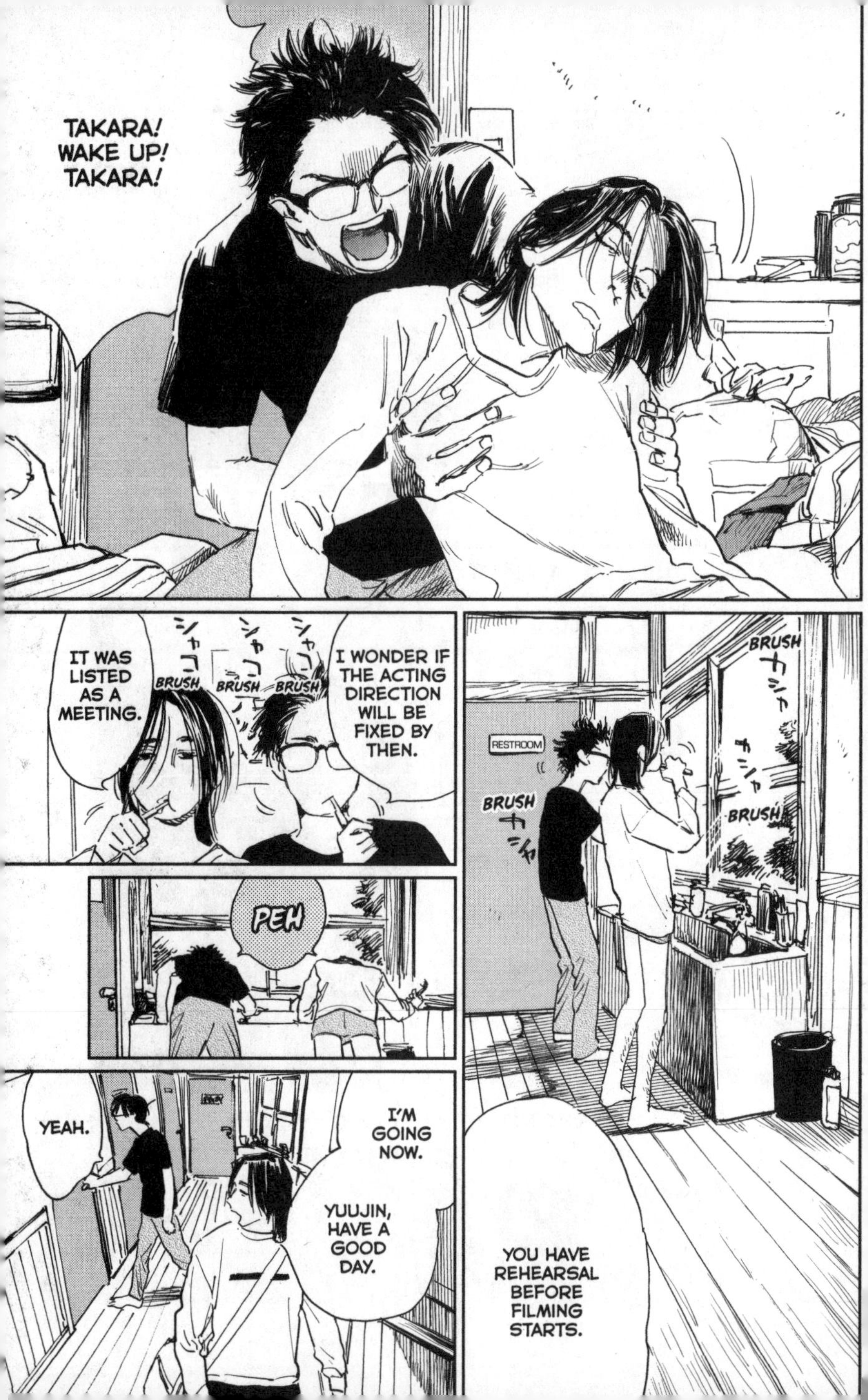
TAKARA! WAKE UP! TAKARA!
BRUSH
BRUSH
RESTROOM
BRUSH
YOU HAVE REHEARSAL BEFORE FILMING STARTS.
I WONDER IF THE ACTING DIRECTION WILL BE FIXED BY THEN.
BRUSH
BRUSH
BRUSH
IT WAS LISTED AS A MEETING.
PEH
I'M GOING NOW.
YUUJIN, HAVE A GOOD DAY.
YEAH.

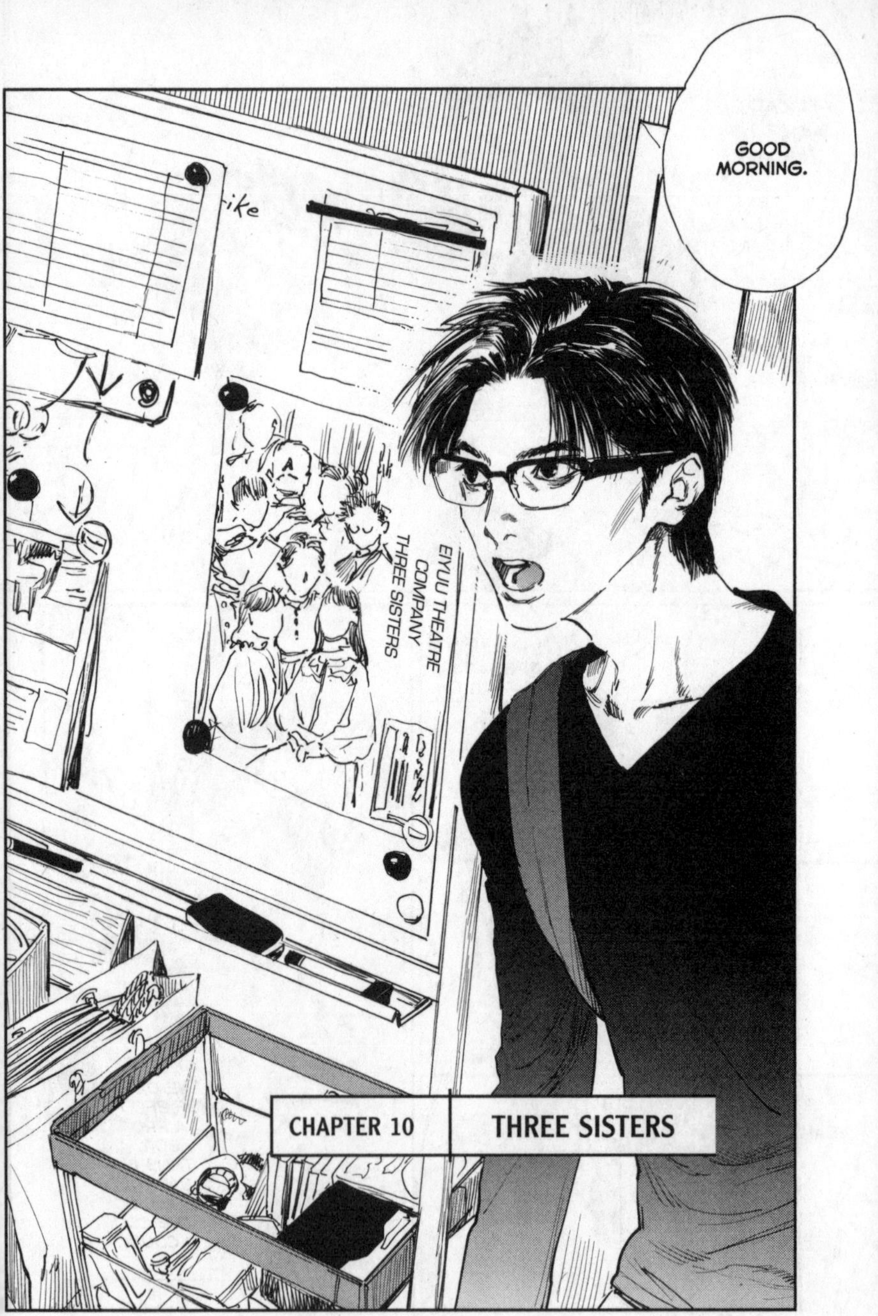
GOOD MORNING.
EIYUU THEATRE COMPANY
THREE SISTERS
CHAPTER 10
THREE SISTERS

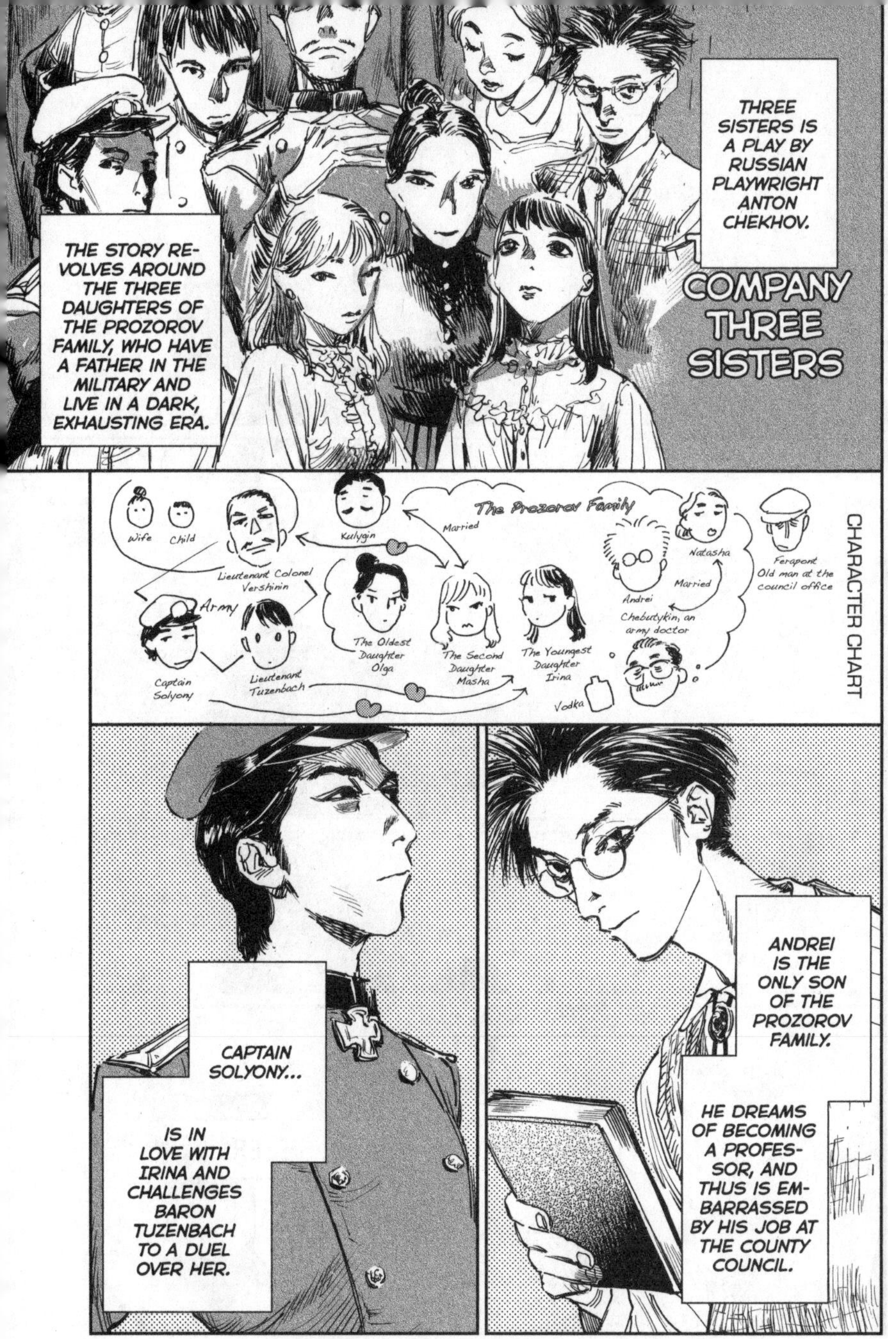
THREE SISTERS IS A PLAY BY RUSSIAN PLAYWRIGHT ANTON CHEKHOV.
COMPANY THREE SISTERS
THE STORY REVOLVES AROUND THE THREE DAUGHTERS OF THE PROZOROV FAMILY, WHO HAVE A FATHER IN THE MILITARY AND LIVE IN A DARK, EXHAUSTING ERA.
CHARACTER CHART
Ferapont Old man at the council office
The Prozorov Family
Natasha
Married
Andrei
Chebutykin, an army doctor
Kulygin
Married
Wife
Child
Lieutenant Colonel Vershinin
Army
The Oldest Daughter Olga
The Second Daughter Masha
The Youngest Daughter Irina
Vodka
Captain Solyony
Lieutenant Tuzenbach
ANDREI IS THE ONLY SON OF THE PROZOROV FAMILY.
HE DREAMS OF BECOMING A PROFESSOR, AND THUS IS EMBARRASSED BY HIS JOB AT THE COUNTY COUNCIL.
CAPTAIN SOLYONY...
IS IN LOVE WITH IRINA AND CHALLENGES BARON TUZENBACH TO A DUEL OVER HER.

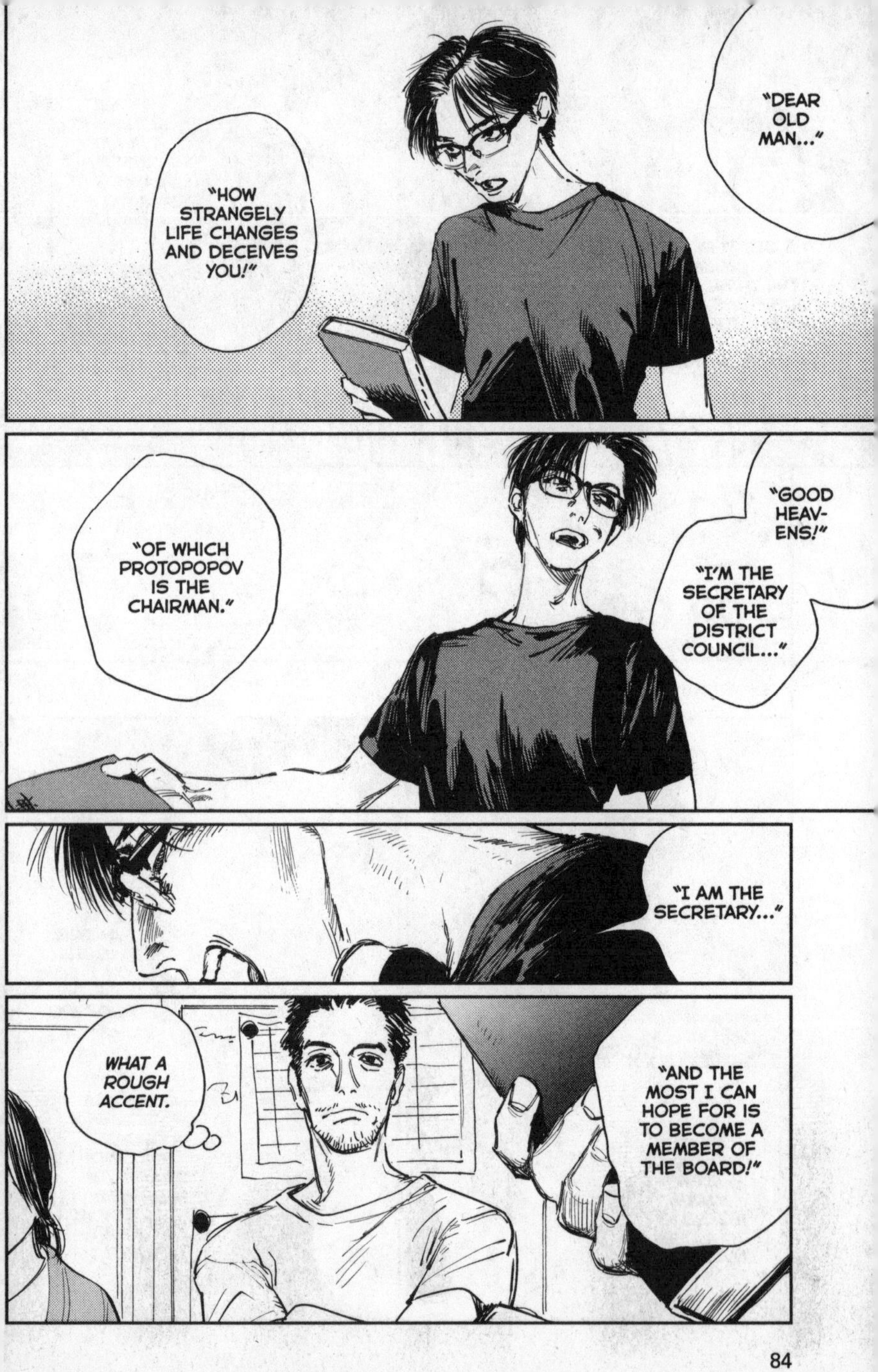
"DEAR OLD MAN..."
"HOW STRANGELY LIFE CHANGES AND DECEIVES YOU!"
"GOOD HEAVENS!"
"I'M THE SECRETARY OF THE DISTRICT COUNCIL..."
"OF WHICH PROTOPOPOV IS THE CHAIRMAN."
"I AM THE SECRETARY..."
"AND THE MOST I CAN HOPE FOR IS TO BECOME A MEMBER OF THE BOARD!"
WHAT A ROUGH ACCENT.

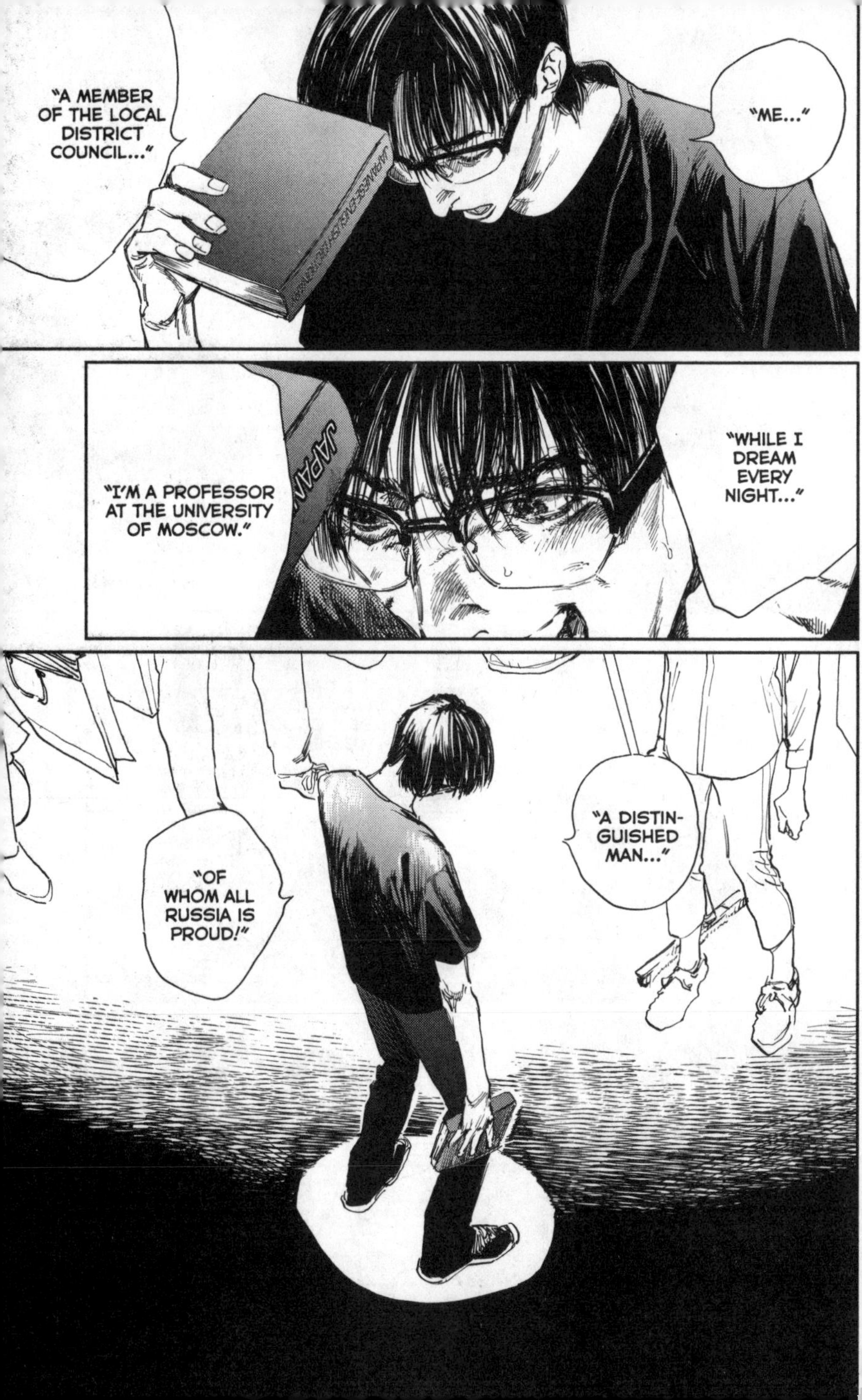
"ME..."
"A MEMBER OF THE LOCAL DISTRICT COUNCIL..."
"WHILE I DREAM EVERY NIGHT..."
"I'M A PROFESSOR AT THE UNIVERSITY OF MOSCOW."
"A DISTIN-GUISHED MAN..."
"OF WHOM ALL RUSSIA IS PROUD!"

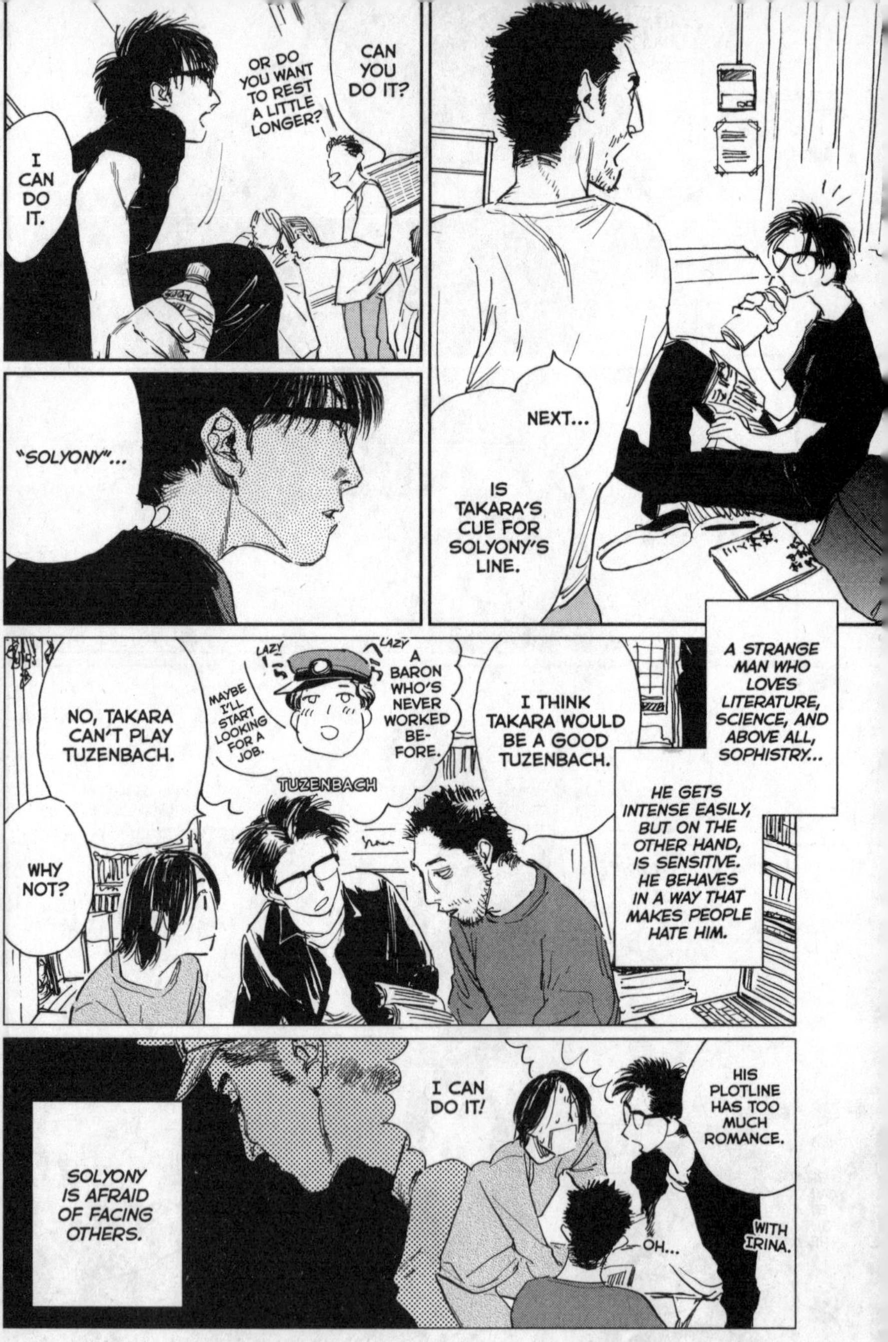
NEXT...
IS TAKARA'S CUE FOR SOLYONY'S LINE.
CAN YOU DO IT?
OR DO YOU WANT TO REST A LITTLE LONGER?
I CAN DO IT.
"SOLYONY"...
A STRANGE MAN WHO LOVES LITERATURE, SCIENCE, AND ABOVE ALL, SOPHISTRY...
HE GETS INTENSE EASILY, BUT ON THE OTHER HAND, IS SENSITIVE. HE BEHAVES IN A WAY THAT MAKES PEOPLE HATE HIM.
I THINK TAKARA WOULD BE A GOOD TUZENBACH.
A BARON WHO'S NEVER WORKED BEFORE.
LAZY
LAZY
MAYBE I'LL START LOOKING FOR A JOB.
TUZENBACH
NO, TAKARA CAN'T PLAY TUZENBACH.
WHY NOT?
HIS PLOTLINE HAS TOO MUCH ROMANCE.
WITH IRINA.
I CAN DO IT!
OH...
SOLYONY IS AFRAID OF FACING OTHERS.

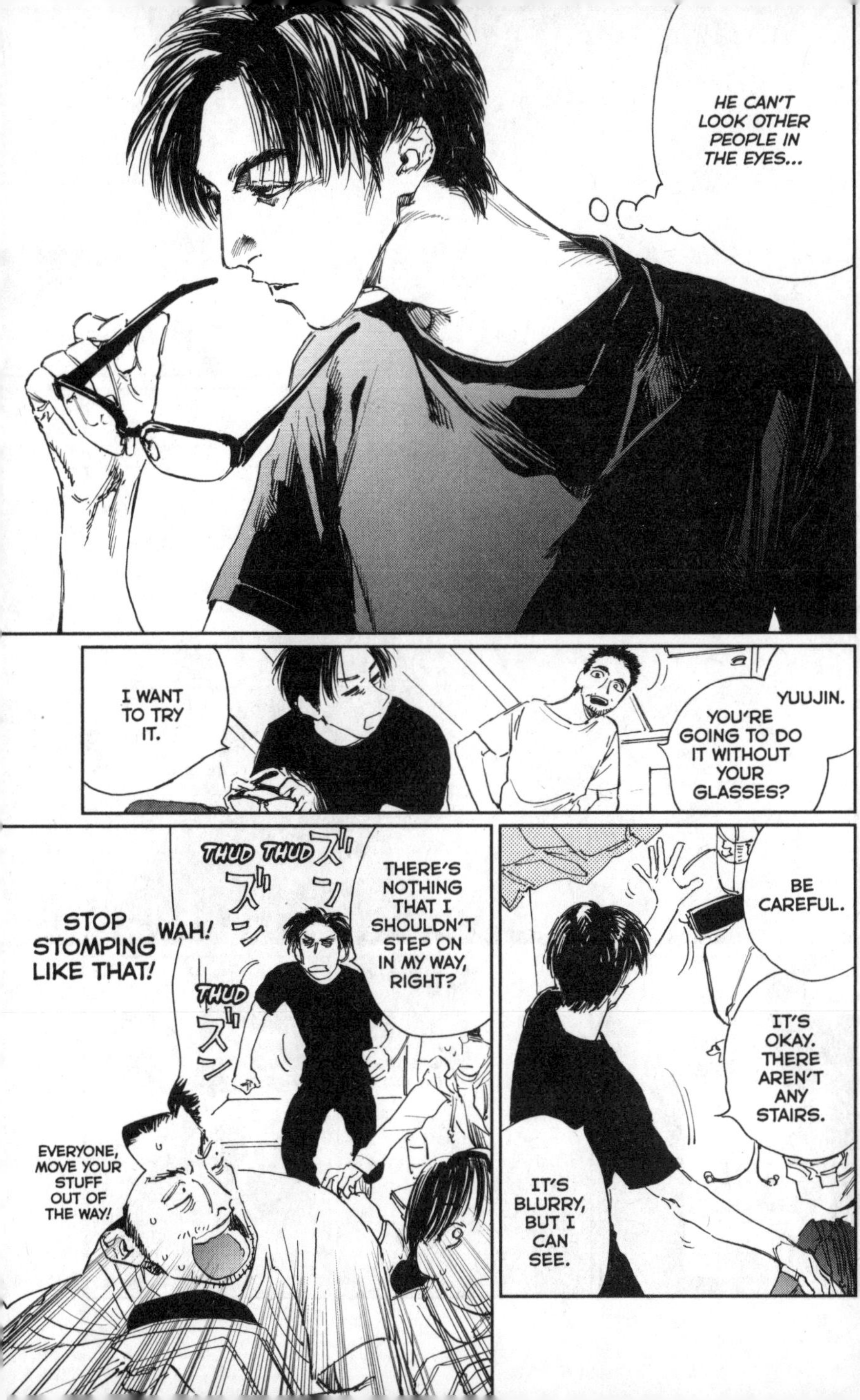
HE CAN'T LOOK OTHER PEOPLE IN THE EYES...
YUUJIN. YOU'RE GOING TO DO IT WITHOUT YOUR GLASSES?
I WANT TO TRY IT.
BE CAREFUL.
IT'S OKAY. THERE AREN'T ANY STAIRS.
IT'S BLURRY, BUT I CAN SEE.
THERE'S NOTHING THAT I SHOULDN'T STEP ON IN MY WAY, RIGHT?
THUD THUD
WAH!
STOP STOMPING LIKE THAT!
THUD
EVERYONE, MOVE YOUR STUFF OUT OF THE WAY!

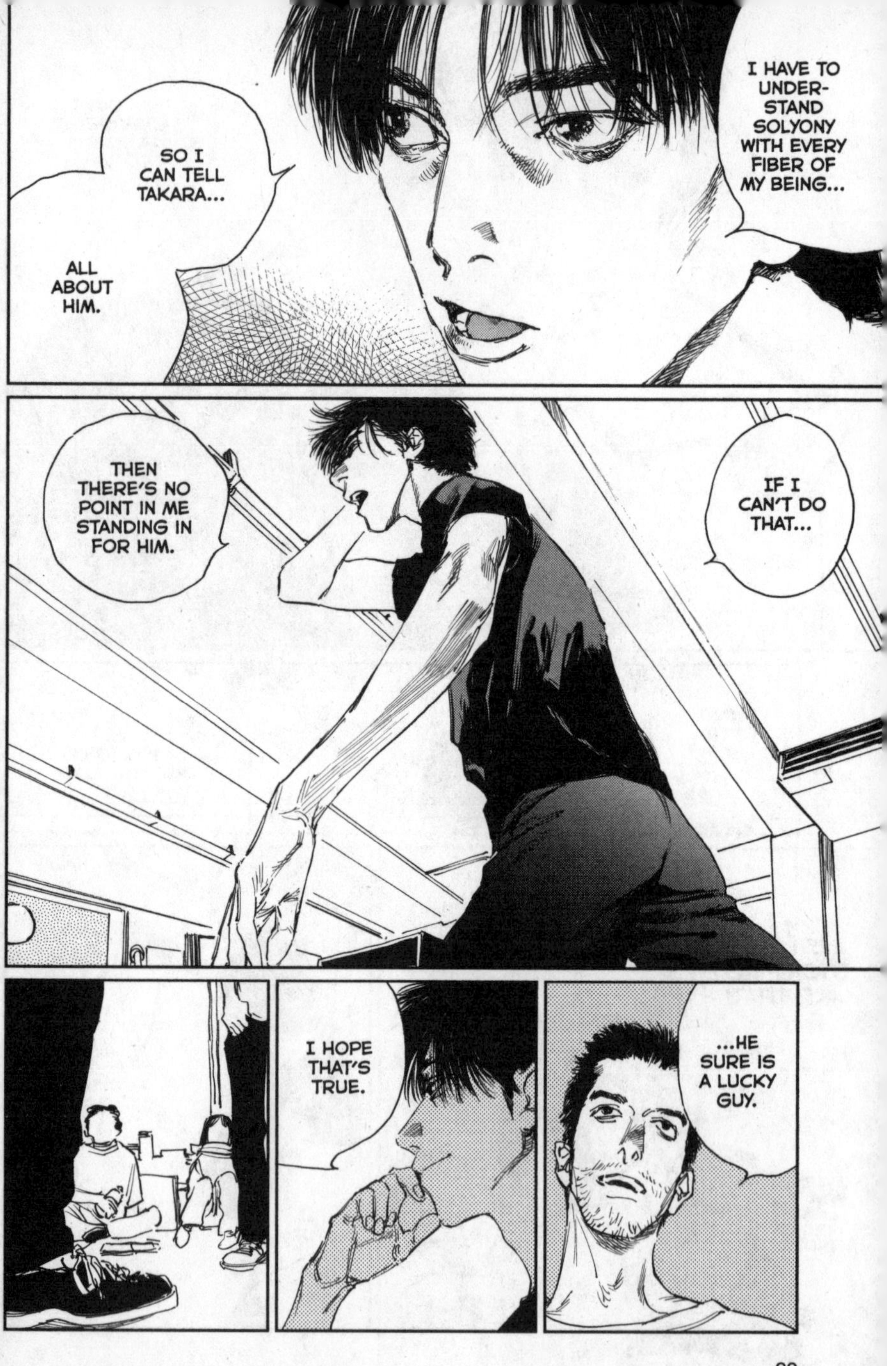
I HAVE TO UNDER-STAND SOLYONY WITH EVERY FIBER OF MY BEING...
SO I CAN TELL TAKARA...
ALL ABOUT HIM.
IF I CAN'T DO THAT...
THEN THERE'S NO POINT IN ME STANDING IN FOR HIM.
...HE SURE IS A LUCKY GUY.
I HOPE THAT'S TRUE.

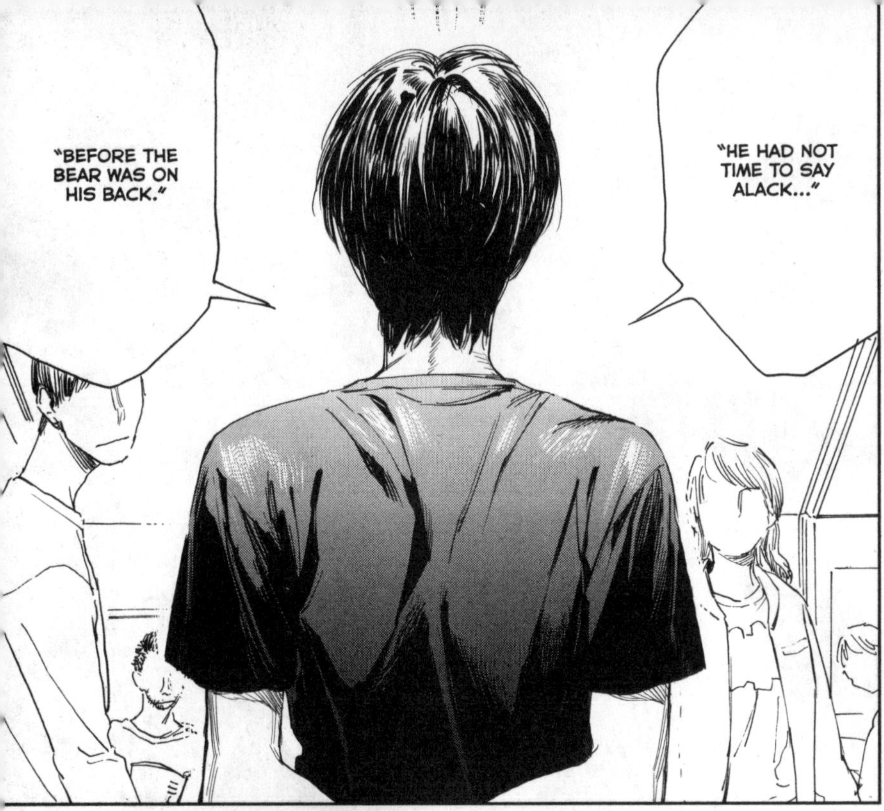
"HE HAD NOT TIME TO SAY ALACK..."
"BEFORE THE BEAR WAS ON HIS BACK."
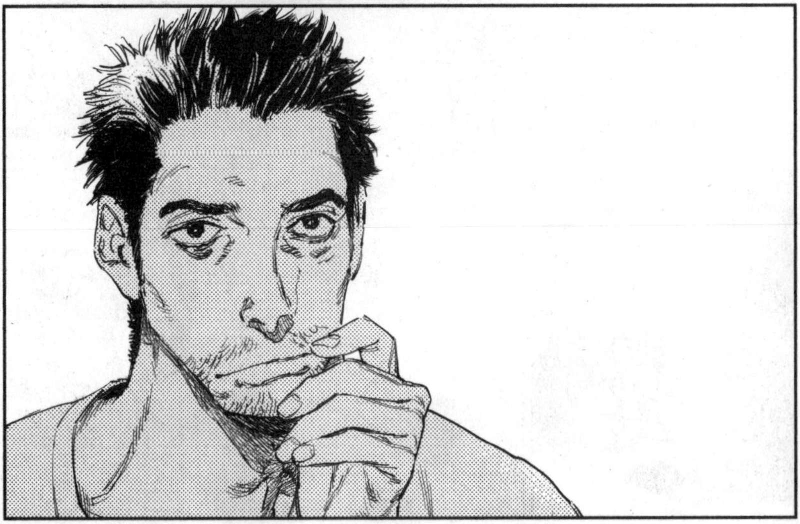

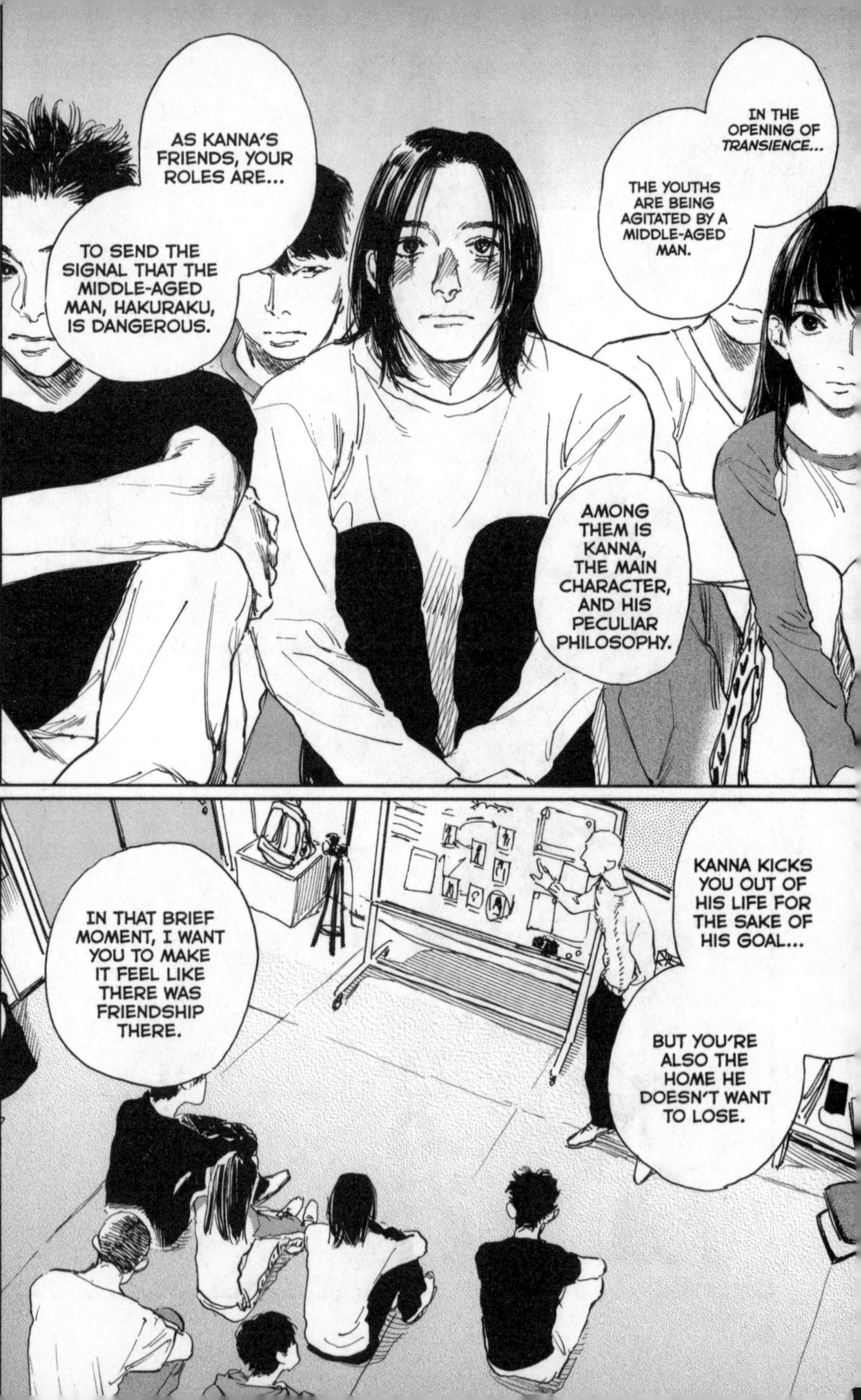
IN THE OPENING OF *TRANSIENCE*...
THE YOUTHS ARE BEING AGITATED BY A MIDDLE-AGED MAN.
AMONG THEM IS KANNA, THE MAIN CHARACTER, AND HIS PECULIAR PHILOSOPHY.
AS KANNA'S FRIENDS, YOUR ROLES ARE...
TO SEND THE SIGNAL THAT THE MIDDLE-AGED MAN, HAKURAKU, IS DANGEROUS.
KANNA KICKS YOU OUT OF HIS LIFE FOR THE SAKE OF HIS GOAL...
BUT YOU'RE ALSO THE HOME HE DOESN'T WANT TO LOSE.
IN THAT BRIEF MOMENT, I WANT YOU TO MAKE IT FEEL LIKE THERE WAS FRIENDSHIP THERE.

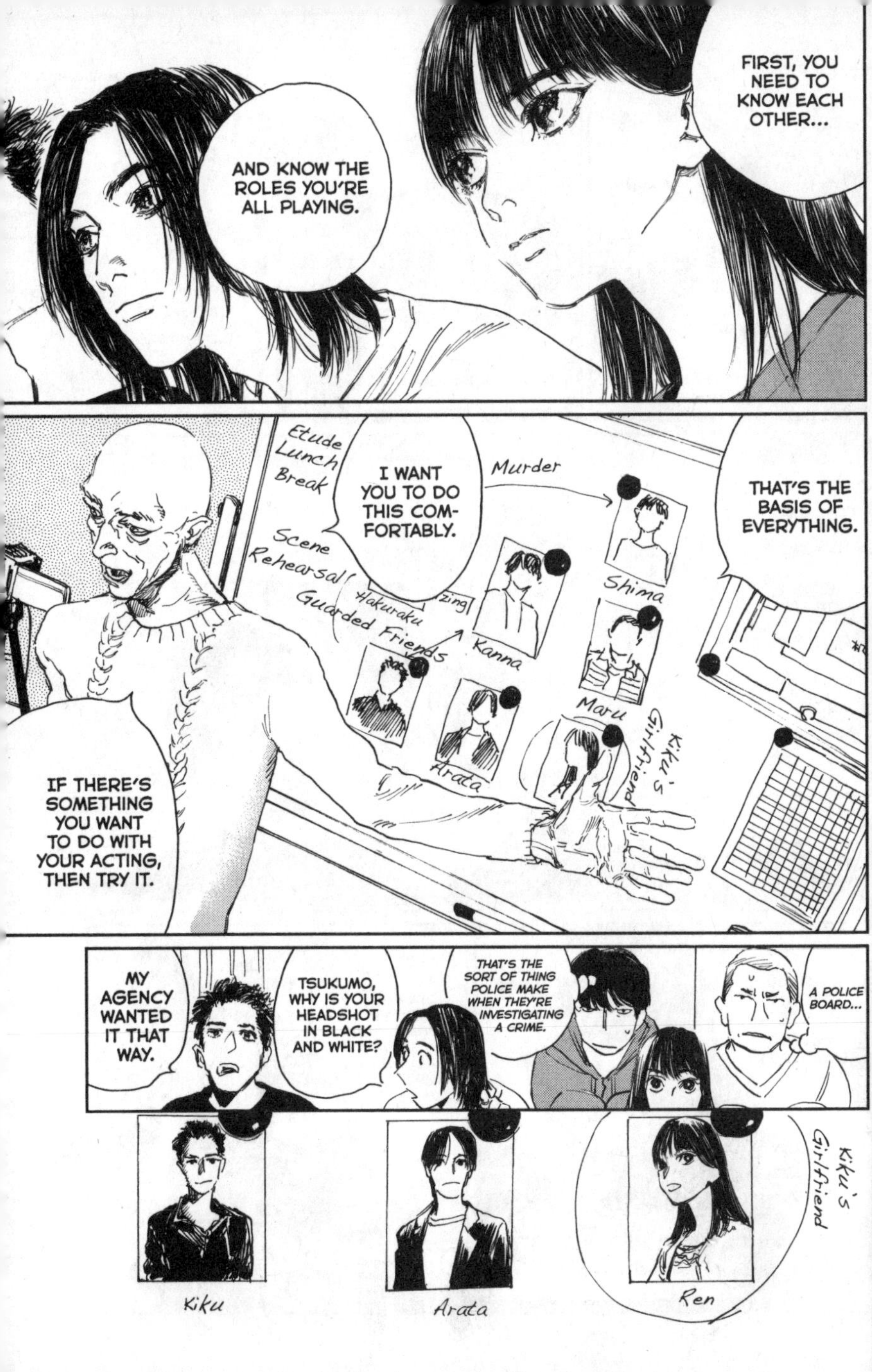
FIRST, YOU NEED TO KNOW EACH OTHER...
AND KNOW THE ROLES YOU'RE ALL PLAYING.
THAT'S THE BASIS OF EVERYTHING.
Murder
Shima
Maru
Kiku's Girlfriend
Kanna
Arata
Etude Lunch Break
I WANT YOU TO DO THIS COM-FORTABLY.
Scene Rehearsal
Hakuraku Guarded Friends
IF THERE'S SOMETHING YOU WANT TO DO WITH YOUR ACTING, THEN TRY IT.
A POLICE BOARD...
THAT'S THE SORT OF THING POLICE MAKE WHEN THEY'RE INVESTIGATING A CRIME.
TSUKUMO, WHY IS YOUR HEADSHOT IN BLACK AND WHITE?
MY AGENCY WANTED IT THAT WAY.
Kiku's Girlfriend
Ren
Arata
Kiku

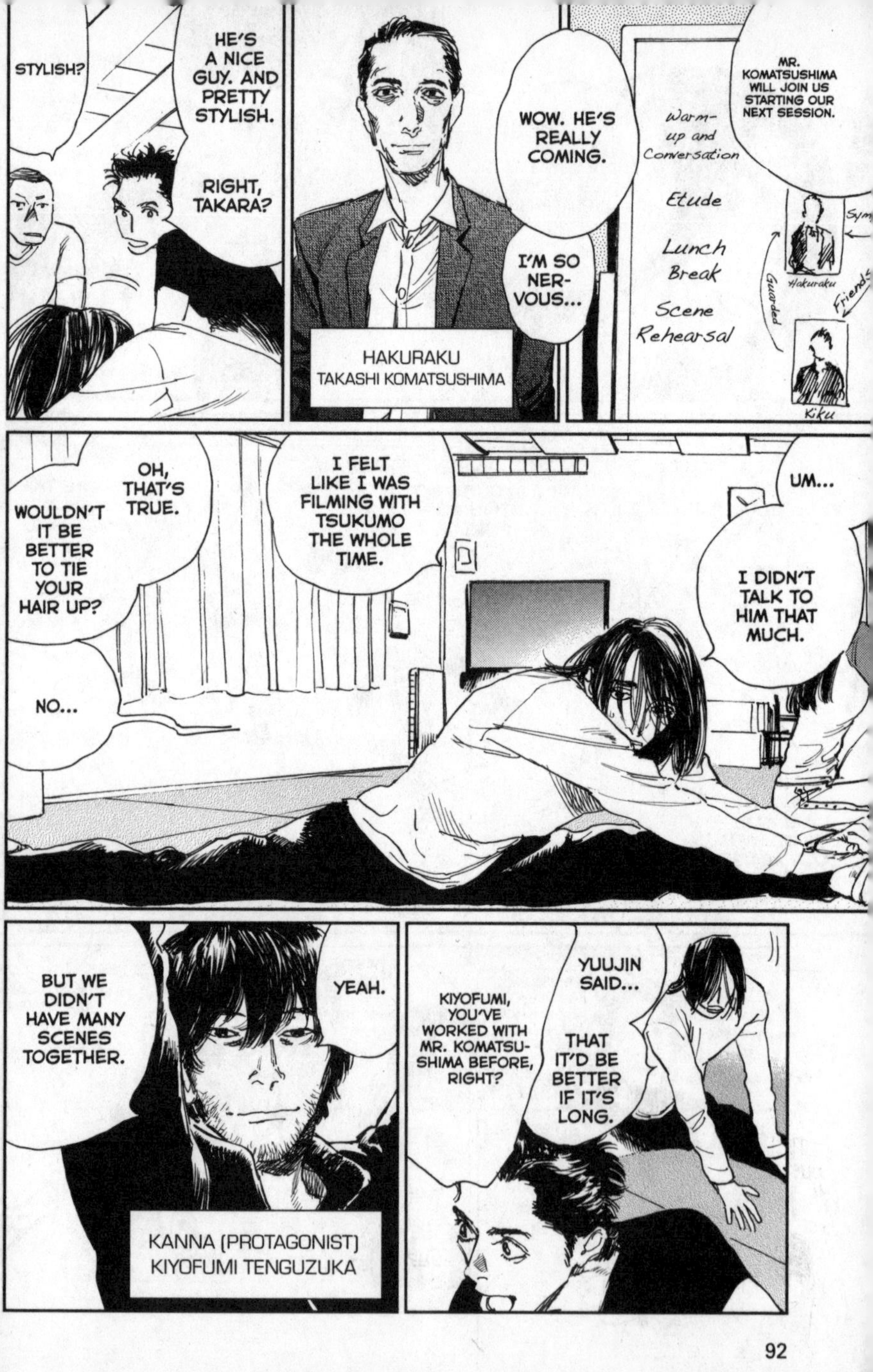
MR. KOMATSUSHIMA WILL JOIN US STARTING OUR NEXT SESSION.
Warm-up and Conversation
Etude
Lunch Break
Scene Rehearsal
Hakuraku
Guarded
Friends
Kiku
WOW. HE'S REALLY COMING.
I'M SO NER-VOUS...
HAKURAKU
TAKASHI KOMATSUSHIMA
HE'S A NICE GUY. AND PRETTY STYLISH.
RIGHT, TAKARA?
STYLISH?
UM...
I DIDN'T TALK TO HIM THAT MUCH.
I FELT LIKE I WAS FILMING WITH TSUKUMO THE WHOLE TIME.
OH, THAT'S TRUE.
WOULDN'T IT BE BETTER TO TIE YOUR HAIR UP?
NO...
YUUJIN SAID...
THAT IT'D BE BETTER IF IT'S LONG.
KIYOFUMI, YOU'VE WORKED WITH MR. KOMATSU-SHIMA BEFORE, RIGHT?
YEAH.
BUT WE DIDN'T HAVE MANY SCENES TOGETHER.
KANNA [PROTAGONIST]
KIYOFUMI TENGUZUKA

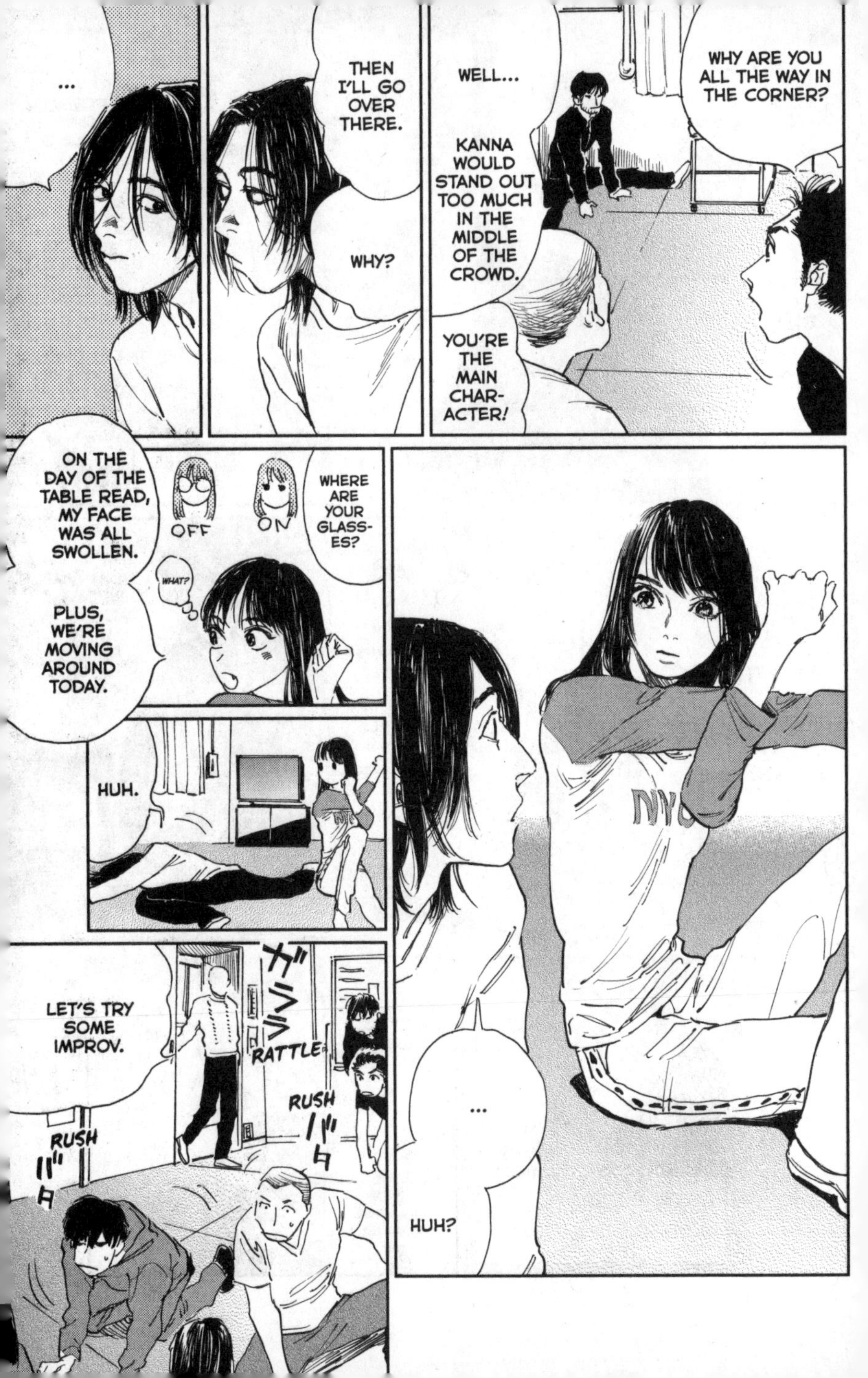
WHY ARE YOU ALL THE WAY IN THE CORNER?
WELL...
KANNA WOULD STAND OUT TOO MUCH IN THE MIDDLE OF THE CROWD.
YOU'RE THE MAIN CHARACTER!
THEN I'LL GO OVER THERE.
WHY?
...
...
HUH?
WHERE ARE YOUR GLASSES?
OFF
ON
WHAT?
ON THE DAY OF THE TABLE READ, MY FACE WAS ALL SWOLLEN.
PLUS, WE'RE MOVING AROUND TODAY.
HUH.
LET'S TRY SOME IMPROV.
ガラ
RATTLE
バタ
RUSH
バタ
RUSH

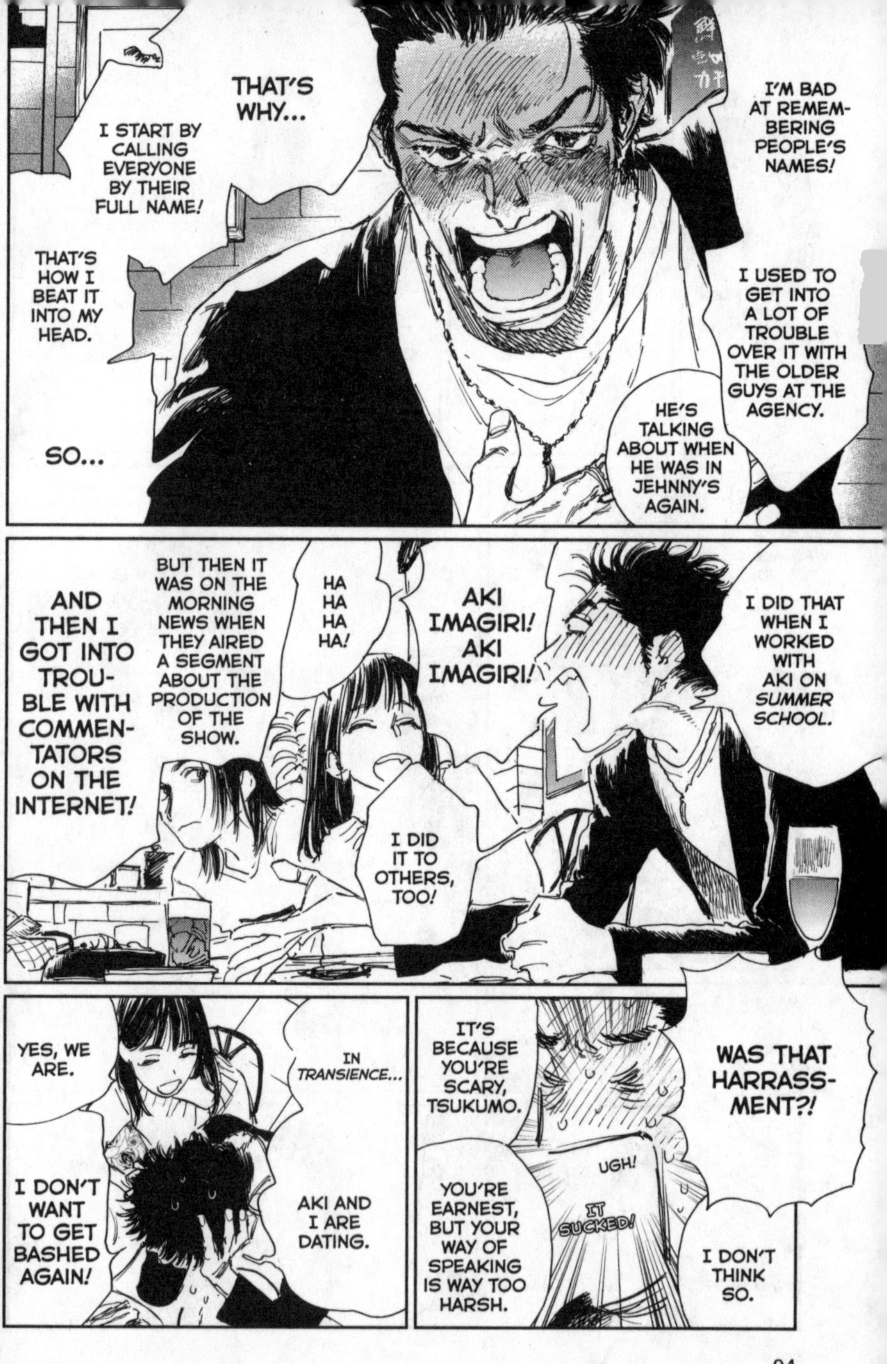
I'M BAD AT REMEMBERING PEOPLE'S NAMES!
THAT'S WHY...
I START BY CALLING EVERYONE BY THEIR FULL NAME!
I USED TO GET INTO A LOT OF TROUBLE OVER IT WITH THE OLDER GUYS AT THE AGENCY.
HE'S TALKING ABOUT WHEN HE WAS IN JEHNNY'S AGAIN.
THAT'S HOW I BEAT IT INTO MY HEAD.
SO...
I DID THAT WHEN I WORKED WITH AKI ON *SUMMER SCHOOL.*
AKI IMAGIRI! AKI IMAGIRI!
HA HA HA HA!
BUT THEN IT WAS ON THE MORNING NEWS WHEN THEY AIRED A SEGMENT ABOUT THE PRODUCTION OF THE SHOW.
AND THEN I GOT INTO TROUBLE WITH COMMENTATORS ON THE INTERNET!
I DID IT TO OTHERS, TOO!
WAS THAT HARRASSMENT?!
IT'S BECAUSE YOU'RE SCARY, TSUKUMO.
UGH!
IT SUCKED!
I DON'T THINK SO.
YOU'RE EARNEST, BUT YOUR WAY OF SPEAKING IS WAY TOO HARSH.
IN *TRANSIENCE...*
YES, WE ARE.
AKI AND I ARE DATING.
I DON'T WANT TO GET BASHED AGAIN!

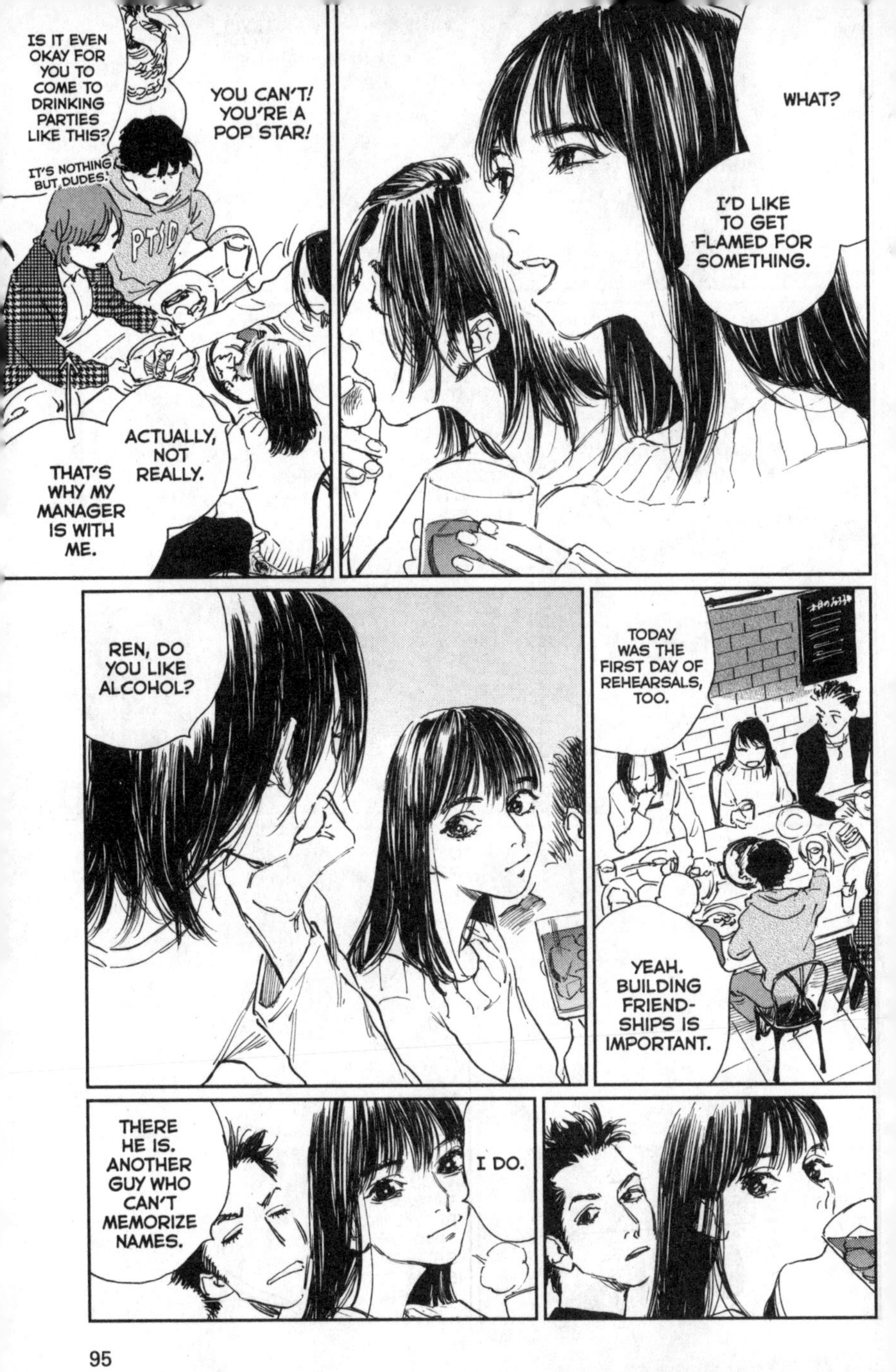
WHAT?
I'D LIKE TO GET FLAMED FOR SOMETHING.
IS IT EVEN OKAY FOR YOU TO COME TO DRINKING PARTIES LIKE THIS?
YOU CAN'T! YOU'RE A POP STAR!
IT'S NOTHING BUT DUDES.
ACTUALLY, NOT REALLY.
THAT'S WHY MY MANAGER IS WITH ME.
TODAY WAS THE FIRST DAY OF REHEARSALS, TOO.
YEAH. BUILDING FRIEND-SHIPS IS IMPORTANT.
REN, DO YOU LIKE ALCOHOL?
I DO.
THERE HE IS. ANOTHER GUY WHO CAN'T MEMORIZE NAMES.

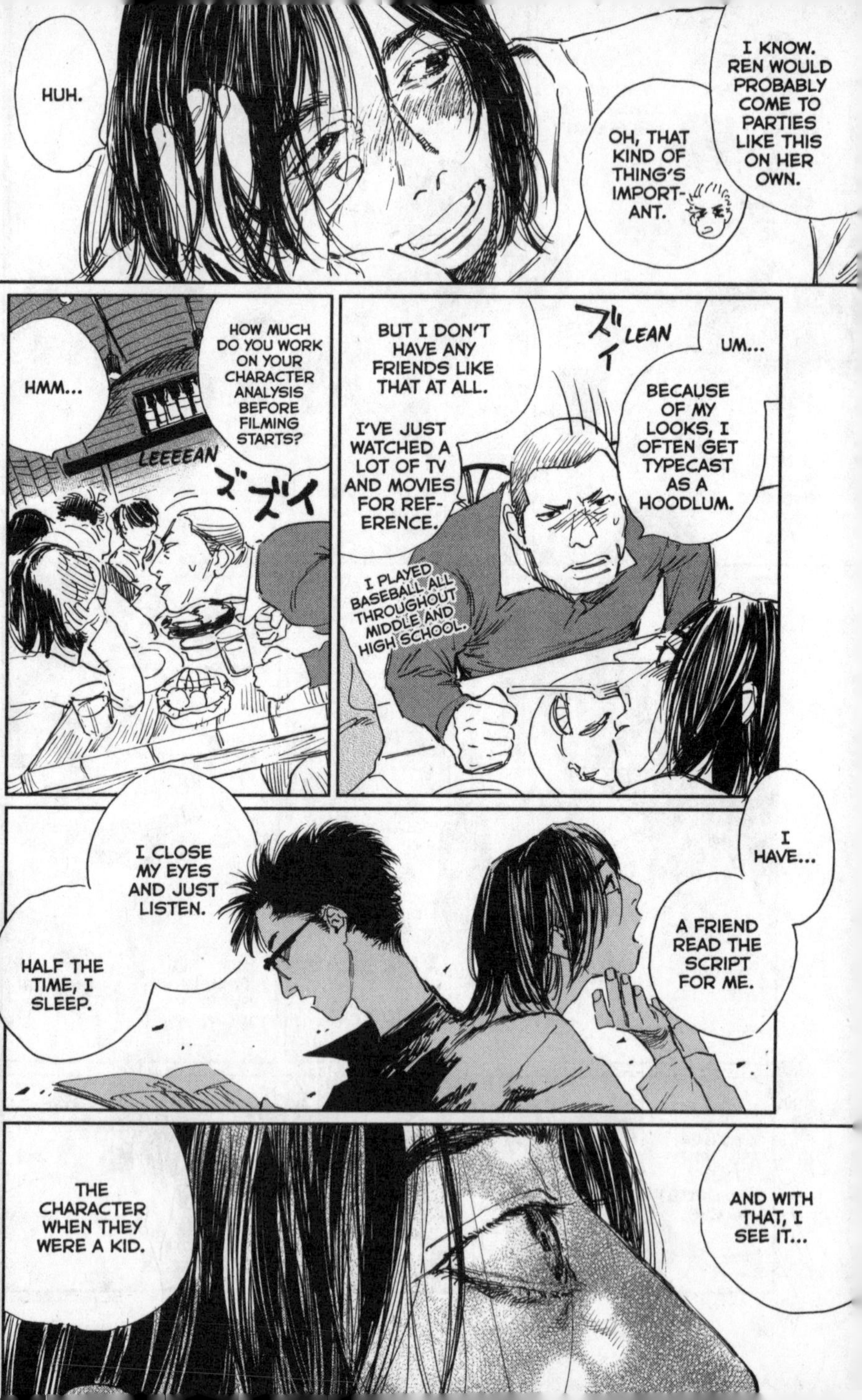
I KNOW. REN WOULD PROBABLY COME TO PARTIES LIKE THIS ON HER OWN.
OH, THAT KIND OF THING'S IMPORT-ANT.
HUH.
UM...
BECAUSE OF MY LOOKS, I OFTEN GET TYPECAST AS A HOODLUM.
ズイ LEAN
BUT I DON'T HAVE ANY FRIENDS LIKE THAT AT ALL.
I'VE JUST WATCHED A LOT OF TV AND MOVIES FOR REF-ERENCE.
I PLAYED BASEBALL ALL THROUGHOUT MIDDLE AND HIGH SCHOOL.
HOW MUCH DO YOU WORK ON YOUR CHARACTER ANALYSIS BEFORE FILMING STARTS?
HMM...
ズズイ LEEEEAN
I HAVE...
A FRIEND READ THE SCRIPT FOR ME.
I CLOSE MY EYES AND JUST LISTEN.
HALF THE TIME, I SLEEP.
AND WITH THAT, I SEE IT...
THE CHARACTER WHEN THEY WERE A KID.

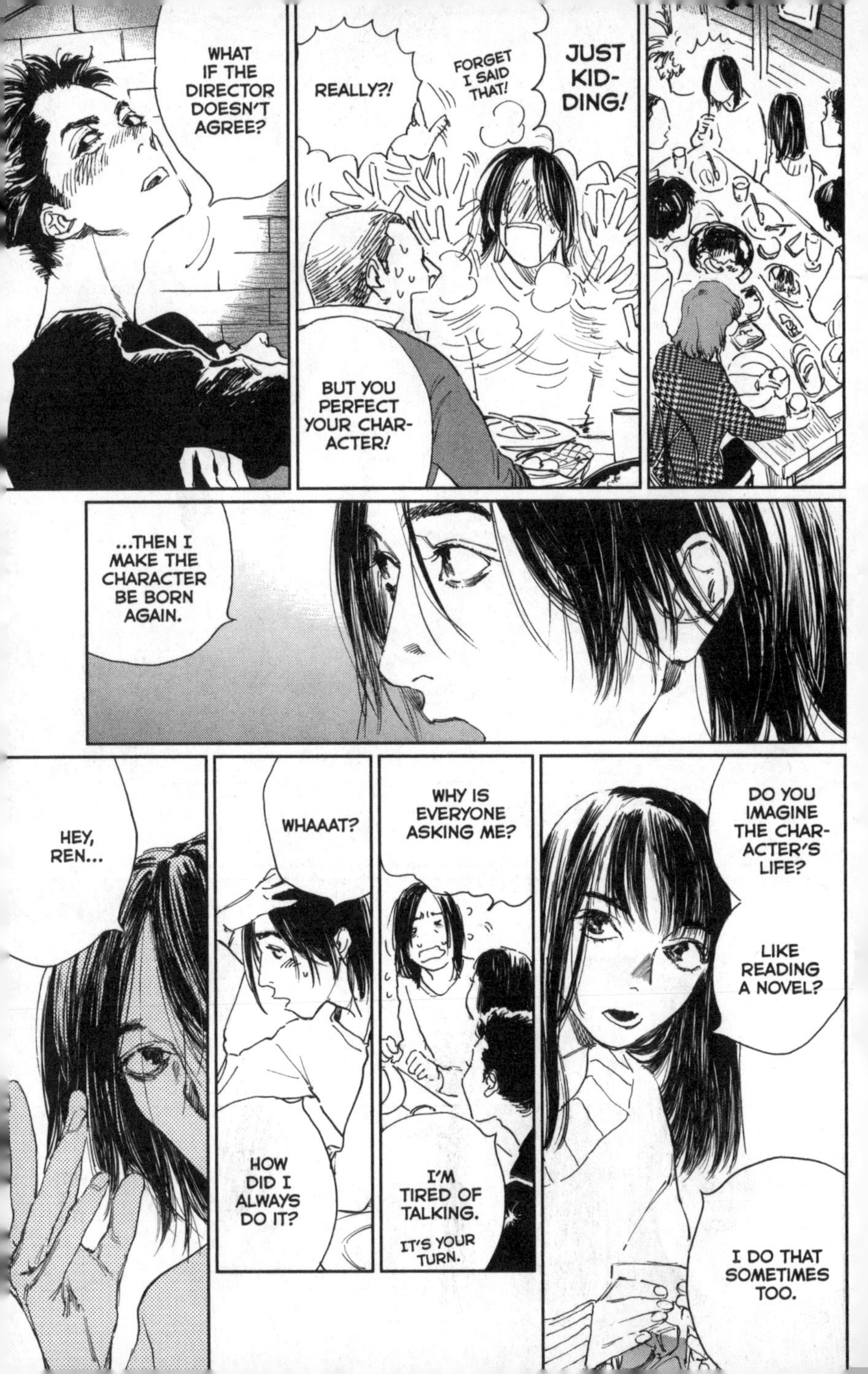
JUST KIDDING!
FORGET I SAID THAT!
REALLY?!
BUT YOU PERFECT YOUR CHARACTER!
WHAT IF THE DIRECTOR DOESN'T AGREE?
...THEN I MAKE THE CHARACTER BE BORN AGAIN.
DO YOU IMAGINE THE CHARACTER'S LIFE?
LIKE READING A NOVEL?
I DO THAT SOMETIMES TOO.
WHY IS EVERYONE ASKING ME?
I'M TIRED OF TALKING.
IT'S YOUR TURN.
WHAAAT?
HOW DID I ALWAYS DO IT?
HEY, REN...

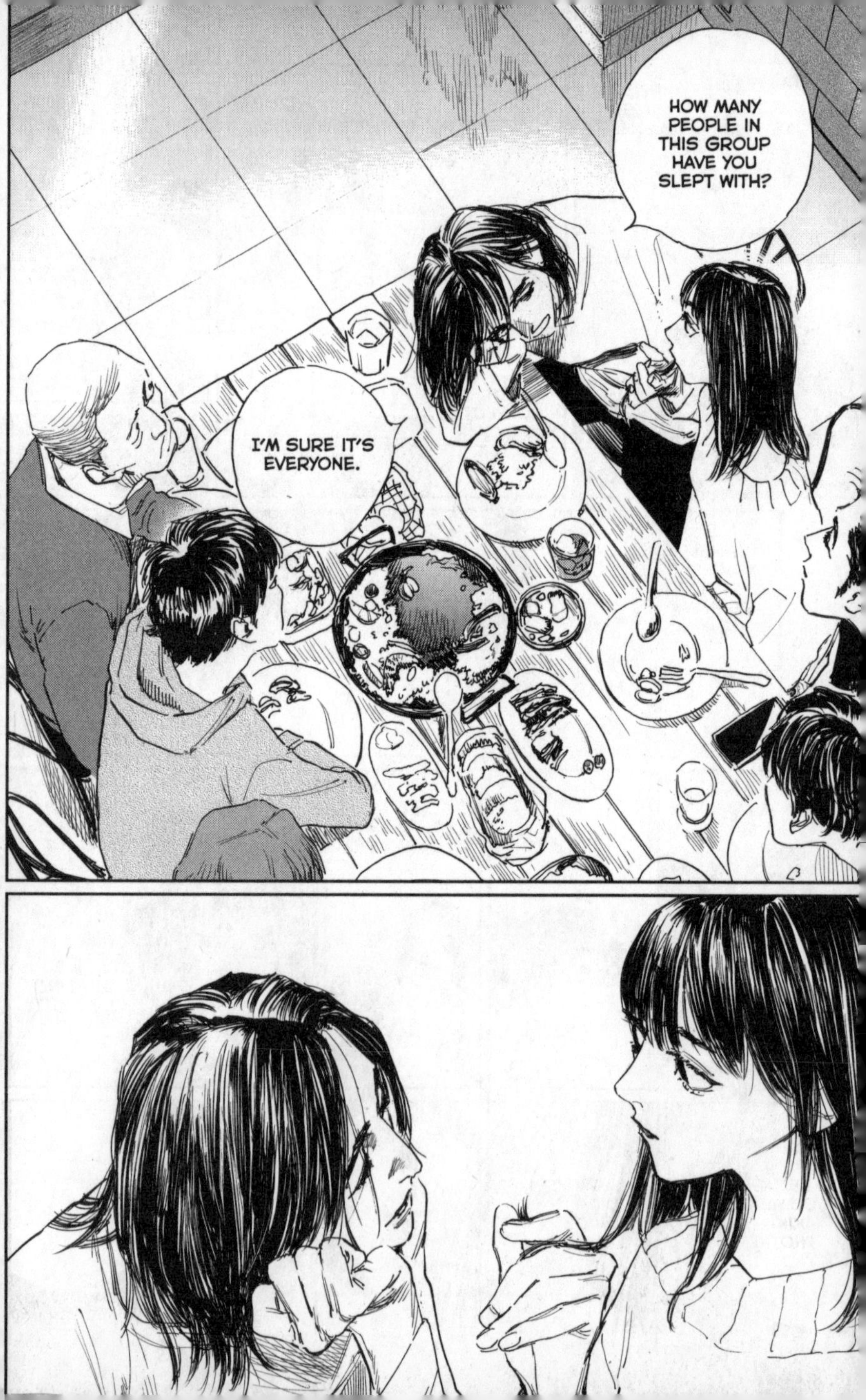
HOW MANY PEOPLE IN THIS GROUP HAVE YOU SLEPT WITH?
I'M SURE IT'S EVERYONE.

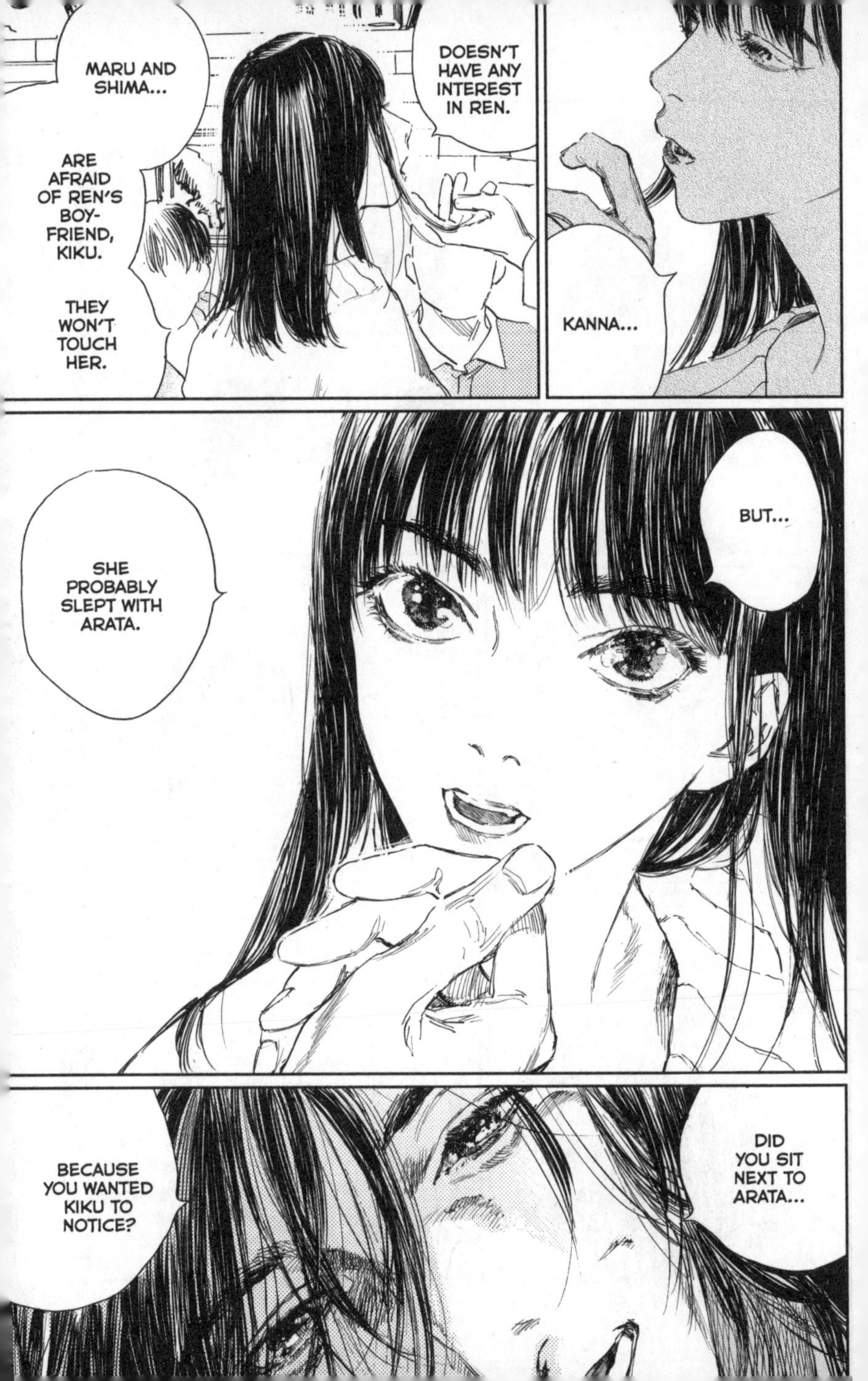
KANNA...
DOESN'T HAVE ANY INTEREST IN REN.
MARU AND SHIMA...
ARE AFRAID OF REN'S BOY-FRIEND, KIKU.
THEY WON'T TOUCH HER.
BUT...
SHE PROBABLY SLEPT WITH ARATA.
DID YOU SIT NEXT TO ARATA...
BECAUSE YOU WANTED KIKU TO NOTICE?

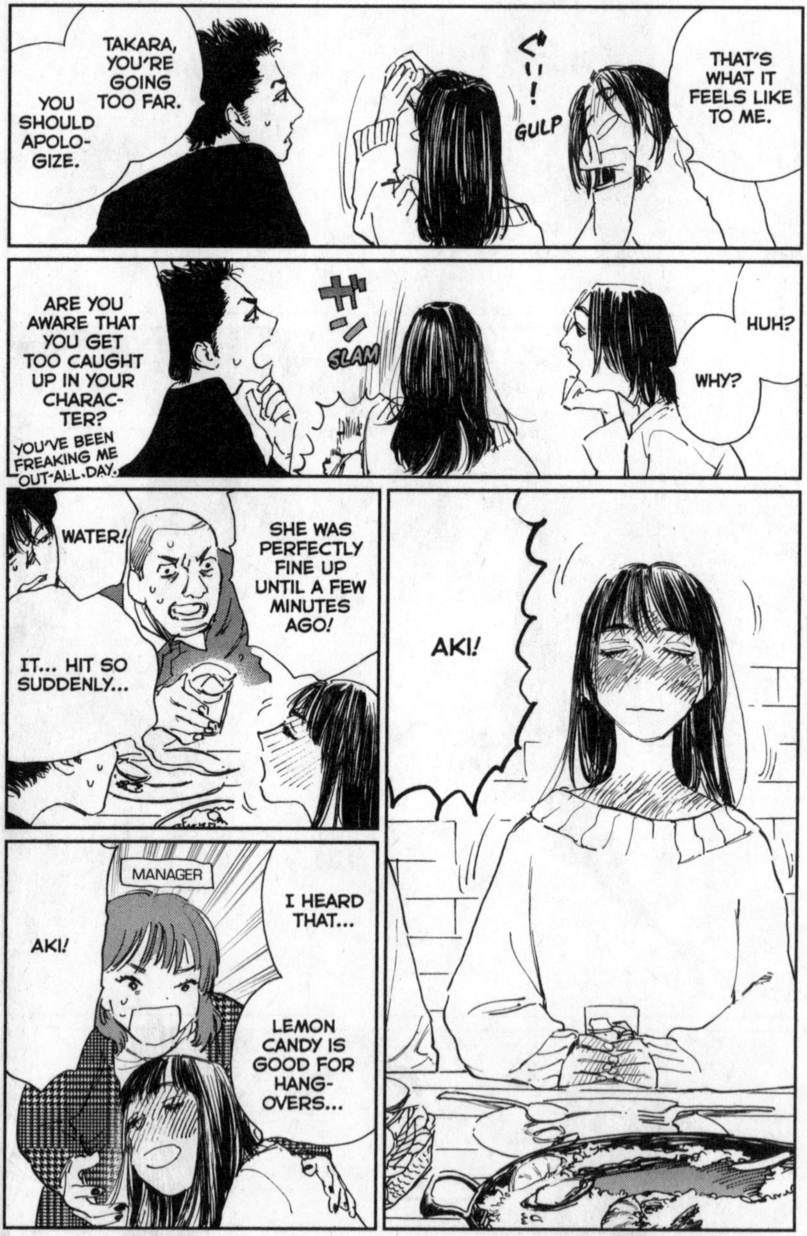
THAT'S WHAT IT FEELS LIKE TO ME.
ぐい!
GULP
TAKARA, YOU'RE GOING TOO FAR.
YOU SHOULD APOLOGIZE.
HUH?
WHY?
ガン
SLAM
ARE YOU AWARE THAT YOU GET TOO CAUGHT UP IN YOUR CHARACTER?
YOU'VE BEEN FREAKING ME OUT ALL DAY.
AKI!
SHE WAS PERFECTLY FINE UP UNTIL A FEW MINUTES AGO!
WATER!
IT... HIT SO SUDDENLY...
I HEARD THAT...
LEMON CANDY IS GOOD FOR HANGOVERS...
MANAGER
AKI!

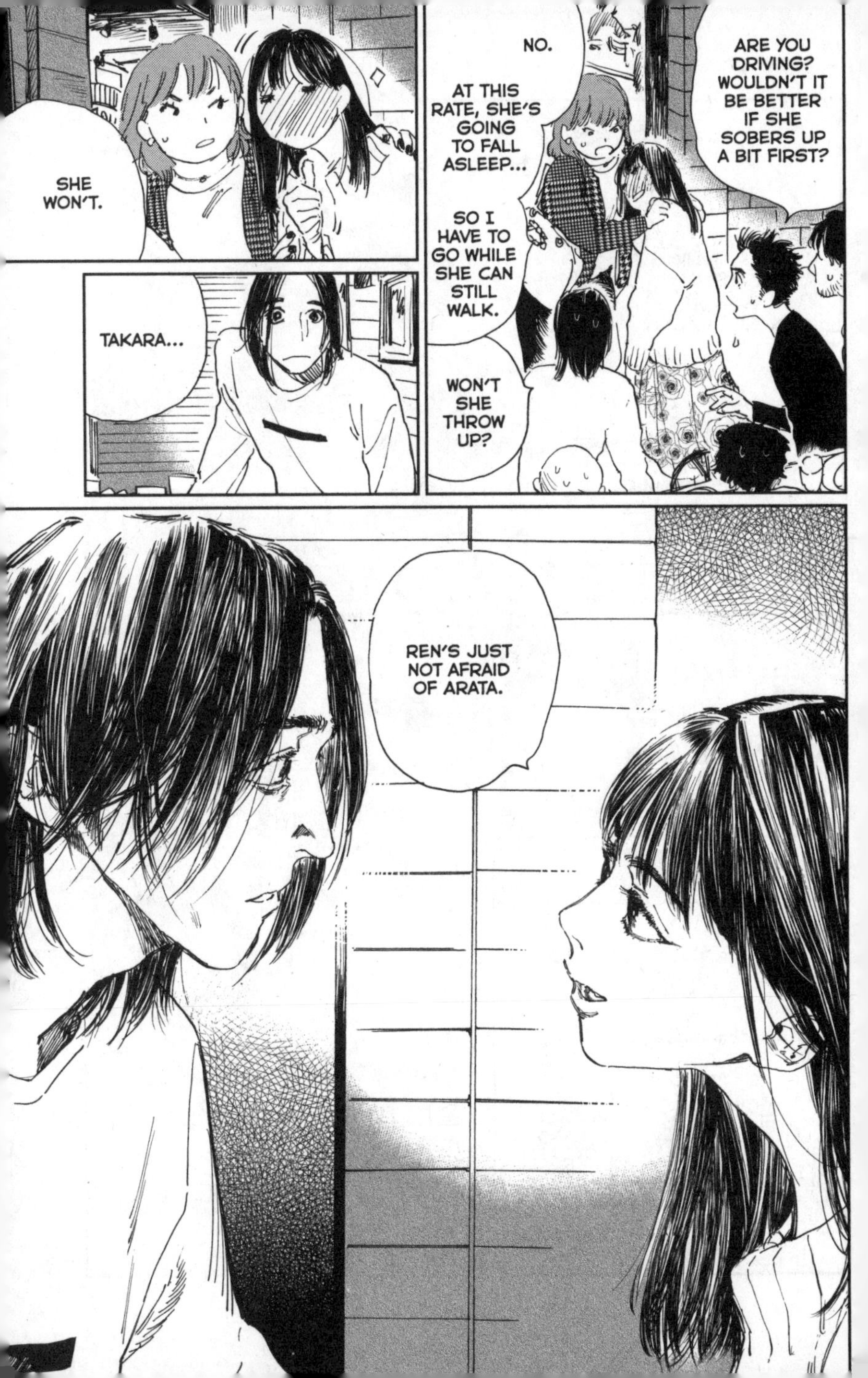
ARE YOU DRIVING? WOULDN'T IT BE BETTER IF SHE SOBERS UP A BIT FIRST?
NO.
AT THIS RATE, SHE'S GOING TO FALL ASLEEP...
SO I HAVE TO GO WHILE SHE CAN STILL WALK.
WON'T SHE THROW UP?
SHE WON'T.
TAKARA...
REN'S JUST NOT AFRAID OF ARATA.

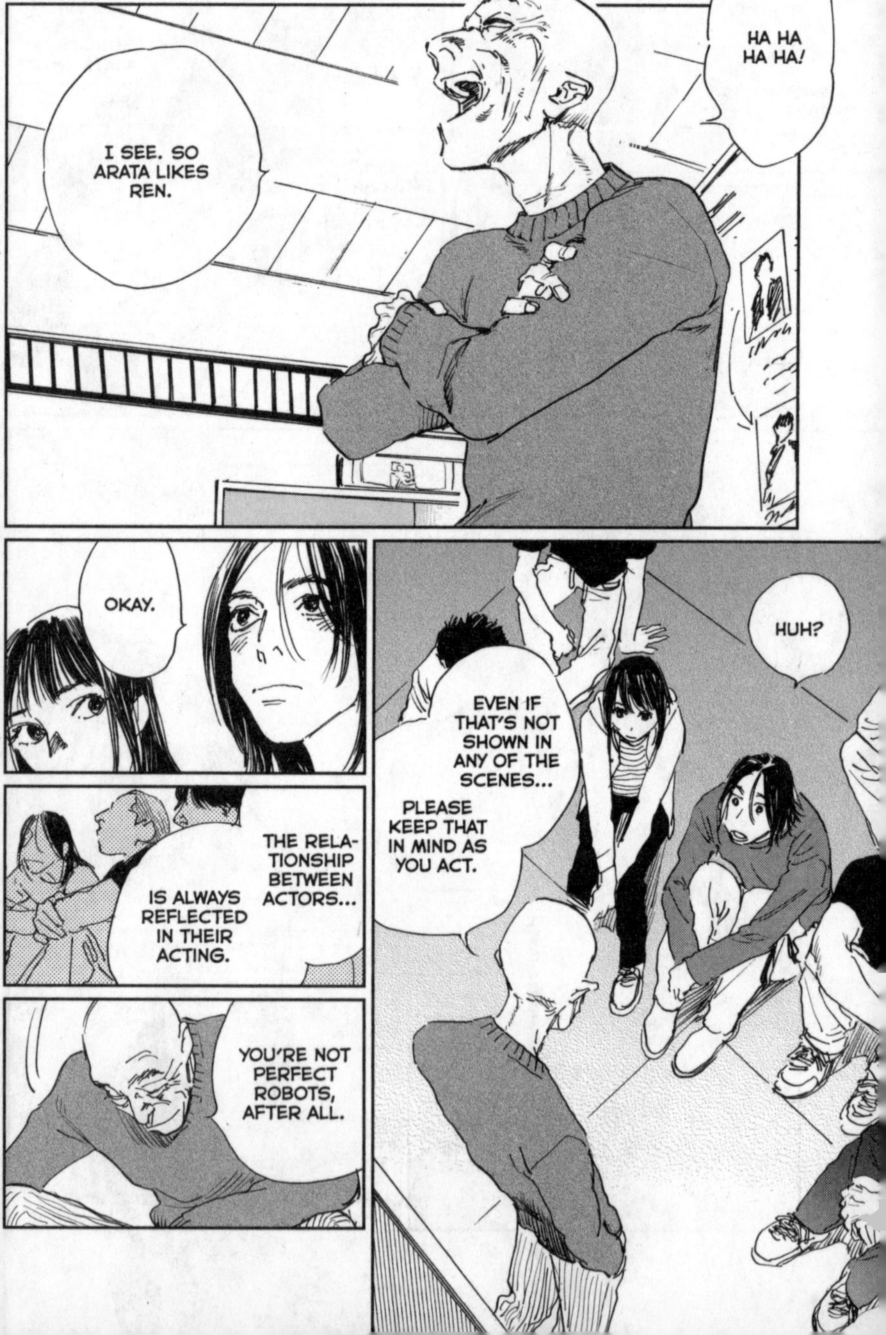
HA HA HA HA!
I SEE. SO ARATA LIKES REN.
HUH?
EVEN IF THAT'S NOT SHOWN IN ANY OF THE SCENES...
PLEASE KEEP THAT IN MIND AS YOU ACT.
OKAY.
THE RELATIONSHIP BETWEEN ACTORS...
IS ALWAYS REFLECTED IN THEIR ACTING.
YOU'RE NOT PERFECT ROBOTS, AFTER ALL.

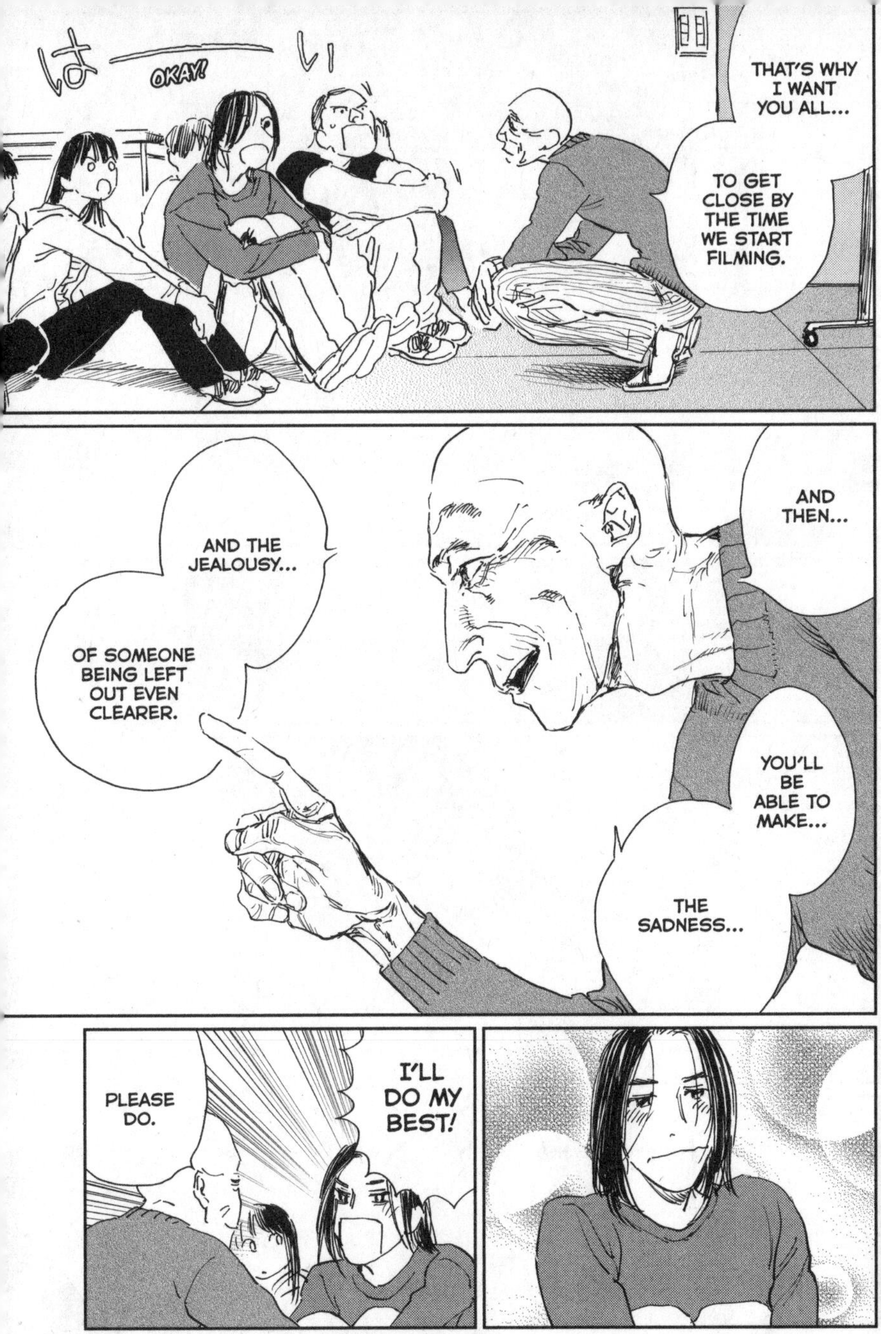
THAT'S WHY I WANT YOU ALL...
TO GET CLOSE BY THE TIME WE START FILMING.
はーーーい
OKAY!
AND THEN...
YOU'LL BE ABLE TO MAKE...
THE SADNESS...
AND THE JEALOUSY...
OF SOMEONE BEING LEFT OUT EVEN CLEARER.
I'LL DO MY BEST!
PLEASE DO.

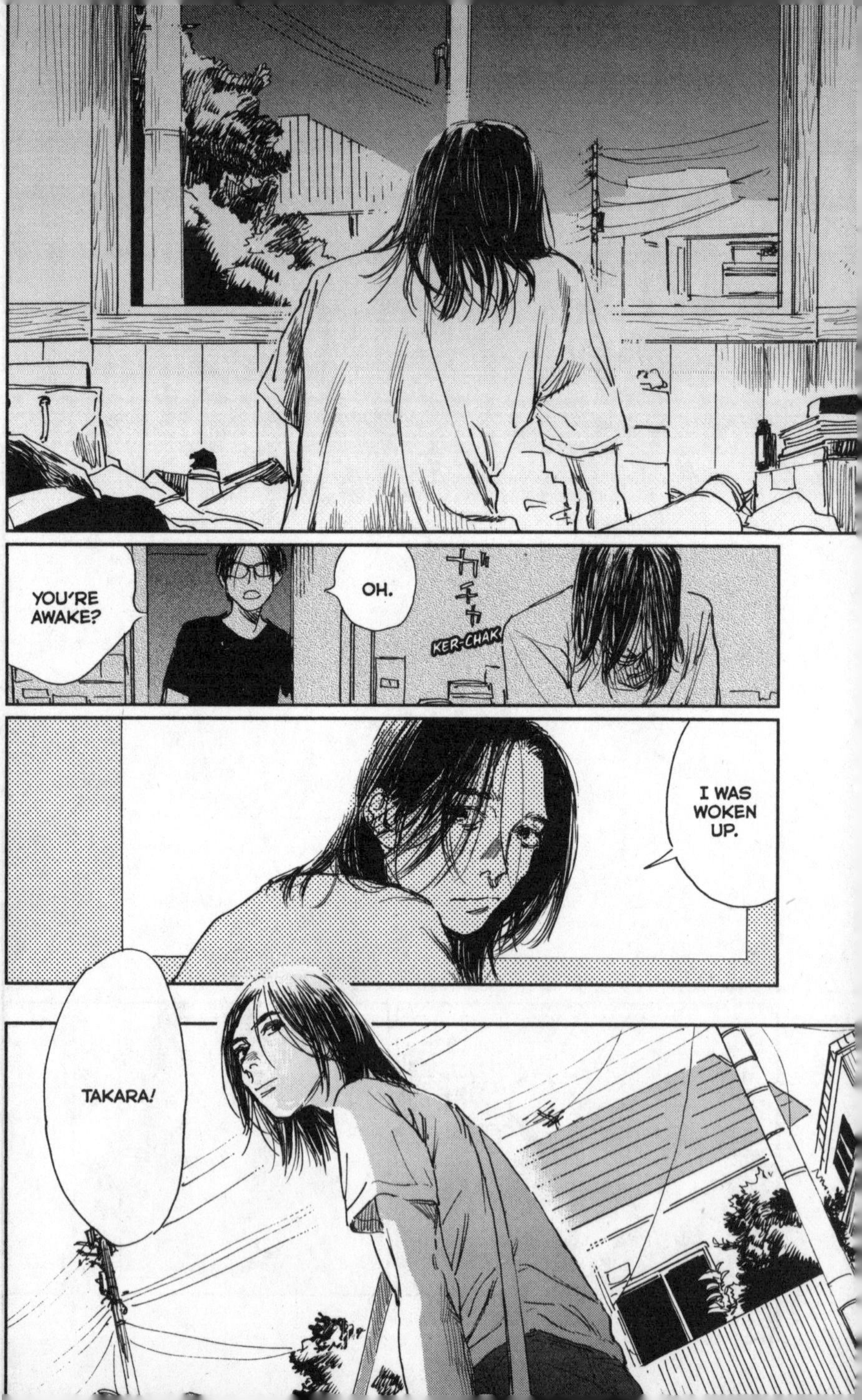
ガチャ
KER-CHAK
OH.
YOU'RE AWAKE?
I WAS WOKEN UP.
TAKARA!

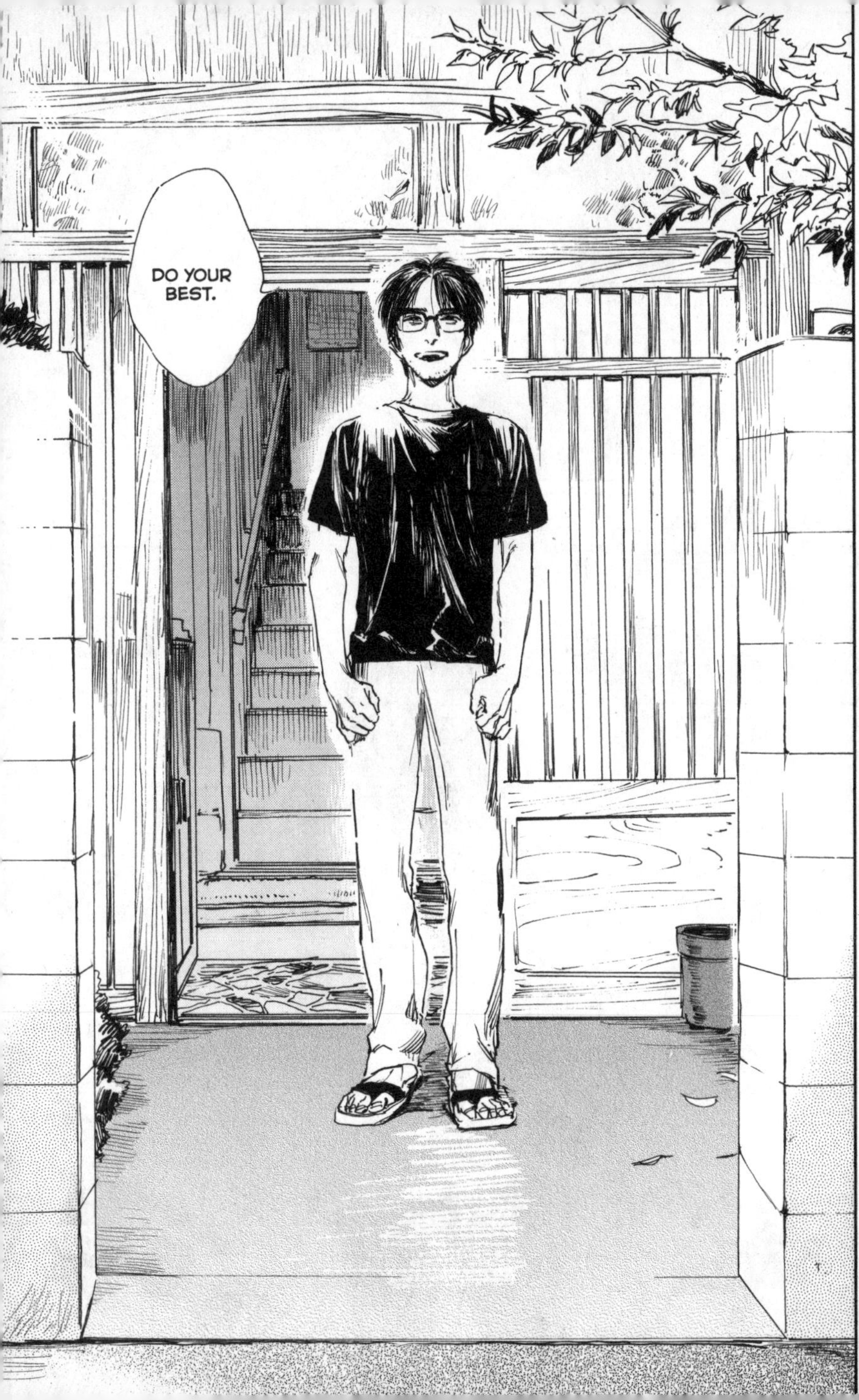
DO YOUR BEST.

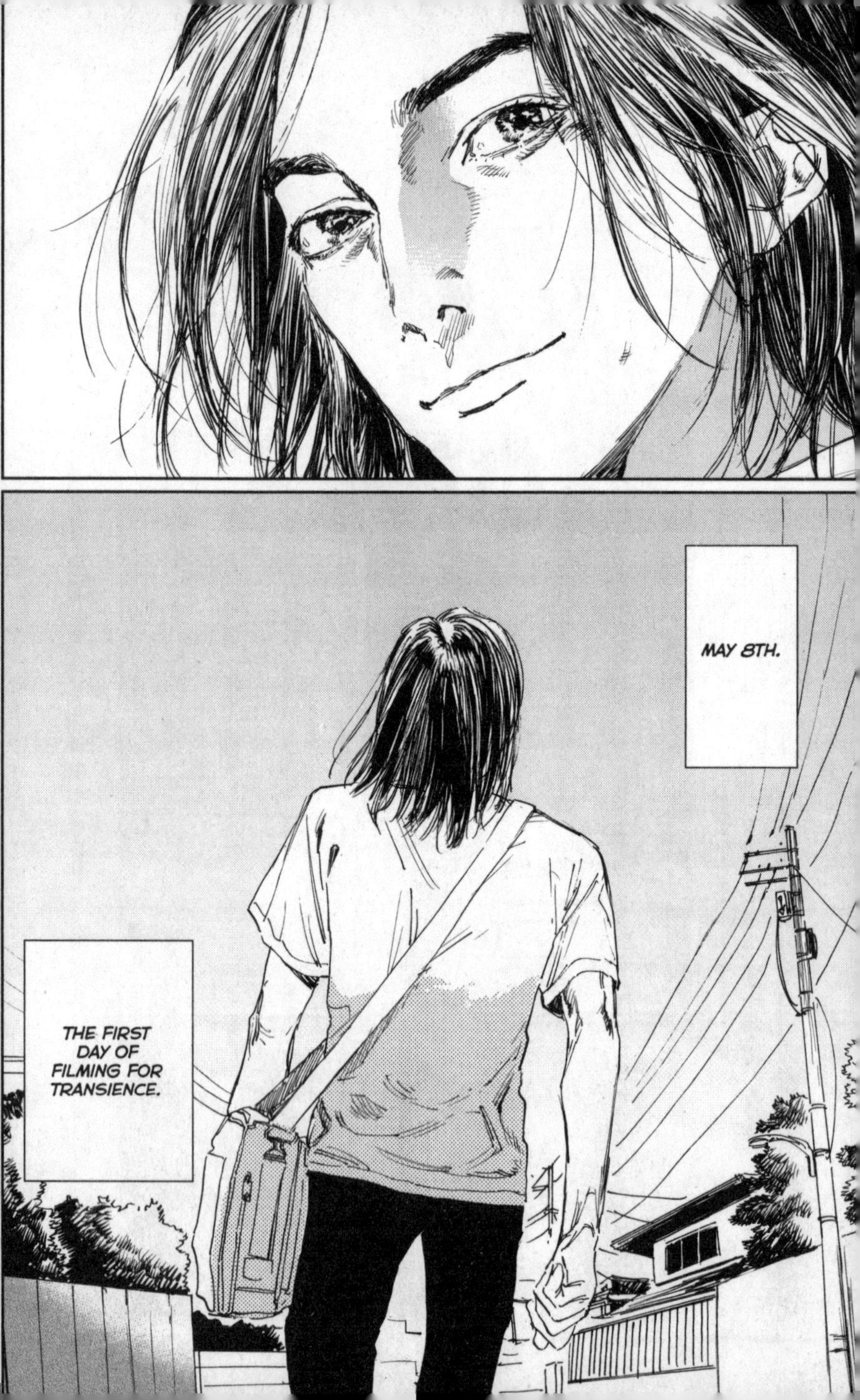
MAY 8TH.
THE FIRST DAY OF FILMING FOR TRANSIENCE.

DOUBLE

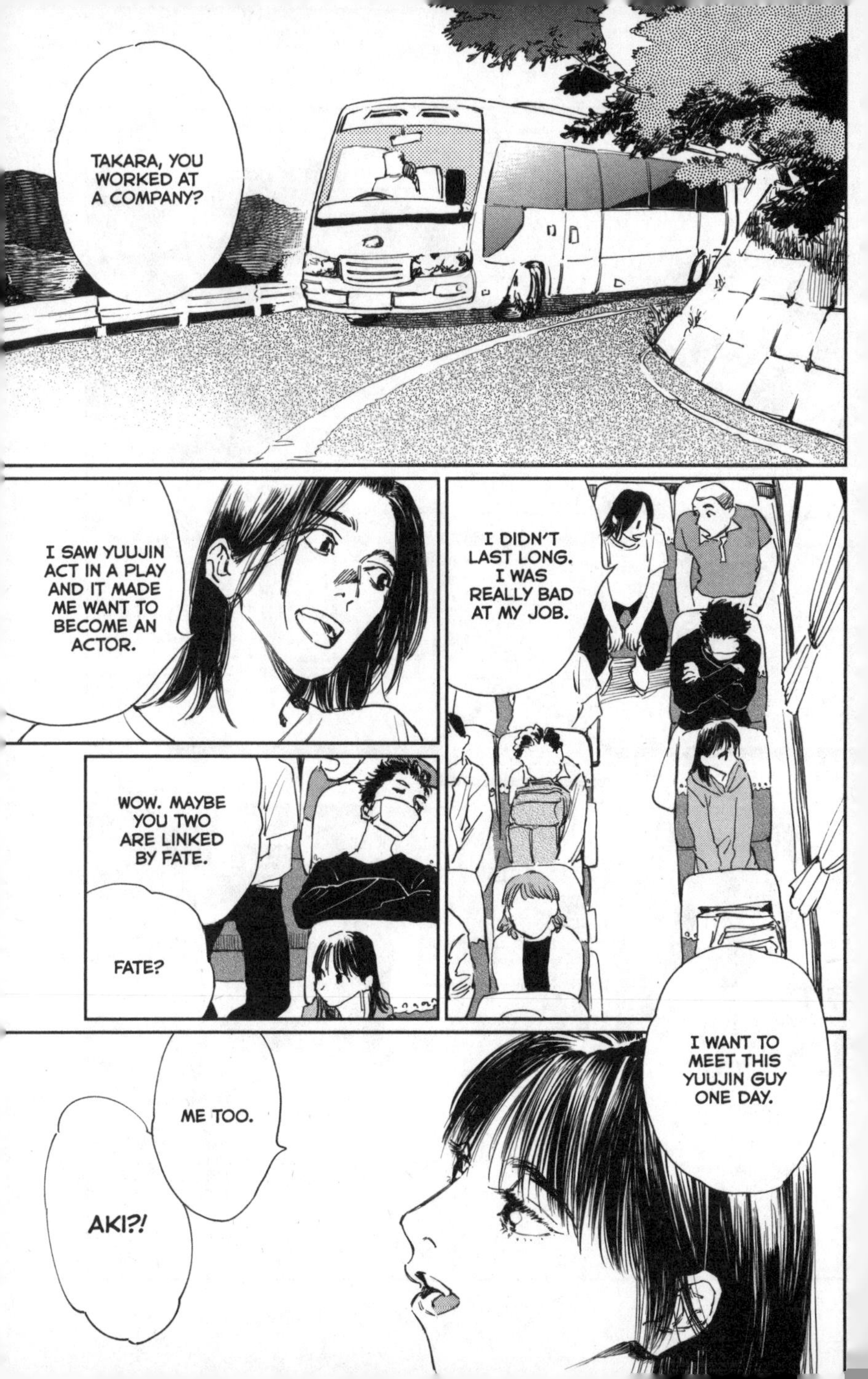
TAKARA, YOU WORKED AT A COMPANY?
I DIDN'T LAST LONG. I WAS REALLY BAD AT MY JOB.
I SAW YUUJIN ACT IN A PLAY AND IT MADE ME WANT TO BECOME AN ACTOR.
WOW. MAYBE YOU TWO ARE LINKED BY FATE.
FATE?
I WANT TO MEET THIS YUUJIN GUY ONE DAY.
ME TOO.
AKI?!

CHAPTER 11 SLEEPING WHILE ANGRY

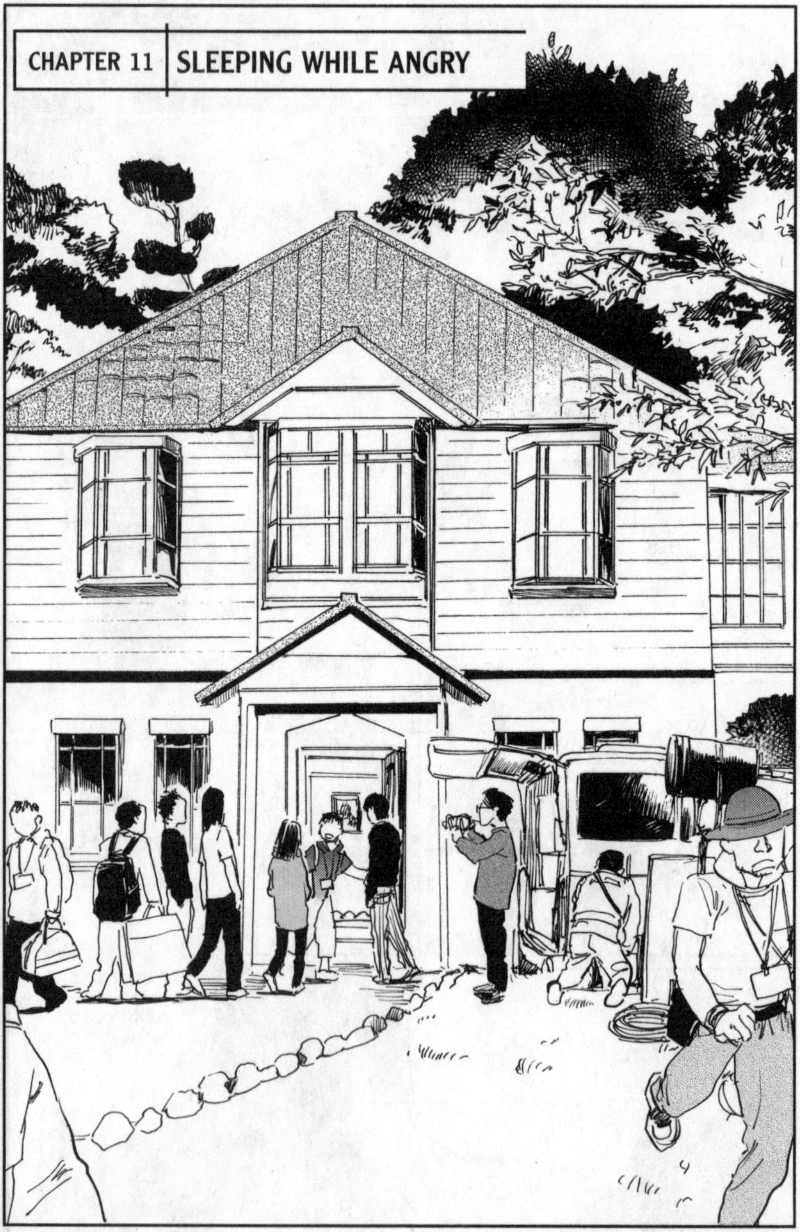

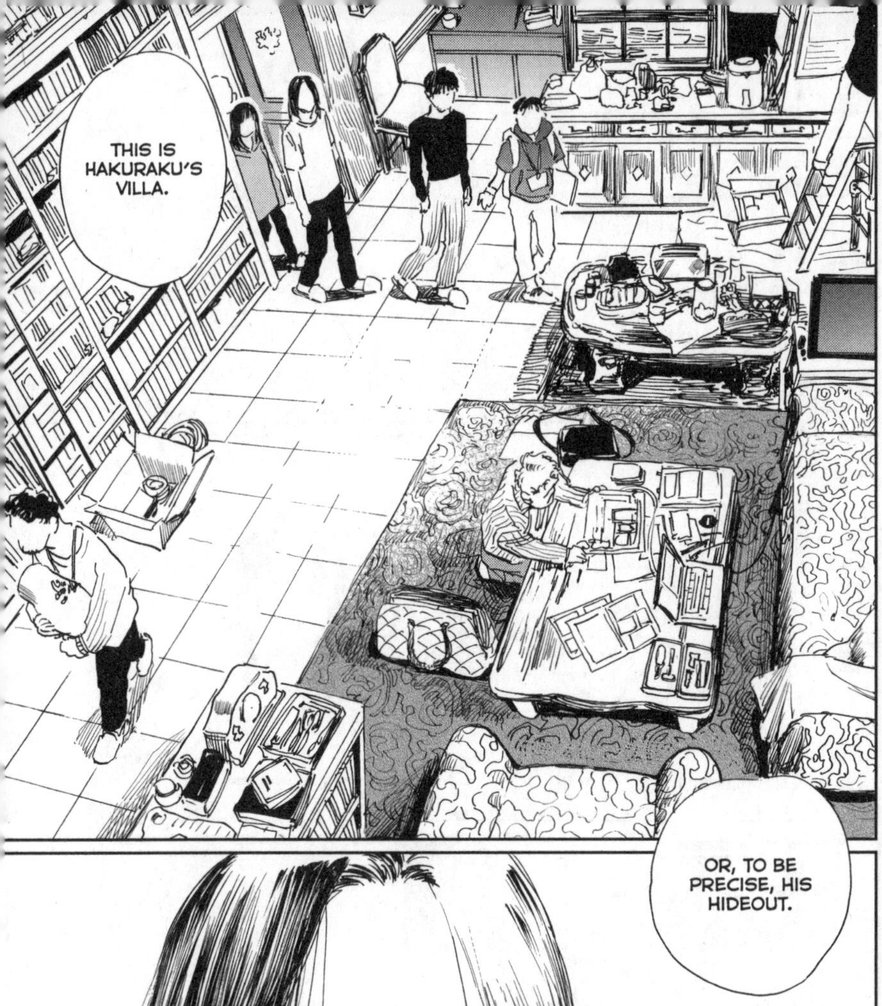
THIS IS HAKURAKU'S VILLA.
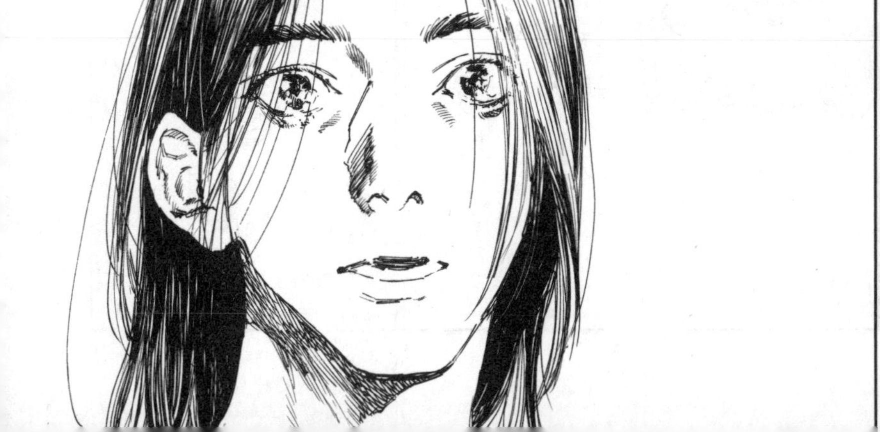
OR, TO BE PRECISE, HIS HIDEOUT.

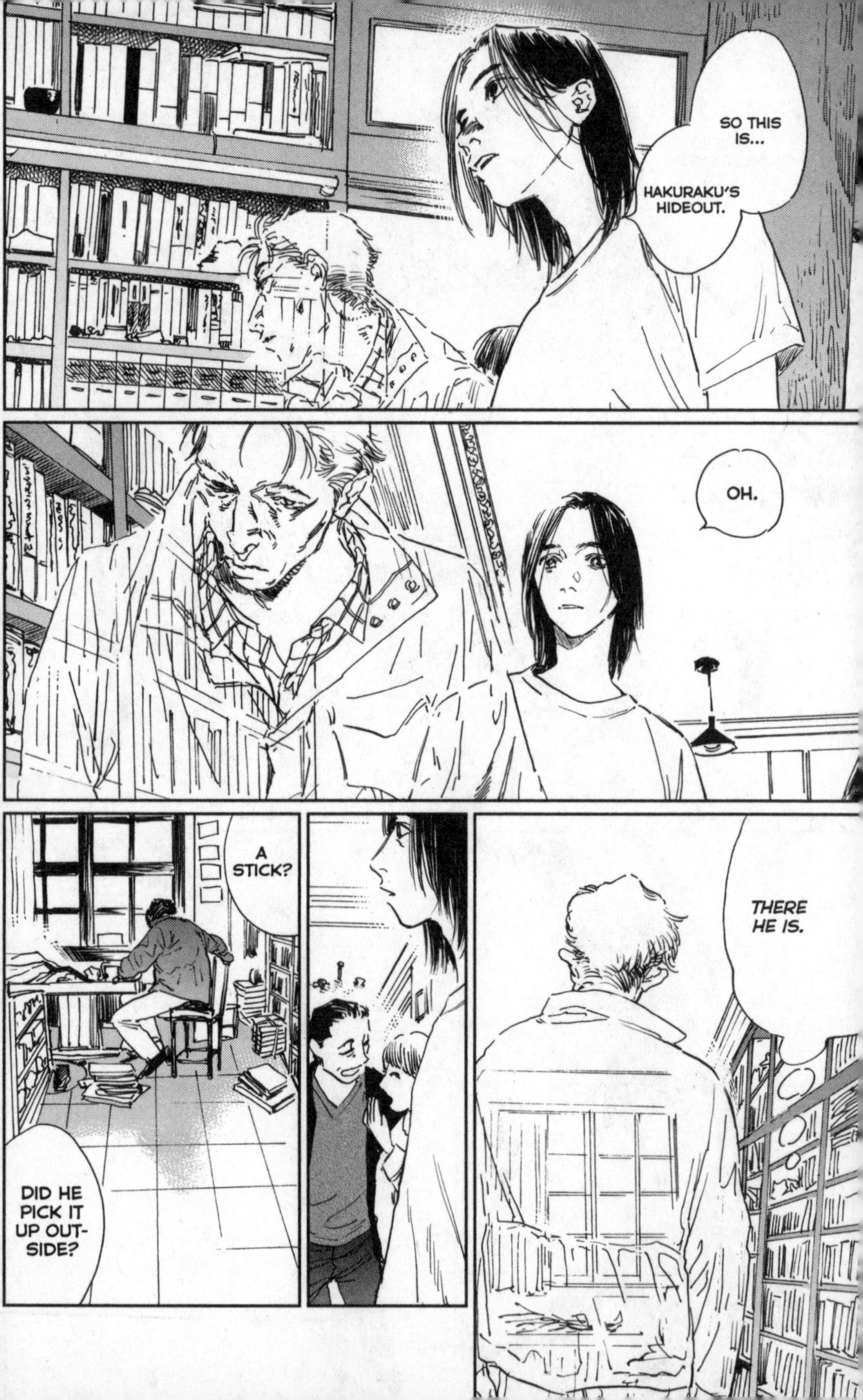
SO THIS IS... HAKURAKU'S HIDEOUT.
OH.
THERE HE IS.
A STICK?
DID HE PICK IT UP OUT-SIDE?

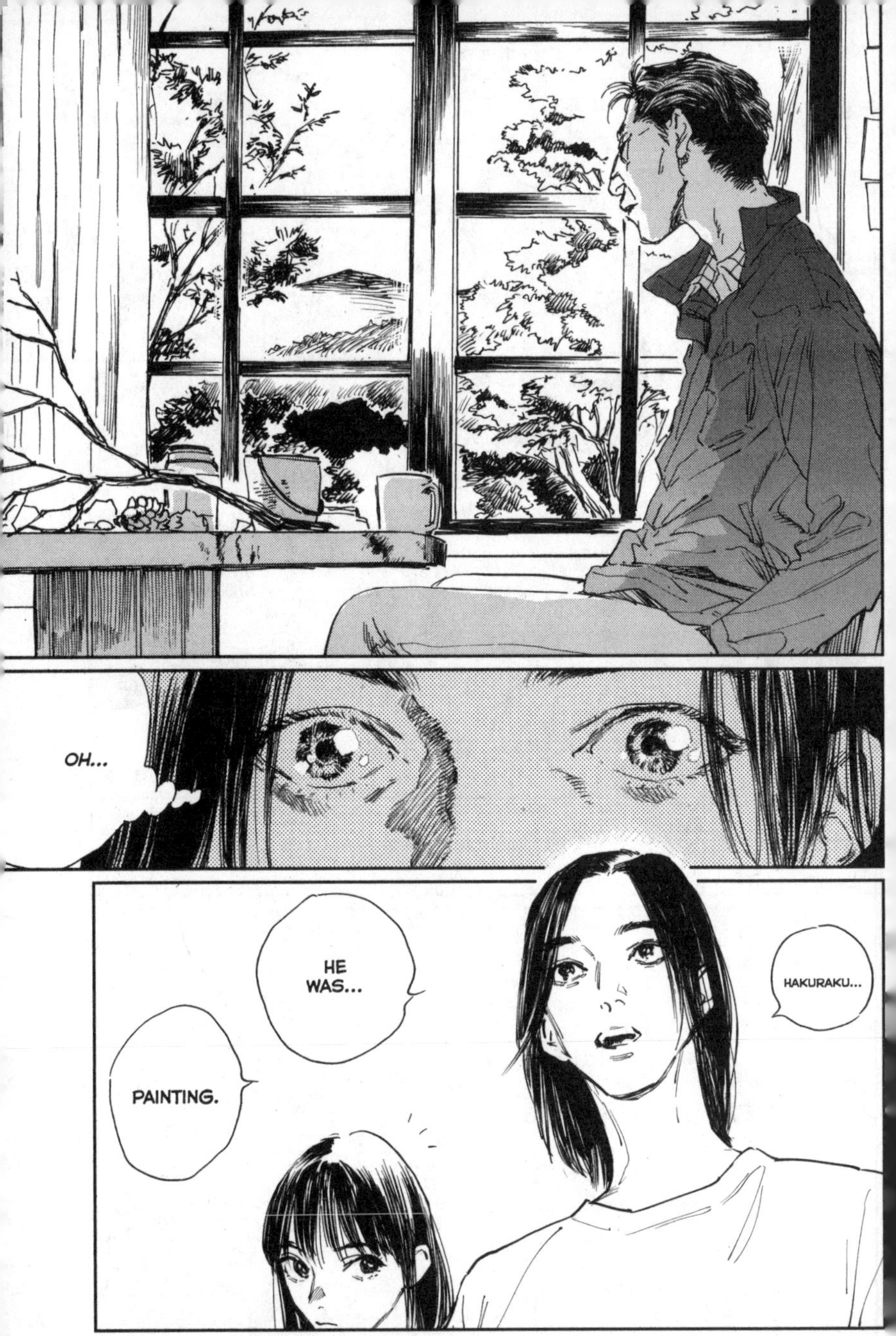
OH...
HAKURAKU...
HE WAS...
PAINTING.

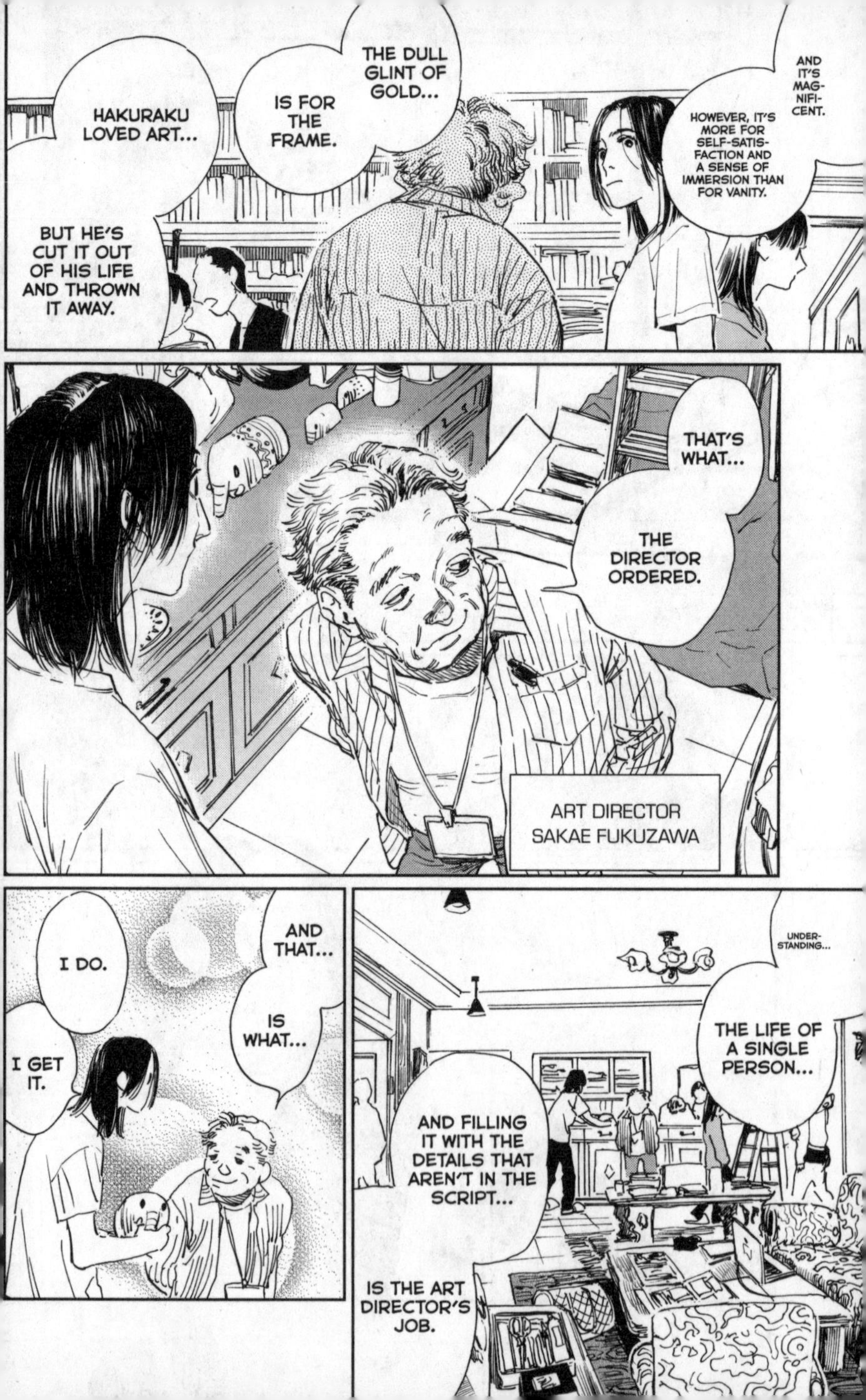
AND IT'S MAGNIFICENT.
HOWEVER, IT'S MORE FOR SELF-SATISFACTION AND A SENSE OF IMMERSION THAN FOR VANITY.
THE DULL GLINT OF GOLD...
IS FOR THE FRAME.
HAKURAKU LOVED ART...
BUT HE'S CUT IT OUT OF HIS LIFE AND THROWN IT AWAY.
THAT'S WHAT...
THE DIRECTOR ORDERED.
ART DIRECTOR SAKAE FUKUZAWA
UNDERSTANDING...
THE LIFE OF A SINGLE PERSON...
AND FILLING IT WITH THE DETAILS THAT AREN'T IN THE SCRIPT...
IS THE ART DIRECTOR'S JOB.
AND THAT...
IS WHAT...
I DO.
I GET IT.

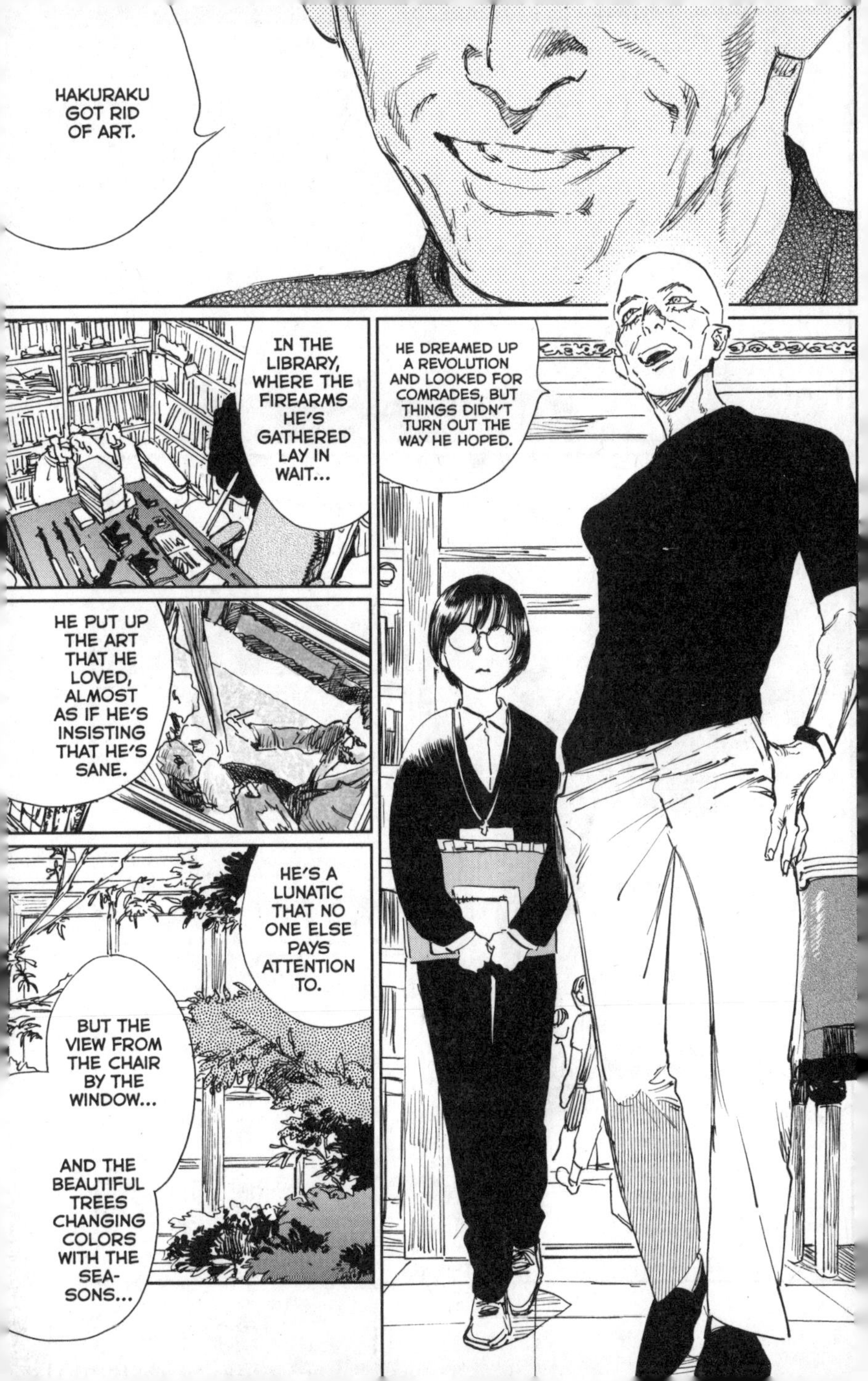
HAKURAKU GOT RID OF ART.
HE DREAMED UP A REVOLUTION AND LOOKED FOR COMRADES, BUT THINGS DIDN'T TURN OUT THE WAY HE HOPED.
IN THE LIBRARY, WHERE THE FIREARMS HE'S GATHERED LAY IN WAIT...
HE PUT UP THE ART THAT HE LOVED, ALMOST AS IF HE'S INSISTING THAT HE'S SANE.
HE'S A LUNATIC THAT NO ONE ELSE PAYS ATTENTION TO.
BUT THE VIEW FROM THE CHAIR BY THE WINDOW...
AND THE BEAUTIFUL TREES CHANGING COLORS WITH THE SEA-SONS...

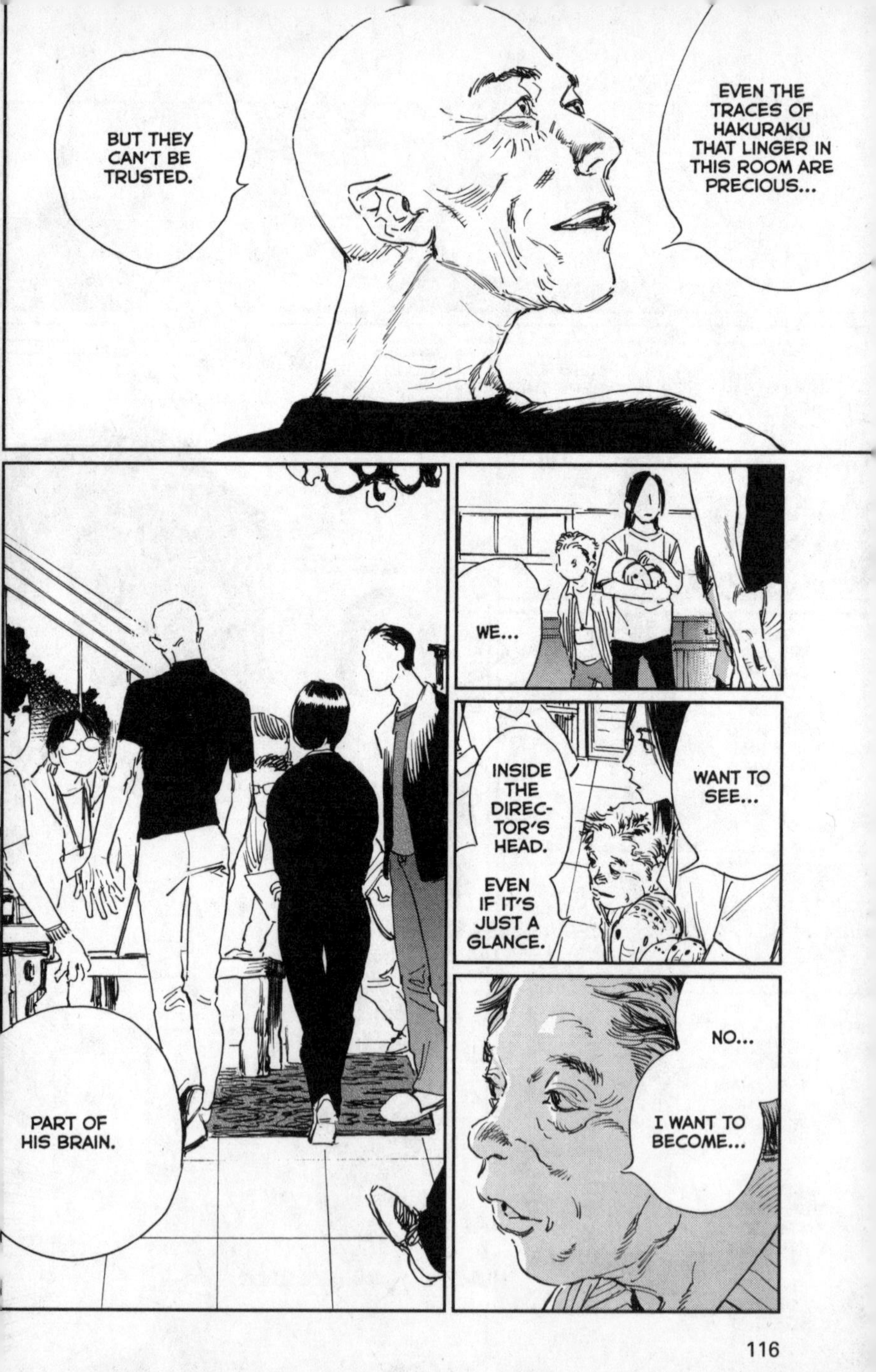
EVEN THE TRACES OF HAKURAKU THAT LINGER IN THIS ROOM ARE PRECIOUS...
BUT THEY CAN'T BE TRUSTED.
WE...
WANT TO SEE...
INSIDE THE DIREC-TOR'S HEAD.
EVEN IF IT'S JUST A GLANCE.
NO...
I WANT TO BECOME...
PART OF HIS BRAIN.

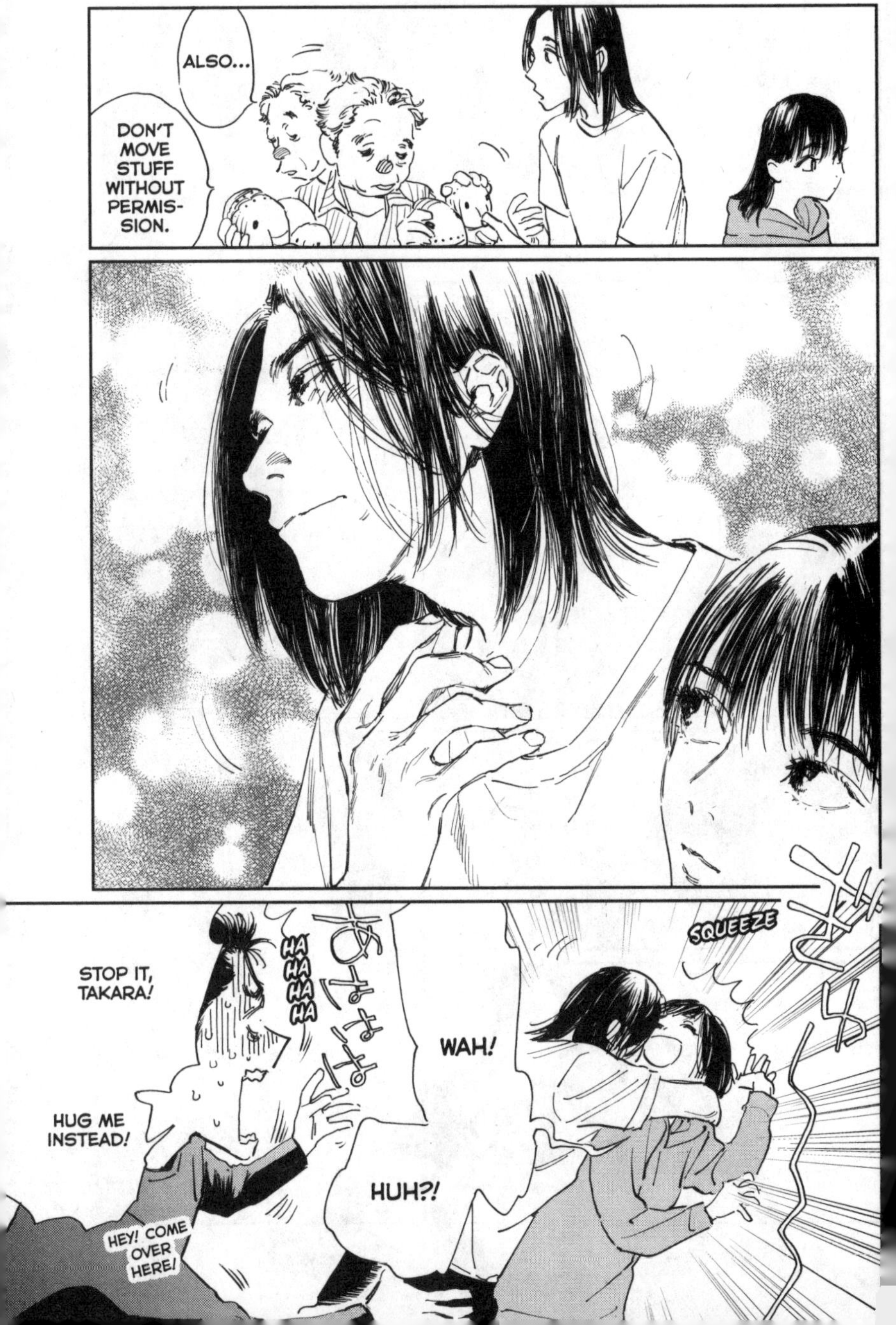
ALSO...
DON'T MOVE STUFF WITHOUT PERMIS-SION.
SQUEEZE
WAH!
HUH?!
HA HA HA HA
STOP IT, TAKARA!
HUG ME INSTEAD!
HEY! COME OVER HERE!

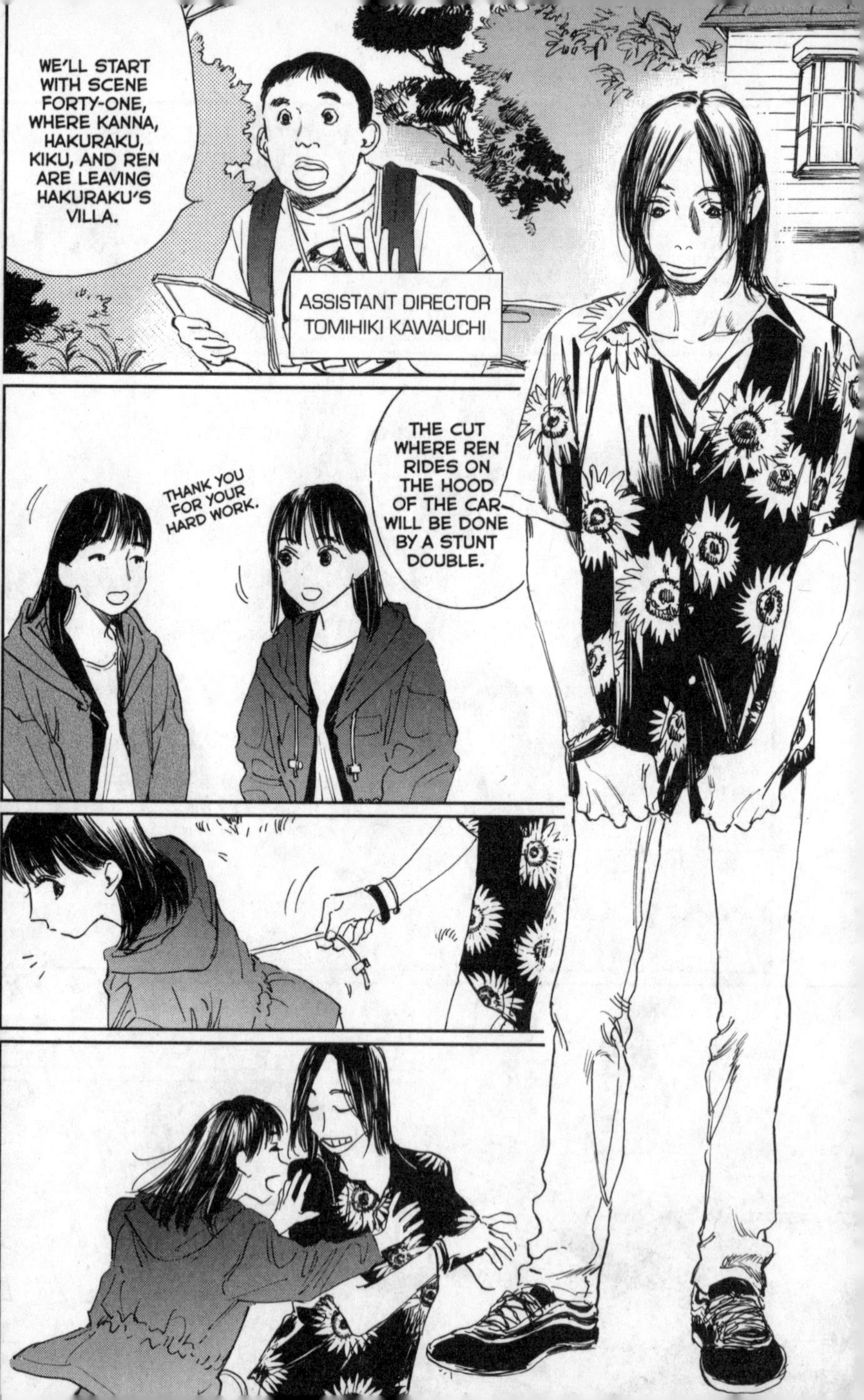
WE'LL START WITH SCENE FORTY-ONE, WHERE KANNA, HAKURAKU, KIKU, AND REN ARE LEAVING HAKURAKU'S VILLA.
ASSISTANT DIRECTOR TOMIHIKI KAWAUCHI
THE CUT WHERE REN RIDES ON THE HOOD OF THE CAR WILL BE DONE BY A STUNT DOUBLE.
THANK YOU FOR YOUR HARD WORK.

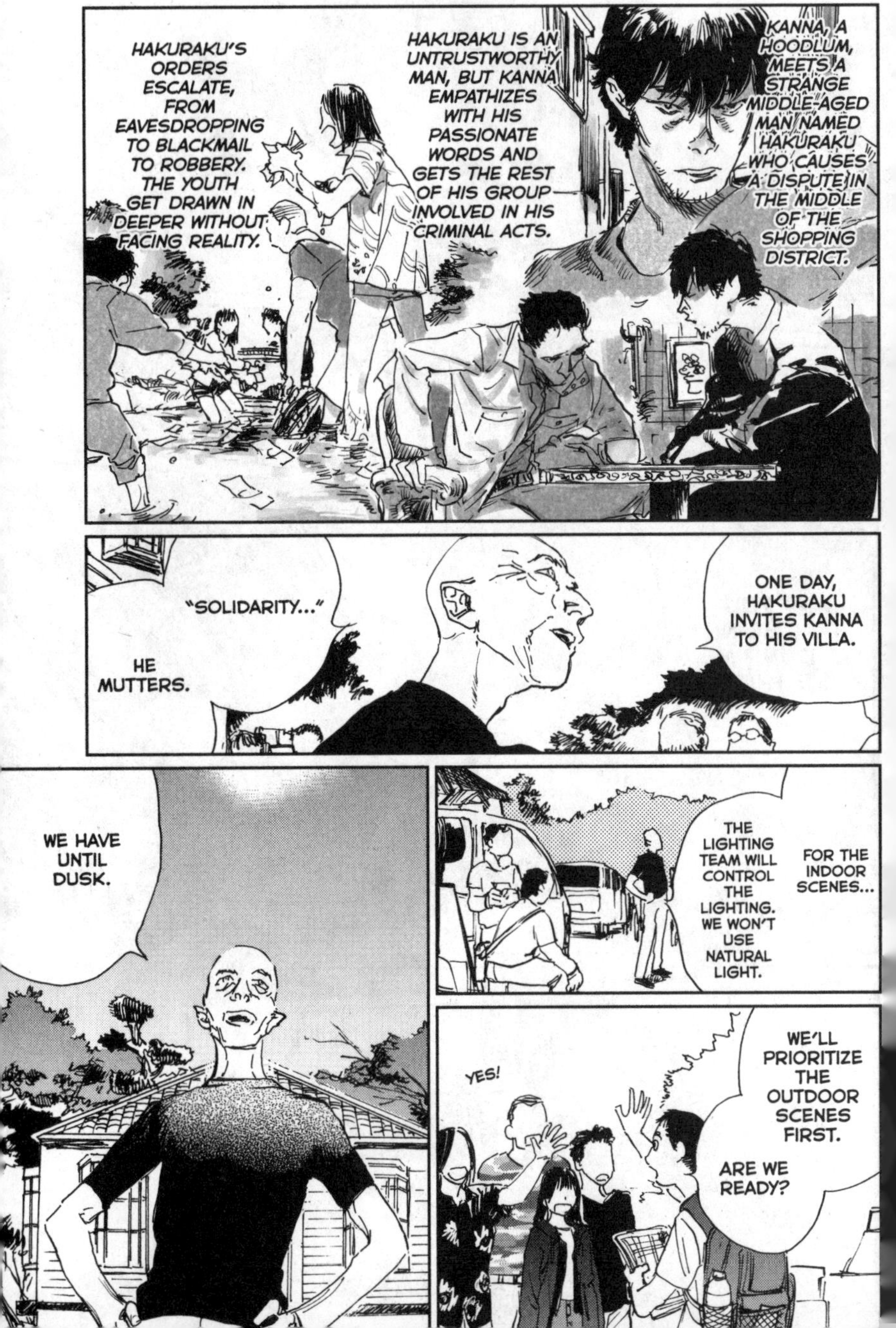
KANNA, A HOODLUM, MEETS A STRANGE MIDDLE-AGED MAN NAMED HAKURAKU WHO CAUSES A DISPUTE IN THE MIDDLE OF THE SHOPPING DISTRICT.
HAKURAKU IS AN UNTRUSTWORTHY MAN, BUT KANNA EMPATHIZES WITH HIS PASSIONATE WORDS AND GETS THE REST OF HIS GROUP INVOLVED IN HIS CRIMINAL ACTS.
HAKURAKU'S ORDERS ESCALATE, FROM EAVESDROPPING TO BLACKMAIL TO ROBBERY. THE YOUTH GET DRAWN IN DEEPER WITHOUT FACING REALITY.
ONE DAY, HAKURAKU INVITES KANNA TO HIS VILLA.
"SOLIDARITY..."
HE MUTTERS.
FOR THE INDOOR SCENES...
THE LIGHTING TEAM WILL CONTROL THE LIGHTING. WE WON'T USE NATURAL LIGHT.
WE'LL PRIORITIZE THE OUTDOOR SCENES FIRST.
ARE WE READY?
YES!
WE HAVE UNTIL DUSK.

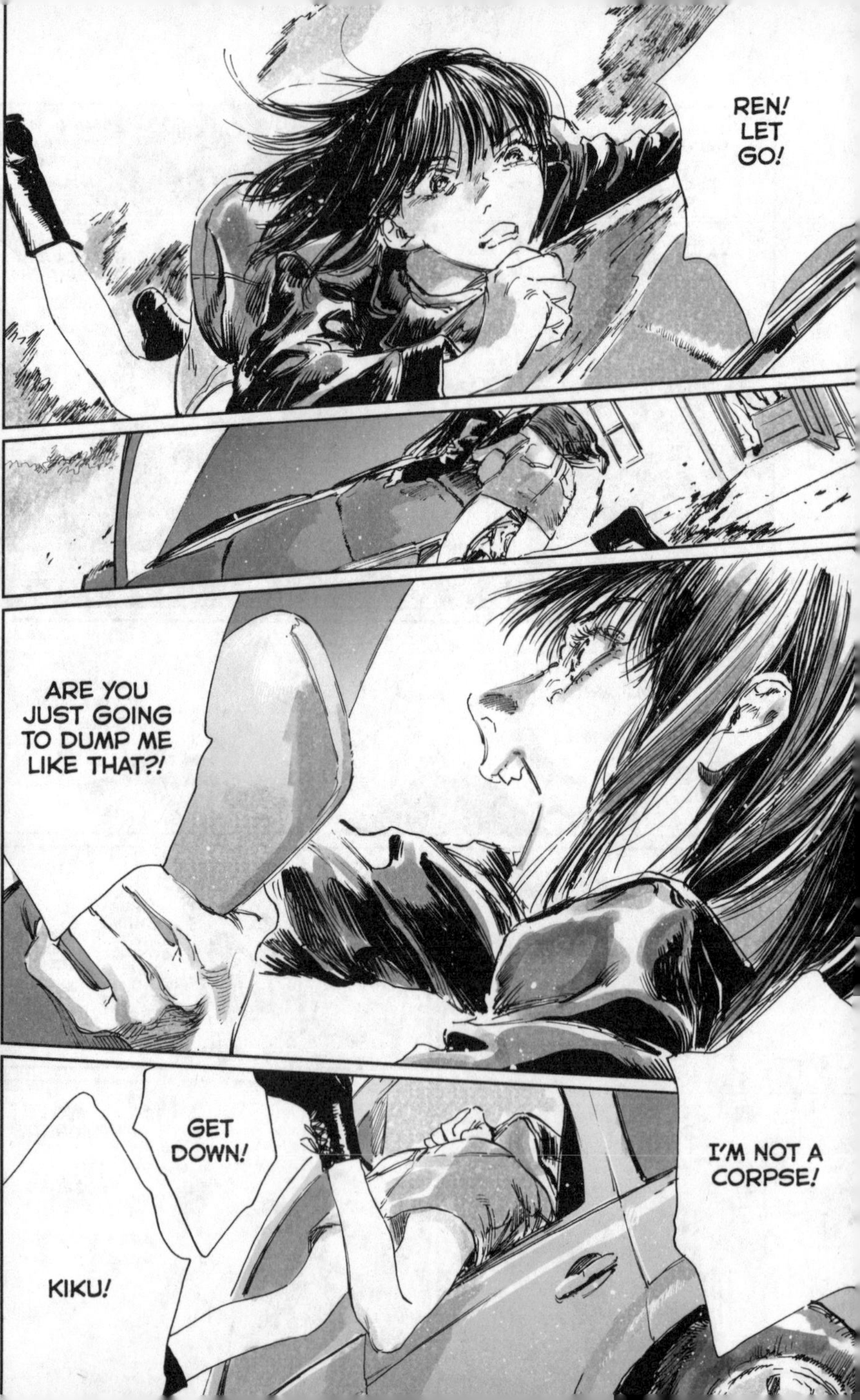
REN! LET GO!
ARE YOU JUST GOING TO DUMP ME LIKE THAT?!
I'M NOT A CORPSE!
GET DOWN!
KIKU!

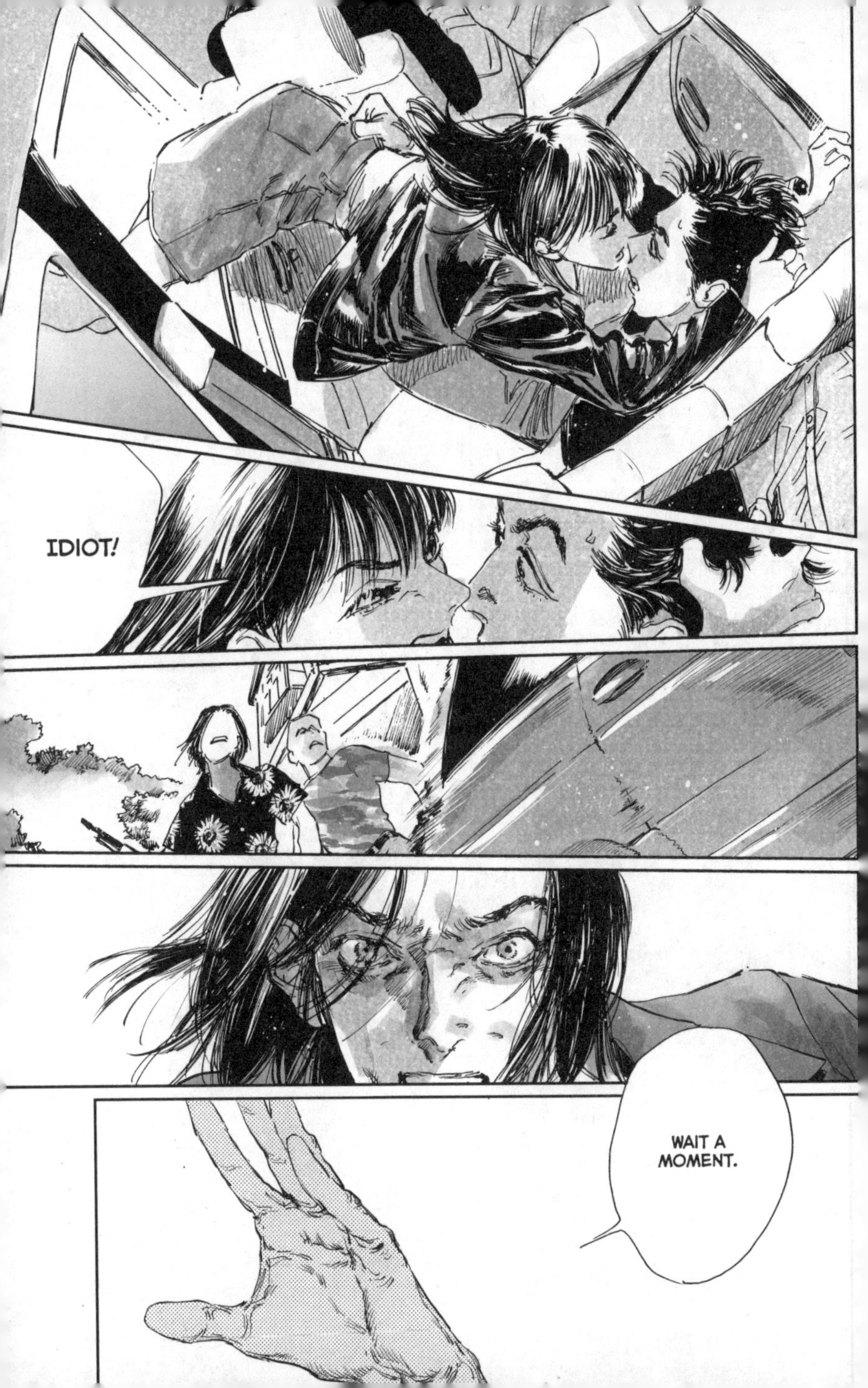
IDIOT!
WAIT A MOMENT.

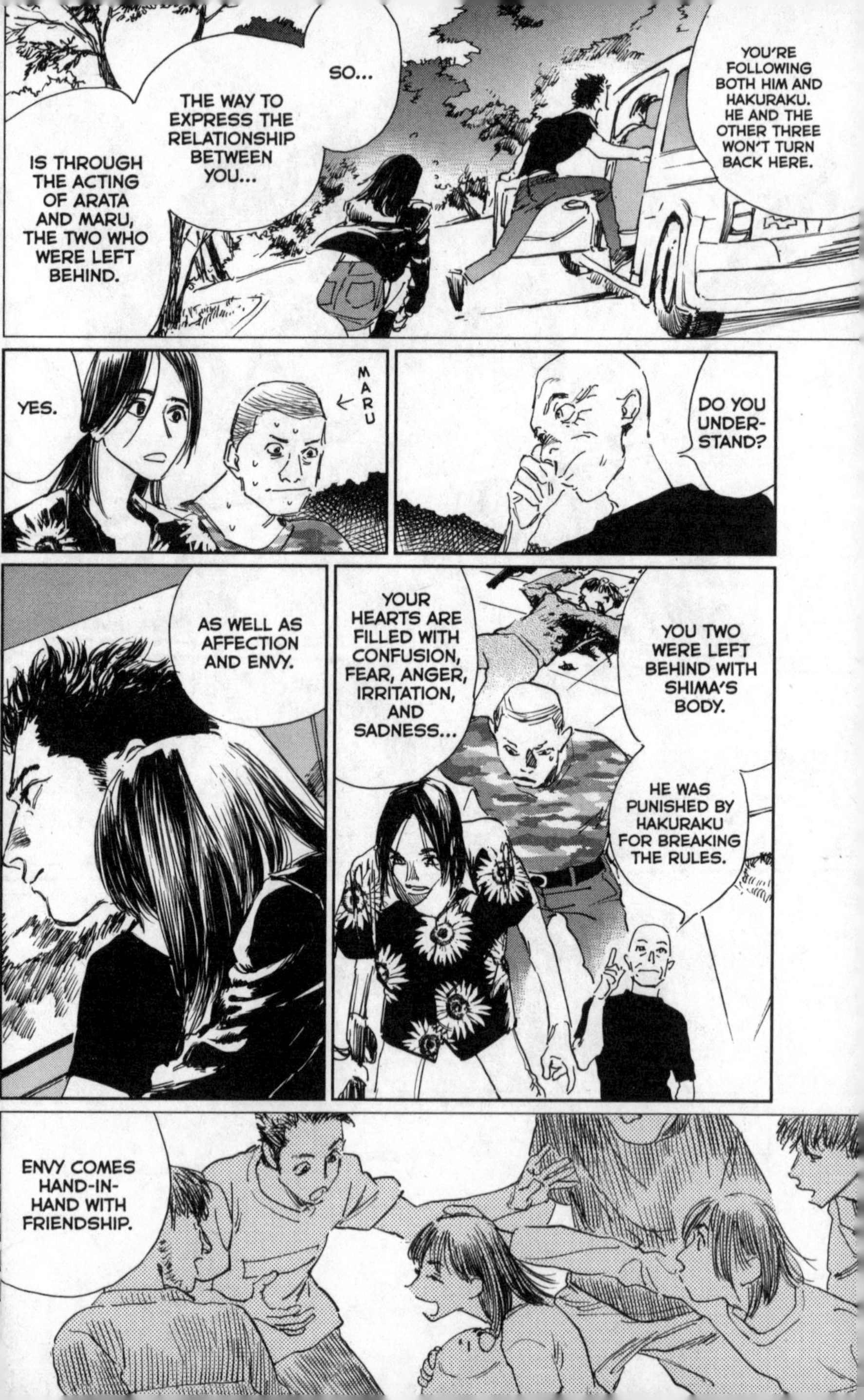
YOU'RE FOLLOWING BOTH HIM AND HAKURAKU. HE AND THE OTHER THREE WON'T TURN BACK HERE.
SO...
THE WAY TO EXPRESS THE RELATIONSHIP BETWEEN YOU...
IS THROUGH THE ACTING OF ARATA AND MARU, THE TWO WHO WERE LEFT BEHIND.
DO YOU UNDERSTAND?
MARU
YES.
YOU TWO WERE LEFT BEHIND WITH SHIMA'S BODY.
HE WAS PUNISHED BY HAKURAKU FOR BREAKING THE RULES.
YOUR HEARTS ARE FILLED WITH CONFUSION, FEAR, ANGER, IRRITATION, AND SADNESS...
AS WELL AS AFFECTION AND ENVY.
ENVY COMES HAND-IN-HAND WITH FRIENDSHIP.

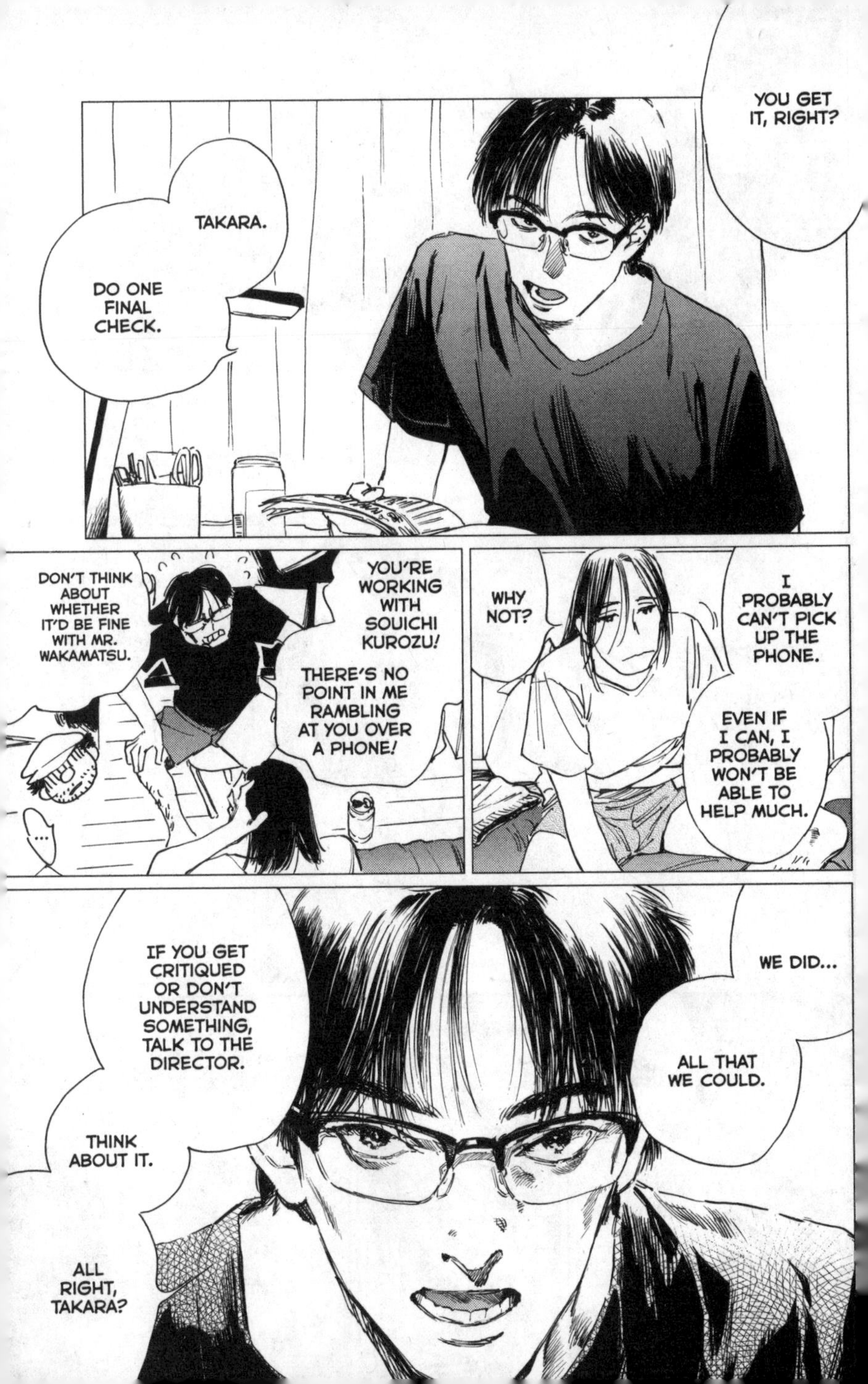
YOU GET IT, RIGHT?
TAKARA.
DO ONE FINAL CHECK.
I PROBABLY CAN'T PICK UP THE PHONE.
WHY NOT?
EVEN IF I CAN, I PROBABLY WON'T BE ABLE TO HELP MUCH.
YOU'RE WORKING WITH SOUICHI KUROZU!
THERE'S NO POINT IN ME RAMBLING AT YOU OVER A PHONE!
DON'T THINK ABOUT WHETHER IT'D BE FINE WITH MR. WAKAMATSU.
...
WE DID...
ALL THAT WE COULD.
IF YOU GET CRITIQUED OR DON'T UNDERSTAND SOMETHING, TALK TO THE DIRECTOR.
THINK ABOUT IT.
ALL RIGHT, TAKARA?

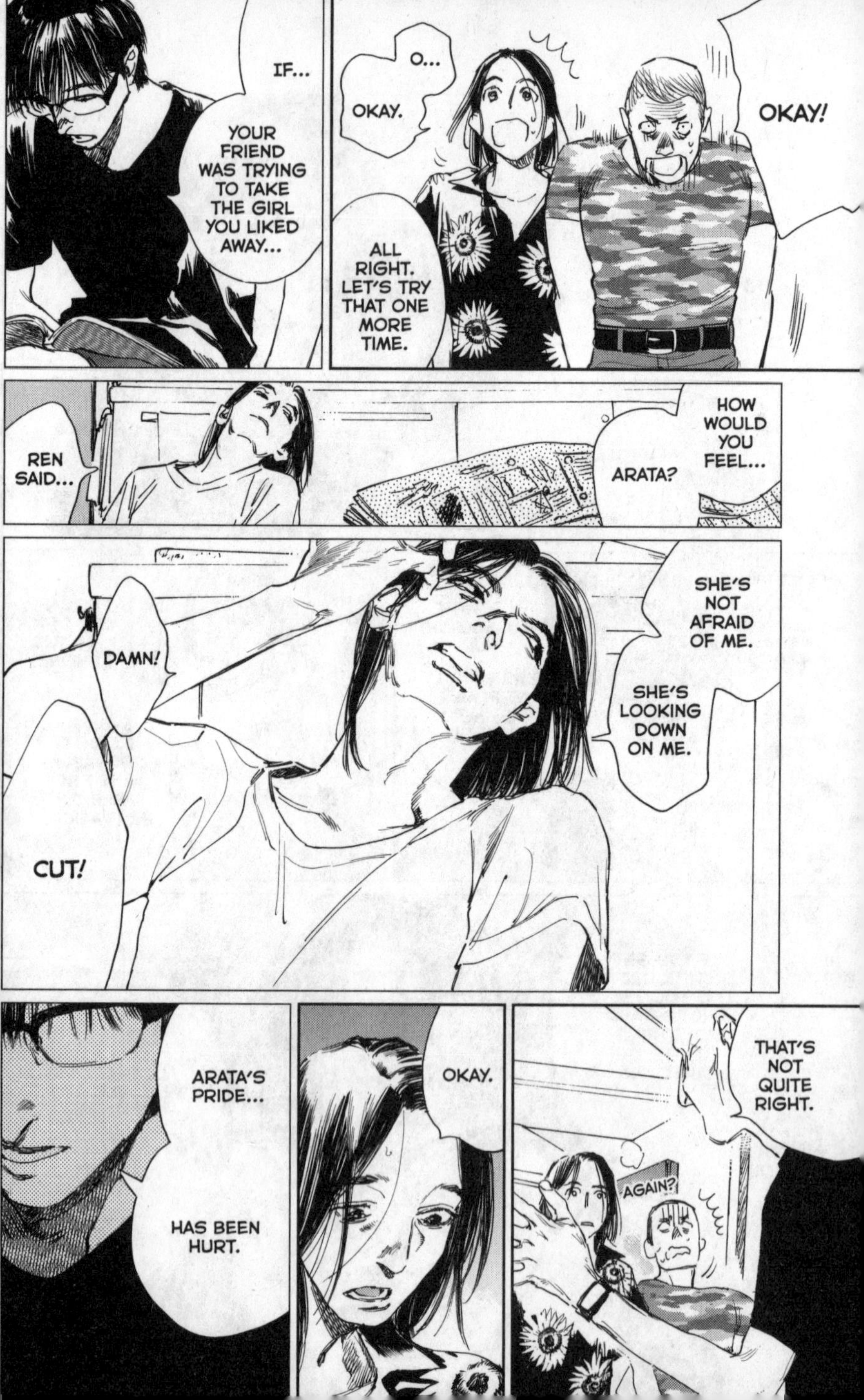
OKAY!
O...
OKAY.
ALL RIGHT. LET'S TRY THAT ONE MORE TIME.
IF...
YOUR FRIEND WAS TRYING TO TAKE THE GIRL YOU LIKED AWAY...
HOW WOULD YOU FEEL...
ARATA?
REN SAID...
SHE'S NOT AFRAID OF ME.
SHE'S LOOKING DOWN ON ME.
DAMN!
CUT!
THAT'S NOT QUITE RIGHT.
AGAIN?
OKAY.
ARATA'S PRIDE...
HAS BEEN HURT.

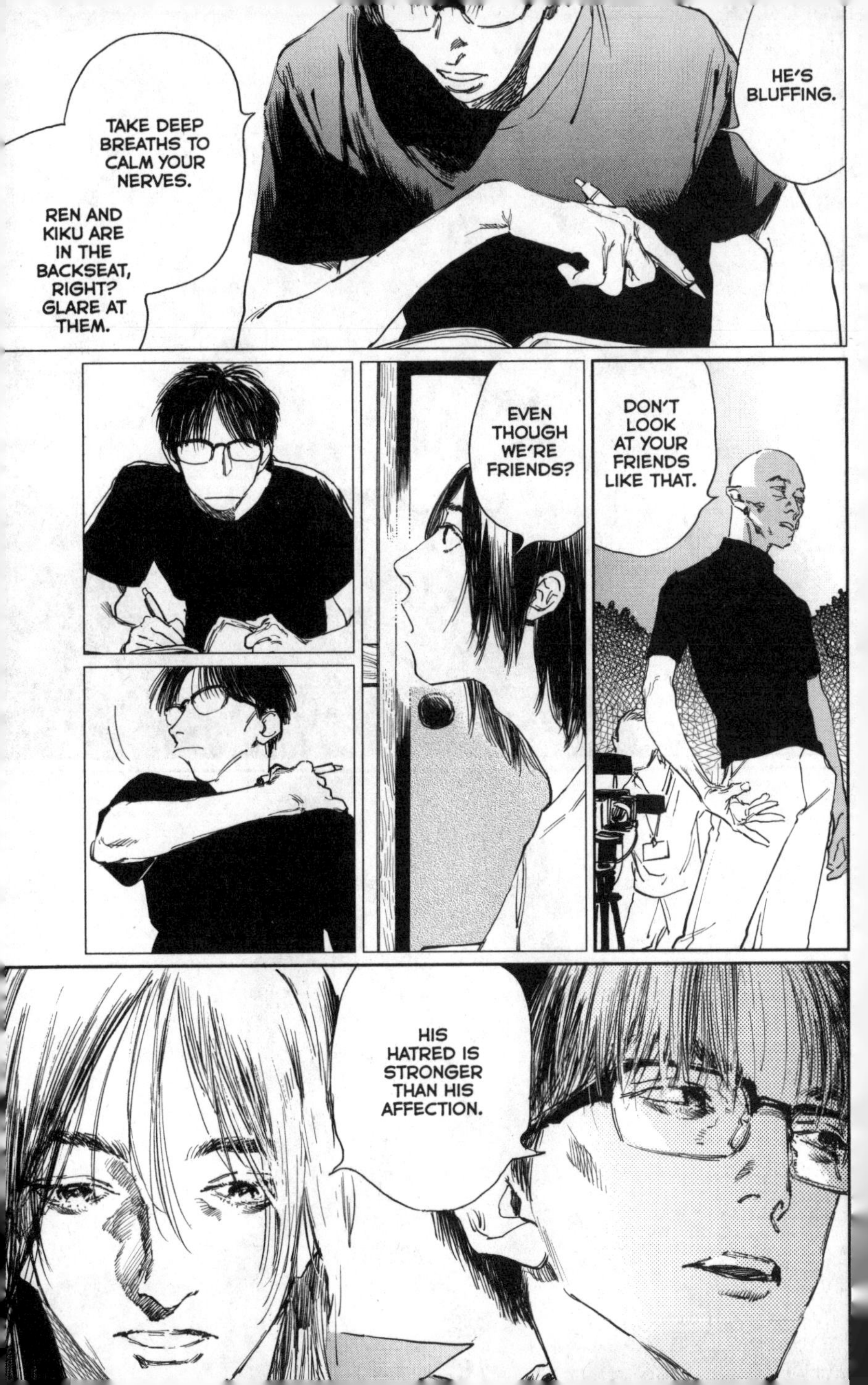
HE'S BLUFFING.
TAKE DEEP BREATHS TO CALM YOUR NERVES.
REN AND KIKU ARE IN THE BACKSEAT, RIGHT? GLARE AT THEM.
DON'T LOOK AT YOUR FRIENDS LIKE THAT.
EVEN THOUGH WE'RE FRIENDS?
HIS HATRED IS STRONGER THAN HIS AFFECTION.

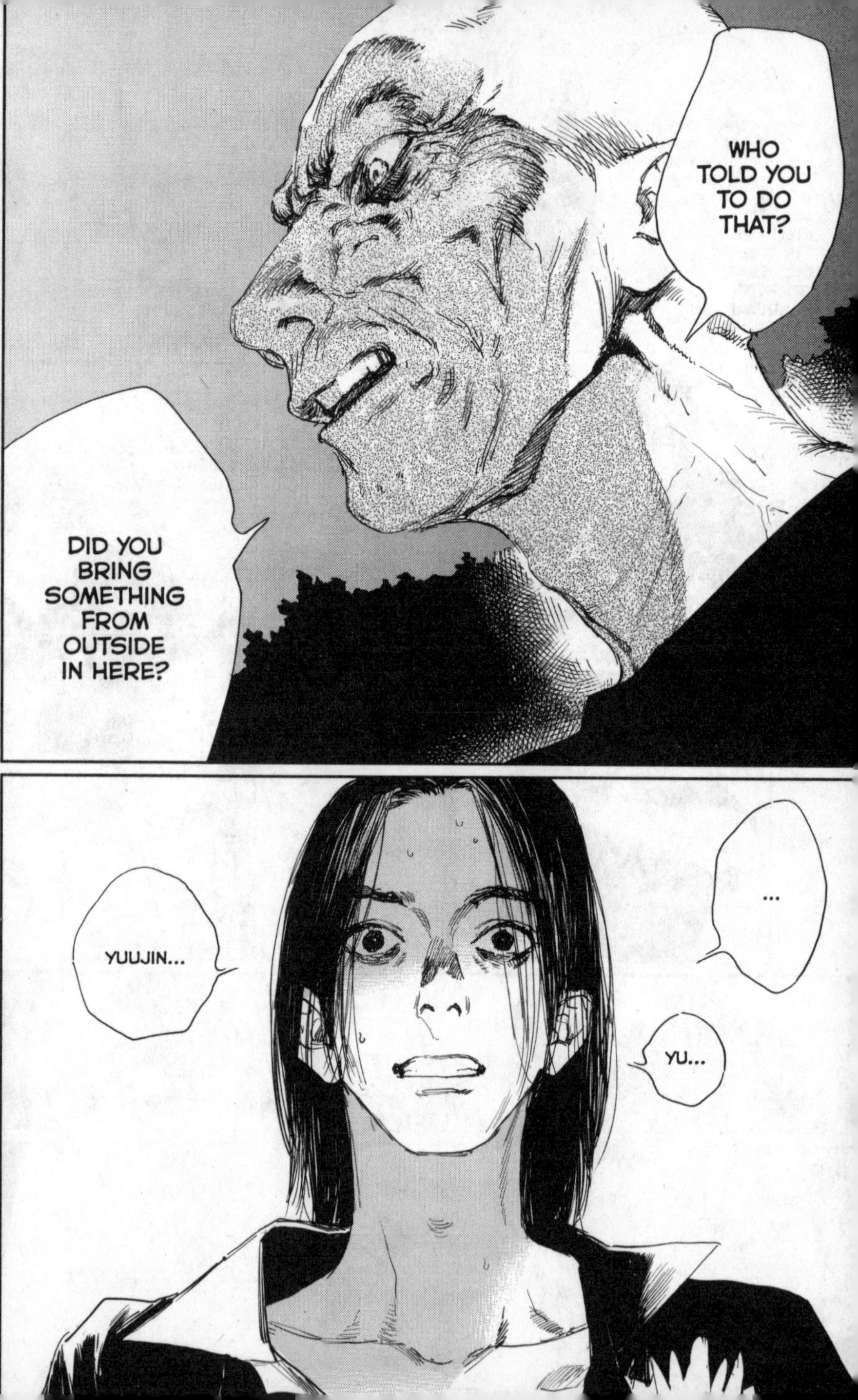
WHO TOLD YOU TO DO THAT?
DID YOU BRING SOMETHING FROM OUTSIDE IN HERE?
...
YU...
YUUJIN...

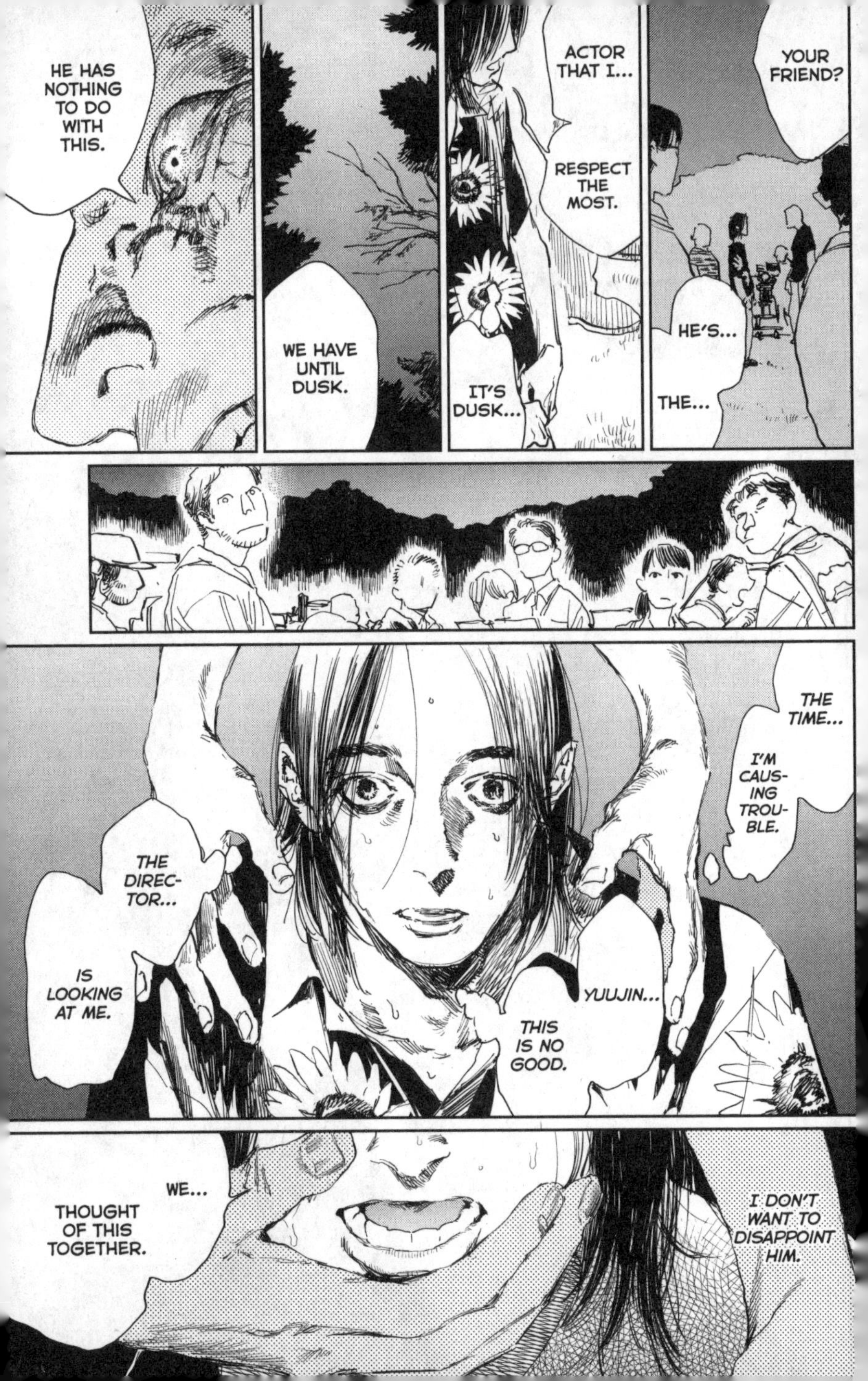
YOUR FRIEND?
HE'S...
THE...
ACTOR THAT I...
RESPECT THE MOST.
IT'S DUSK...
WE HAVE UNTIL DUSK.
HE HAS NOTHING TO DO WITH THIS.
THE TIME...
I'M CAUSING TROUBLE.
YUUJIN...
THIS IS NO GOOD.
THE DIRECTOR...
IS LOOKING AT ME.
I DON'T WANT TO DISAPPOINT HIM.
WE...
THOUGHT OF THIS TOGETHER.

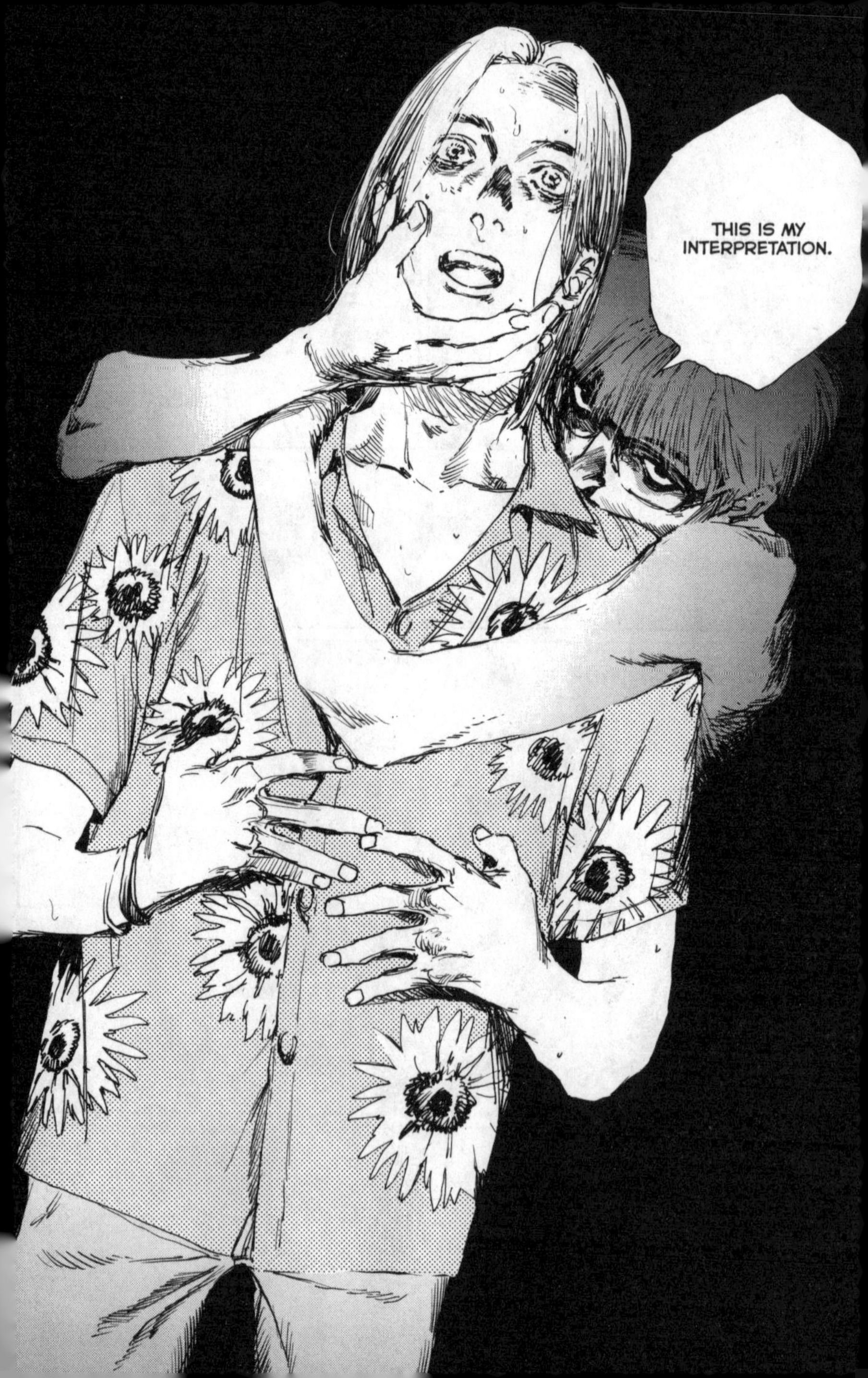
THIS IS MY INTERPRETATION.

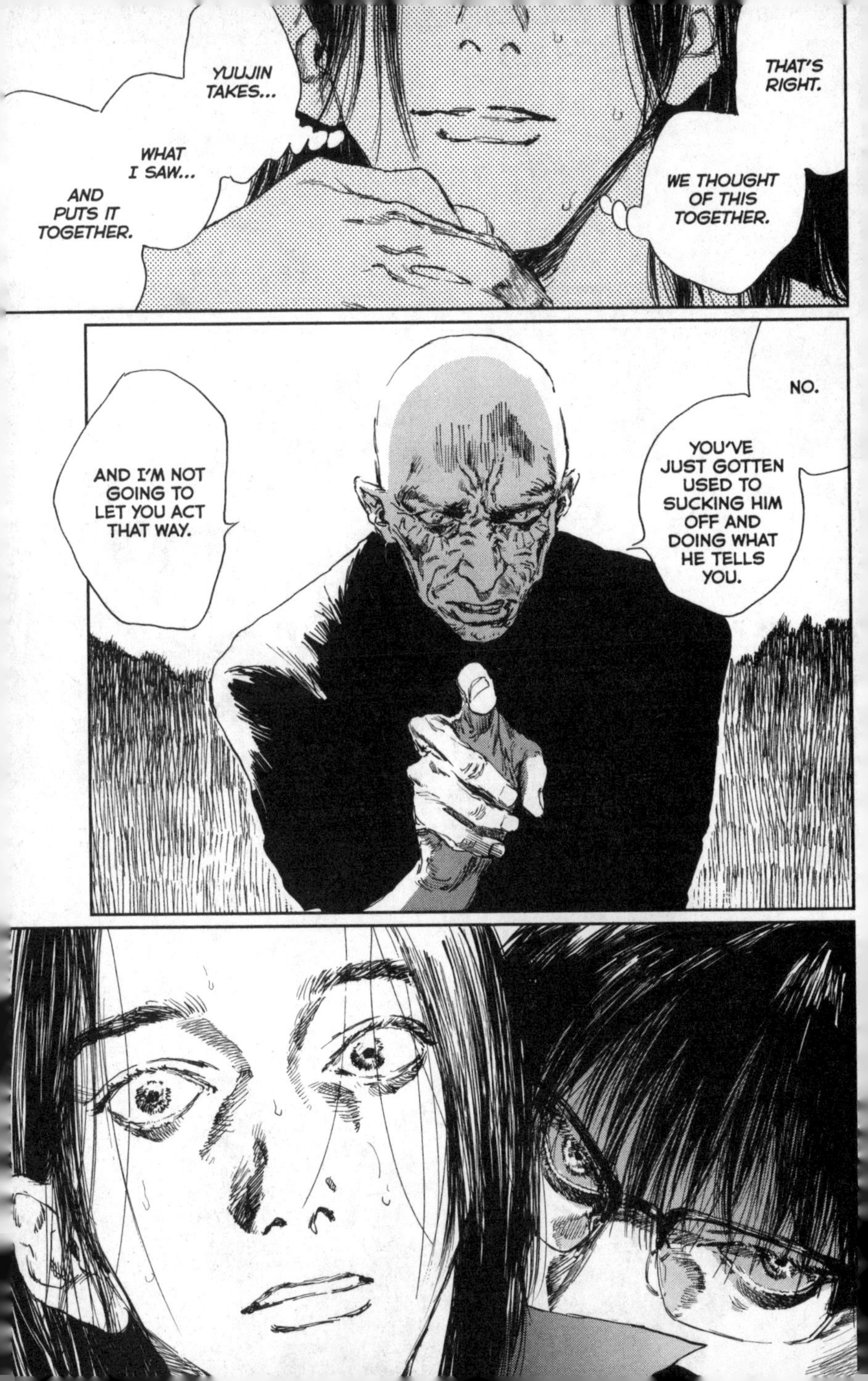
THAT'S RIGHT.
WE THOUGHT OF THIS TOGETHER.
YUUJIN TAKES...
WHAT I SAW...
AND PUTS IT TOGETHER.
NO.
YOU'VE JUST GOTTEN USED TO SUCKING HIM OFF AND DOING WHAT HE TELLS YOU.
AND I'M NOT GOING TO LET YOU ACT THAT WAY.

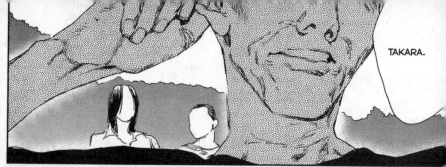

TAKARA.

DIE FOR ME?

WOULD YOU...

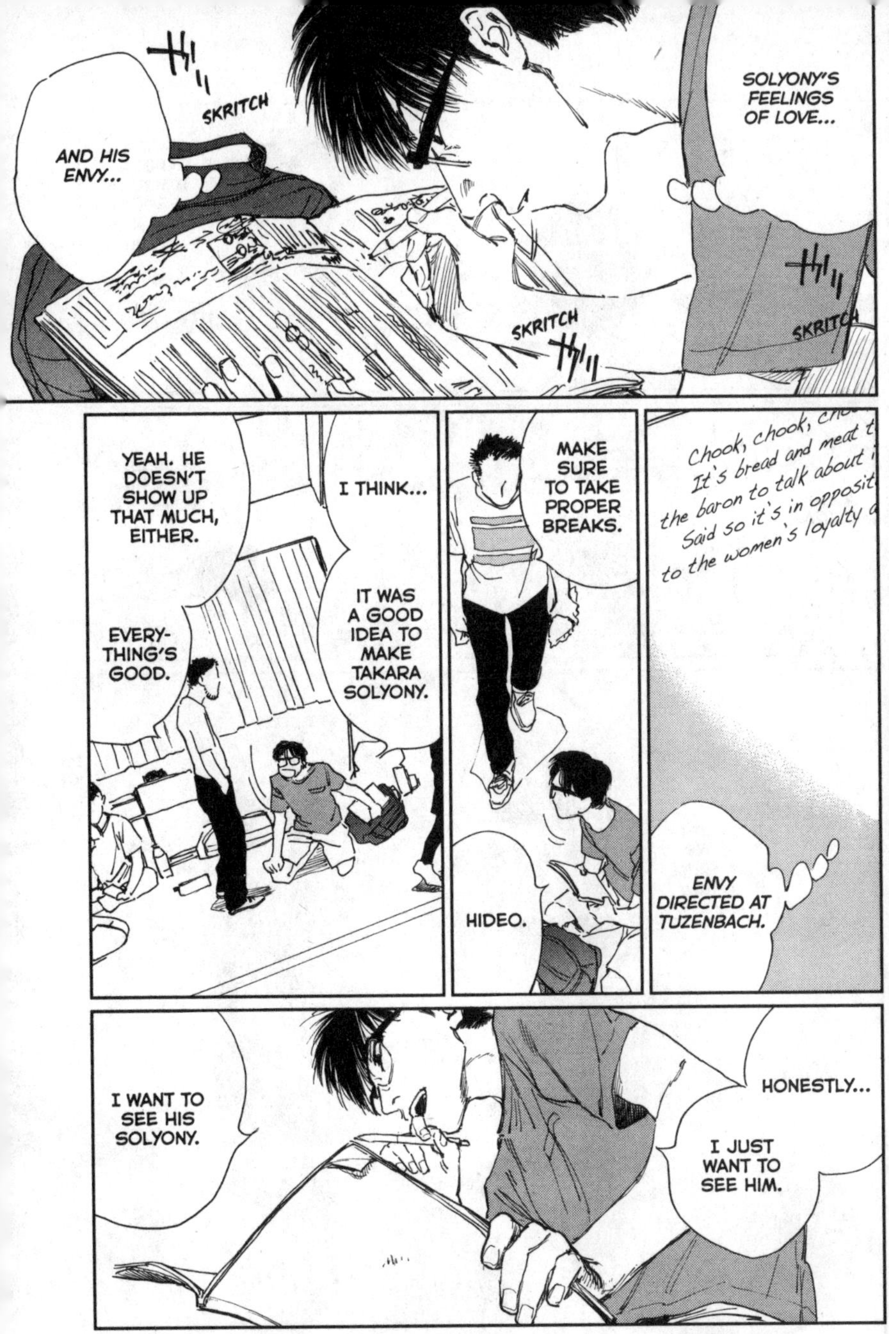
SOLYONY'S FEELINGS OF LOVE...
SKRITCH
SKRITCH
AND HIS ENVY...
SKRITCH
Chook, chook,
It's bread and meat
the baron to talk about
Said so it's in
to the women's loyalty
ENVY DIRECTED AT TUZENBACH.
MAKE SURE TO TAKE PROPER BREAKS.
HIDEO.
I THINK...
IT WAS A GOOD IDEA TO MAKE TAKARA SOLYONY.
YEAH. HE DOESN'T SHOW UP THAT MUCH, EITHER.
EVERYTHING'S GOOD.
HONESTLY...
I JUST WANT TO SEE HIM.
I WANT TO SEE HIS SOLYONY.

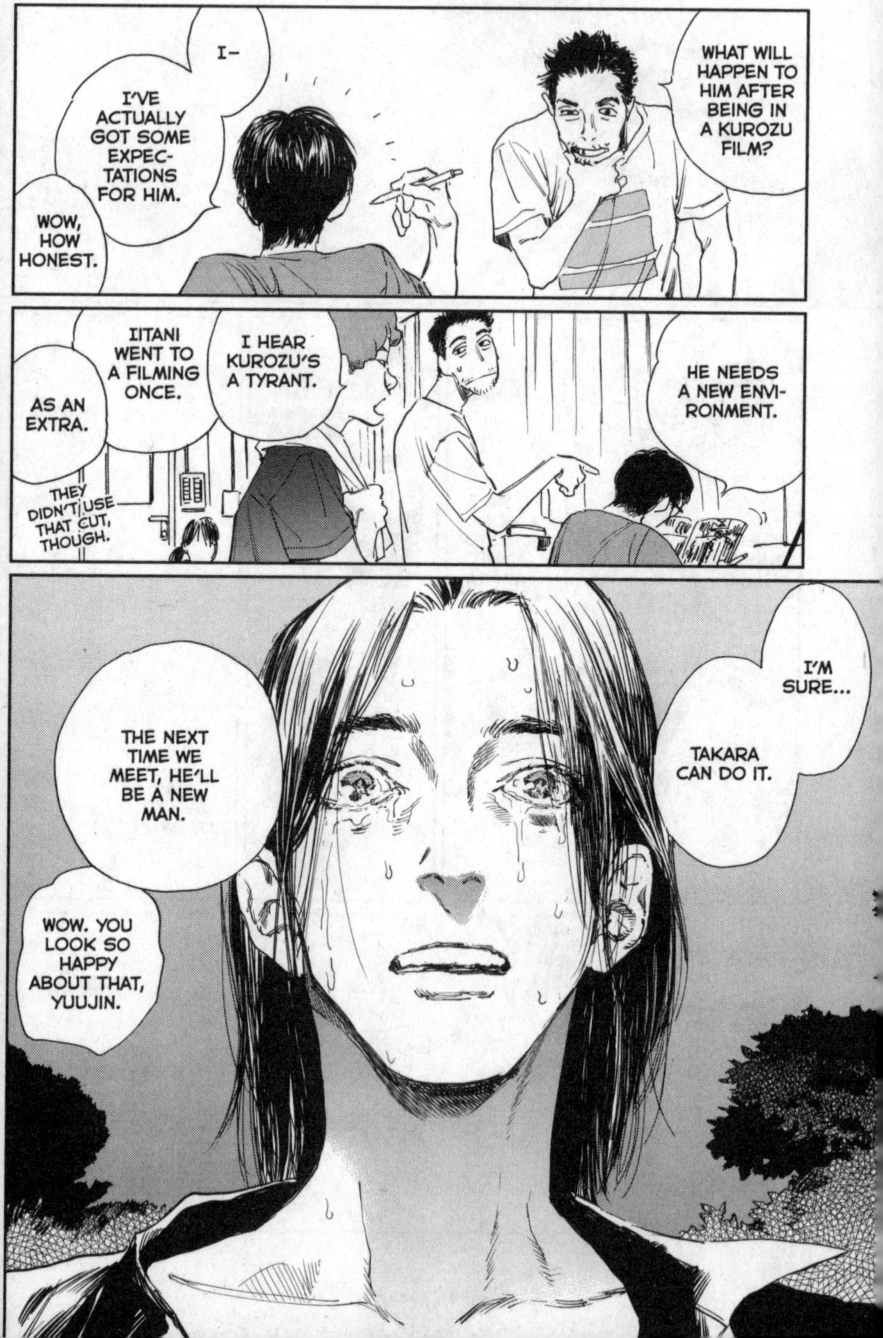
WHAT WILL HAPPEN TO HIM AFTER BEING IN A KUROZU FILM?
I–
I'VE ACTUALLY GOT SOME EXPEC-TATIONS FOR HIM.
WOW, HOW HONEST.
HE NEEDS A NEW ENVI-RONMENT.
I HEAR KUROZU'S A TYRANT.
IITANI WENT TO A FILMING ONCE.
AS AN EXTRA.
THEY DIDN'T USE THAT CUT, THOUGH.
I'M SURE...
TAKARA CAN DO IT.
THE NEXT TIME WE MEET, HE'LL BE A NEW MAN.
WOW. YOU LOOK SO HAPPY ABOUT THAT, YUUJIN.

DOUBLE

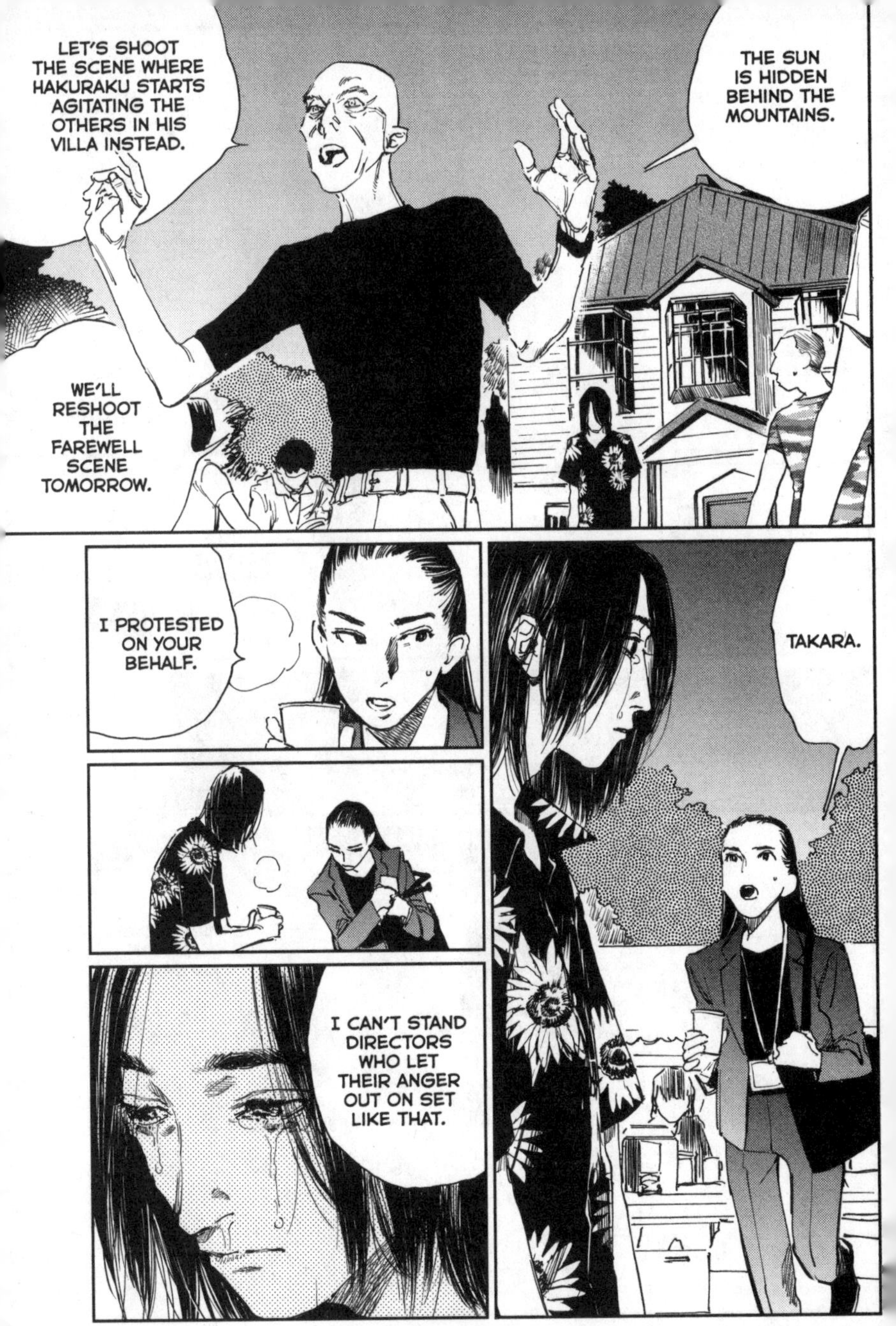
THE SUN IS HIDDEN BEHIND THE MOUNTAINS.
LET'S SHOOT THE SCENE WHERE HAKURAKU STARTS AGITATING THE OTHERS IN HIS VILLA INSTEAD.
WE'LL RESHOOT THE FAREWELL SCENE TOMORROW.
TAKARA.
I PROTESTED ON YOUR BEHALF.
I CAN'T STAND DIRECTORS WHO LET THEIR ANGER OUT ON SET LIKE THAT.

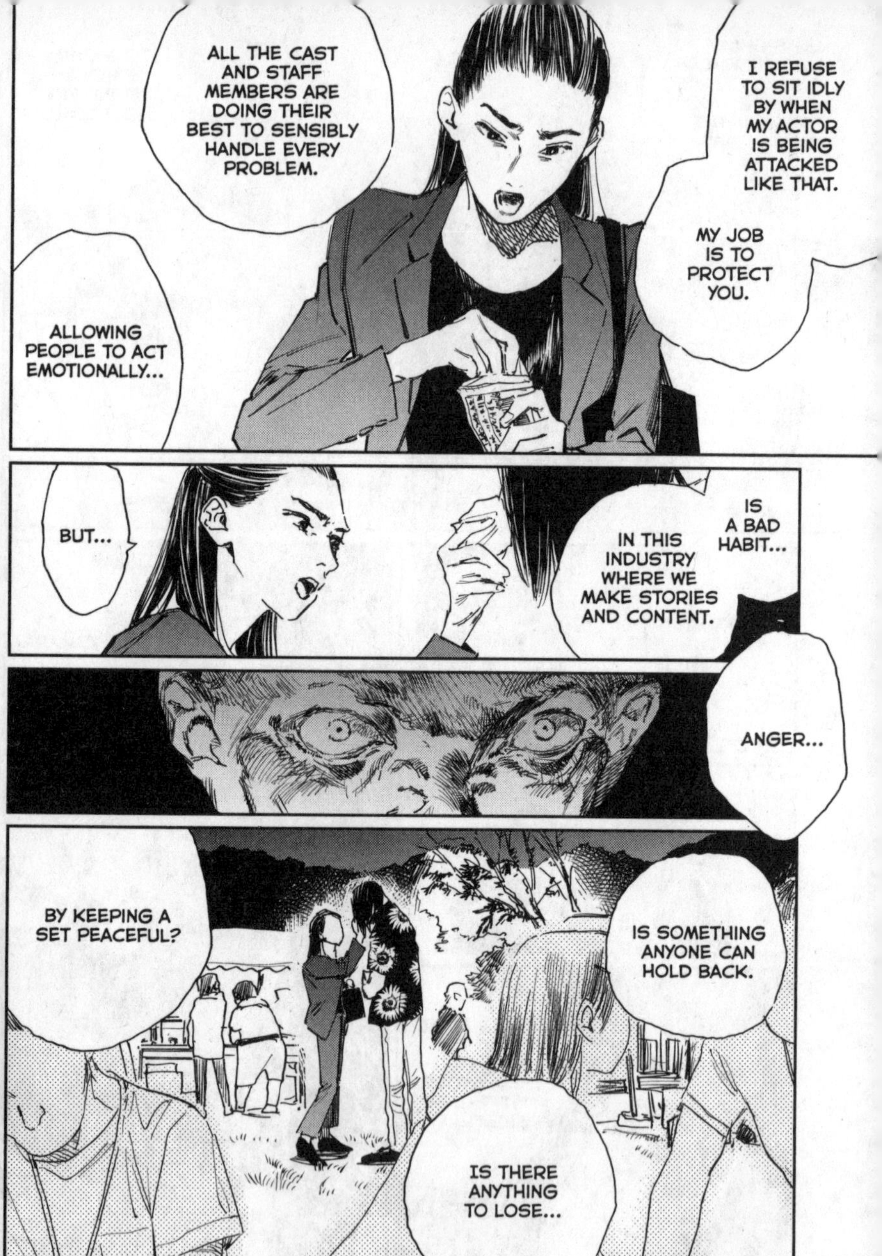

I REFUSE TO SIT IDLY BY WHEN MY ACTOR IS BEING ATTACKED LIKE THAT.
MY JOB IS TO PROTECT YOU.
ALL THE CAST AND STAFF MEMBERS ARE DOING THEIR BEST TO SENSIBLY HANDLE EVERY PROBLEM.
ALLOWING PEOPLE TO ACT EMOTIONALLY...
IS A BAD HABIT...
IN THIS INDUSTRY WHERE WE MAKE STORIES AND CONTENT.
BUT...
ANGER...
IS SOMETHING ANYONE CAN HOLD BACK.
BY KEEPING A SET PEACEFUL?
IS THERE ANYTHING TO LOSE...

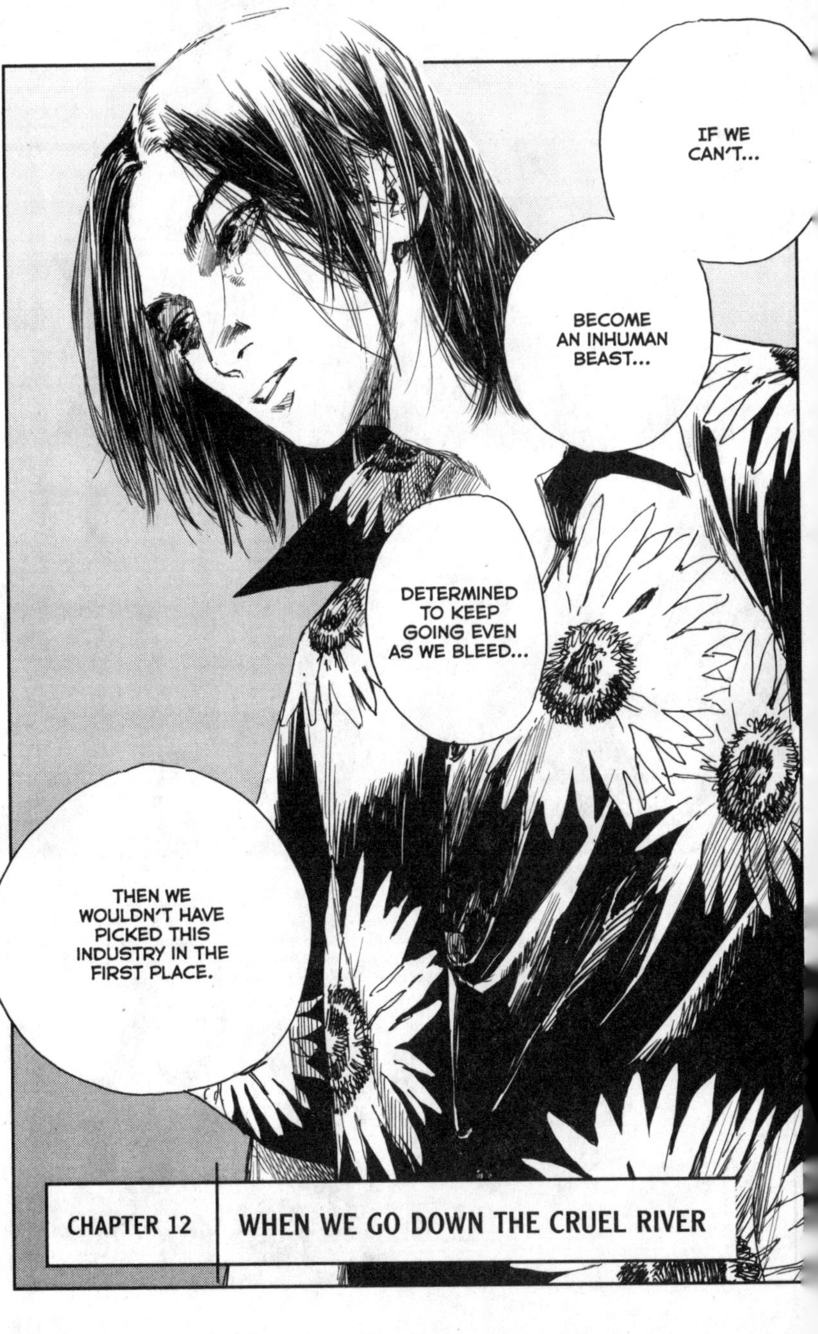
IF WE CAN'T...
BECOME AN INHUMAN BEAST...
DETERMINED TO KEEP GOING EVEN AS WE BLEED...
THEN WE WOULDN'T HAVE PICKED THIS INDUSTRY IN THE FIRST PLACE.

CHAPTER 12 WHEN WE GO DOWN THE CRUEL RIVER

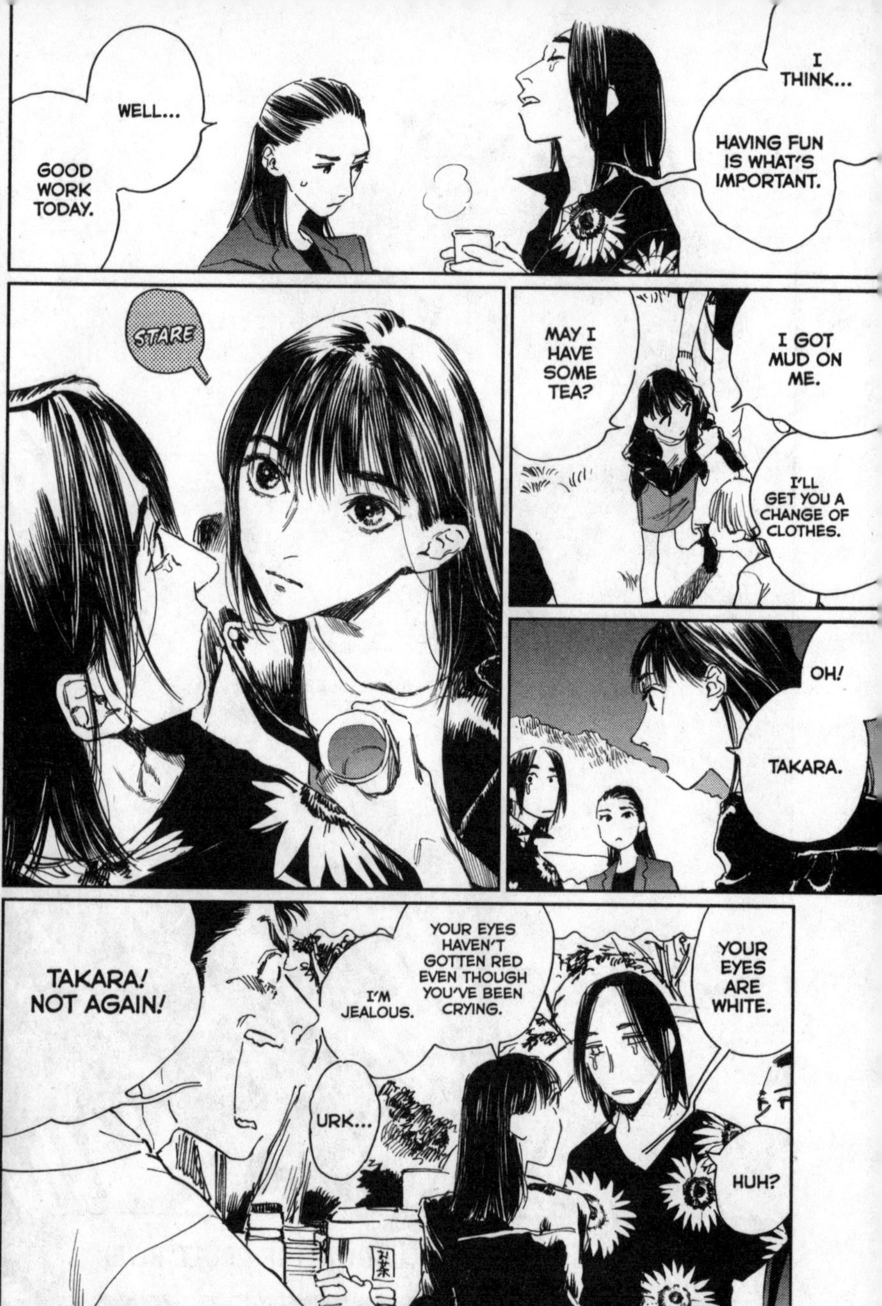
I THINK...
HAVING FUN IS WHAT'S IMPORTANT.
WELL...
GOOD WORK TODAY.
I GOT MUD ON ME.
MAY I HAVE SOME TEA?
I'LL GET YOU A CHANGE OF CLOTHES.
OH!
TAKARA.
STARE
YOUR EYES ARE WHITE.
HUH?
YOUR EYES HAVEN'T GOTTEN RED EVEN THOUGH YOU'VE BEEN CRYING.
I'M JEALOUS.
URK...
TAKARA! NOT AGAIN!

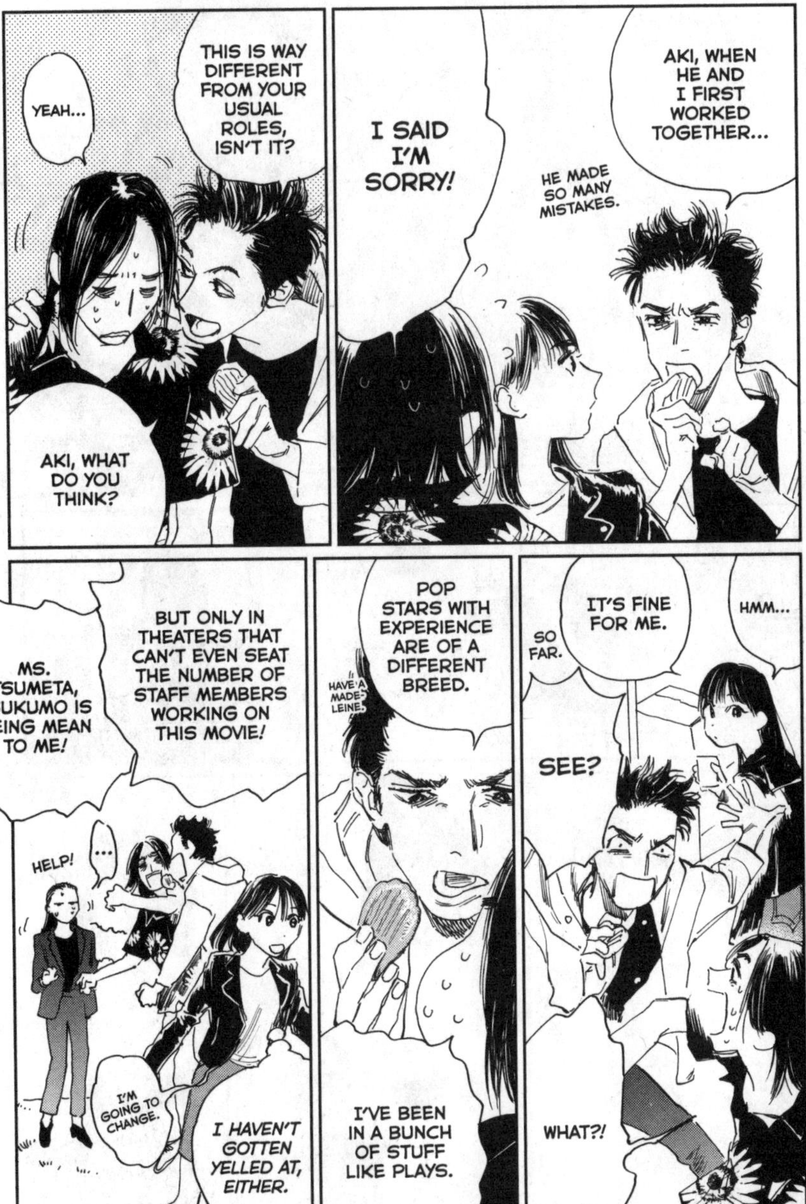
AKI, WHEN HE AND I FIRST WORKED TOGETHER...
HE MADE SO MANY MISTAKES.
I SAID I'M SORRY!
THIS IS WAY DIFFERENT FROM YOUR USUAL ROLES, ISN'T IT?
YEAH...
AKI, WHAT DO YOU THINK?
HMM...
IT'S FINE FOR ME.
SO FAR.
SEE?
WHAT?!
POP STARS WITH EXPERIENCE ARE OF A DIFFERENT BREED.
HAVE A MADE-LEINE.
I'VE BEEN IN A BUNCH OF STUFF LIKE PLAYS.
BUT ONLY IN THEATERS THAT CAN'T EVEN SEAT THE NUMBER OF STAFF MEMBERS WORKING ON THIS MOVIE!
MS. TSUMETA, TSUKUMO IS BEING MEAN TO ME!
...
HELP!
I'M GOING TO CHANGE.
I HAVEN'T GOTTEN YELLED AT, EITHER.

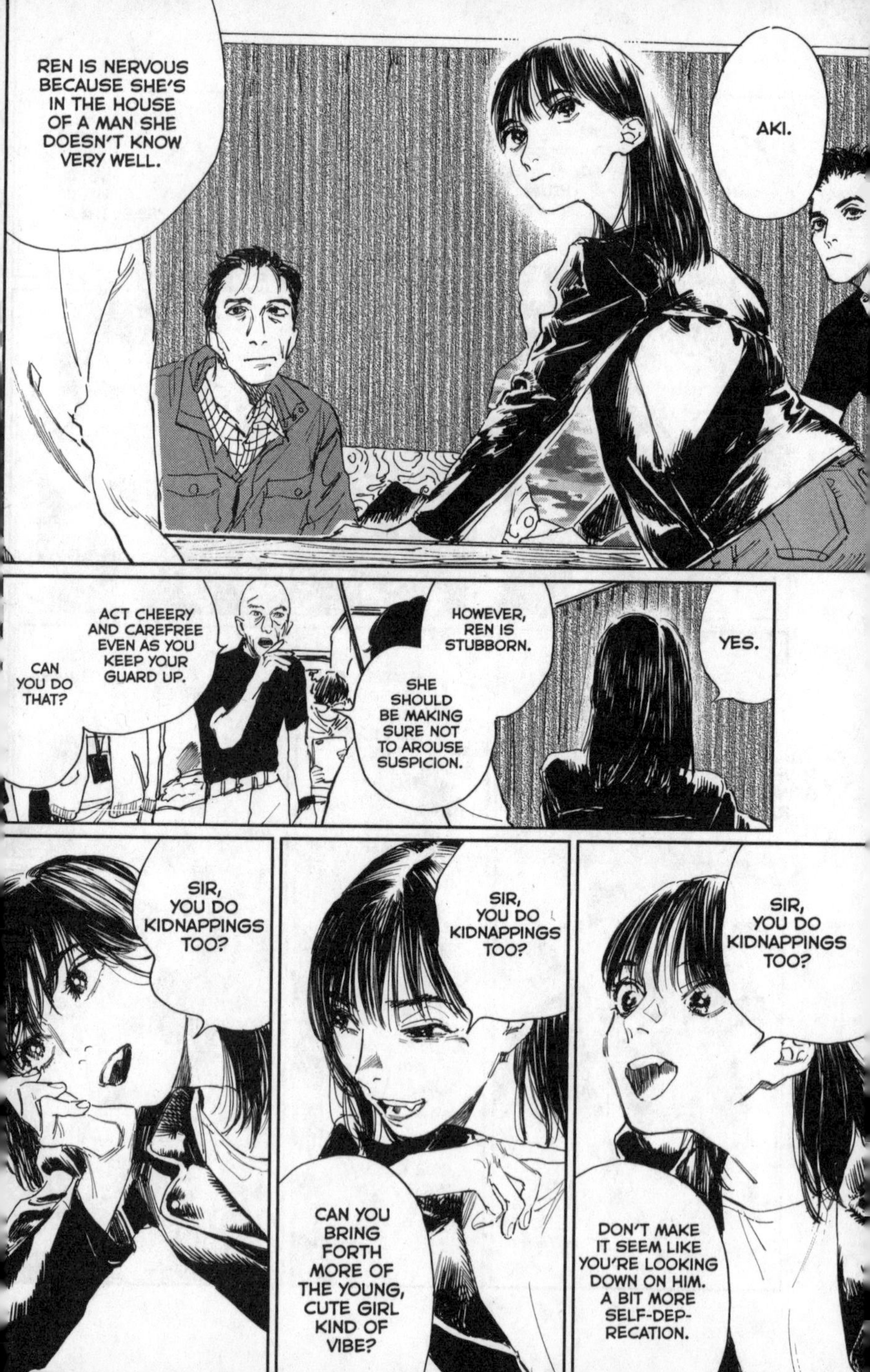
AKI.
REN IS NERVOUS BECAUSE SHE'S IN THE HOUSE OF A MAN SHE DOESN'T KNOW VERY WELL.
YES.
HOWEVER, REN IS STUBBORN.
SHE SHOULD BE MAKING SURE NOT TO AROUSE SUSPICION.
ACT CHEERY AND CAREFREE EVEN AS YOU KEEP YOUR GUARD UP.
CAN YOU DO THAT?
SIR, YOU DO KIDNAPPINGS TOO?
DON'T MAKE IT SEEM LIKE YOU'RE LOOKING DOWN ON HIM. A BIT MORE SELF-DEP-RECATION.
SIR, YOU DO KIDNAPPINGS TOO?
CAN YOU BRING FORTH MORE OF THE YOUNG, CUTE GIRL KIND OF VIBE?
SIR, YOU DO KIDNAPPINGS TOO?

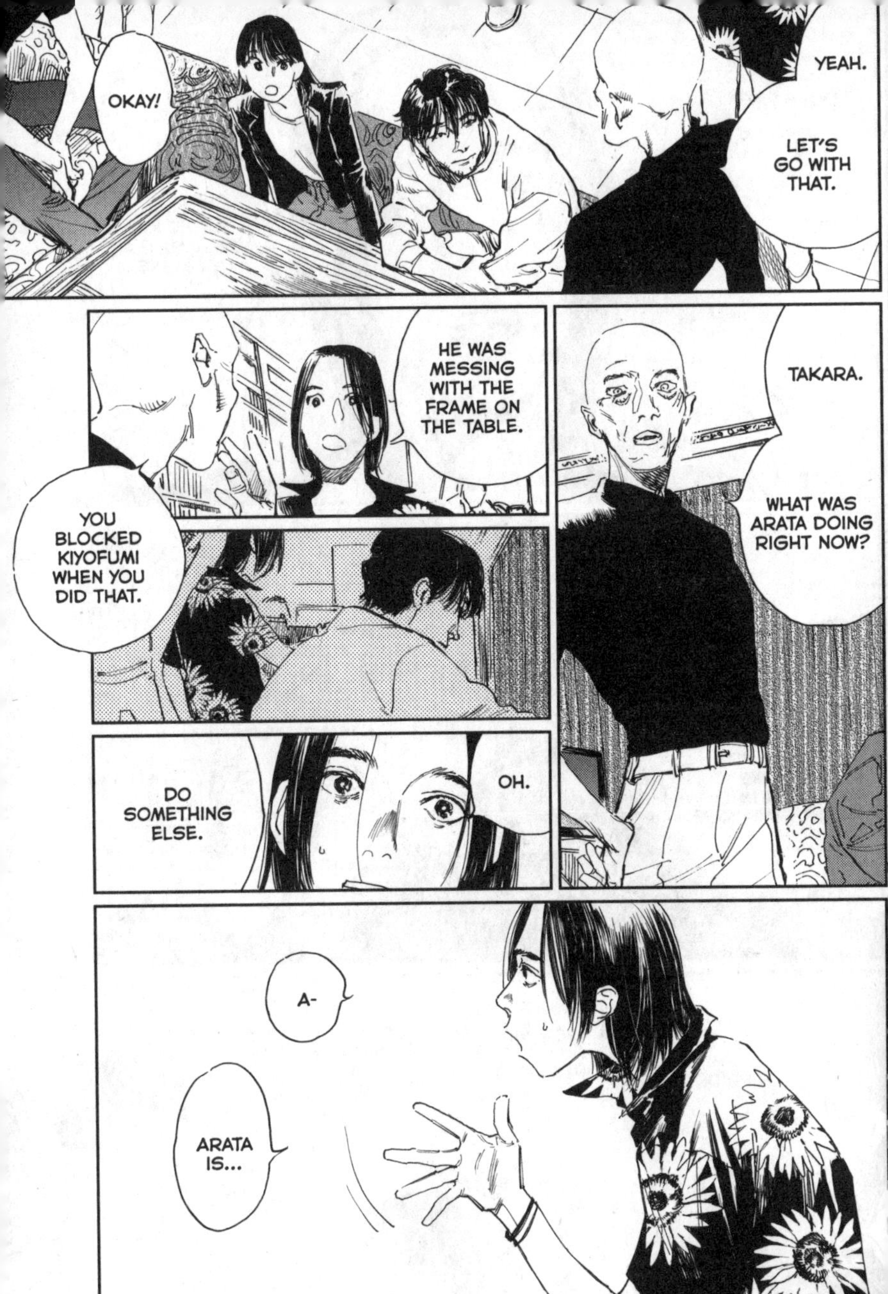
YEAH.
LET'S GO WITH THAT.
OKAY!
TAKARA.
WHAT WAS ARATA DOING RIGHT NOW?
HE WAS MESSING WITH THE FRAME ON THE TABLE.
YOU BLOCKED KIYOFUMI WHEN YOU DID THAT.
OH.
DO SOMETHING ELSE.
A-
ARATA IS...

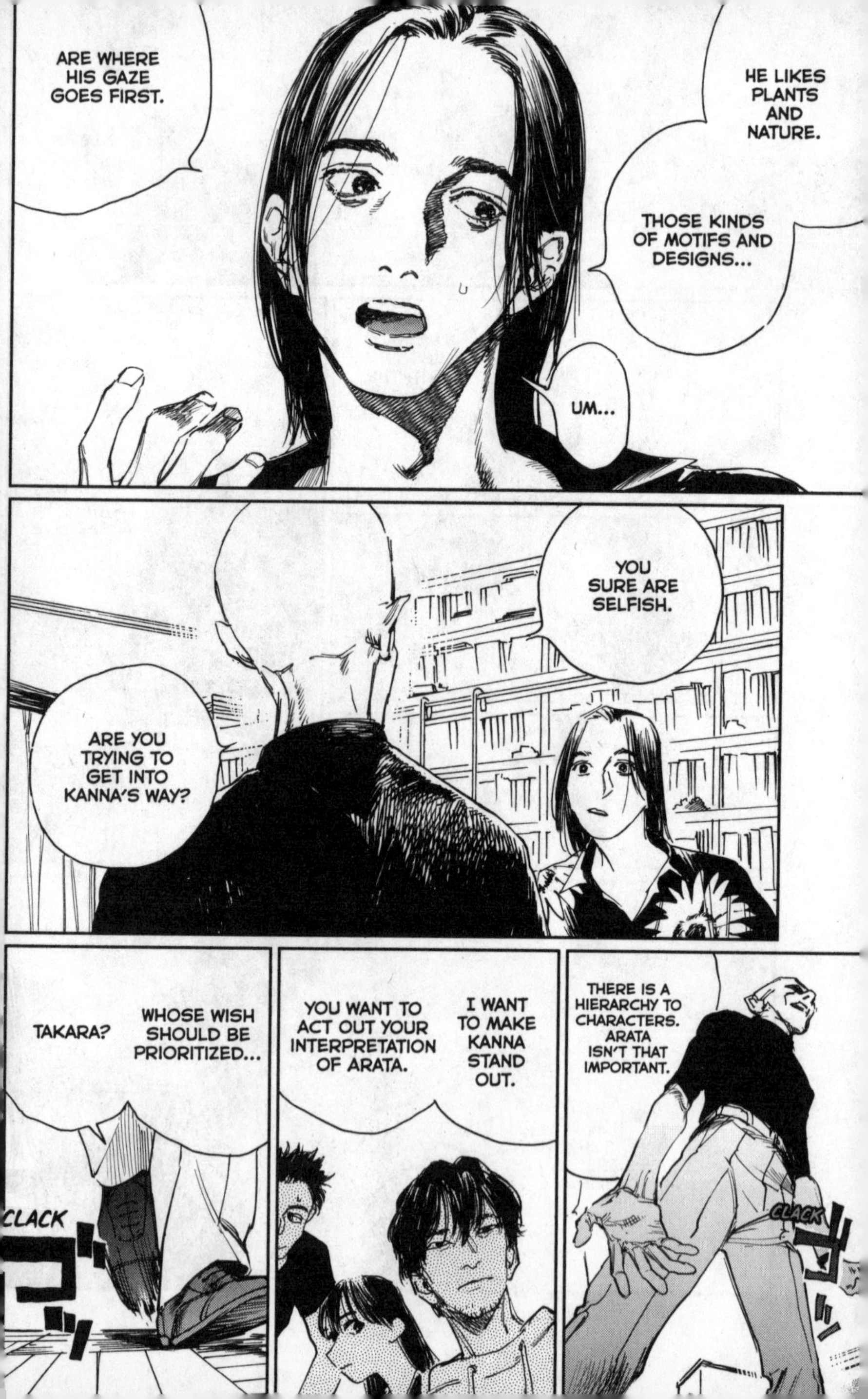

HE LIKES PLANTS AND NATURE.
THOSE KINDS OF MOTIFS AND DESIGNS...
ARE WHERE HIS GAZE GOES FIRST.
UM...
YOU SURE ARE SELFISH.
ARE YOU TRYING TO GET INTO KANNA'S WAY?
THERE IS A HIERARCHY TO CHARACTERS. ARATA ISN'T THAT IMPORTANT.
CLACK
I WANT TO MAKE KANNA STAND OUT.
YOU WANT TO ACT OUT YOUR INTERPRETATION OF ARATA.
WHOSE WISH SHOULD BE PRIORITIZED...
TAKARA?
CLACK

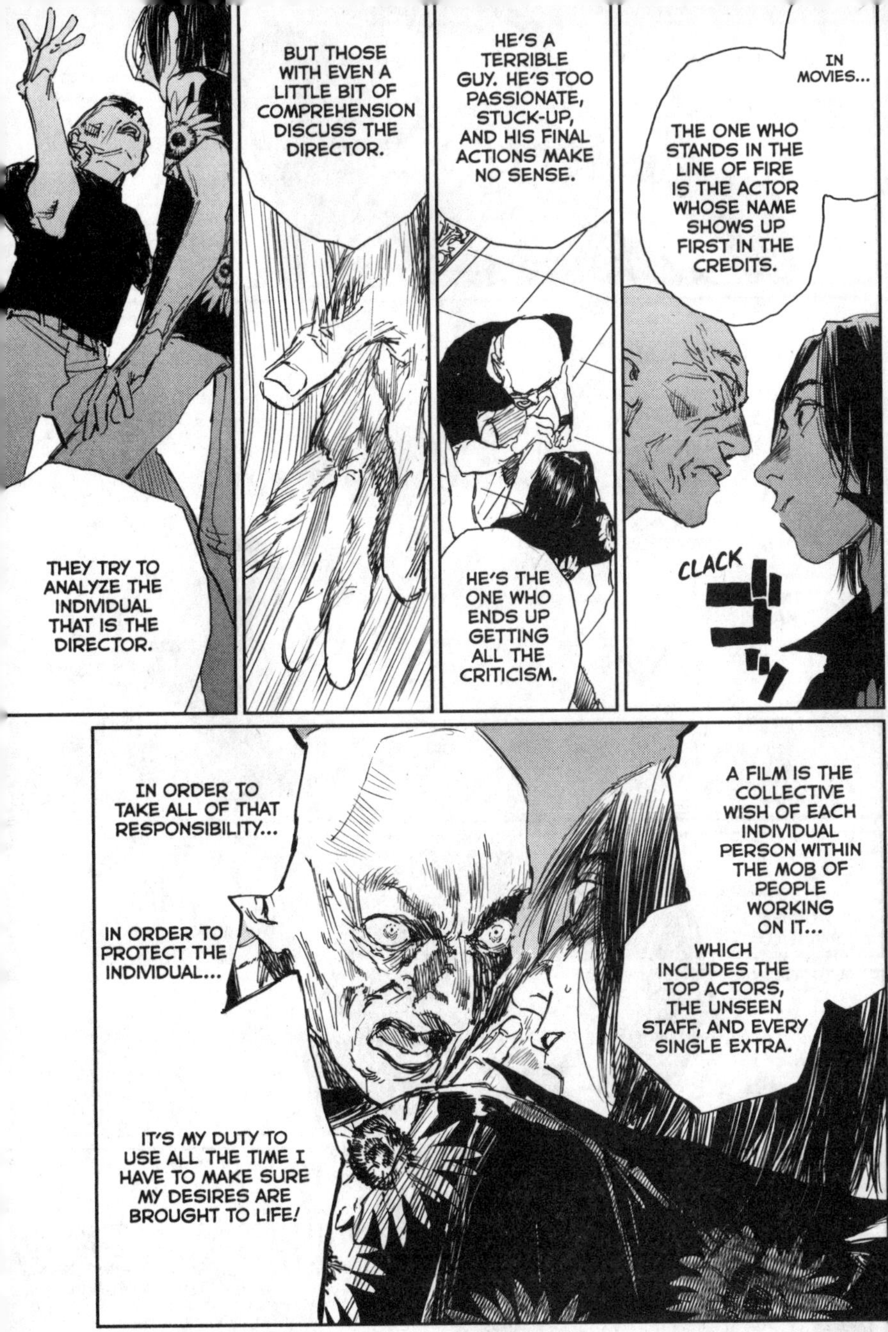
IN MOVIES...
THE ONE WHO STANDS IN THE LINE OF FIRE IS THE ACTOR WHOSE NAME SHOWS UP FIRST IN THE CREDITS.
CLACK
HE'S A TERRIBLE GUY. HE'S TOO PASSIONATE, STUCK-UP, AND HIS FINAL ACTIONS MAKE NO SENSE.
HE'S THE ONE WHO ENDS UP GETTING ALL THE CRITICISM.
BUT THOSE WITH EVEN A LITTLE BIT OF COMPREHENSION DISCUSS THE DIRECTOR.
THEY TRY TO ANALYZE THE INDIVIDUAL THAT IS THE DIRECTOR.
A FILM IS THE COLLECTIVE WISH OF EACH INDIVIDUAL PERSON WITHIN THE MOB OF PEOPLE WORKING ON IT...
WHICH INCLUDES THE TOP ACTORS, THE UNSEEN STAFF, AND EVERY SINGLE EXTRA.
IN ORDER TO TAKE ALL OF THAT RESPONSIBILITY...
IN ORDER TO PROTECT THE INDIVIDUAL...
IT'S MY DUTY TO USE ALL THE TIME I HAVE TO MAKE SURE MY DESIRES ARE BROUGHT TO LIFE!

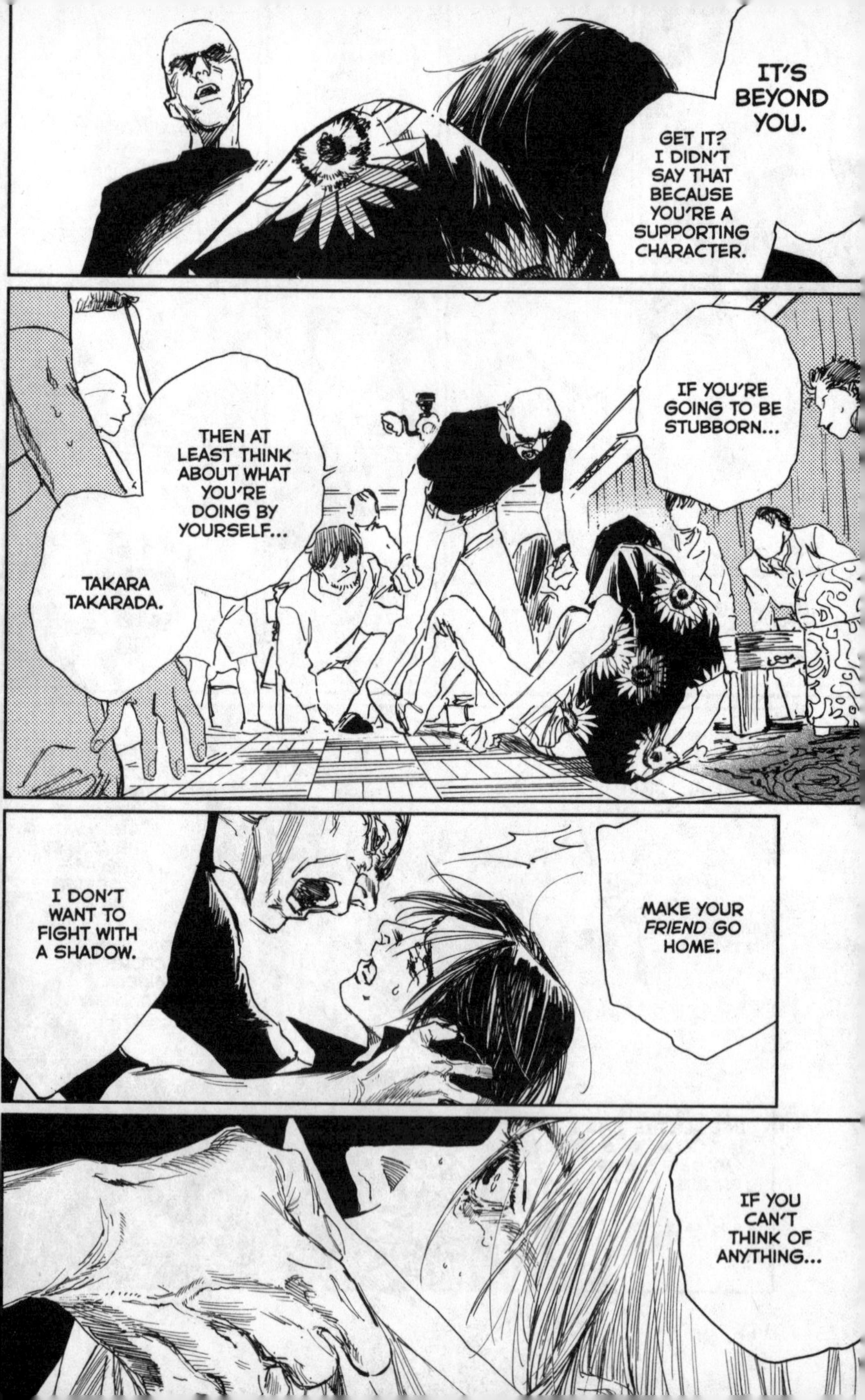
IT'S BEYOND YOU.
GET IT? I DIDN'T SAY THAT BECAUSE YOU'RE A SUPPORTING CHARACTER.
IF YOU'RE GOING TO BE STUBBORN...
THEN AT LEAST THINK ABOUT WHAT YOU'RE DOING BY YOURSELF...
TAKARA TAKARADA.
MAKE YOUR *FRIEND* GO HOME.
I DON'T WANT TO FIGHT WITH A SHADOW.
IF *YOU* CAN'T THINK OF ANYTHING...

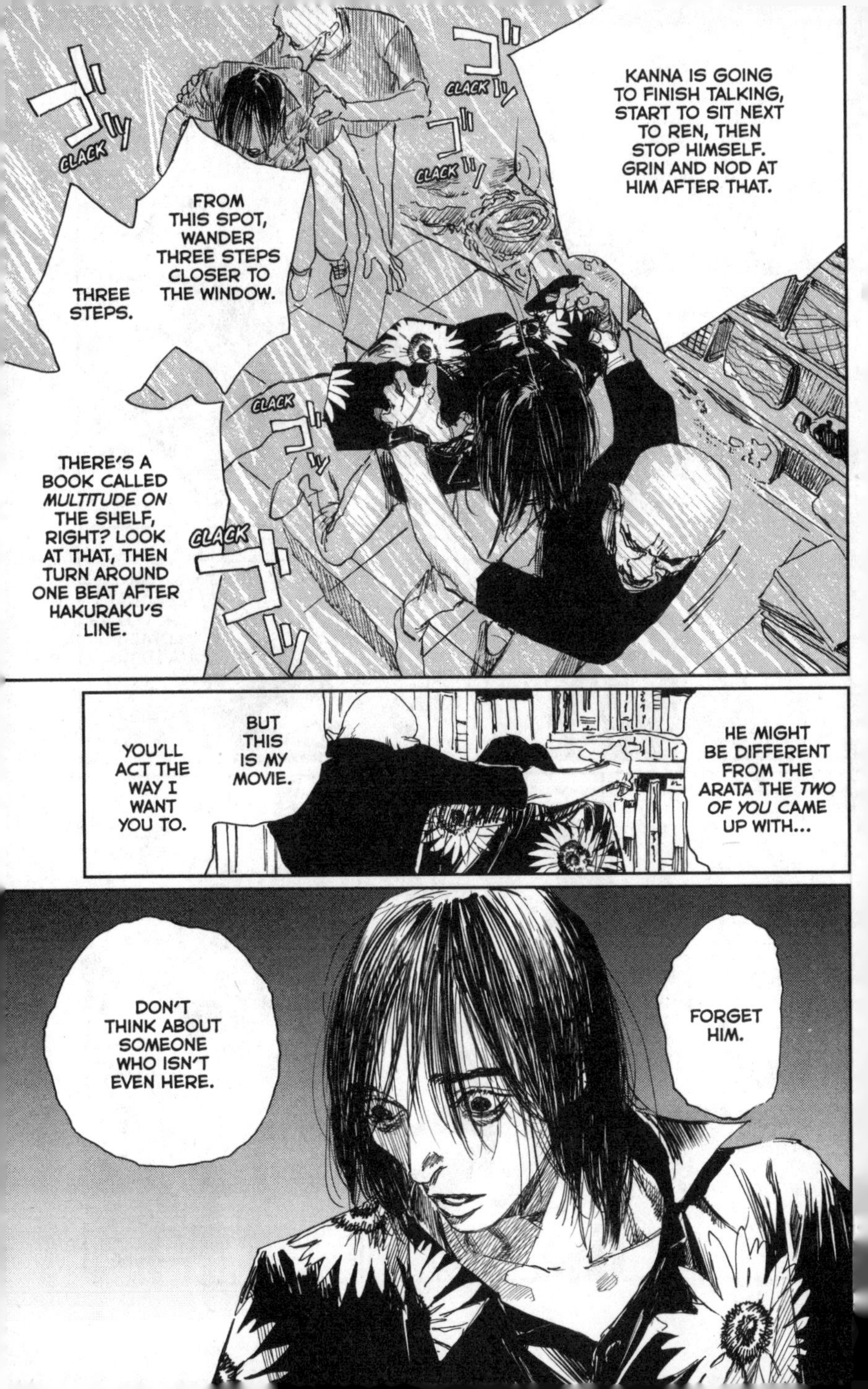
KANNA IS GOING TO FINISH TALKING, START TO SIT NEXT TO REN, THEN STOP HIMSELF. GRIN AND NOD AT HIM AFTER THAT.
CLACK
CLACK
CLACK
FROM THIS SPOT, WANDER THREE STEPS CLOSER TO THE WINDOW.
THREE STEPS.
CLACK
CLACK
THERE'S A BOOK CALLED *MULTITUDE* ON THE SHELF, RIGHT? LOOK AT THAT, THEN TURN AROUND ONE BEAT AFTER HAKURAKU'S LINE.
HE MIGHT BE DIFFERENT FROM THE ARATA THE *TWO OF YOU* CAME UP WITH...
BUT THIS IS MY MOVIE.
YOU'LL ACT THE WAY I WANT YOU TO.
FORGET HIM.
DON'T THINK ABOUT SOMEONE WHO ISN'T EVEN HERE.

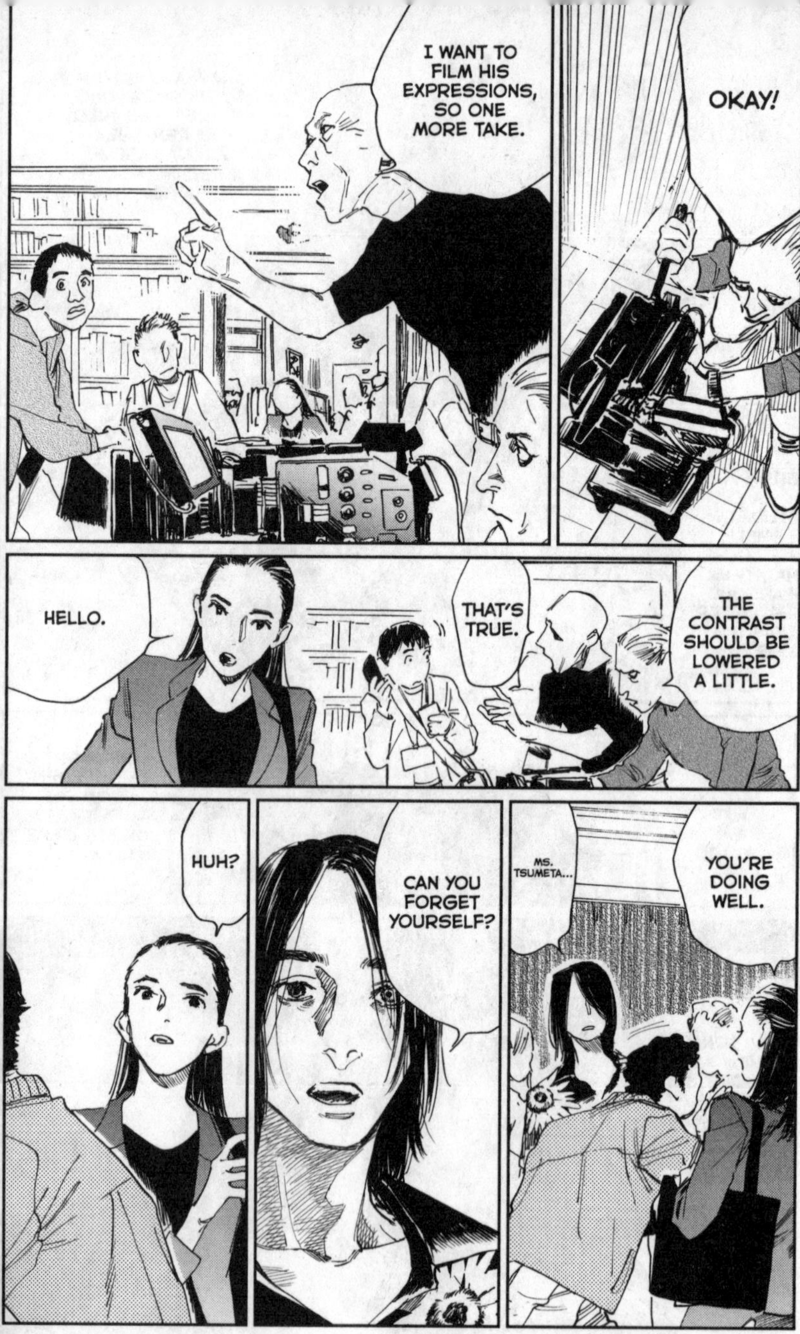
OKAY!
I WANT TO FILM HIS EXPRESSIONS, SO ONE MORE TAKE.
THE CONTRAST SHOULD BE LOWERED A LITTLE.
THAT'S TRUE.
HELLO.
YOU'RE DOING WELL.
MS. TSUMETA...
CAN YOU FORGET YOURSELF?
HUH?

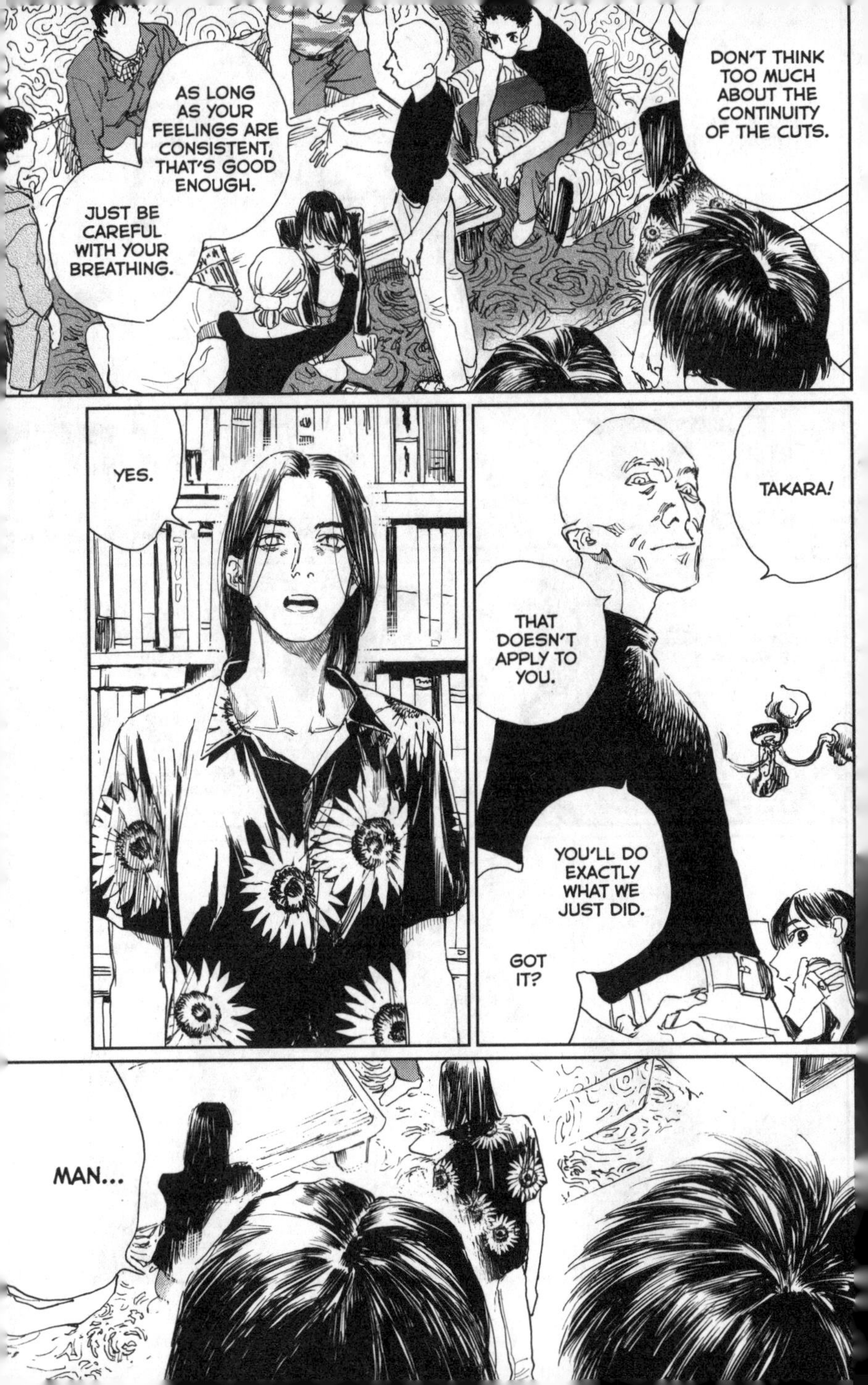
DON'T THINK TOO MUCH ABOUT THE CONTINUITY OF THE CUTS.
AS LONG AS YOUR FEELINGS ARE CONSISTENT, THAT'S GOOD ENOUGH.
JUST BE CAREFUL WITH YOUR BREATHING.
TAKARA!
THAT DOESN'T APPLY TO YOU.
YOU'LL DO EXACTLY WHAT WE JUST DID.
GOT IT?
YES.
MAN...

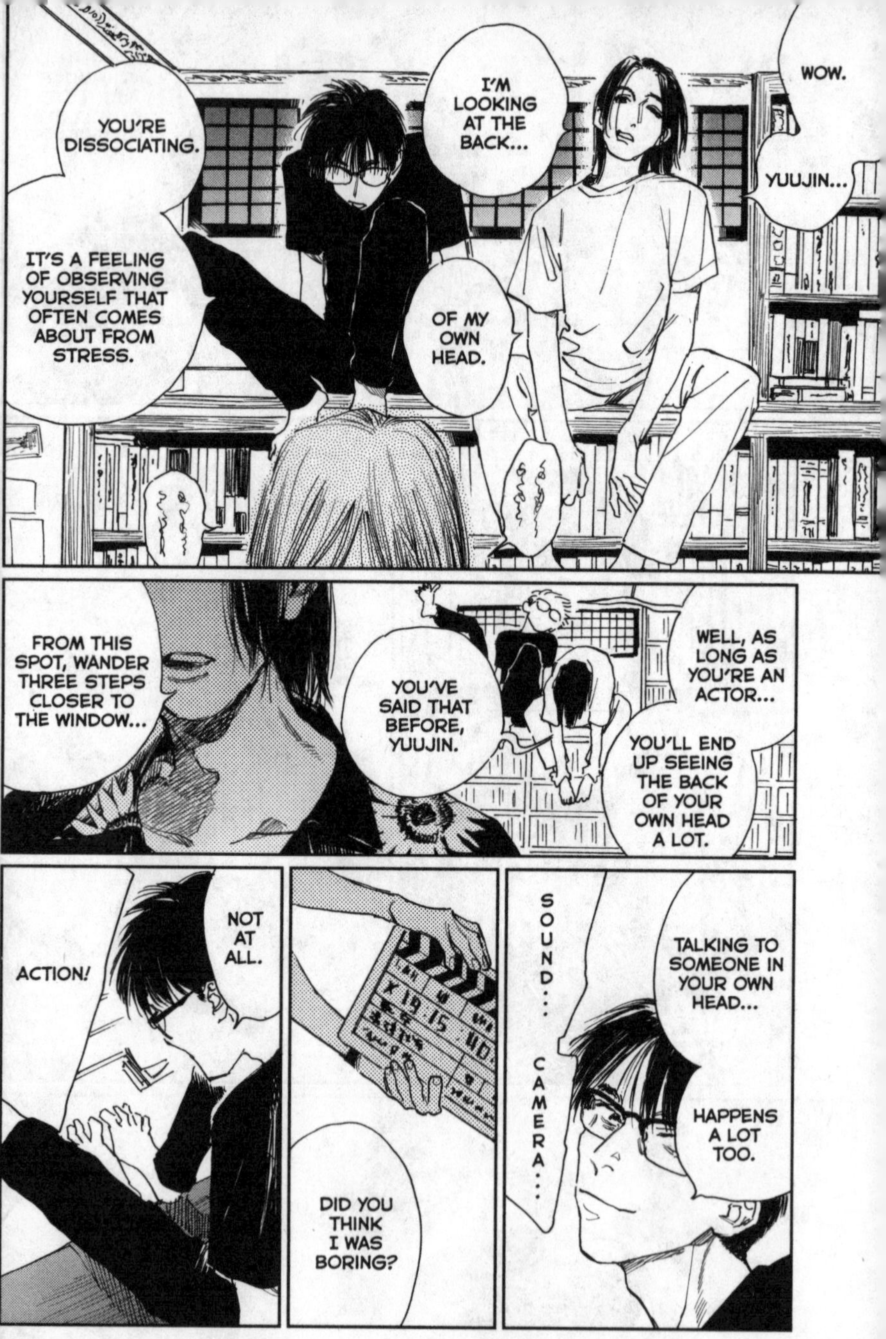
WOW.
YUUJIN...
I'M LOOKING AT THE BACK...
OF MY OWN HEAD.
YOU'RE DISSOCIATING.
IT'S A FEELING OF OBSERVING YOURSELF THAT OFTEN COMES ABOUT FROM STRESS.
WELL, AS LONG AS YOU'RE AN ACTOR...
YOU'LL END UP SEEING THE BACK OF YOUR OWN HEAD A LOT.
YOU'VE SAID THAT BEFORE, YUUJIN.
FROM THIS SPOT, WANDER THREE STEPS CLOSER TO THE WINDOW...
TALKING TO SOMEONE IN YOUR OWN HEAD...
HAPPENS A LOT TOO.
SOUND... CAMERA...
DID YOU THINK I WAS BORING?
NOT AT ALL.
ACTION!

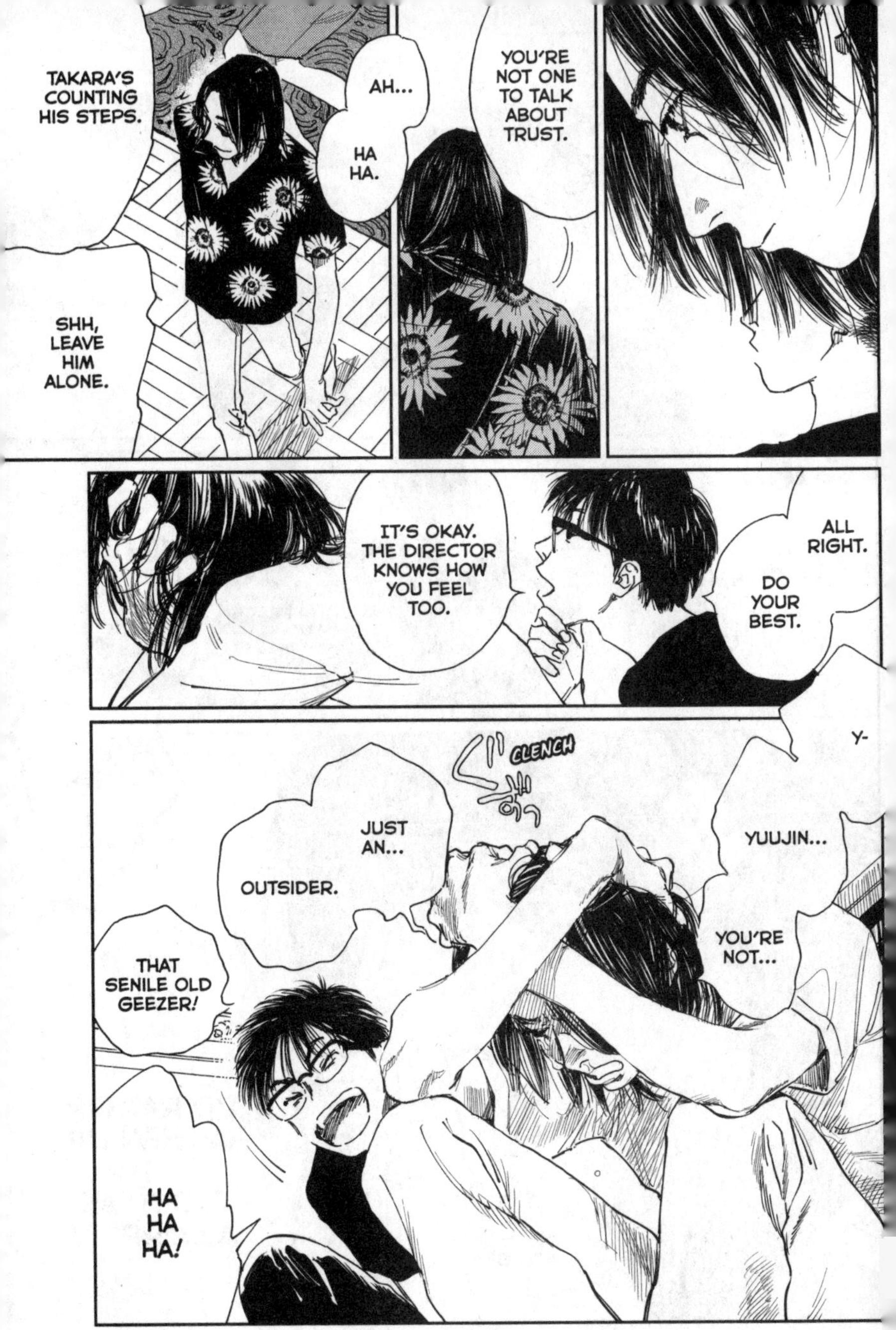
YOU'RE NOT ONE TO TALK ABOUT TRUST.
AH...
HA HA.
TAKARA'S COUNTING HIS STEPS.
SHH, LEAVE HIM ALONE.
ALL RIGHT.
DO YOUR BEST.
IT'S OKAY. THE DIRECTOR KNOWS HOW YOU FEEL TOO.
Y-
YUUJIN...
YOU'RE NOT...
CLENCH
JUST AN...
OUTSIDER.
THAT SENILE OLD GEEZER!
HA HA HA!

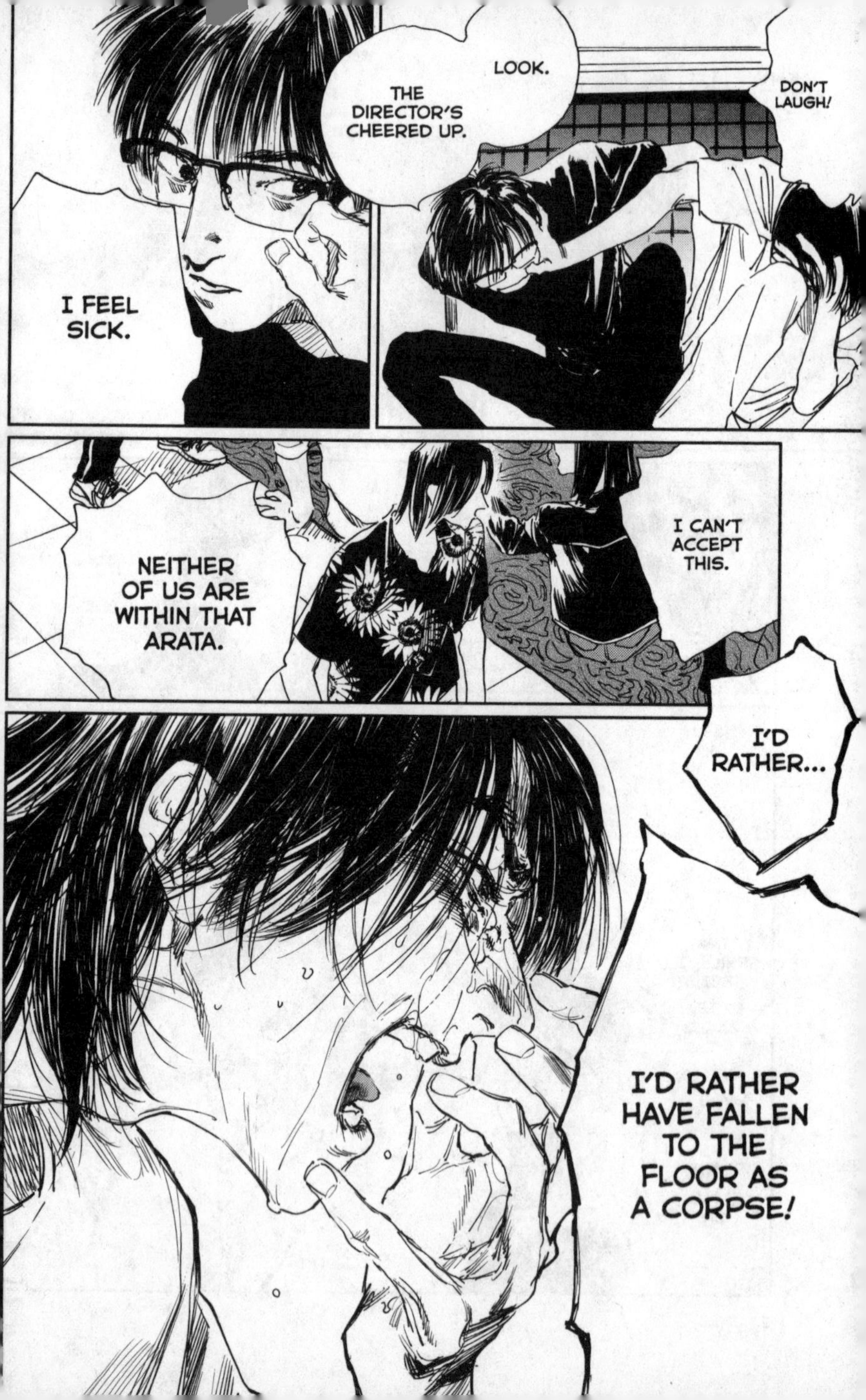
LOOK. THE DIRECTOR'S CHEERED UP.
DON'T LAUGH!
I FEEL SICK.
I CAN'T ACCEPT THIS.
NEITHER OF US ARE WITHIN THAT ARATA.
I'D RATHER...
I'D RATHER HAVE FALLEN TO THE FLOOR AS A CORPSE!

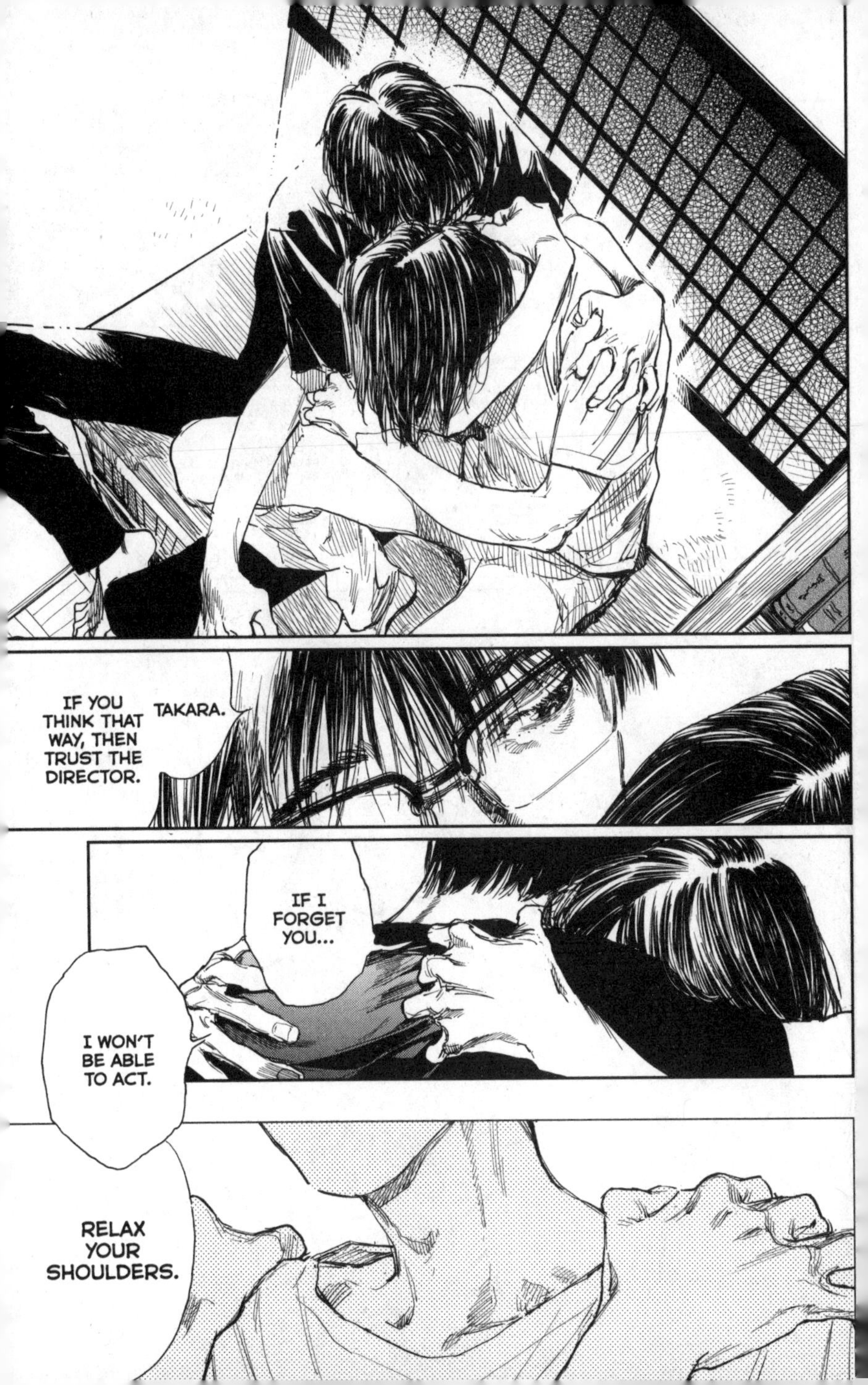
TAKARA.
IF YOU THINK THAT WAY, THEN TRUST THE DIRECTOR.
IF I FORGET YOU...
I WON'T BE ABLE TO ACT.
RELAX YOUR SHOULDERS.

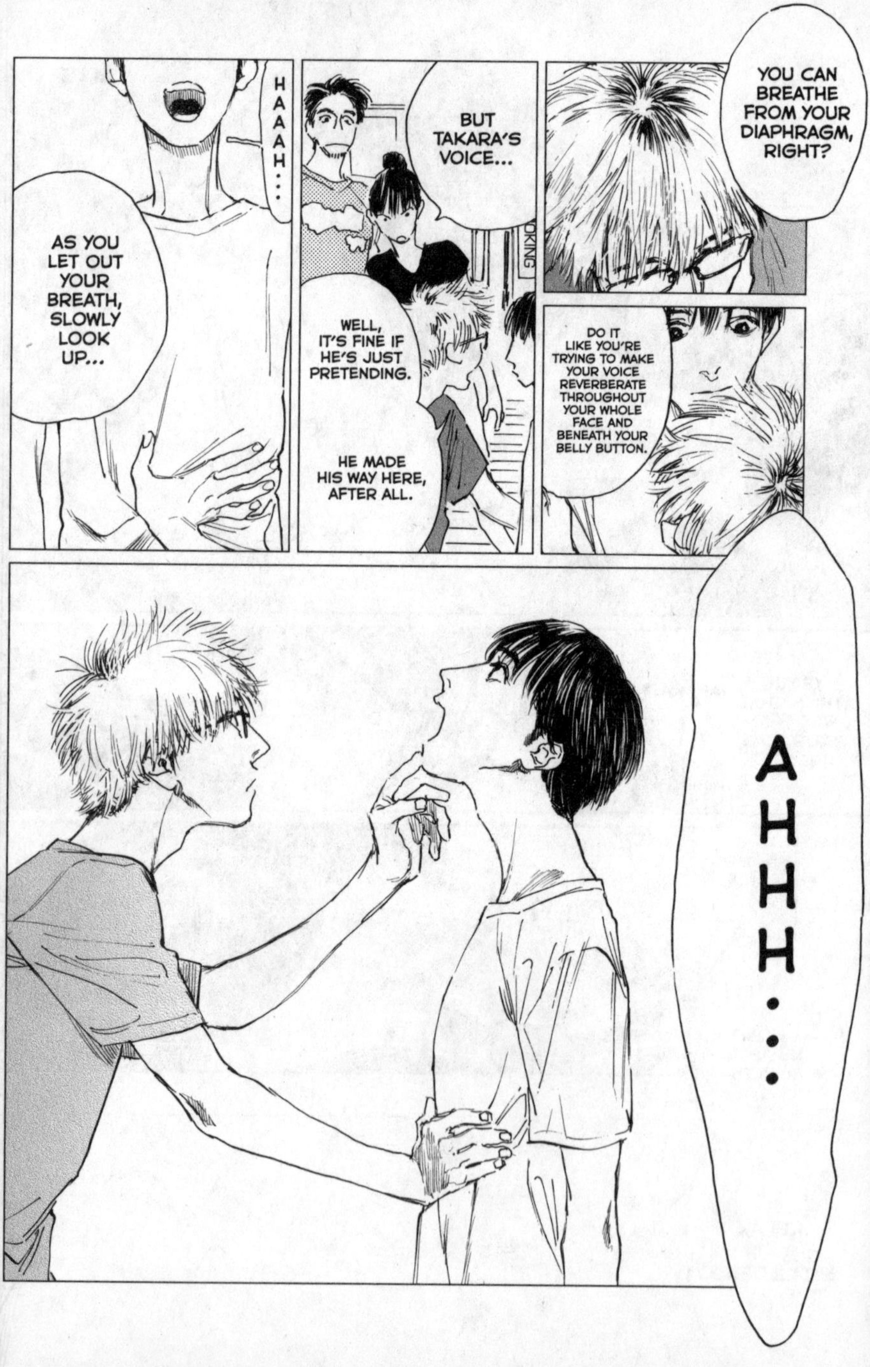
YOU CAN BREATHE FROM YOUR DIAPHRAGM, RIGHT?
DO IT LIKE YOU'RE TRYING TO MAKE YOUR VOICE REVERBERATE THROUGHOUT YOUR WHOLE FACE AND BENEATH YOUR BELLY BUTTON.
BUT TAKARA'S VOICE...
WELL, IT'S FINE IF HE'S JUST PRETENDING.
HE MADE HIS WAY HERE, AFTER ALL.
HAAAAH...
AS YOU LET OUT YOUR BREATH, SLOWLY LOOK UP...
AHHH...

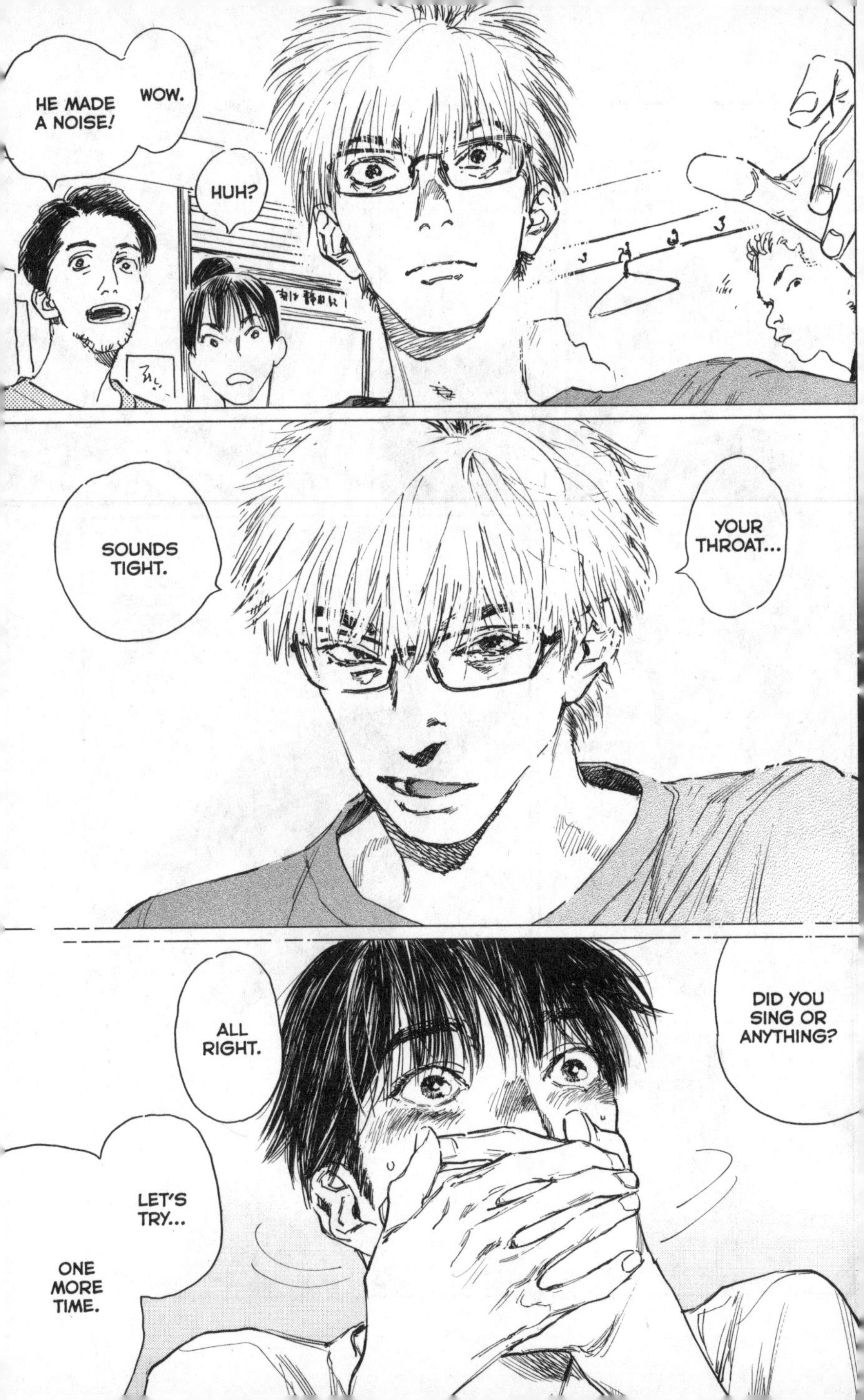
WOW.
HE MADE A NOISE!
HUH?
YOUR THROAT...
SOUNDS TIGHT.
DID YOU SING OR ANYTHING?
ALL RIGHT.
LET'S TRY...
ONE MORE TIME.

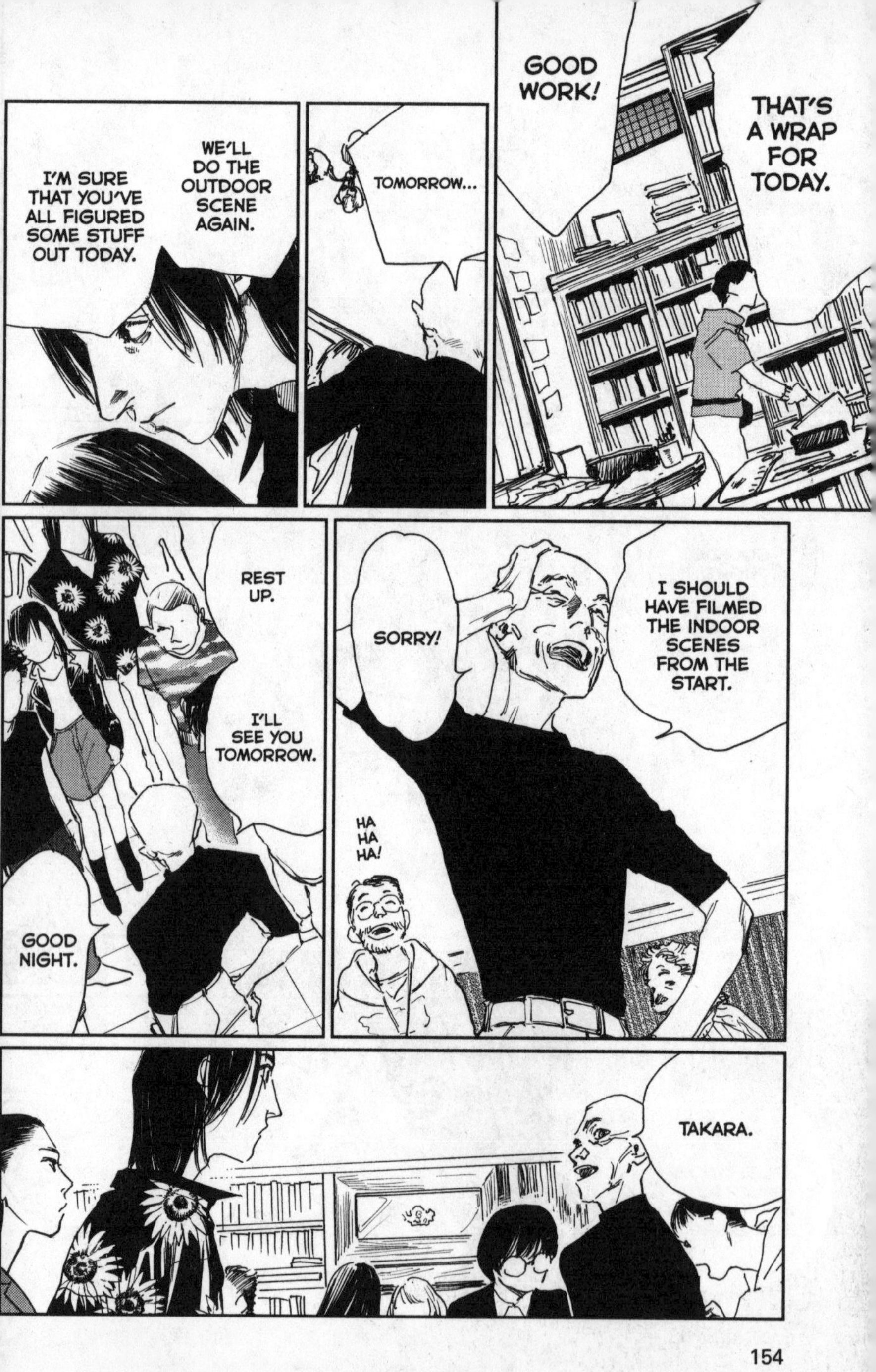
THAT'S A WRAP FOR TODAY.
GOOD WORK!
TOMORROW...
WE'LL DO THE OUTDOOR SCENE AGAIN.
I'M SURE THAT YOU'VE ALL FIGURED SOME STUFF OUT TODAY.
I SHOULD HAVE FILMED THE INDOOR SCENES FROM THE START.
SORRY!
HA HA HA!
REST UP.
I'LL SEE YOU TOMORROW.
GOOD NIGHT.
TAKARA.

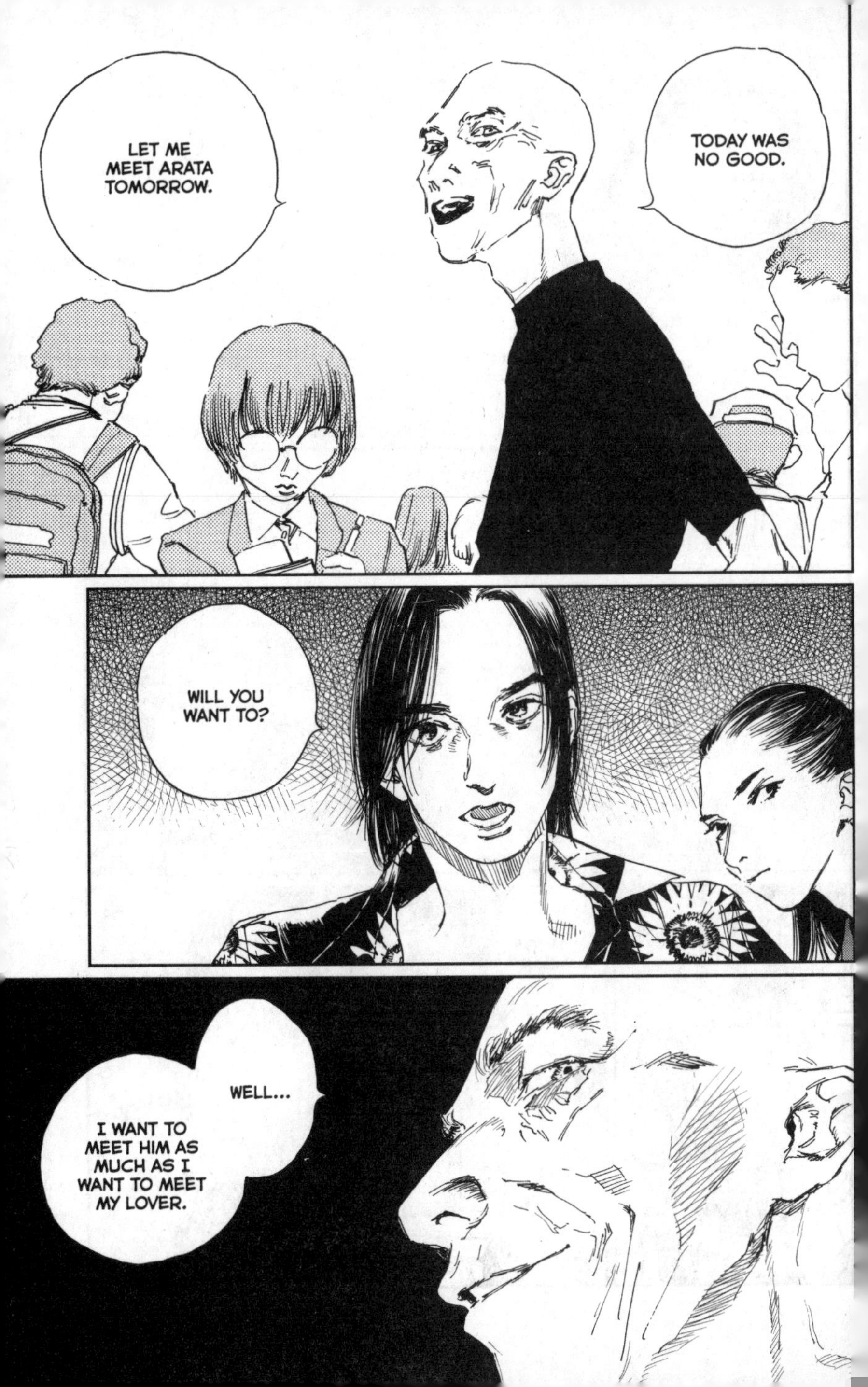
TODAY WAS NO GOOD.
LET ME MEET ARATA TOMORROW.
WILL YOU WANT TO?
WELL...
I WANT TO MEET HIM AS MUCH AS I WANT TO MEET MY LOVER.

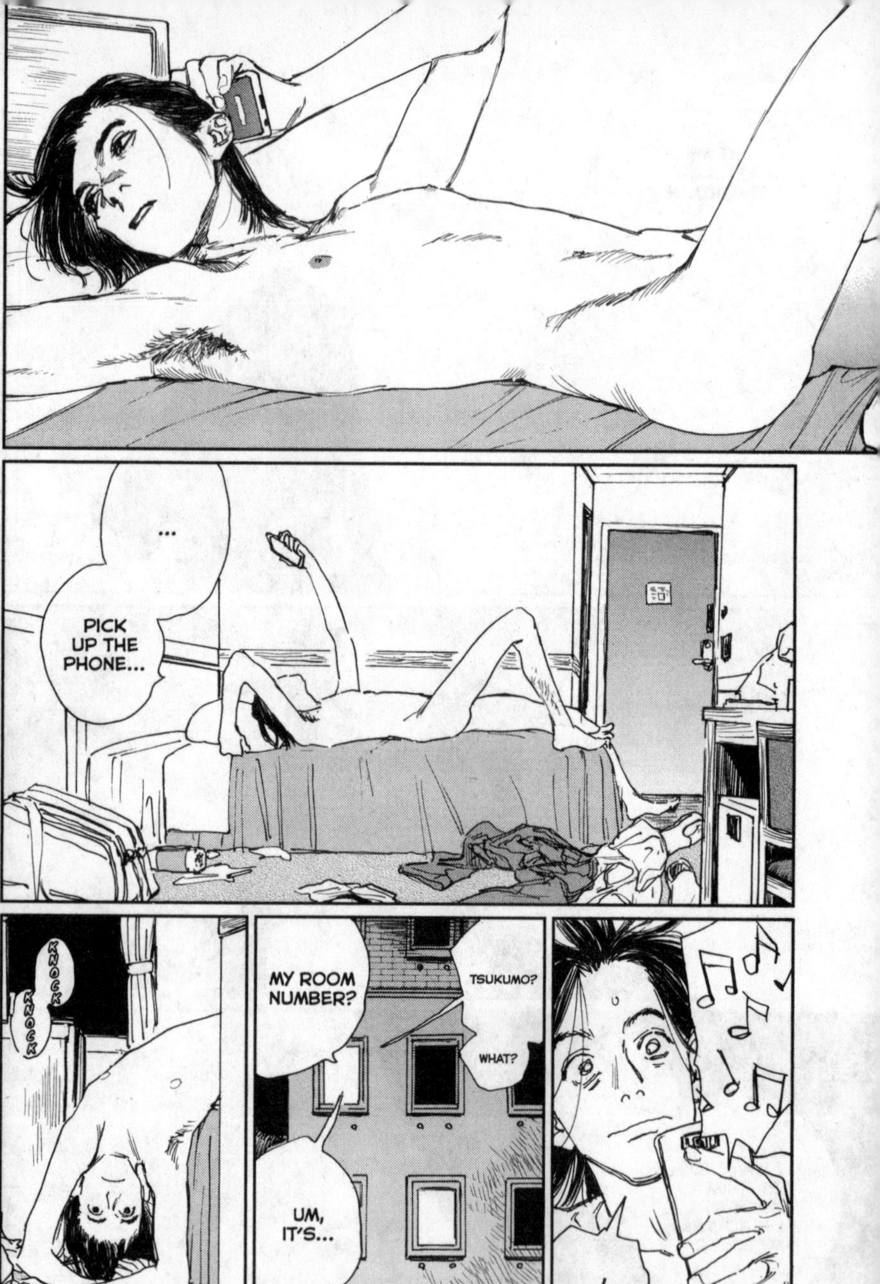
...
PICK UP THE PHONE...
!
TSUKUMO?
MY ROOM NUMBER?
WHAT?
UM, IT'S...
KNOCK KNOCK

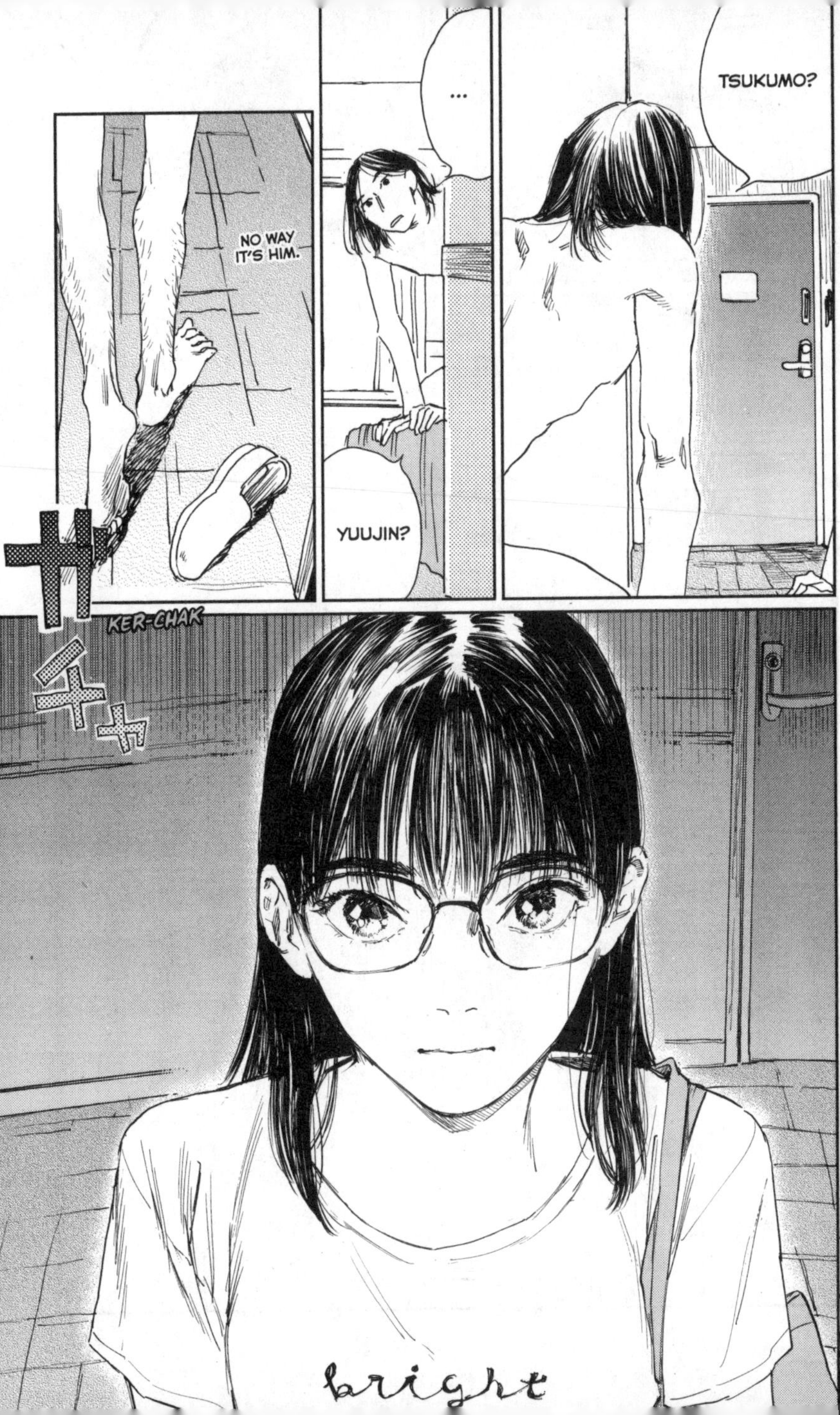
TSUKUMO?
...
YUUJIN?
NO WAY IT'S HIM.
KER-CHAK
bright

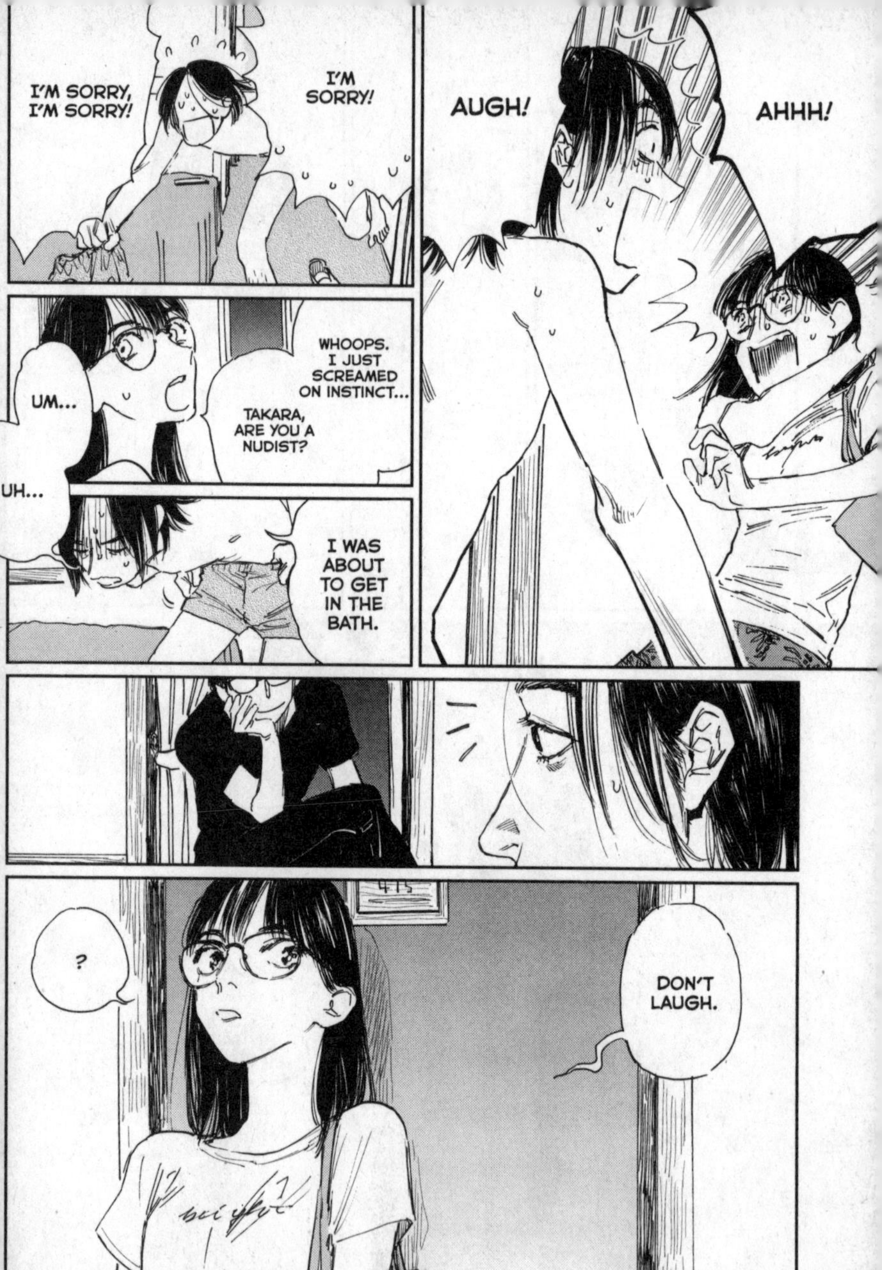
AHHH!
AUGH!
I'M SORRY!
I'M SORRY, I'M SORRY!
WHOOPS. I JUST SCREAMED ON INSTINCT...
TAKARA, ARE YOU A NUDIST?
UM...
I WAS ABOUT TO GET IN THE BATH.
UH...
DON'T LAUGH.
?

DOUBLE

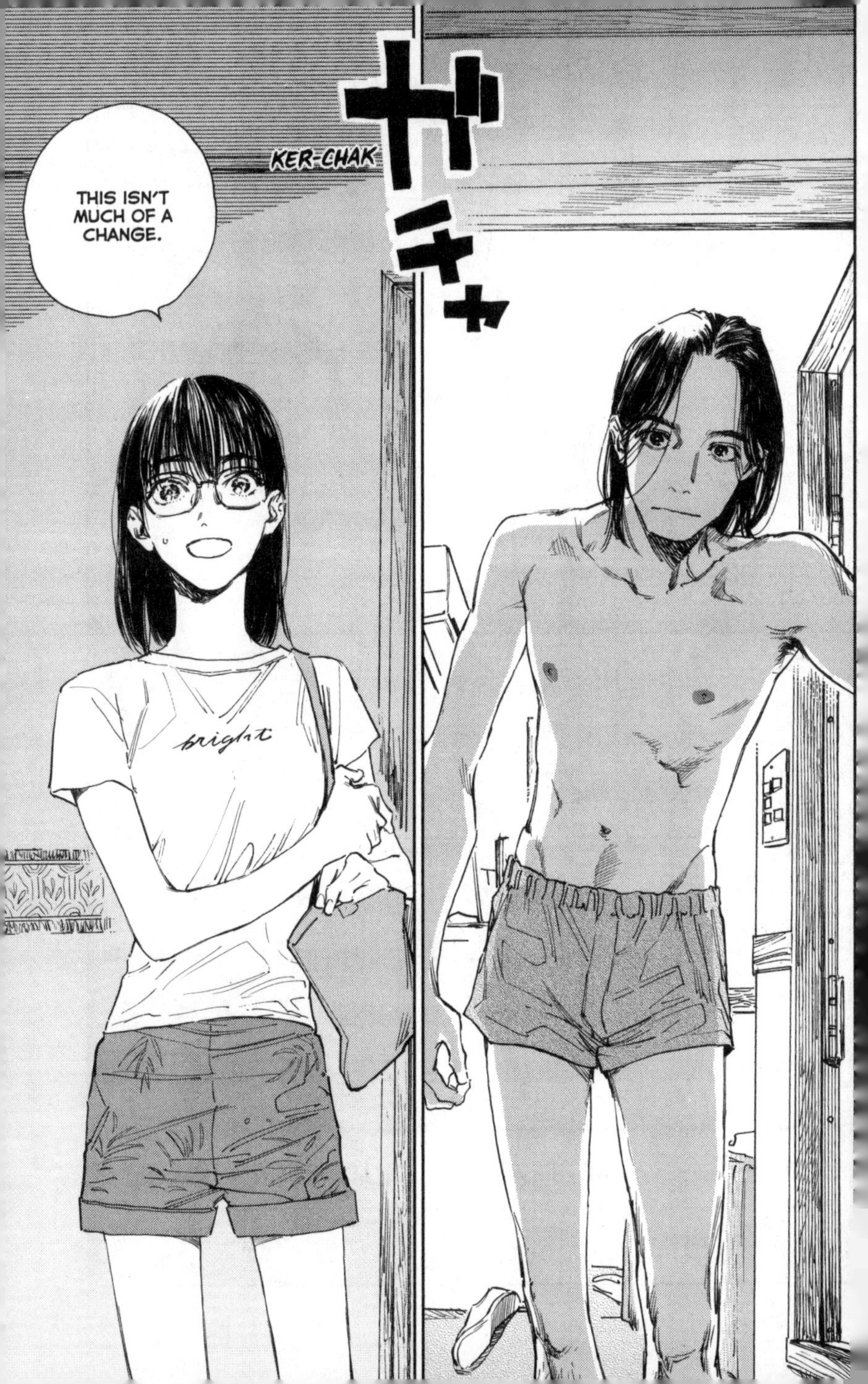
ガチャ
KER-CHAK
THIS ISN'T MUCH OF A CHANGE.
bright

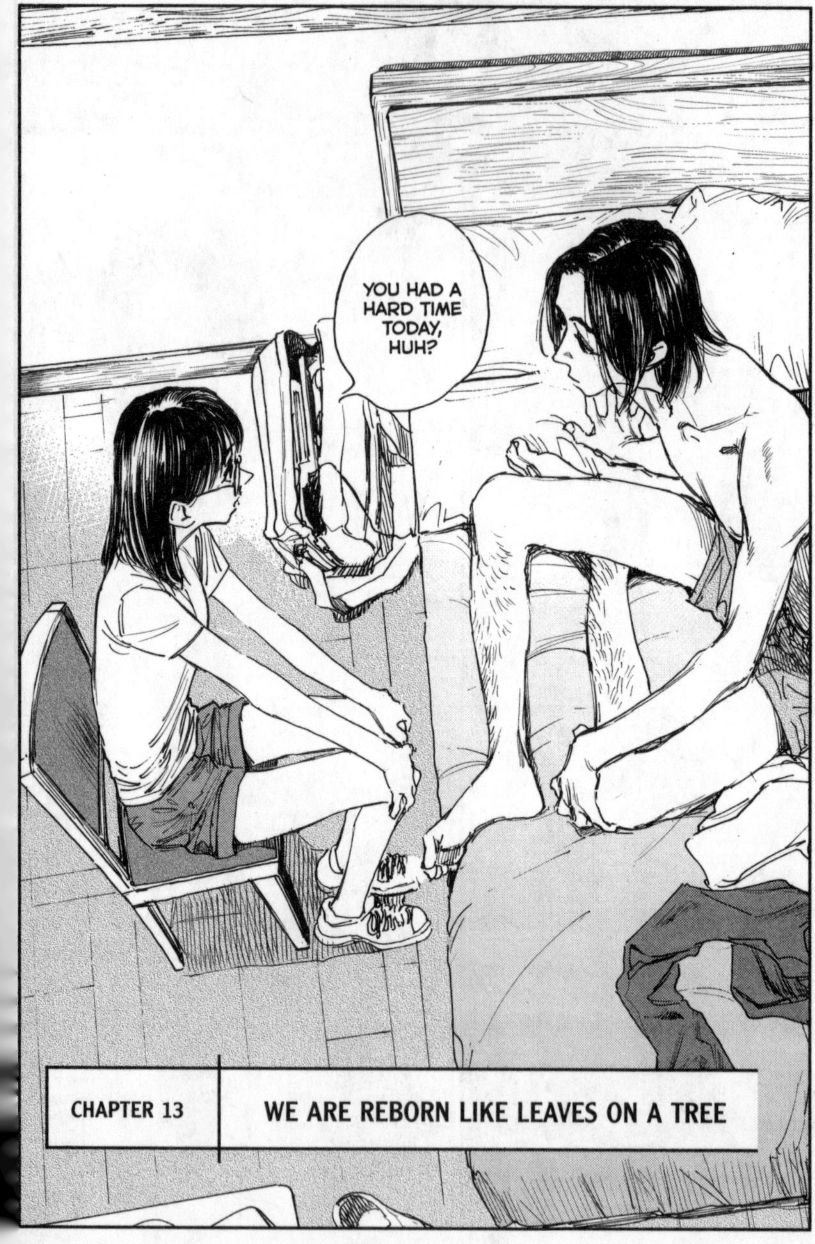
YOU HAD A HARD TIME TODAY, HUH?
CHAPTER 13
WE ARE REBORN LIKE LEAVES ON A TREE

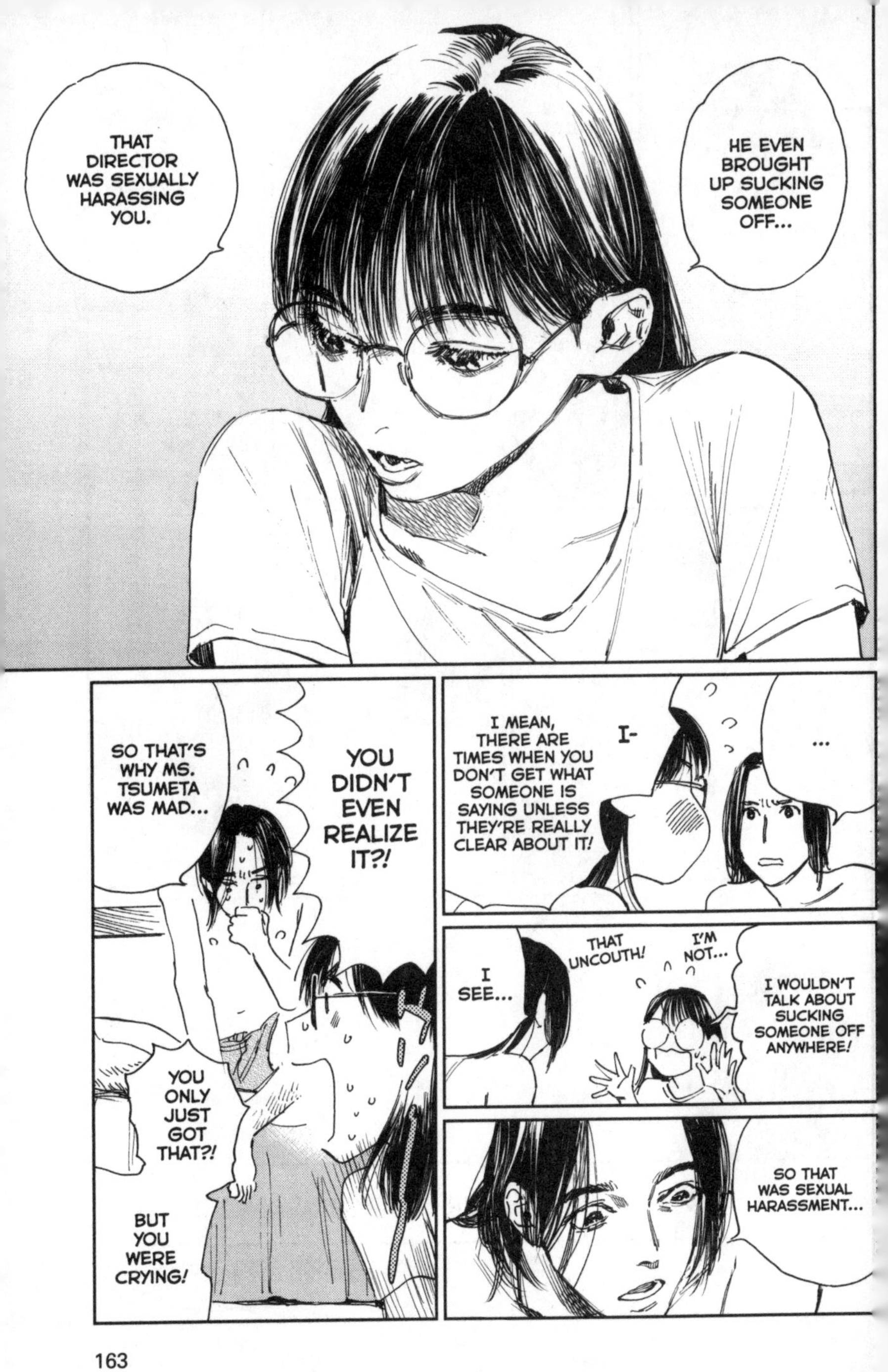
HE EVEN BROUGHT UP SUCKING SOMEONE OFF...
THAT DIRECTOR WAS SEXUALLY HARASSING YOU.
...
I-
I MEAN, THERE ARE TIMES WHEN YOU DON'T GET WHAT SOMEONE IS SAYING UNLESS THEY'RE REALLY CLEAR ABOUT IT!
I WOULDN'T TALK ABOUT SUCKING SOMEONE OFF ANYWHERE!
I'M NOT...
THAT UNCOUTH!
I SEE...
SO THAT WAS SEXUAL HARASSMENT...
YOU DIDN'T EVEN REALIZE IT?!
SO THAT'S WHY MS. TSUMETA WAS MAD...
YOU ONLY JUST GOT THAT?!
BUT YOU WERE CRYING!

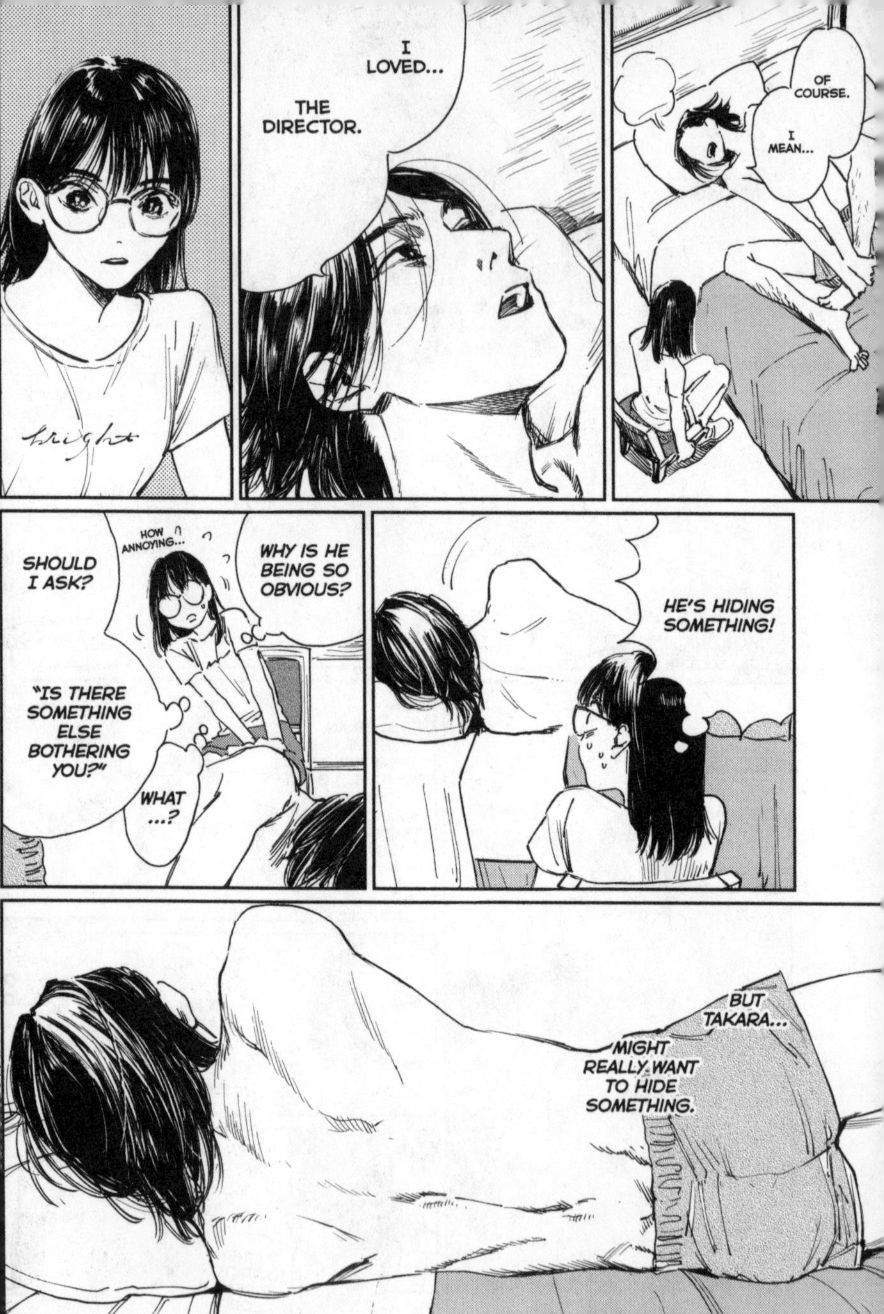
OF COURSE.
I MEAN...
I LOVED...
THE DIRECTOR.
bright
HE'S HIDING SOMETHING!
WHY IS HE BEING SO OBVIOUS?
HOW ANNOYING...
SHOULD I ASK?
"IS THERE SOMETHING ELSE BOTHERING YOU?"
WHAT ...?
BUT TAKARA...
MIGHT REALLY WANT TO HIDE SOMETHING.

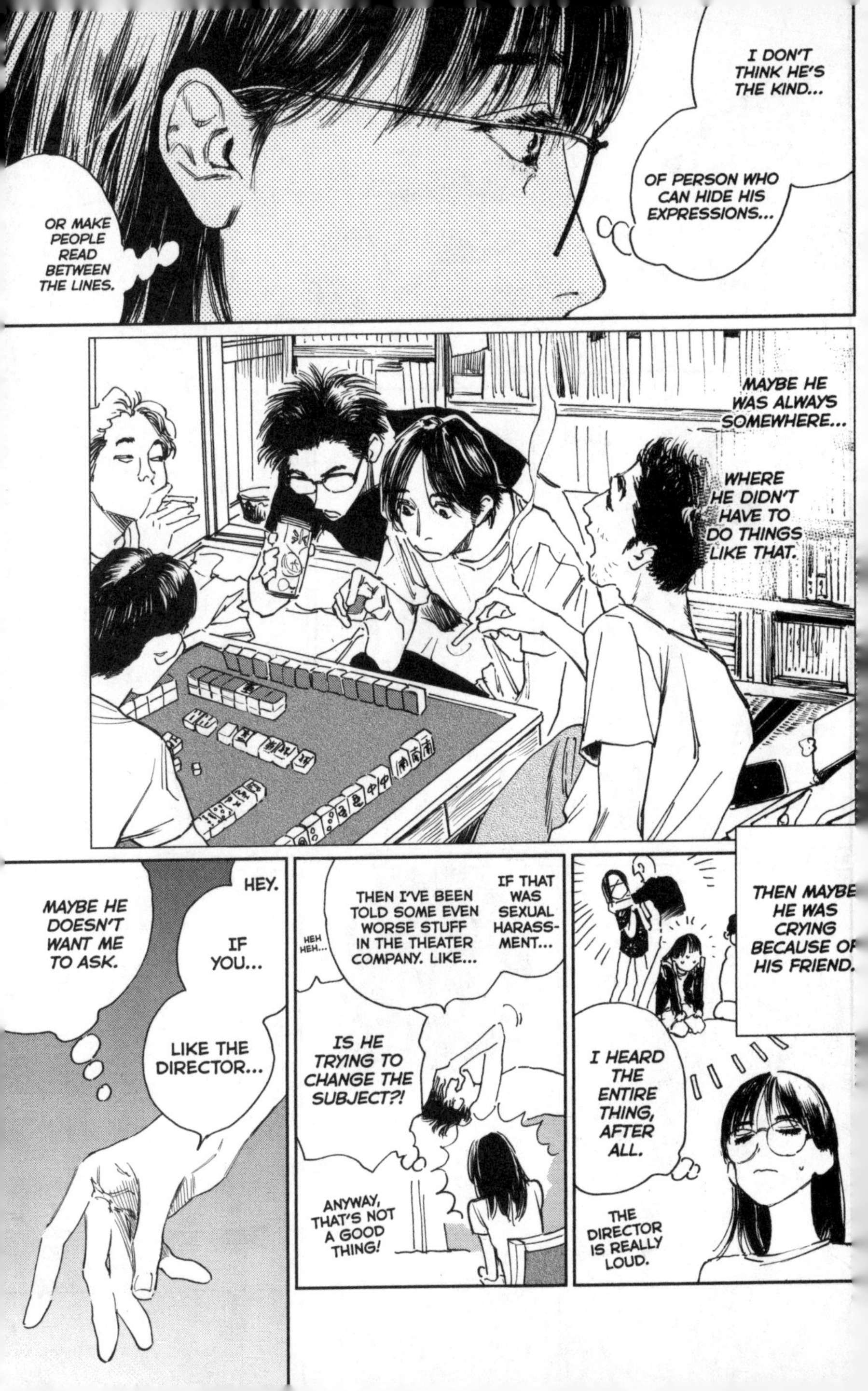
I DON'T THINK HE'S THE KIND...
OF PERSON WHO CAN HIDE HIS EXPRESSIONS...
OR MAKE PEOPLE READ BETWEEN THE LINES.
MAYBE HE WAS ALWAYS SOMEWHERE...
WHERE HE DIDN'T HAVE TO DO THINGS LIKE THAT.
THEN MAYBE HE WAS CRYING BECAUSE OF HIS FRIEND.
I HEARD THE ENTIRE THING, AFTER ALL.
THE DIRECTOR IS REALLY LOUD.
IF THAT WAS SEXUAL HARASSMENT...
THEN I'VE BEEN TOLD SOME EVEN WORSE STUFF IN THE THEATER COMPANY. LIKE...
HEH HEH...
IS HE TRYING TO CHANGE THE SUBJECT?!
ANYWAY, THAT'S NOT A GOOD THING!
HEY.
IF YOU...
LIKE THE DIRECTOR...
MAYBE HE DOESN'T WANT ME TO ASK.

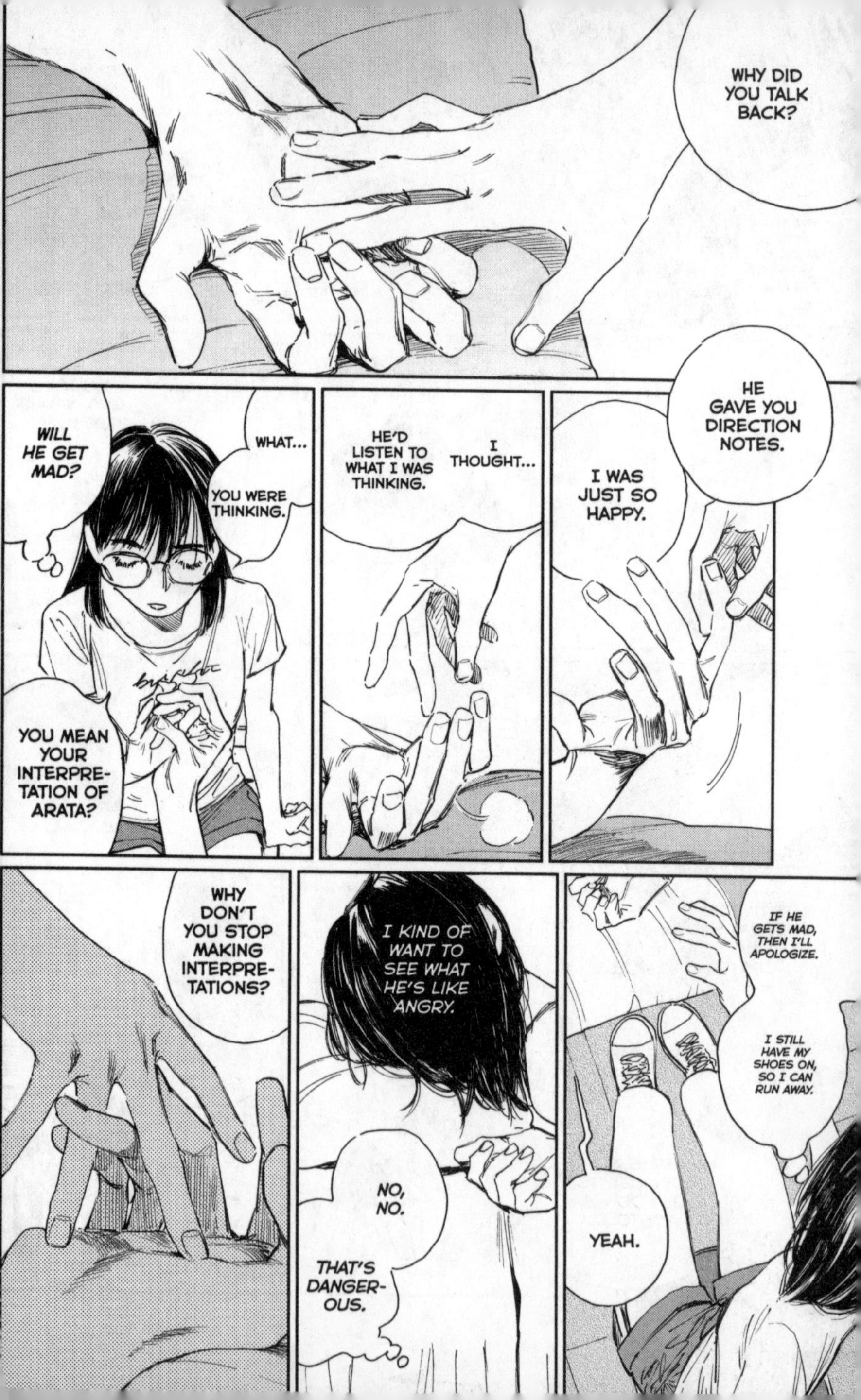
WHY DID YOU TALK BACK?
HE GAVE YOU DIRECTION NOTES.
I WAS JUST SO HAPPY.
I THOUGHT...
HE'D LISTEN TO WHAT I WAS THINKING.
WHAT... YOU WERE THINKING.
WILL HE GET MAD?
YOU MEAN YOUR INTERPRETATION OF ARATA?
IF HE GETS MAD, THEN I'LL APOLOGIZE.
I STILL HAVE MY SHOES ON, SO I CAN RUN AWAY.
YEAH.
I KIND OF WANT TO SEE WHAT HE'S LIKE ANGRY.
NO, NO.
THAT'S DANGEROUS.
WHY DON'T YOU STOP MAKING INTERPRETATIONS?

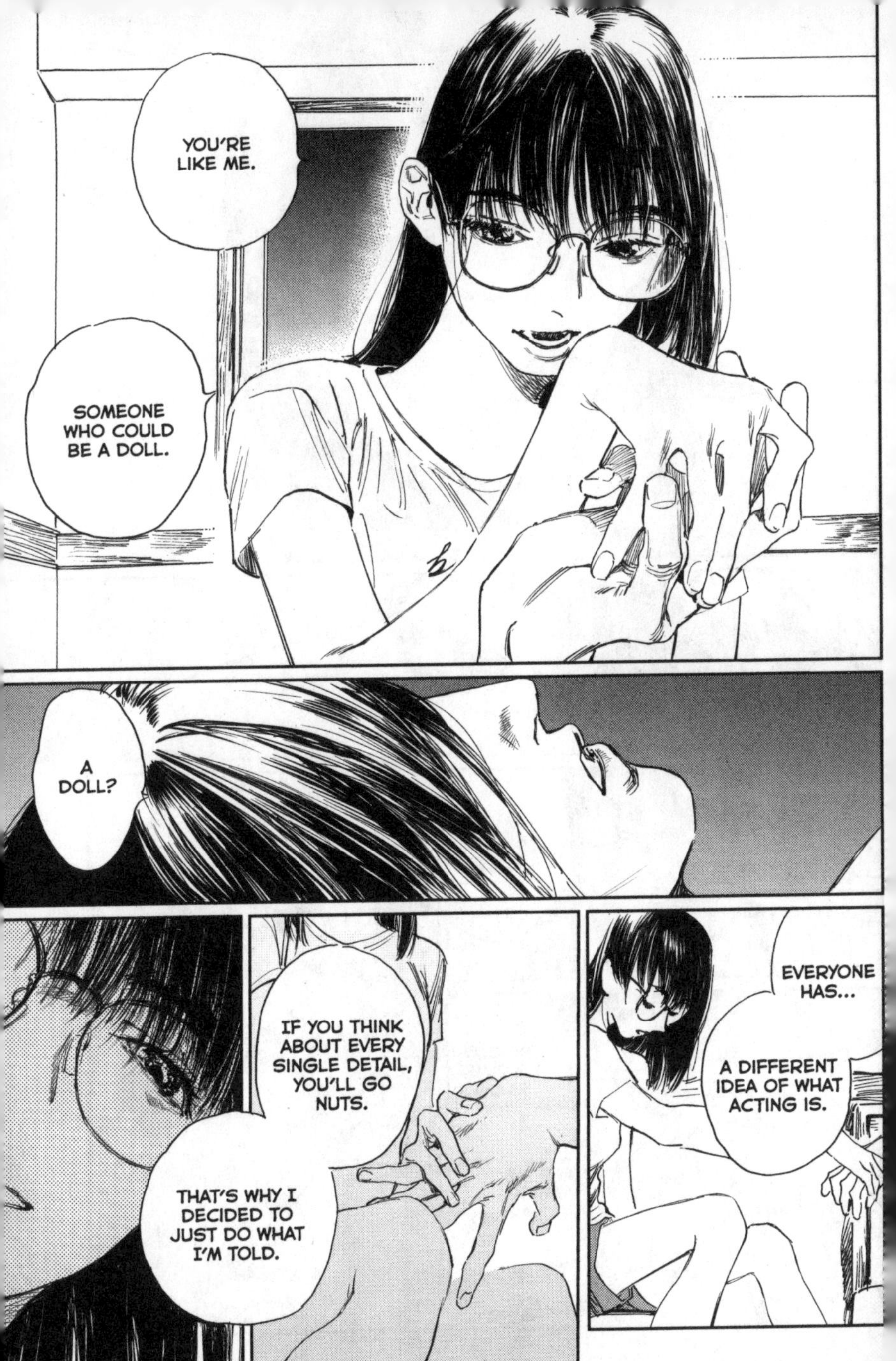
YOU'RE LIKE ME.
SOMEONE WHO COULD BE A DOLL.
A DOLL?
EVERYONE HAS...
A DIFFERENT IDEA OF WHAT ACTING IS.
IF YOU THINK ABOUT EVERY SINGLE DETAIL, YOU'LL GO NUTS.
THAT'S WHY I DECIDED TO JUST DO WHAT I'M TOLD.

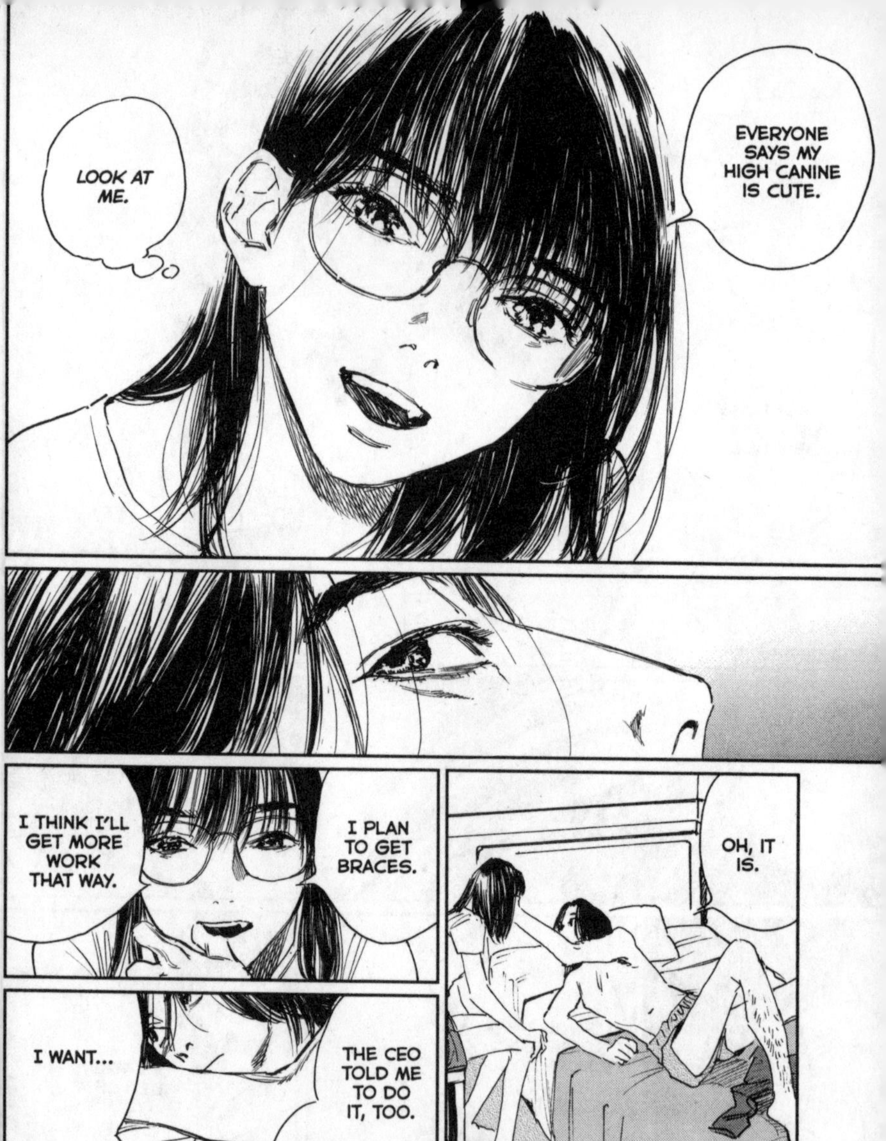
EVERYONE SAYS MY HIGH CANINE IS CUTE.
LOOK AT ME.
OH, IT IS.
I PLAN TO GET BRACES.
I THINK I'LL GET MORE WORK THAT WAY.
THE CEO TOLD ME TO DO IT, TOO.
IT'LL MAKE ME MORE POPULAR.
I WANT...
A LOT OF DIFFERENT PEOPLE TO LIKE ME.

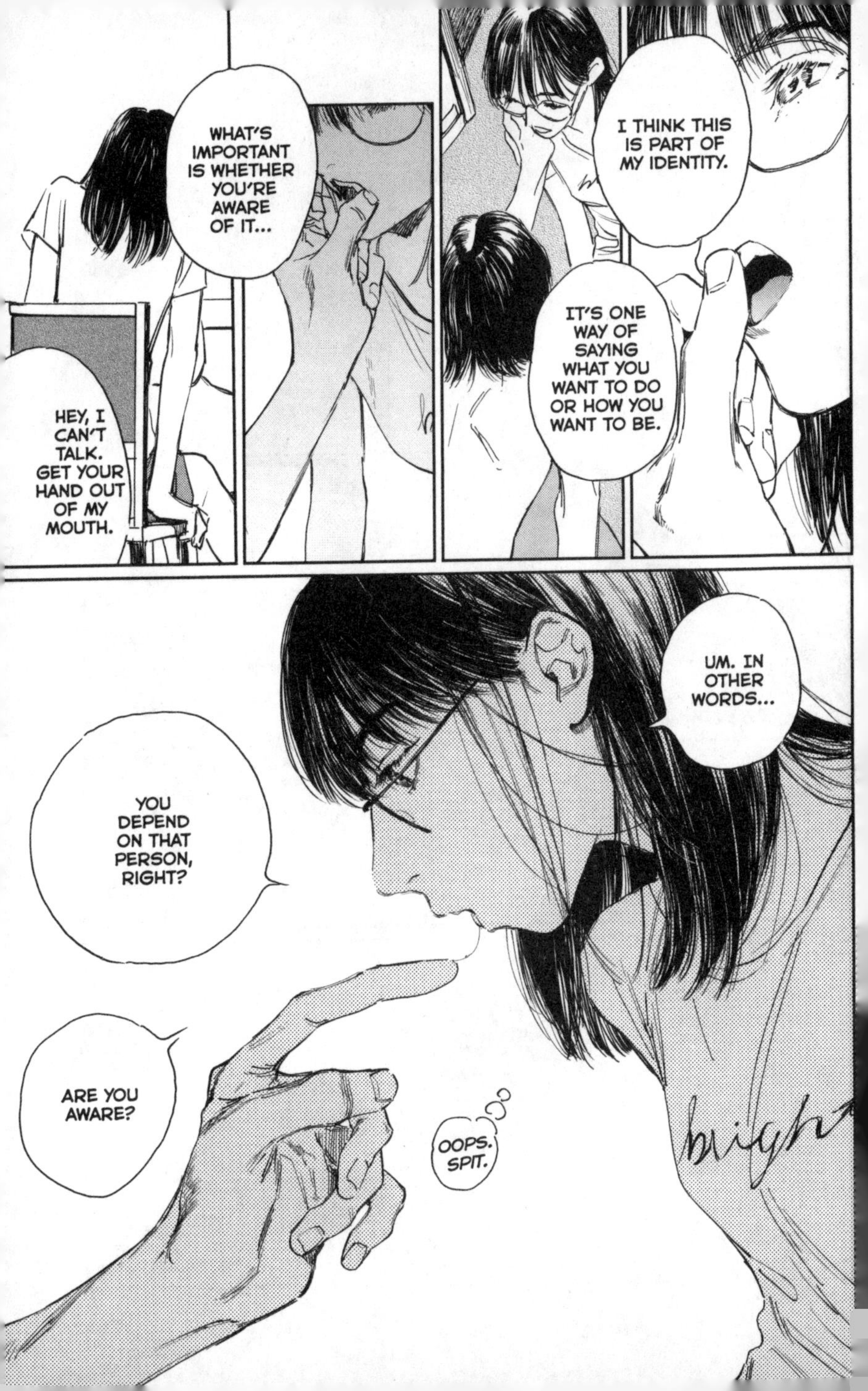
I THINK THIS IS PART OF MY IDENTITY.
IT'S ONE WAY OF SAYING WHAT YOU WANT TO DO OR HOW YOU WANT TO BE.
WHAT'S IMPORTANT IS WHETHER YOU'RE AWARE OF IT...
HEY, I CAN'T TALK. GET YOUR HAND OUT OF MY MOUTH.
UM. IN OTHER WORDS...
YOU DEPEND ON THAT PERSON, RIGHT?
ARE YOU AWARE?
OOPS. SPIT.

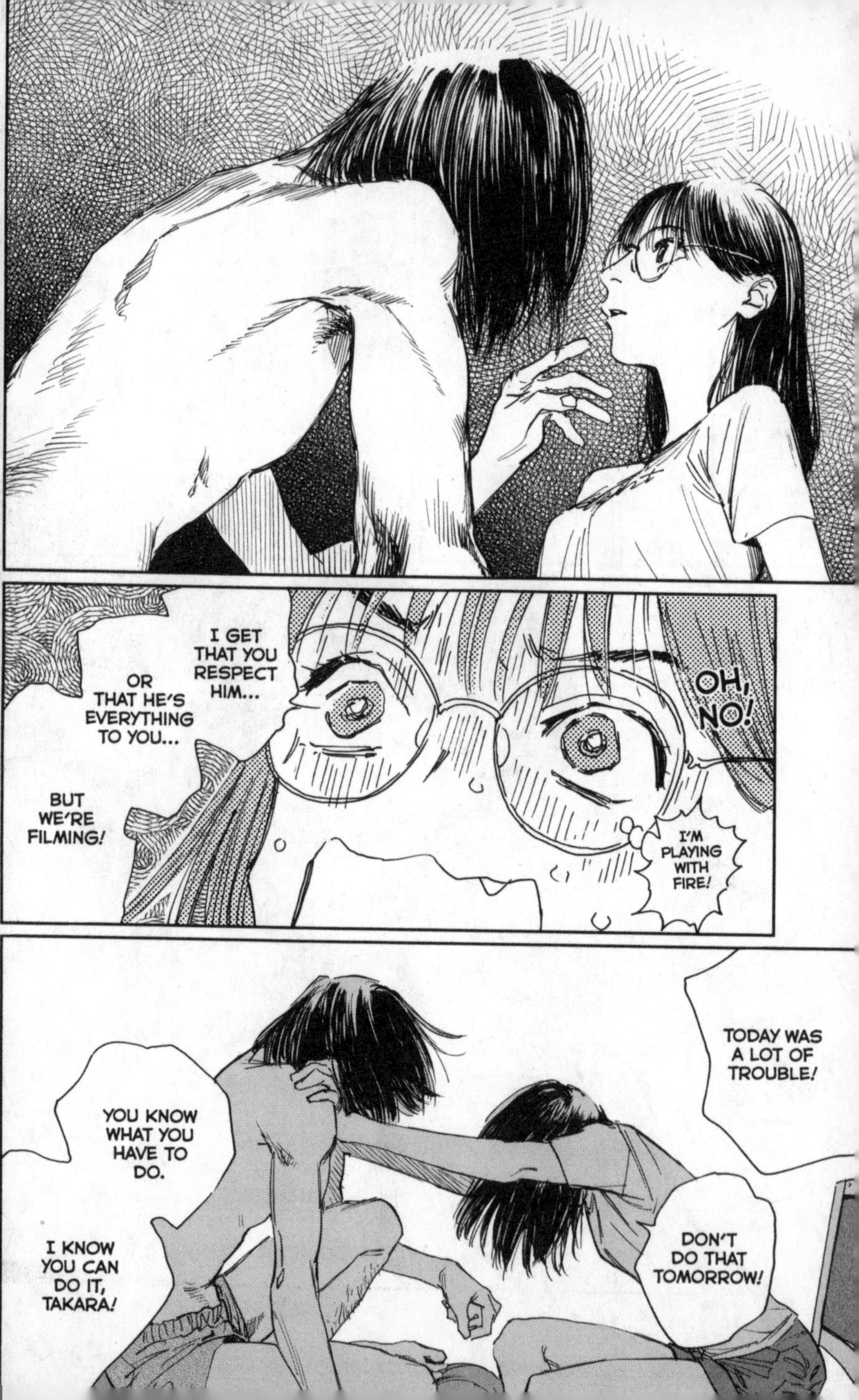
OH, NO!
I'M PLAYING WITH FIRE!
I GET THAT YOU RESPECT HIM...
OR THAT HE'S EVERYTHING TO YOU...
BUT WE'RE FILMING!
TODAY WAS A LOT OF TROUBLE!
DON'T DO THAT TOMORROW!
YOU KNOW WHAT YOU HAVE TO DO.
I KNOW YOU CAN DO IT, TAKARA!

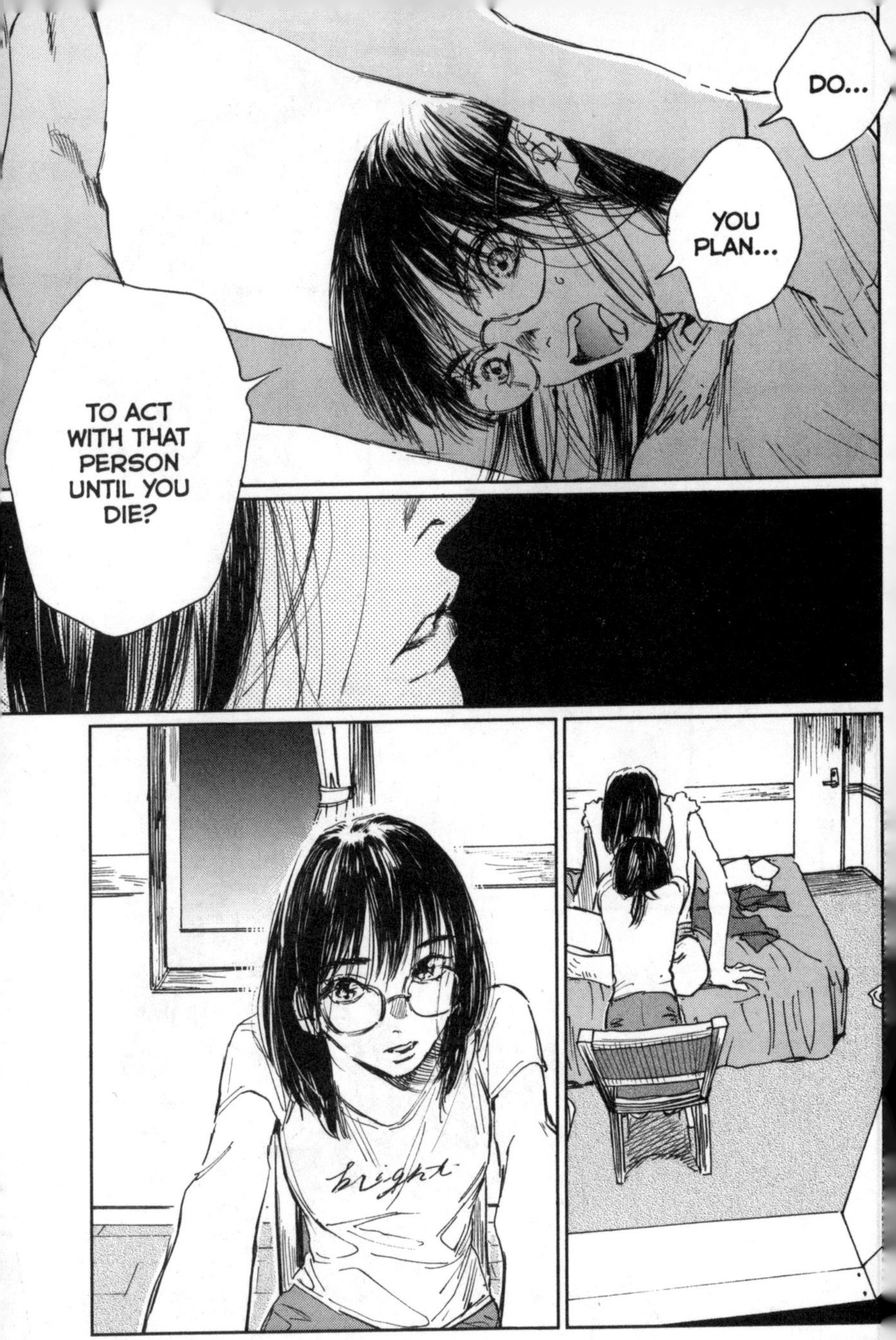
DO...
YOU PLAN...
TO ACT WITH THAT PERSON UNTIL YOU DIE?
bright

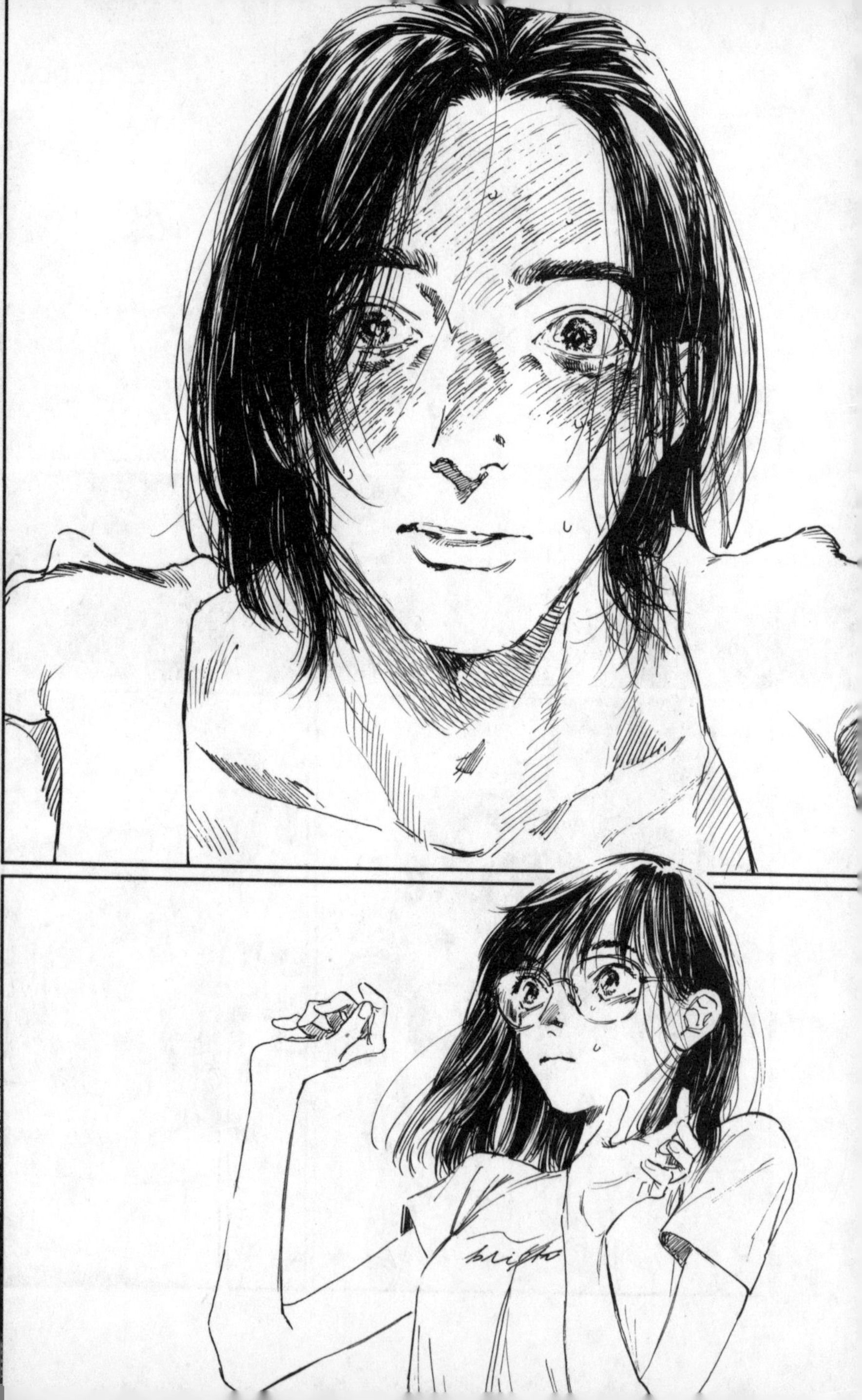

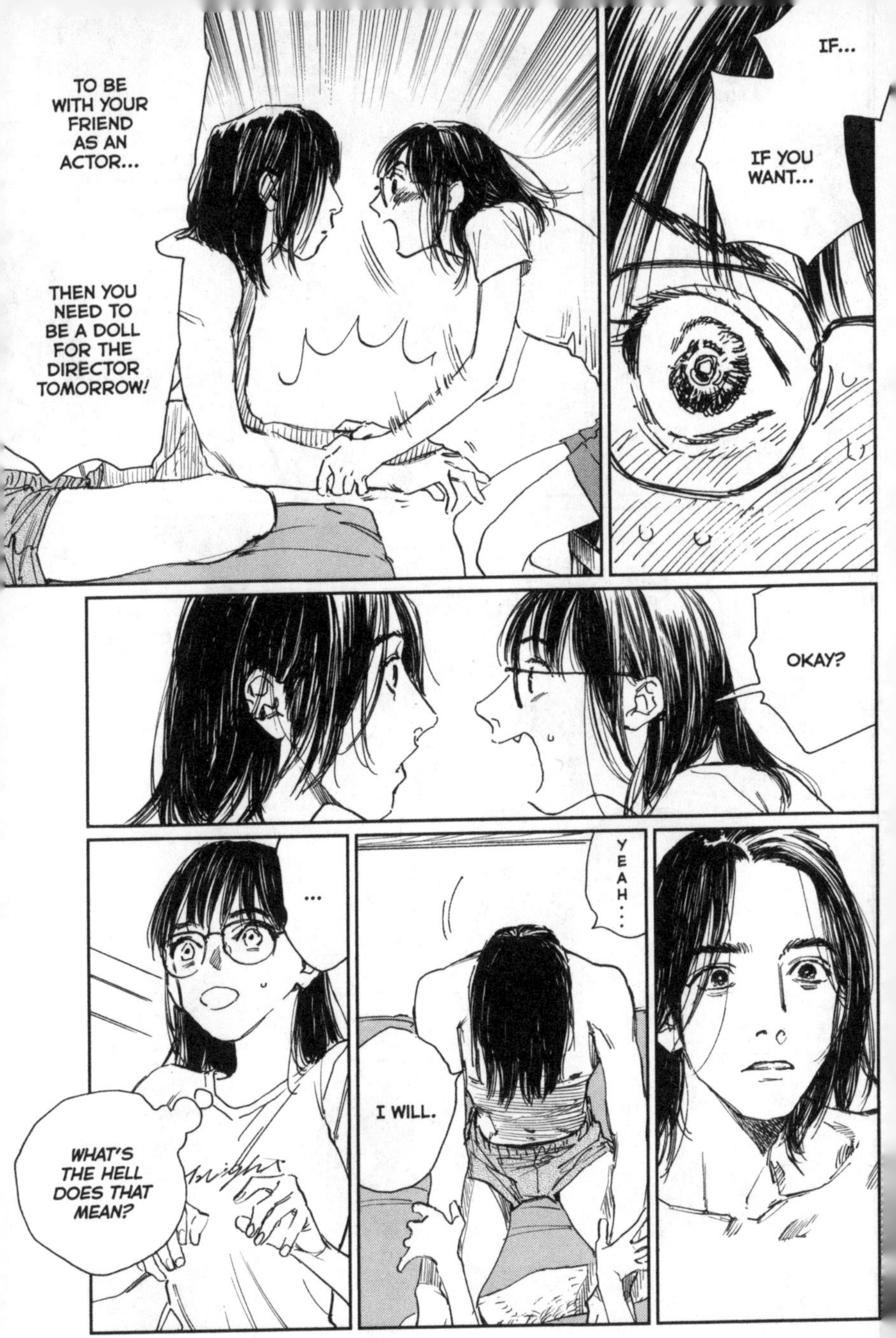
IF...
IF YOU WANT...
TO BE WITH YOUR FRIEND AS AN ACTOR...
THEN YOU NEED TO BE A DOLL FOR THE DIRECTOR TOMORROW!
OKAY?
YEAH...
I WILL.
...
WHAT'S THE HELL DOES THAT MEAN?

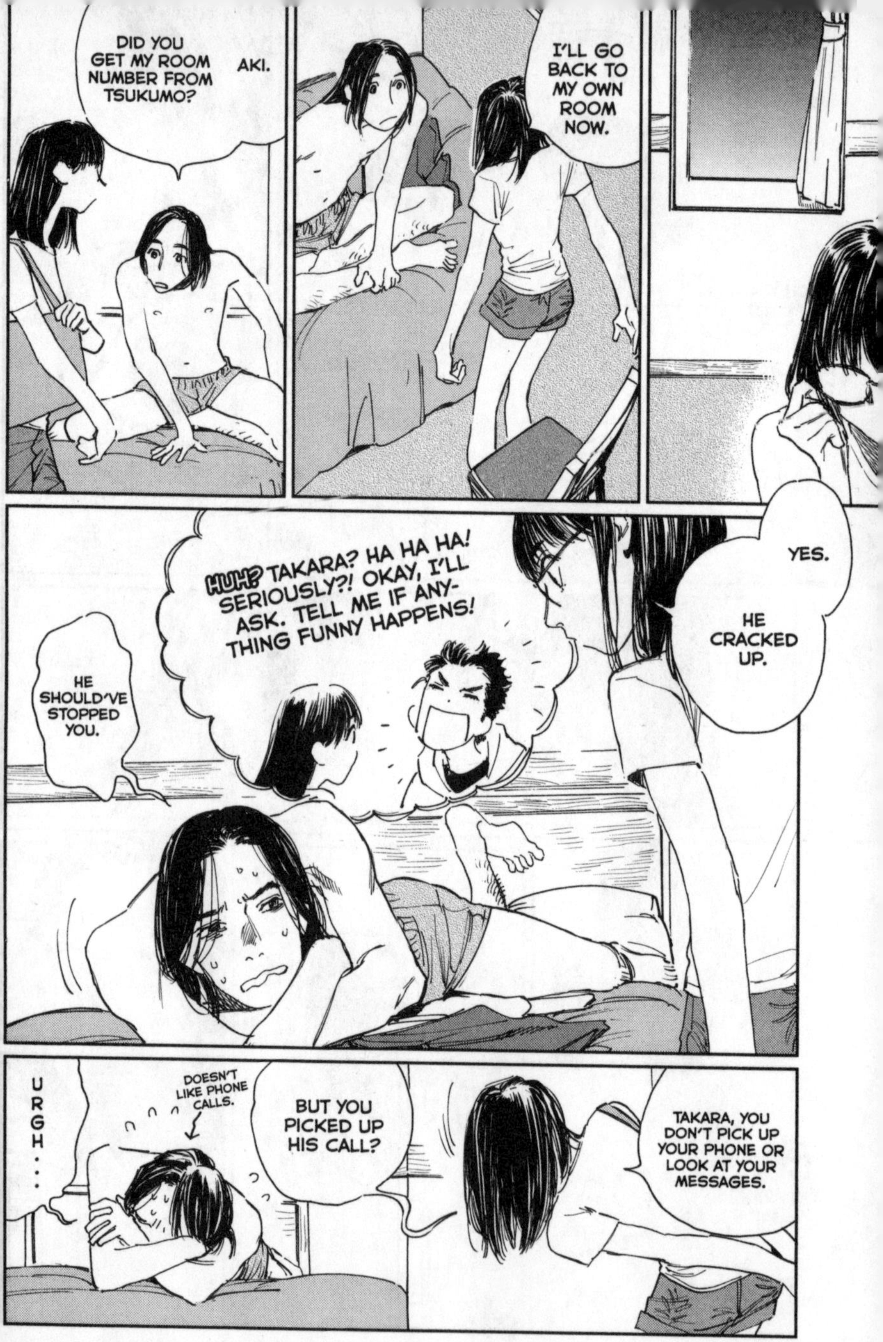

I'LL GO BACK TO MY OWN ROOM NOW.
AKI.
DID YOU GET MY ROOM NUMBER FROM TSUKUMO?
YES.
HE CRACKED UP.
HUH? TAKARA? HA HA HA! SERIOUSLY?! OKAY, I'LL ASK. TELL ME IF ANY-THING FUNNY HAPPENS!
HE SHOULD'VE STOPPED YOU.
TAKARA, YOU DON'T PICK UP YOUR PHONE OR LOOK AT YOUR MESSAGES.
BUT YOU PICKED UP HIS CALL?
DOESN'T LIKE PHONE CALLS.
URGH...

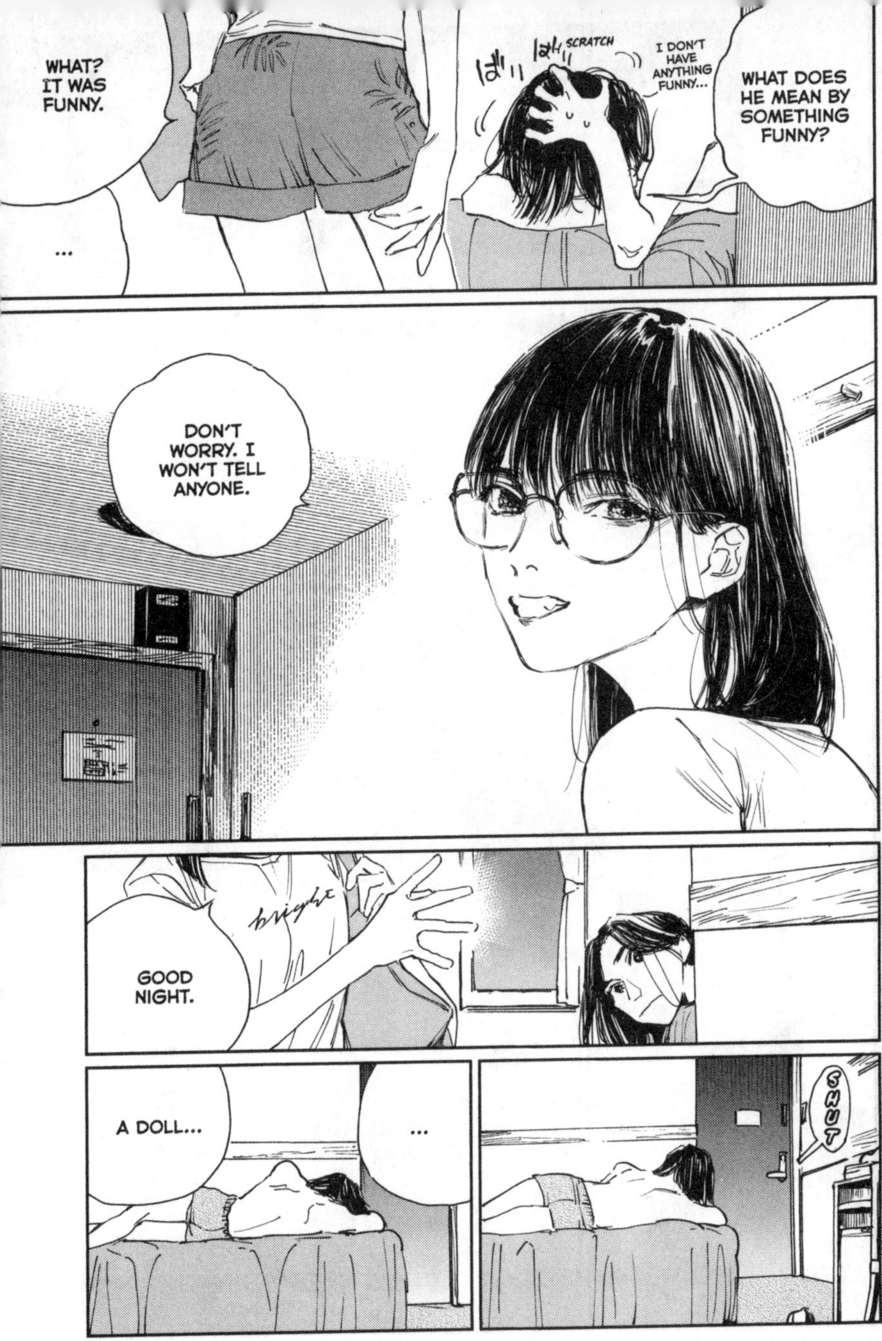
WHAT DOES HE MEAN BY SOMETHING FUNNY?
SCRATCH
I DON'T HAVE ANYTHING FUNNY...
WHAT? IT WAS FUNNY.
...
DON'T WORRY. I WON'T TELL ANYONE.
GOOD NIGHT.
SHUT
...
A DOLL...

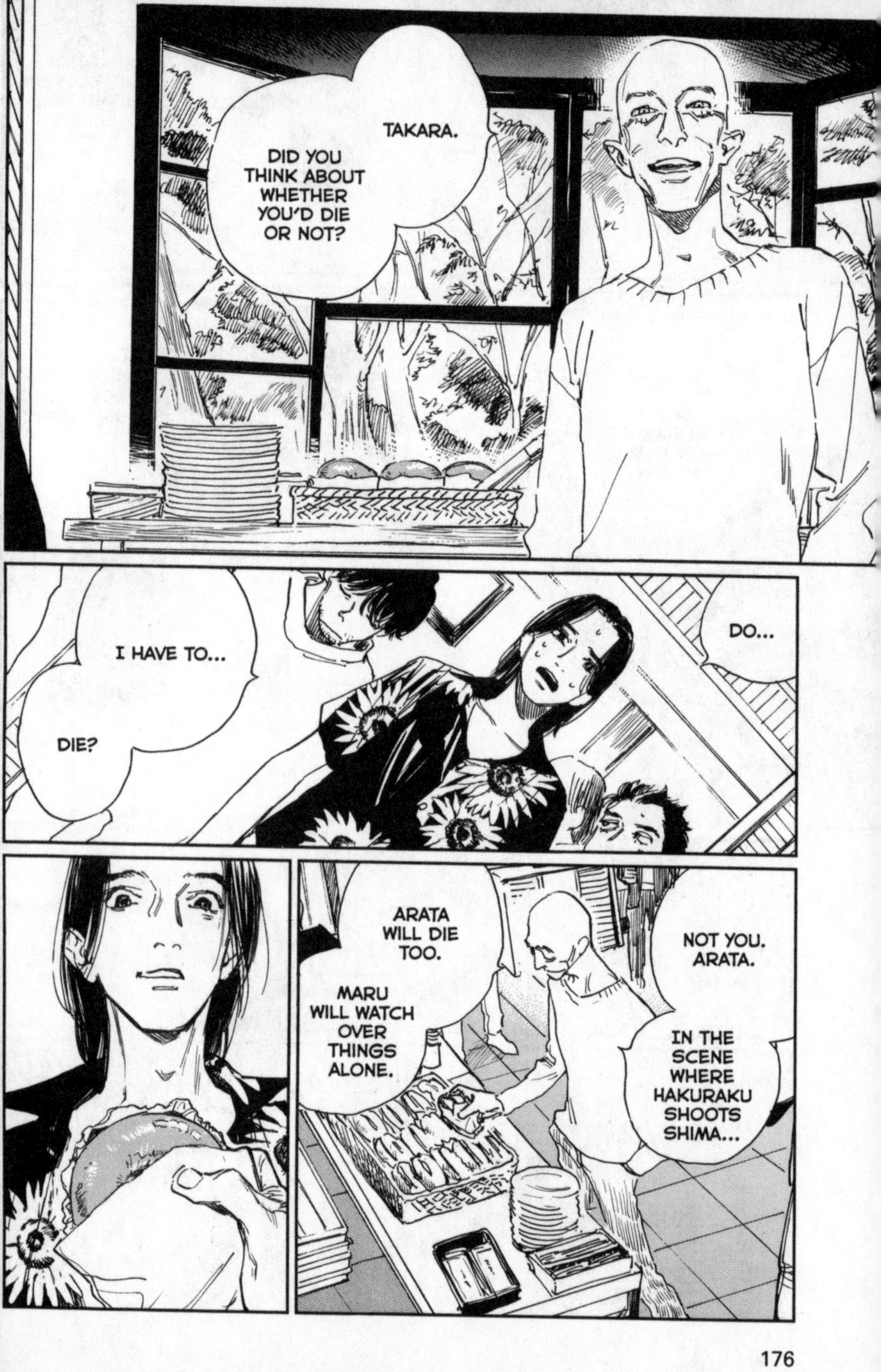
TAKARA.
DID YOU THINK ABOUT WHETHER YOU'D DIE OR NOT?
DO...
I HAVE TO...
DIE?
NOT YOU. ARATA.
IN THE SCENE WHERE HAKURAKU SHOOTS SHIMA...
ARATA WILL DIE TOO.
MARU WILL WATCH OVER THINGS ALONE.

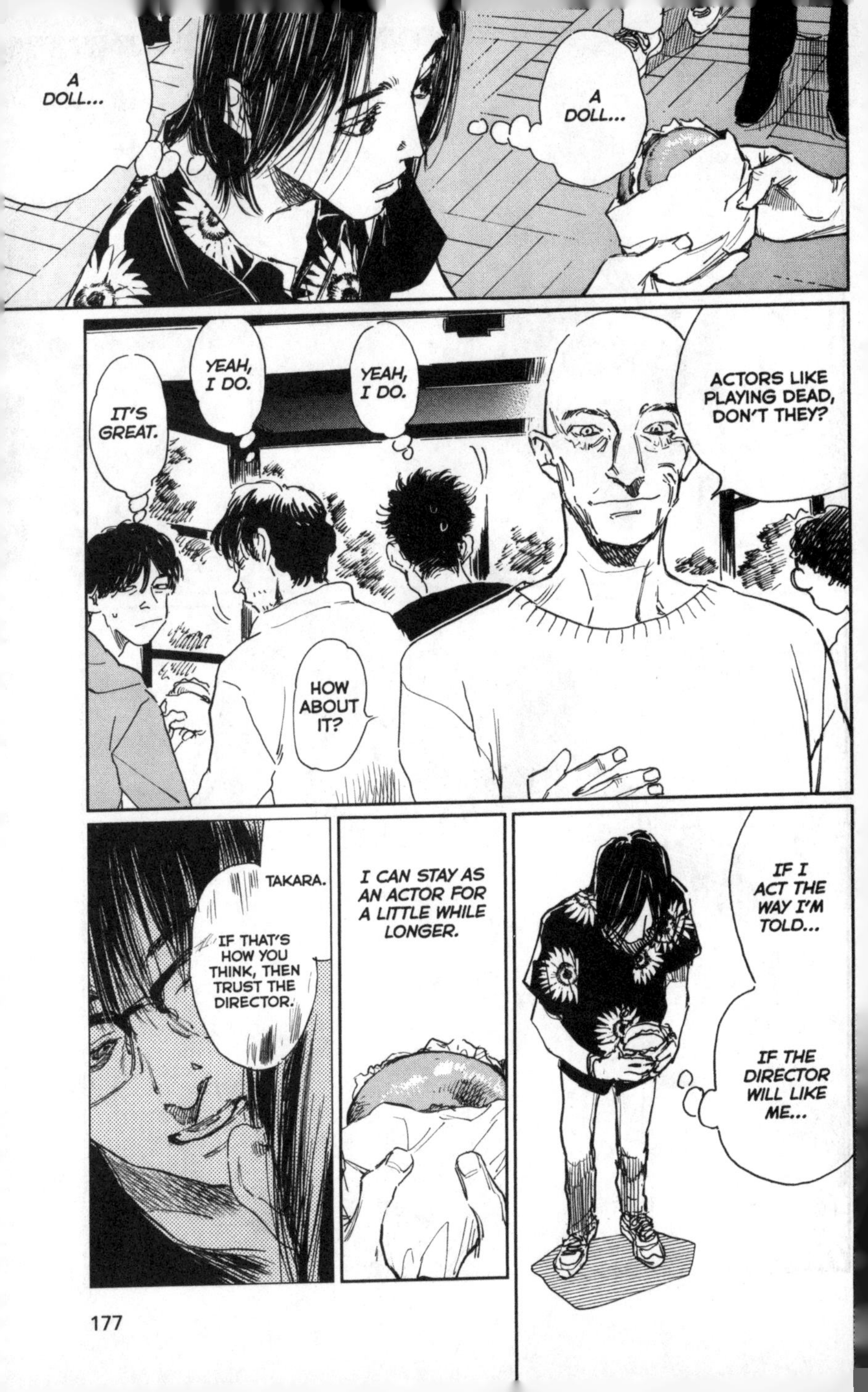
A DOLL...
A DOLL...
ACTORS LIKE PLAYING DEAD, DON'T THEY?
YEAH, I DO.
YEAH, I DO.
IT'S GREAT.
HOW ABOUT IT?
IF I ACT THE WAY I'M TOLD...
IF THE DIRECTOR WILL LIKE ME...
I CAN STAY AS AN ACTOR FOR A LITTLE WHILE LONGER.
TAKARA.
IF THAT'S HOW YOU THINK, THEN TRUST THE DIRECTOR.

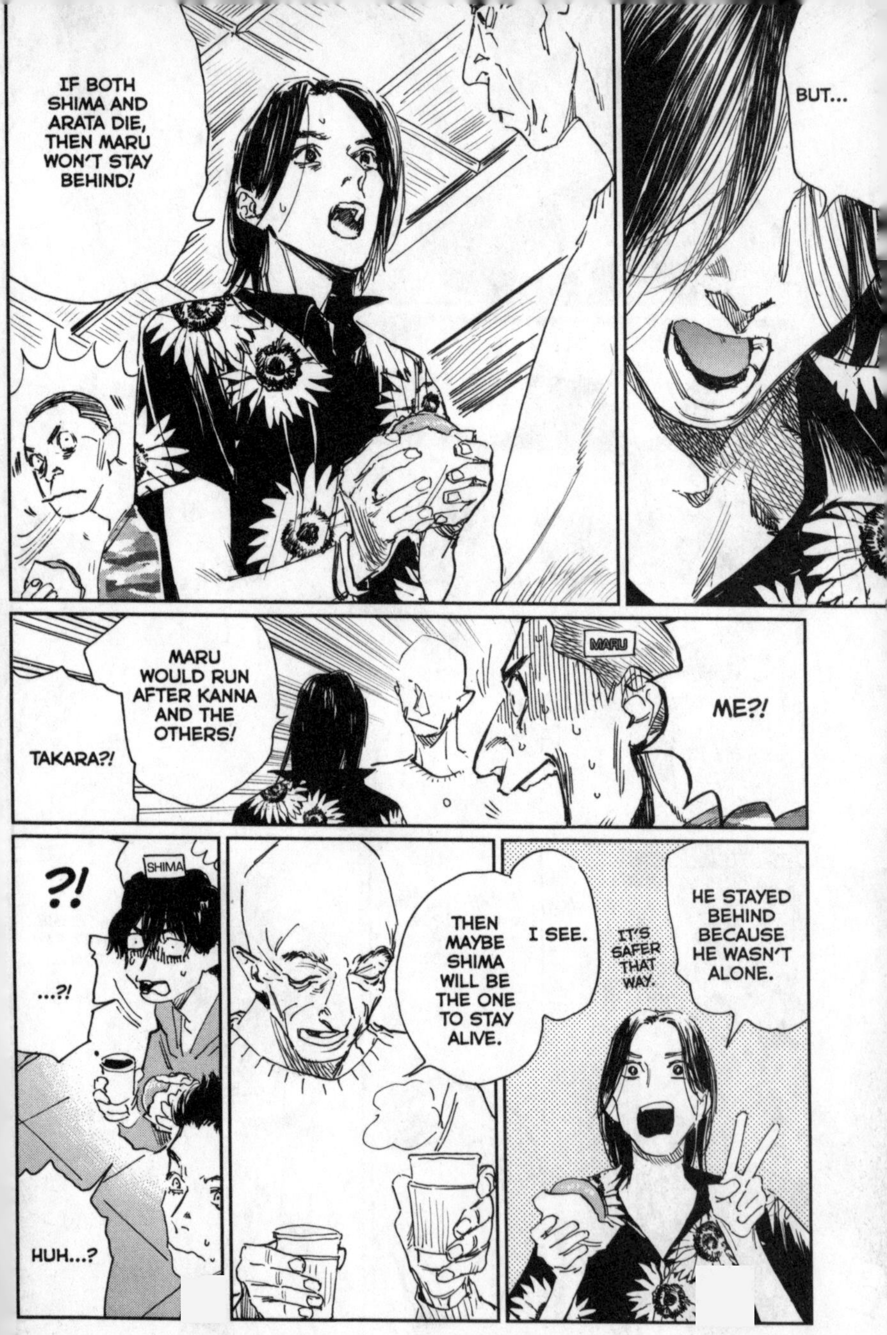
BUT...
IF BOTH SHIMA AND ARATA DIE, THEN MARU WON'T STAY BEHIND!
MARU
ME?!
MARU WOULD RUN AFTER KANNA AND THE OTHERS!
TAKARA?!
HE STAYED BEHIND BECAUSE HE WASN'T ALONE.
IT'S SAFER THAT WAY.
I SEE.
THEN MAYBE SHIMA WILL BE THE ONE TO STAY ALIVE.
SHIMA
?!
...?!
HUH...?

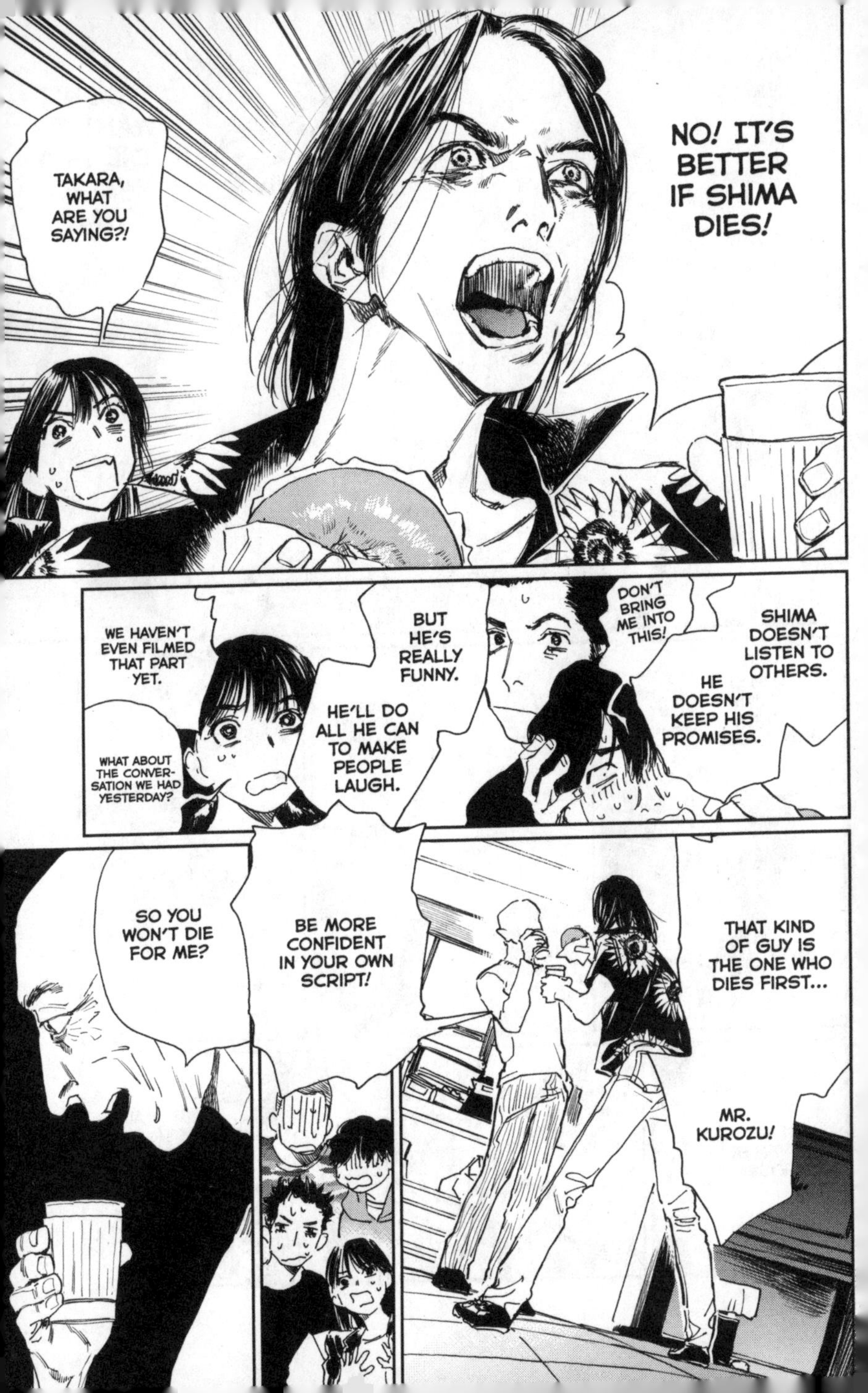
NO! IT'S BETTER IF SHIMA DIES!
TAKARA, WHAT ARE YOU SAYING?!
SHIMA DOESN'T LISTEN TO OTHERS.
HE DOESN'T KEEP HIS PROMISES.
DON'T BRING ME INTO THIS!
BUT HE'S REALLY FUNNY.
HE'LL DO ALL HE CAN TO MAKE PEOPLE LAUGH.
WE HAVEN'T EVEN FILMED THAT PART YET.
WHAT ABOUT THE CONVERSATION WE HAD YESTERDAY?
THAT KIND OF GUY IS THE ONE WHO DIES FIRST...
MR. KUROZU!
BE MORE CONFIDENT IN YOUR OWN SCRIPT!
SO YOU WON'T DIE FOR ME?

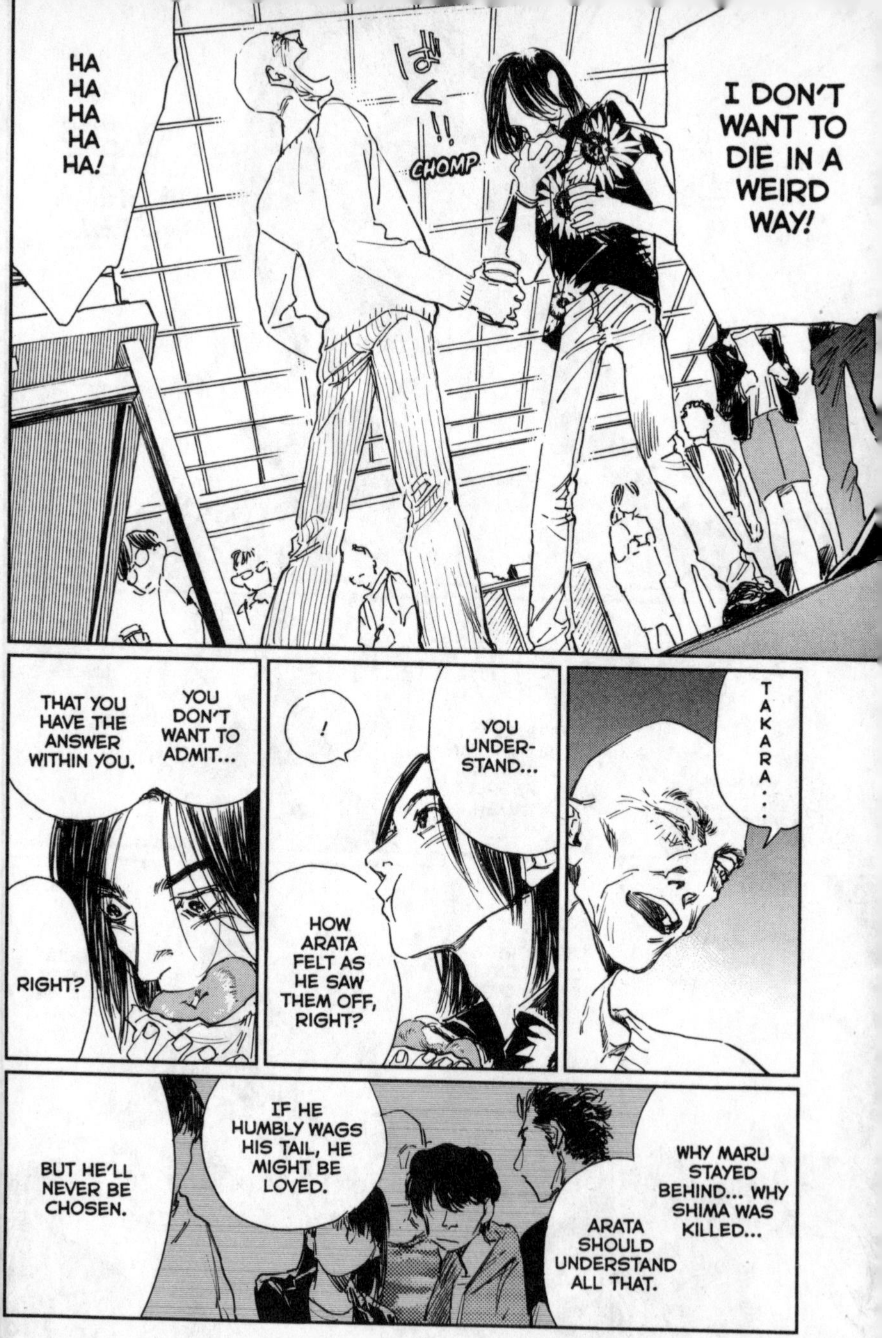
I DON'T WANT TO DIE IN A WEIRD WAY!
ばく!!
CHOMP
HA HA HA HA HA!
TAKARA...
YOU UNDERSTAND...
!
HOW ARATA FELT AS HE SAW THEM OFF, RIGHT?
YOU DON'T WANT TO ADMIT...
THAT YOU HAVE THE ANSWER WITHIN YOU.
RIGHT?
WHY MARU STAYED BEHIND... WHY SHIMA WAS KILLED...
ARATA SHOULD UNDERSTAND ALL THAT.
IF HE HUMBLY WAGS HIS TAIL, HE MIGHT BE LOVED.
BUT HE'LL NEVER BE CHOSEN.

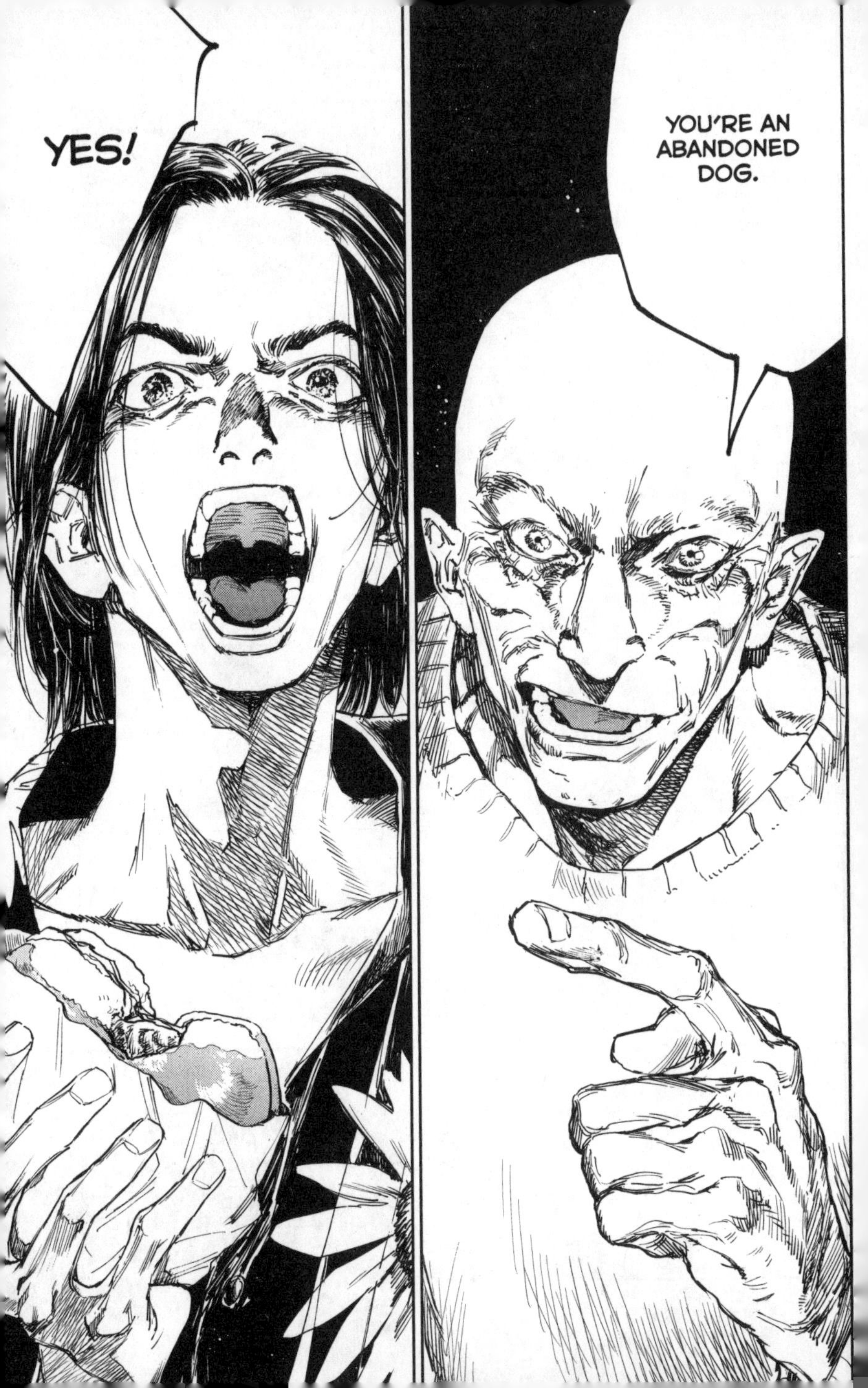
YOU'RE AN ABANDONED DOG.
YES!

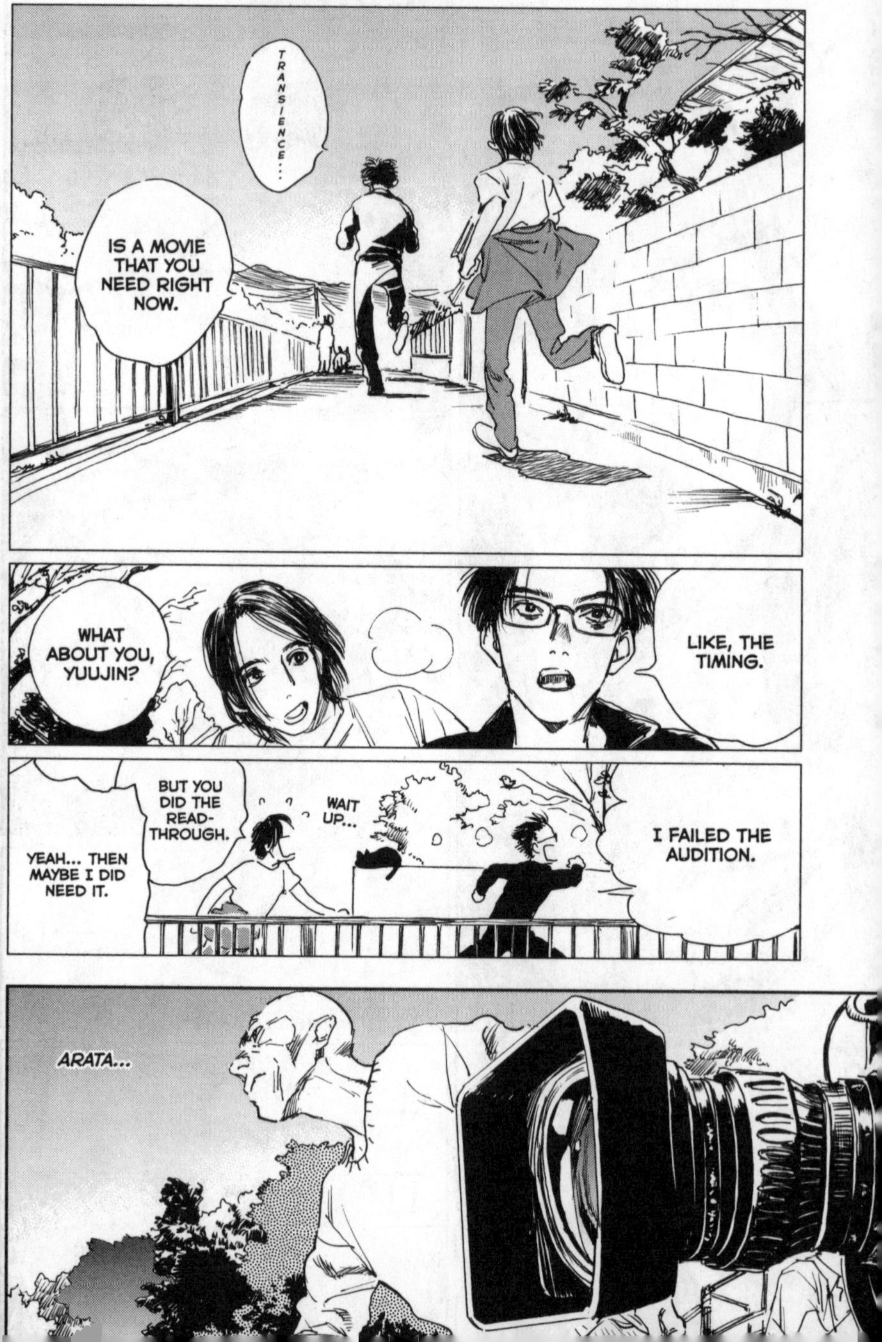
TRANSIENCE...
IS A MOVIE THAT YOU NEED RIGHT NOW.
LIKE, THE TIMING.
WHAT ABOUT YOU, YUUJIN?
I FAILED THE AUDITION.
WAIT UP...
BUT YOU DID THE READ-THROUGH.
YEAH... THEN MAYBE I DID NEED IT.
ARATA...

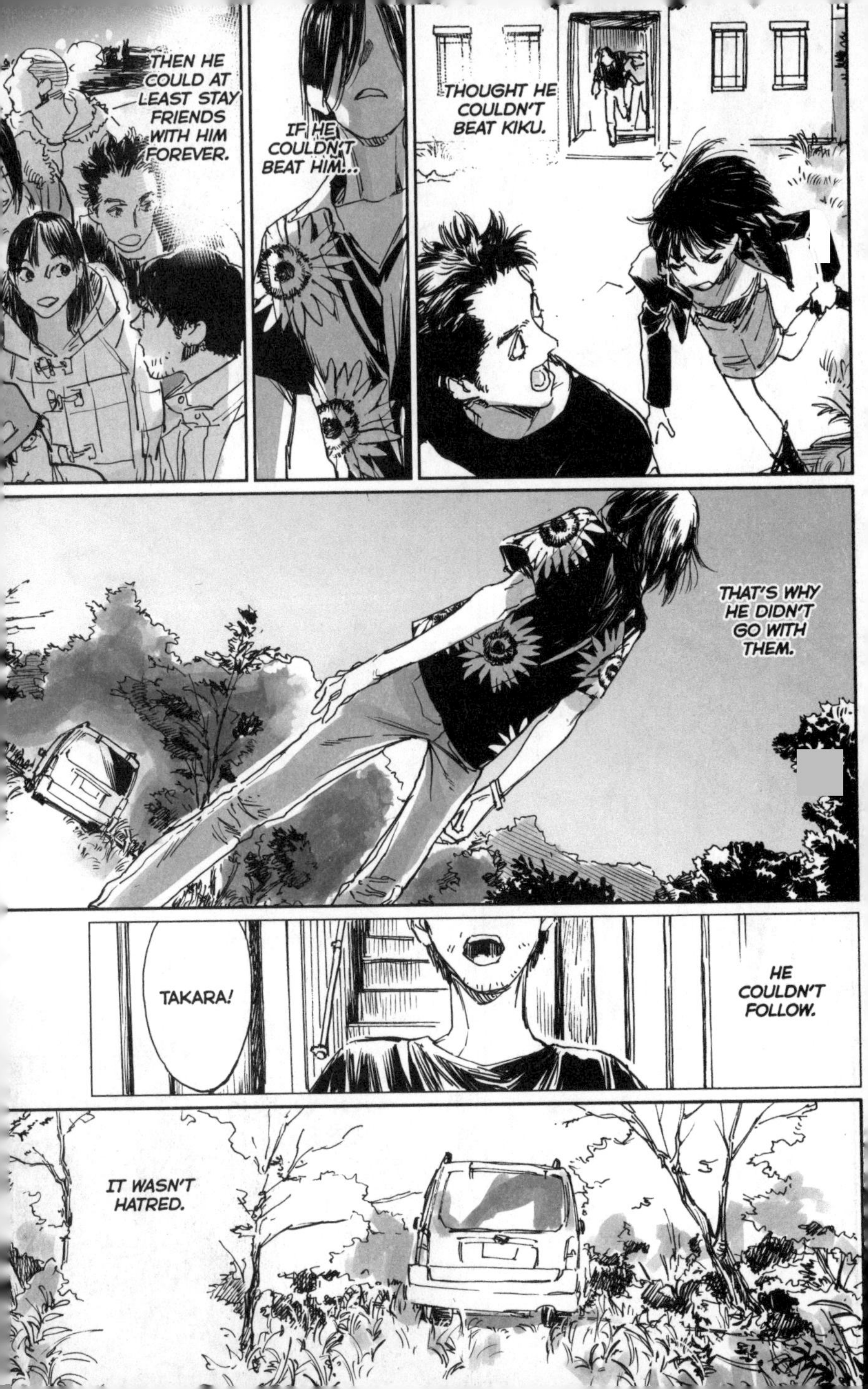

THOUGHT HE COULDN'T BEAT KIKU.
IF HE COULDN'T BEAT HIM...
THEN HE COULD AT LEAST STAY FRIENDS WITH HIM FOREVER.
THAT'S WHY HE DIDN'T GO WITH THEM.
HE COULDN'T FOLLOW.
TAKARA!
IT WASN'T HATRED.

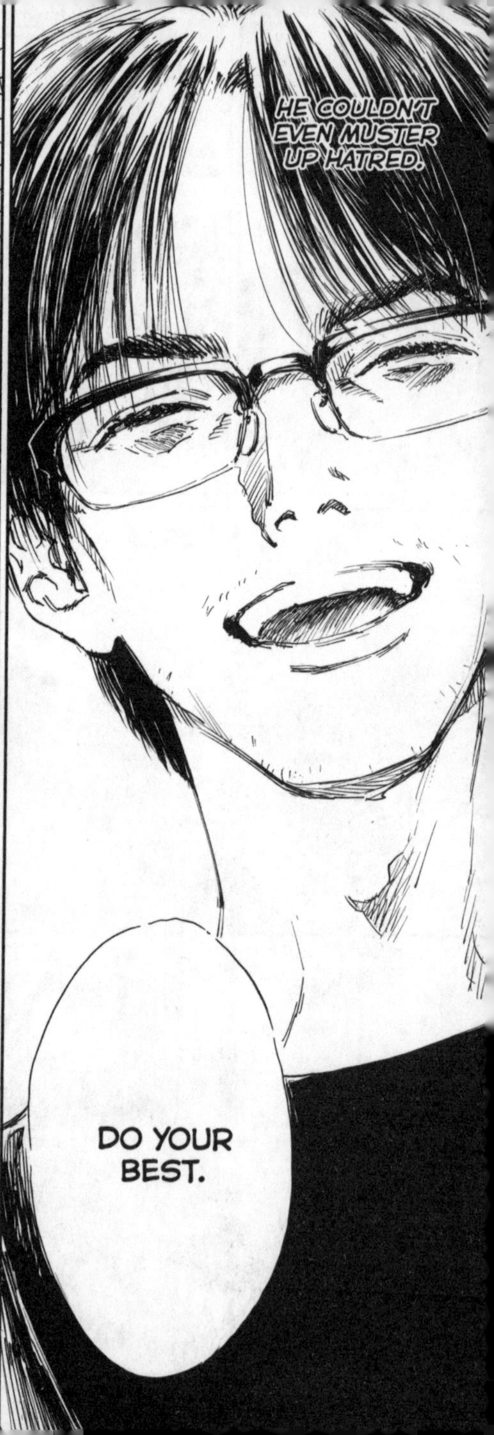
HE COULDN'T EVEN MUSTER UP HATRED.
DO YOUR BEST.
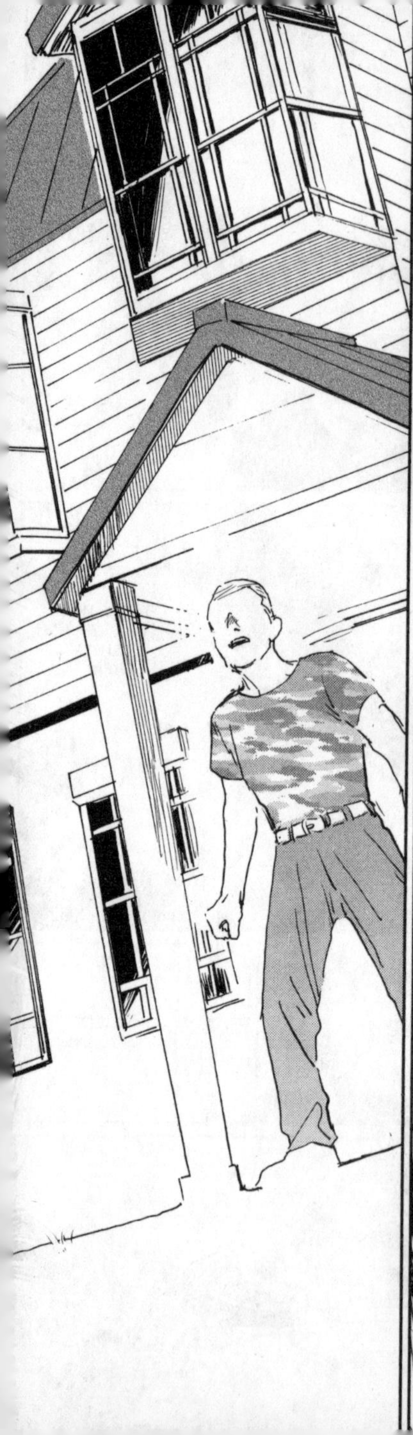

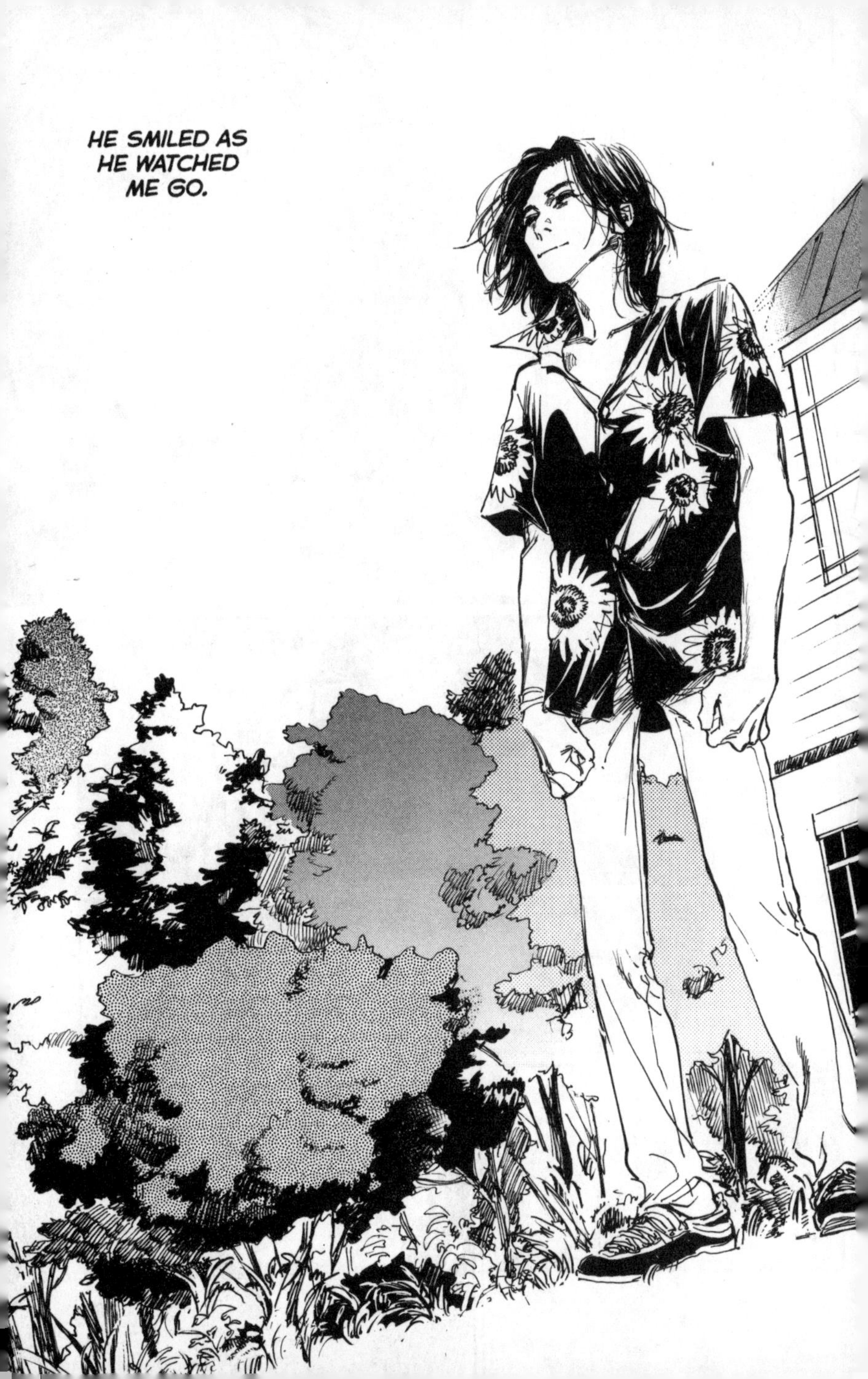
HE SMILED AS HE WATCHED ME GO.

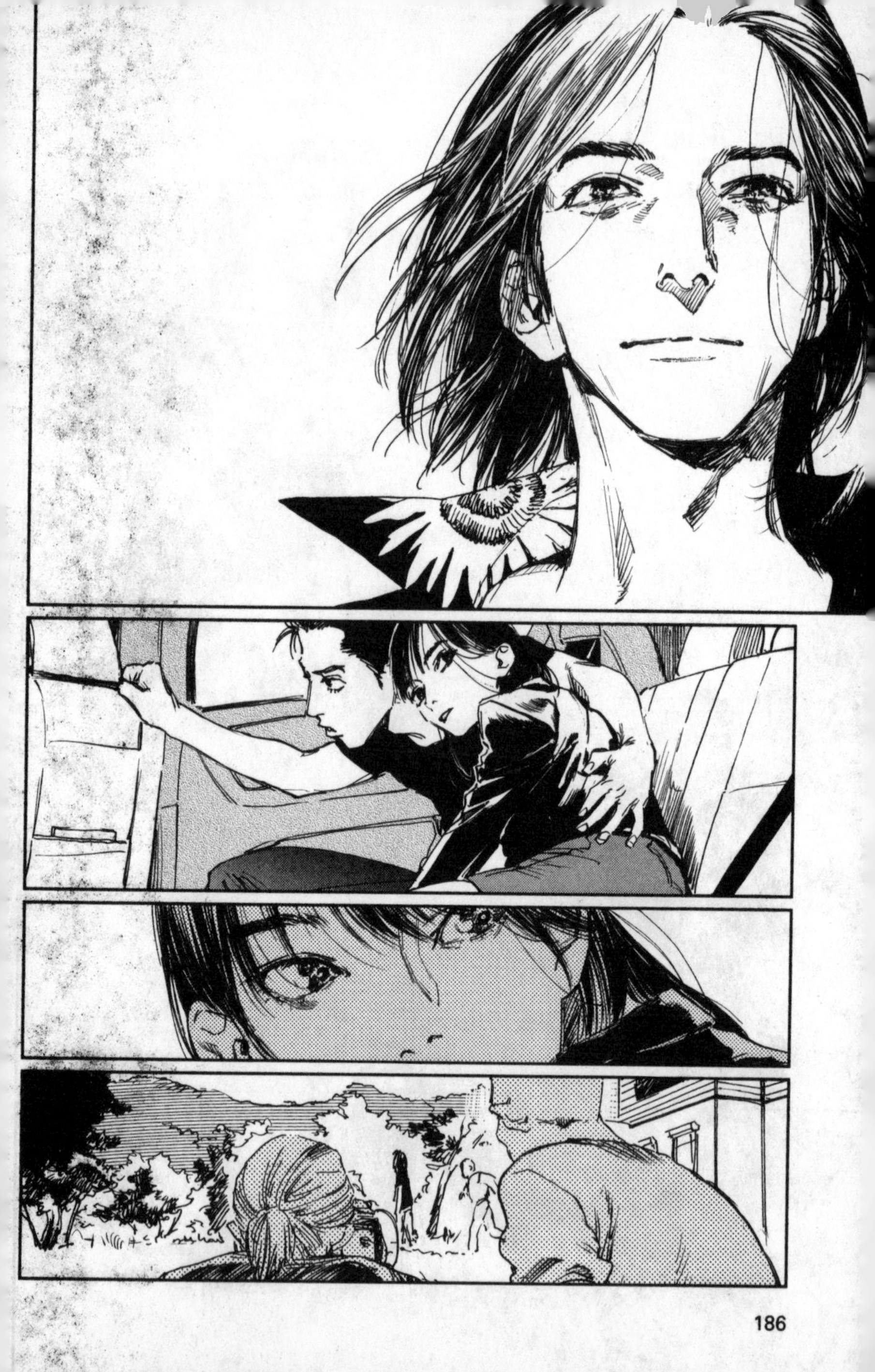

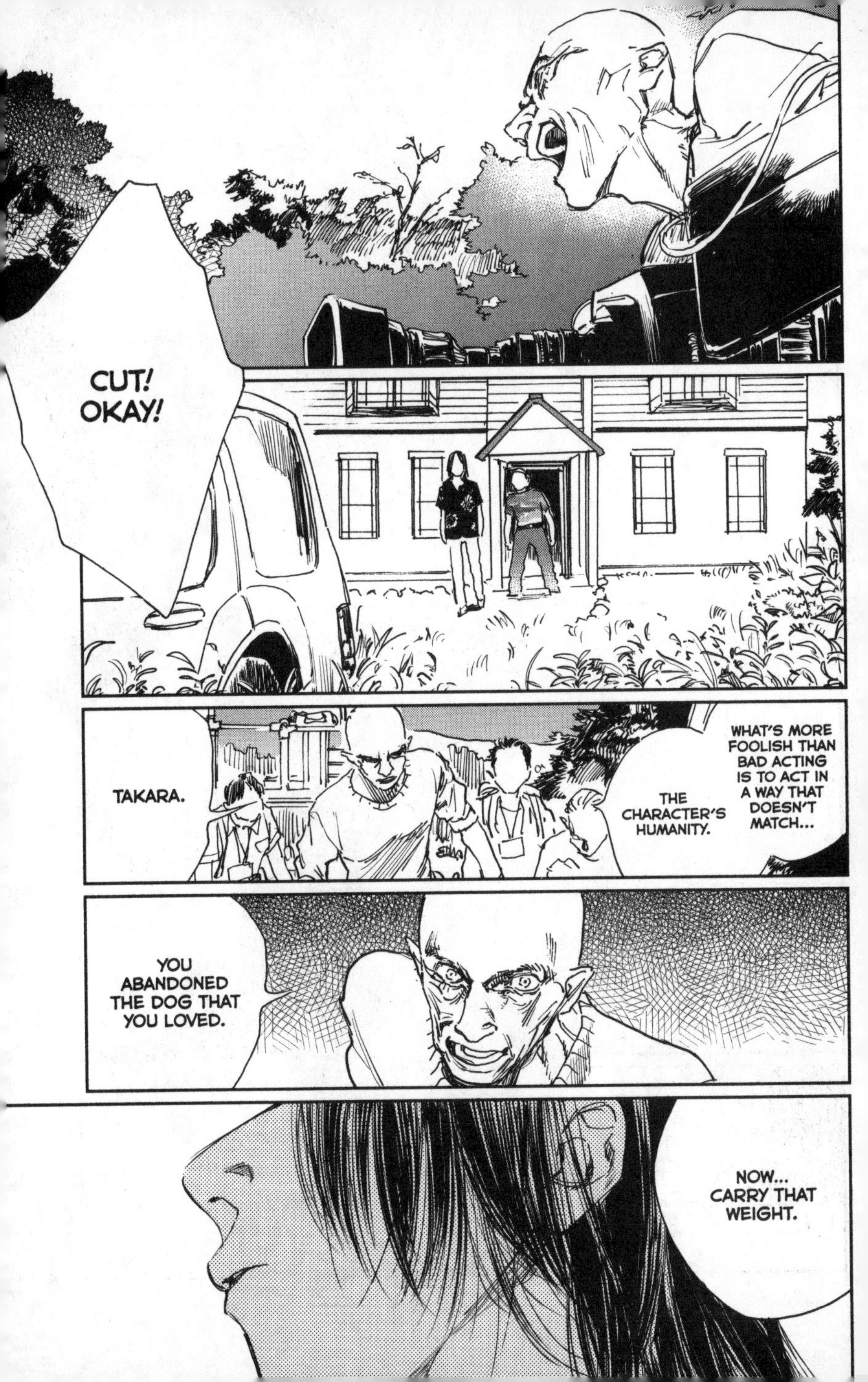
CUT! OKAY!
WHAT'S MORE FOOLISH THAN BAD ACTING IS TO ACT IN A WAY THAT DOESN'T MATCH...
THE CHARACTER'S HUMANITY.
TAKARA.
YOU ABANDONED THE DOG THAT YOU LOVED.
NOW... CARRY THAT WEIGHT.

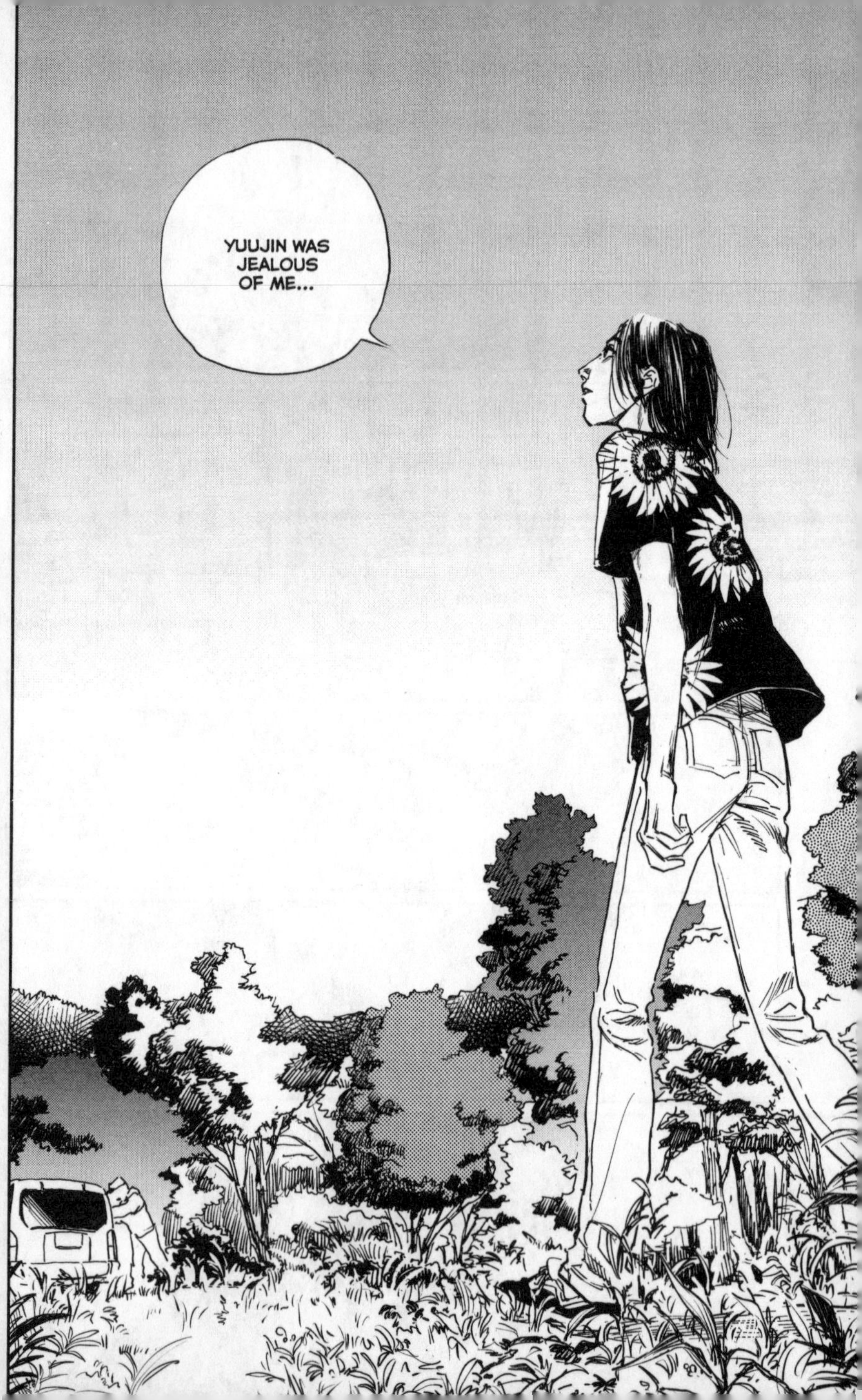
YUUJIN WAS JEALOUS OF ME...

DOUBLE VOL. 2 COMPLETE

CONTINUED IN VOL. | 3

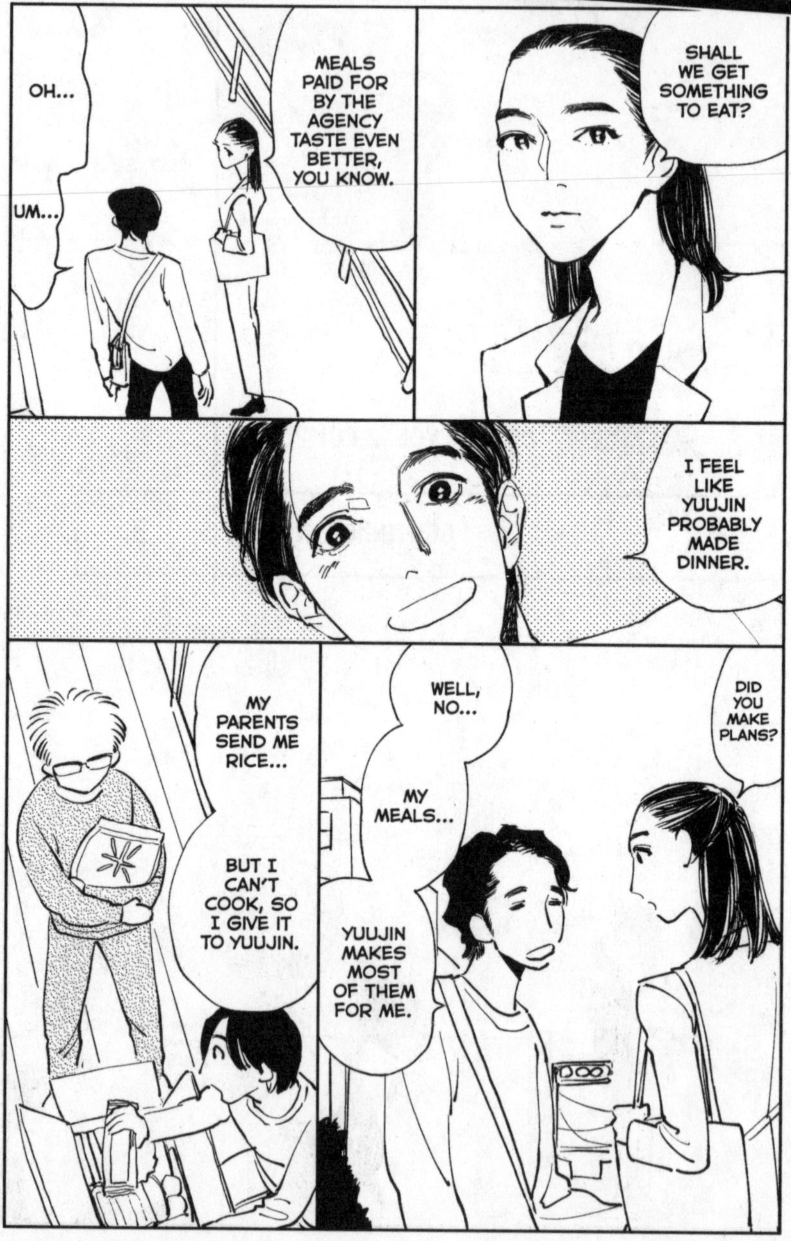
SHALL WE GET SOMETHING TO EAT?
MEALS PAID FOR BY THE AGENCY TASTE EVEN BETTER, YOU KNOW.
OH...
UM...
I FEEL LIKE YUUJIN PROBABLY MADE DINNER.
DID YOU MAKE PLANS?
WELL, NO...
MY MEALS...
YUUJIN MAKES MOST OF THEM FOR ME.
MY PARENTS SEND ME RICE...
BUT I CAN'T COOK, SO I GIVE IT TO YUUJIN.

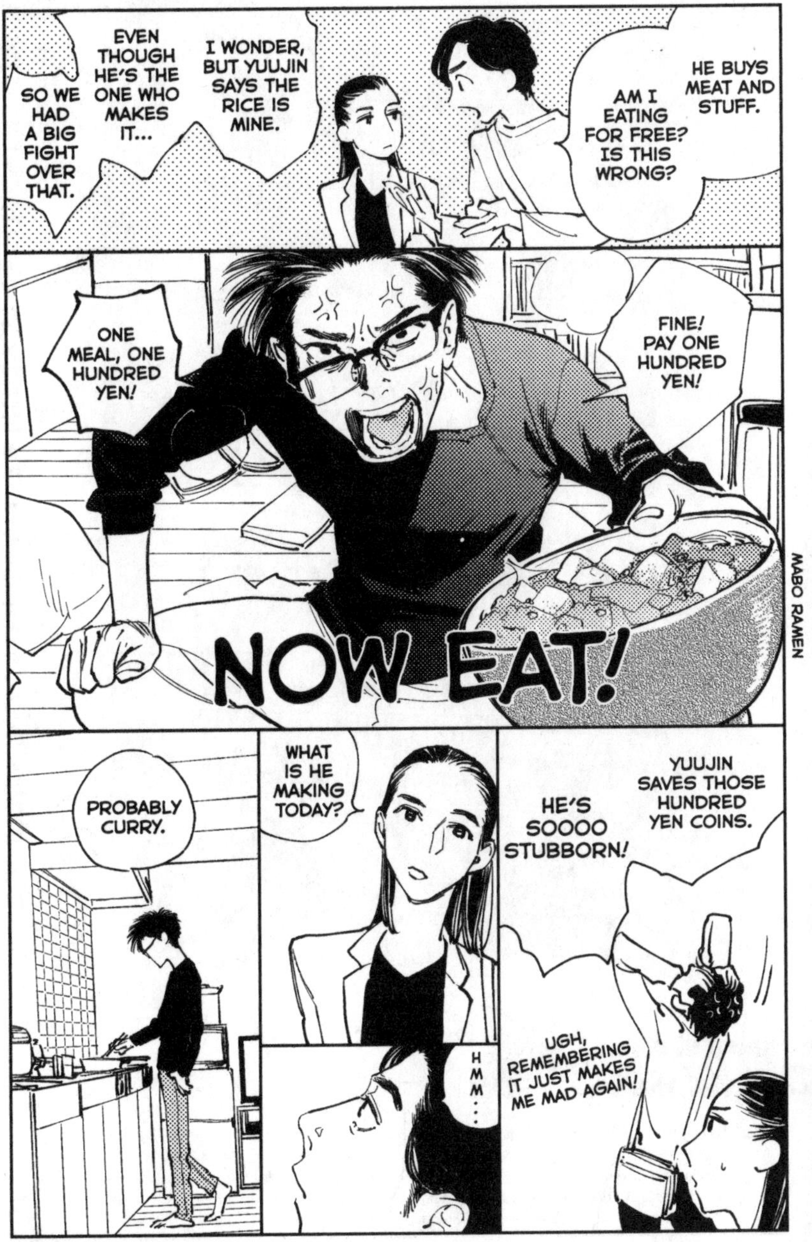
HE BUYS MEAT AND STUFF.
AM I EATING FOR FREE? IS THIS WRONG?
I WONDER, BUT YUUJIN SAYS THE RICE IS MINE.
EVEN THOUGH HE'S THE ONE WHO MAKES IT...
SO WE HAD A BIG FIGHT OVER THAT.
FINE! PAY ONE HUNDRED YEN!
ONE MEAL, ONE HUNDRED YEN!
NOW EAT!
MABO RAMEN
YUUJIN SAVES THOSE HUNDRED YEN COINS.
HE'S SOOOO STUBBORN!
UGH, REMEMBERING IT JUST MAKES ME MAD AGAIN!
WHAT IS HE MAKING TODAY?
HMM...
PROBABLY CURRY.

THE END

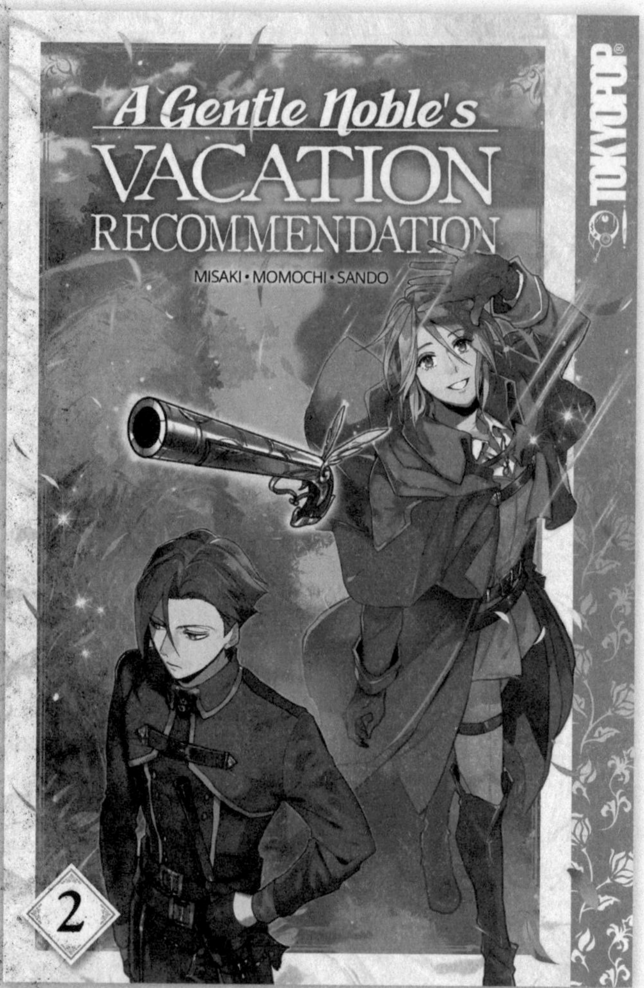
A Gentle Noble's
VACATION
RECOMMENDATION
MISAKI • MOMOCHI • SANDO
TOKYOPOP
2

A GENTLE NOBLE'S VACATION RECOMMENDATION, VOLUME 2

Momochi, Misaki, Sando

FANTASY

After their first successful adventure together, Lizel has officially formed a party with his guard and companion, the famous adventurer Gil. A renowned swordsman known by the moniker Single Stroke for his ability to take down any enemy with just one swipe, Gil has promised to protect Lizel as they become an official part of the adventurer's guild — and the two are already making waves!

It's time for the newly-formed party to prove their mettle!

TOKYOPOP

OSSAN IDOL! VOLUME 2

Mochiko Mochida, Ichika Kino

ICHIKA KINO • MOCHIKO MOCHIDA

IDOL

With the help of producer extraordinaire Kamo Lavender, three (almost) middle-aged men are about to take Japan by storm as a group of Ossan Idols! When Miroku (age 36) accidentally uploaded a video of himself singing and dancing, it quickly went viral. Inspired by his talent and immediate popularity, his friends Yoichi (age 40) and Shiju (age 40) teamed up with him to perform in a competition, where they were discovered by the famous producer himself. Now, the three suddenly have their own radio show, song lyrics, devoted fans, and a debut live performance in a prominent shopping district. Things are really starting to heat up for the unlikely idol group!

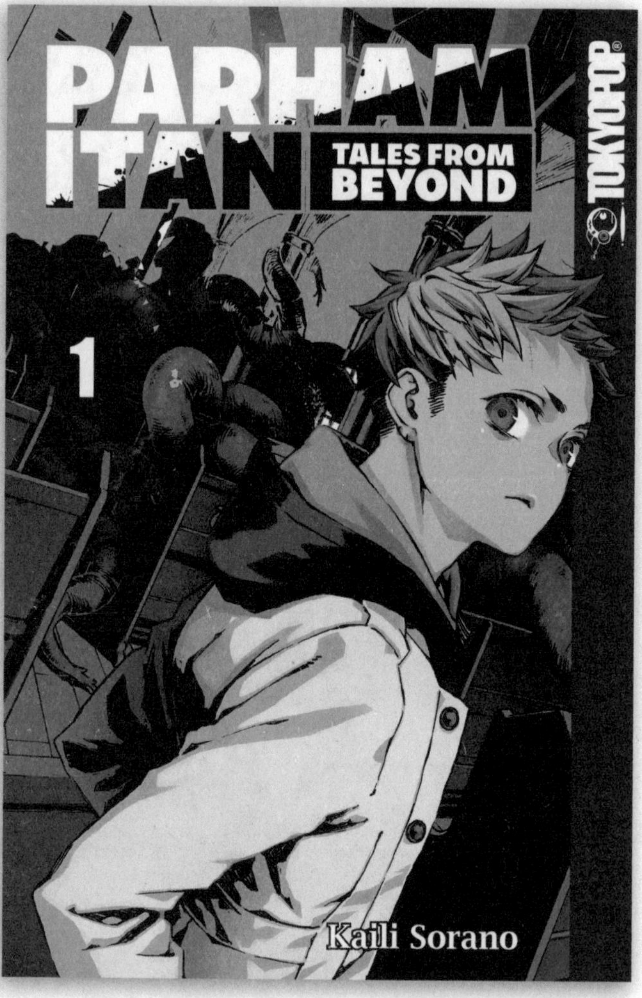
PARHAM ITAN
TALES FROM BEYOND
TOKYOPOP
1
Kaili Sorano

PARHAM ITAN: TALES FROM BEYOND, VOLUME 1

Kaili Sorano

SUPERNATURAL

Yamagishi and Sendo are schoolmates, but that's about as far as their similarities go: one is a short, no-nonsense boxer, while the other is a tall, bookish conspiracy nut. But when they find themselves embroiled in a paranormal phenomenon at school involving plant-faced monster people assimilating innocent victims, it seems they'll have to set aside their differences and work together as best as they can. Of course, it doesn't help that the only one with any answers to this bizarre situation is a mysterious "paranormal investigator" named Akisato, who insists they must find some sort of "key" to stop it all — before giant insects and other preternatural perils from the world "beyond" get to them first. Inspired by Lovecraftian horror and the *Call of Cthulhu*, this is a brand-new manga series from the creator of *Monochrome Factor!*

LAUGHING UNDER THE CLOUDS, VOLUME 2

KarakaraKemuri

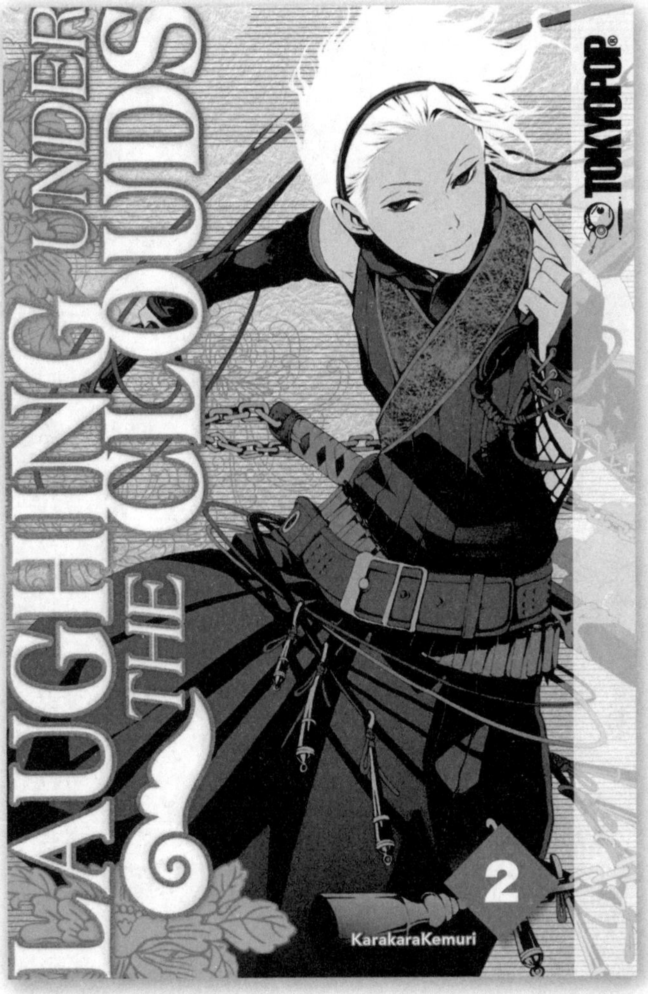

LAUGHING UNDER THE CLOUDS
TOKYOPOP
2
KarakaraKemuri

SUPERNATURAL

A dreaded murderer intrudes on the Kumo family's peace and brings with him news of an ancient calamity: Orochi. As Soramaru realizes his elder brother Tenka has been hiding things from him, he begins to look to outside sources to help him become stronger. At the same time, still other outside forces begin to reach out to Tenka for his knowledge of this ancient evil. The race to find and control Orochi's vessel begins!

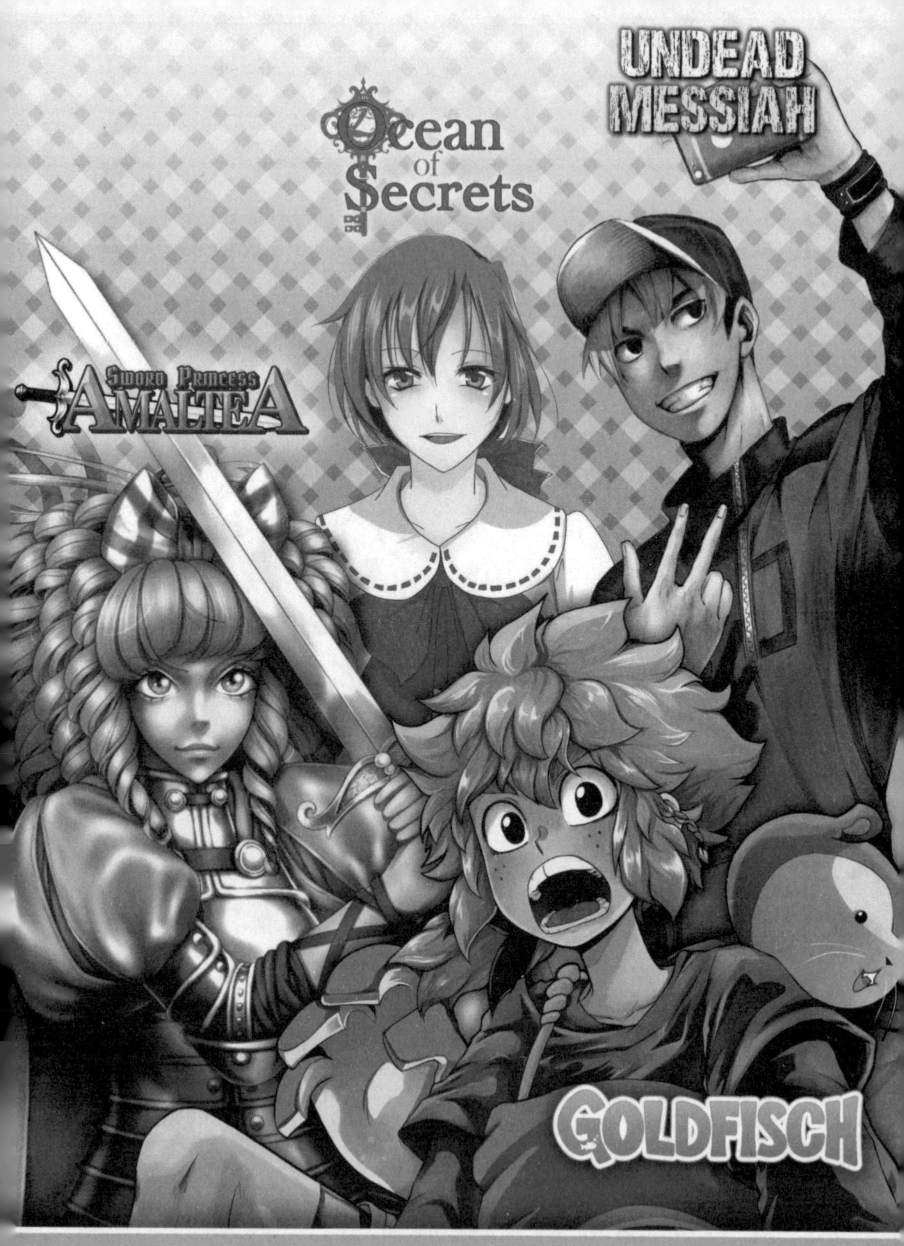
UNDEAD MESSIAH
Ocean of Secrets
Sword Princess AMALTEA
GOLDFISCH

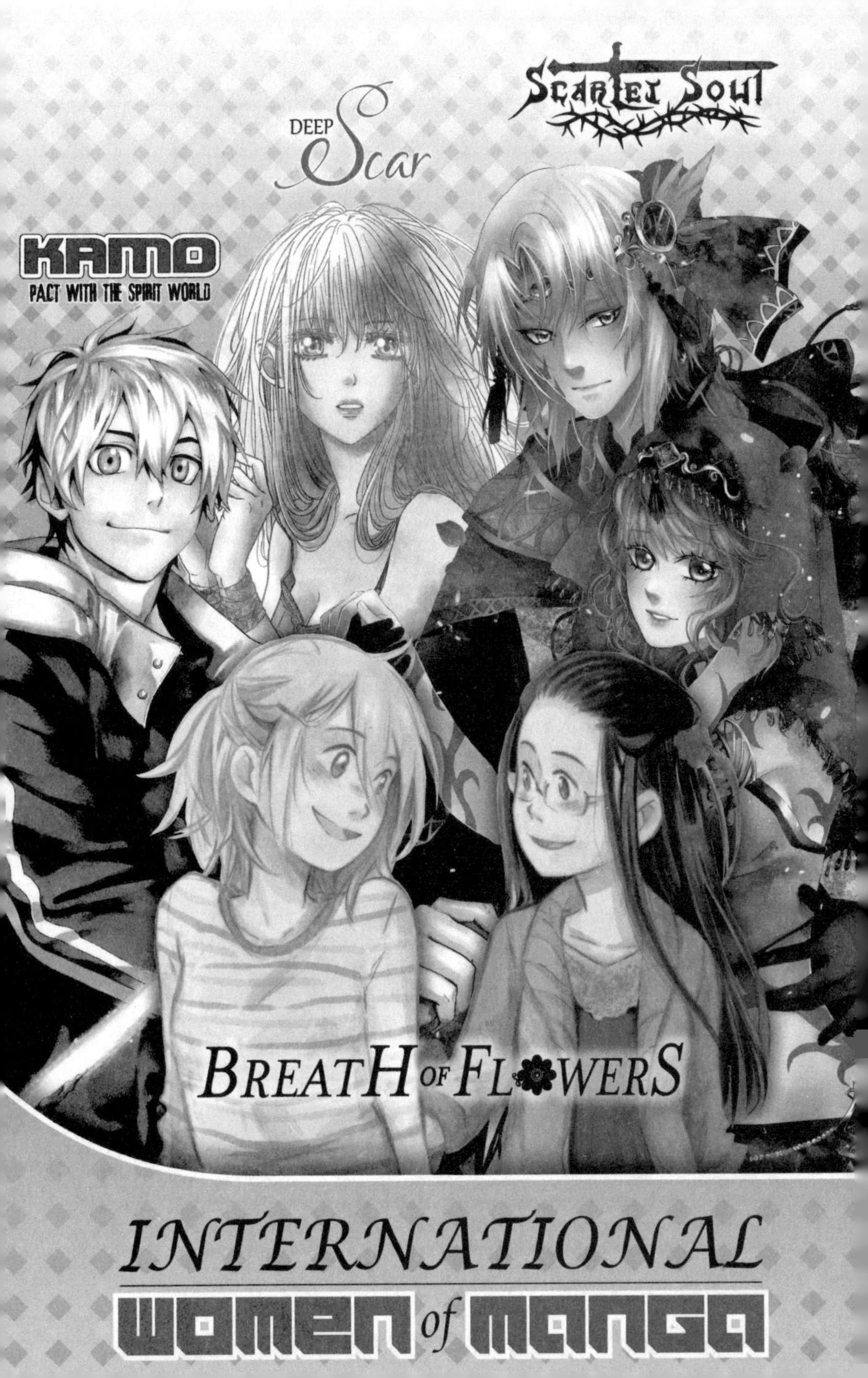

SCARLET SOUL
DEEP Scar
KAMO
PACT WITH THE SPIRIT WORLD
BREATH OF FLOWERS
INTERNATIONAL
WOMEN of MANGA

UNDEAD MESSIAH, VOLUME 1

Gin Zarbo

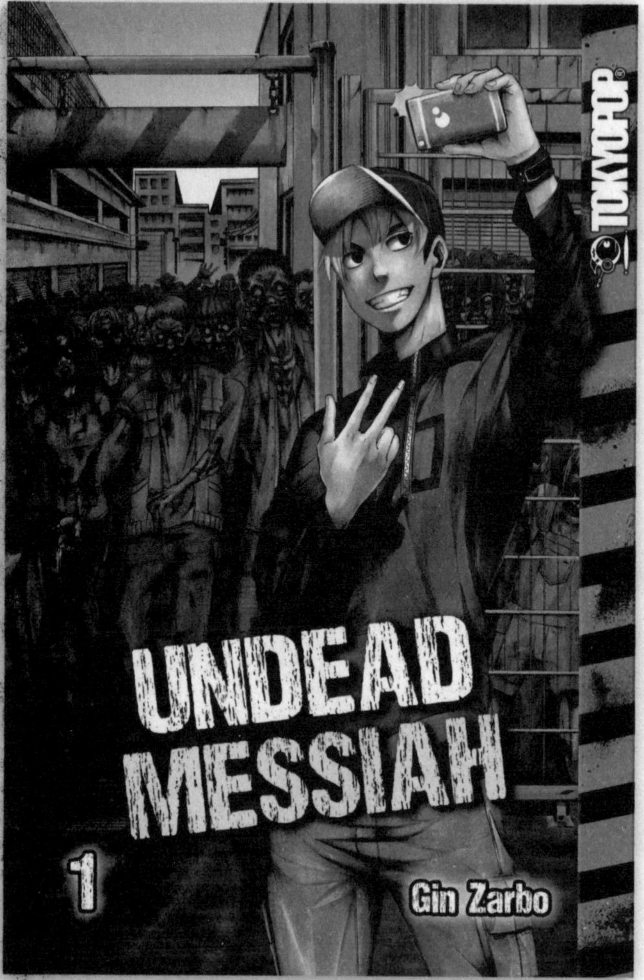
TOKYOPOP
UNDEAD MESSIAH
1
Gin Zarbo

SUPERNATURAL

A pregnant woman is pursued by a supernatural creature. On the internet, videos of a bandaged hero surface. 15-year-old Tim Muley makes a terrible discovery in his neighbor's garden. Three seemingly unrelated events, all of which seem to point to an imminent zombie apocalypse! But this time the story's not about the end of mankind; it's about a new beginning...

KAMO: PACT WITH THE SPIRIT WORLD, VOLUME 1

Ban Zarbo

KAMO
PACT WITH THE SPIRIT WORLD
TOKYOPOP
1
Ban Zarbo

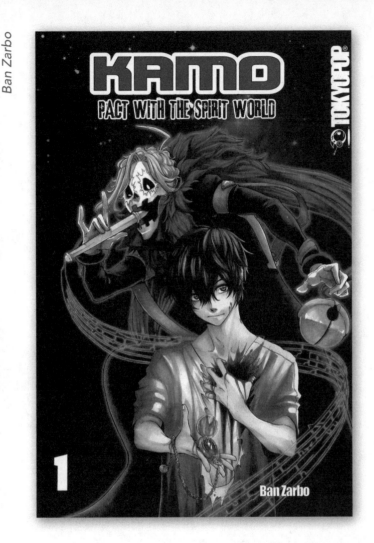

SUPERNATURAL

Born with a failing heart, Kamo has fought death his whole life, but to no avail. As his body weakens and he readies to draw his final breath, he's visited by a powerful spirit named Crimson who offers him a deal: defeat and capture the souls of twelve spirits in exchange for a new heart. It seems too good to be true... and maybe it is. A pact with the spirit world; what could possibly go wrong?

TOKYOPOP

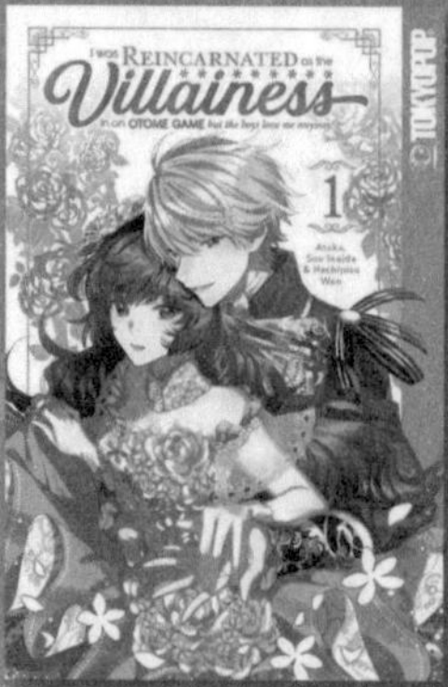
I was REINCARNATED as the Villainess in an OTOME GAME but the boys love me anyway!
1
TOKYOPOP

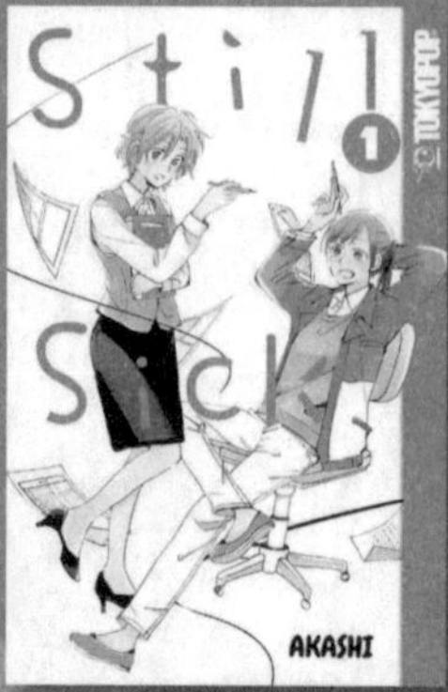
Still Sick
1
AKASHI
TOKYOPOP

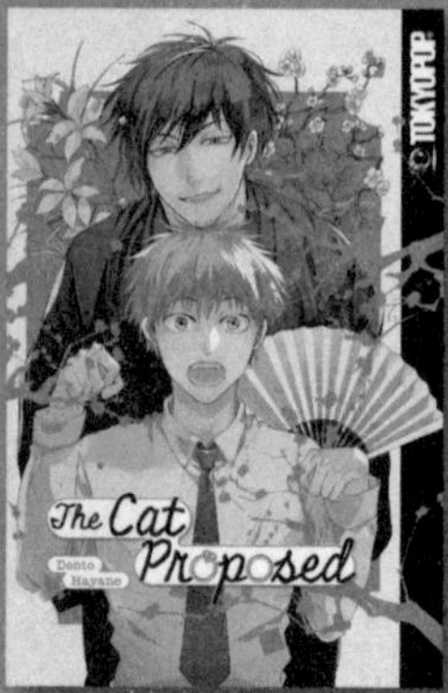
The Cat Proposed
Dento Hayane
TOKYOPOP

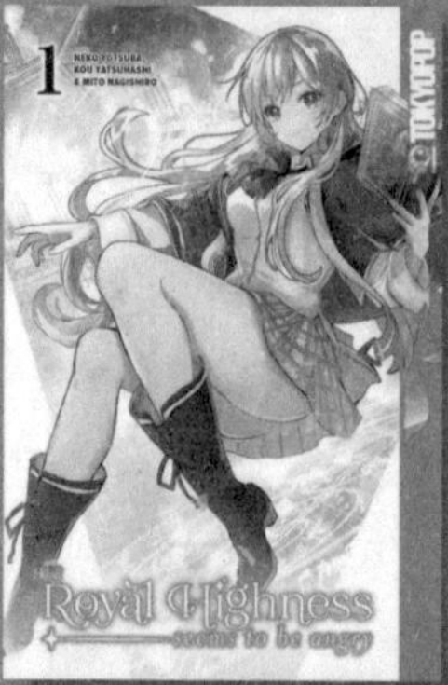
1
Royal Highness seems to be angry
TOKYOPOP

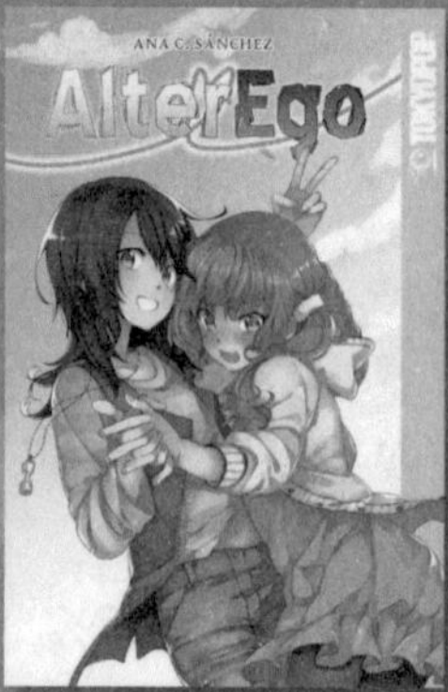
ANA C. SÁNCHEZ
AlterEgo
TOKYOPOP

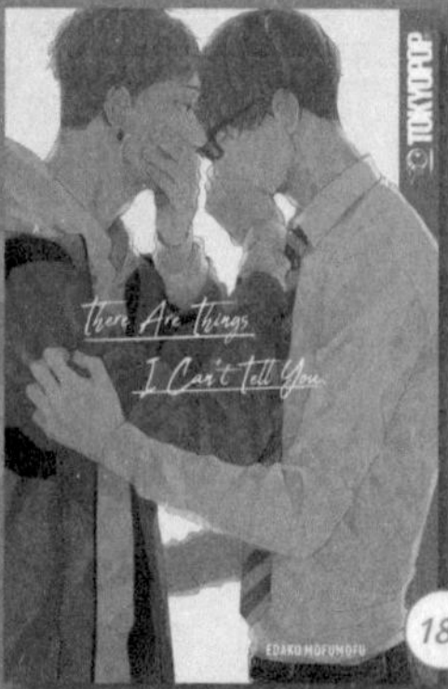
There Are Things I Can't Tell You
EDAKO MOFUMOFU
18+
TOKYOPOP

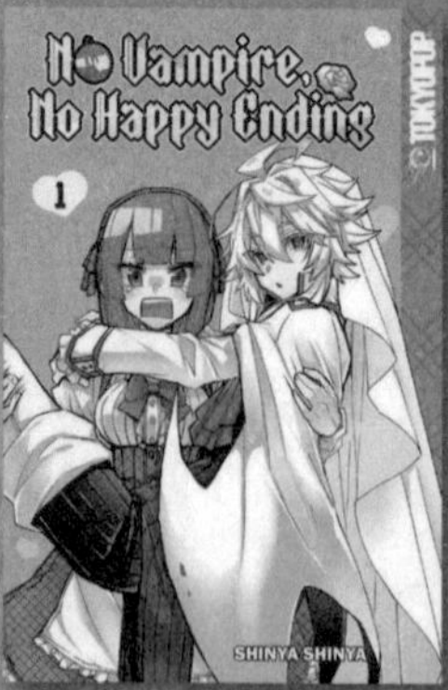
No Vampire, No Happy Ending
1
SHINYA SHINYA
TOKYOPOP

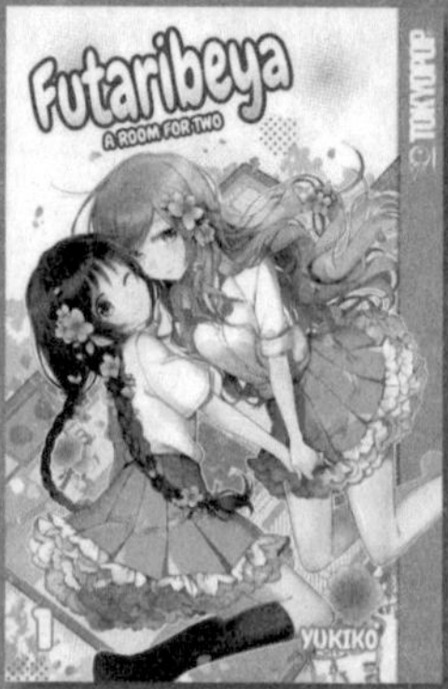
Futaribeya
A ROOM FOR TWO
1
YUKIKO
TOKYOPOP

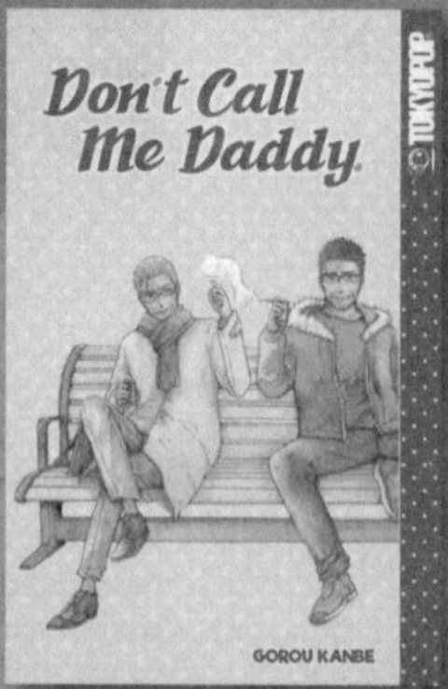
Don't Call Me Daddy
GOROU KANBE
TOKYOPOP

Check out *LOVExLOVE.info* for all kinds of romance!

LOVE x LOVE

TOKYOPOP believes all types of romances deserve to be celebrated. *LOVE x LOVE* was born from that idea and our commitment to representing a variety of stories and voices as diverse as our fans.

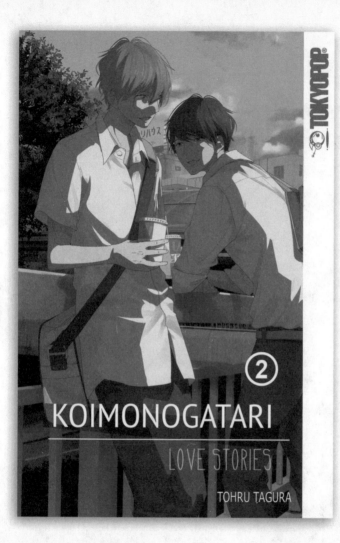

KOIMONOGATARI: LOVE STORIES, VOLUME 2

Tohru Tagura

TOKYOPOP
2
KOIMONOGATARI
LOVE STORIES
TOHRU TAGURA

LOVE-x-LOVE

When Yuiji accidentally finds out his classmate Yamato is gay, he doesn't know how to react. But after spending more time together, the two of them become close friends. While Yamato struggles with his sexuality, Yuiji supports him. Meanwhile, Yuiji is having trouble feeling connected to his long-time girlfriend, realizing that although he still cares about her, the spark in their relationship has faded. Love is a complicated, messy thing — especially in high school, where hurtful rumors and intolerant classmates can make life unbearable. Yamato and Yuiji face their own individual struggles, but together, they learn one very important lesson: it's hard to search for romance if you don't love yourself first.

TOKYOPOP

KATAKOI LAMP
Kyohei Azumi

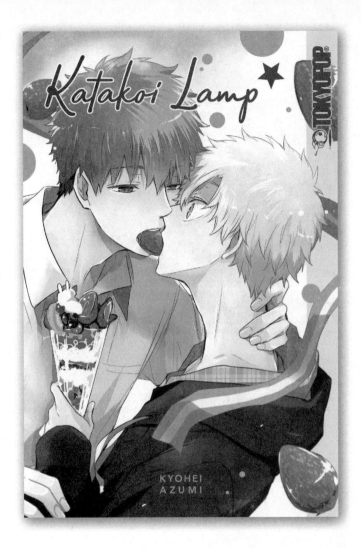

Kazuto Muronoi runs a cute little coffee shop, where many people enjoy doing some work or writing papers for school. Among his coffee shop's regulars is a college student named Jun, who often studies there. It was love at first sight for Kazuto! Will Kazuto be able to find the courage to confess his crush before Jun graduates college and stops frequenting the shop? And to make matters even more complicated... it seems Jun has his sights set on another worker at the café!

OUR NOT-SO-LONELY PLANET TRAVEL GUIDE, VOLUME 2

Mone Sorai

TOKYOPOP
MONE SORAI 2
Our not-so Lonely Planet Travel Guide

LOVE-x-LOVE

Super-serious Asahi Suzumura and easygoing Mitsuki Sayama may seem like an odd couple, but they made a deal — they'll vacation together around the world, and when they return to Japan, they'll get married.

But after the first leg of their journey went so smoothly, perhaps it was inevitable that the next would hit some snags. Despite schedule mishaps and a surprise illness, the amazing food and new friends they find along their journey make up for any troubles. Even though they're far from home, each new destination is an opportunity to become closer to each other.

TOKYOPOP

THE CAT PROPOSED

Dento Hayane

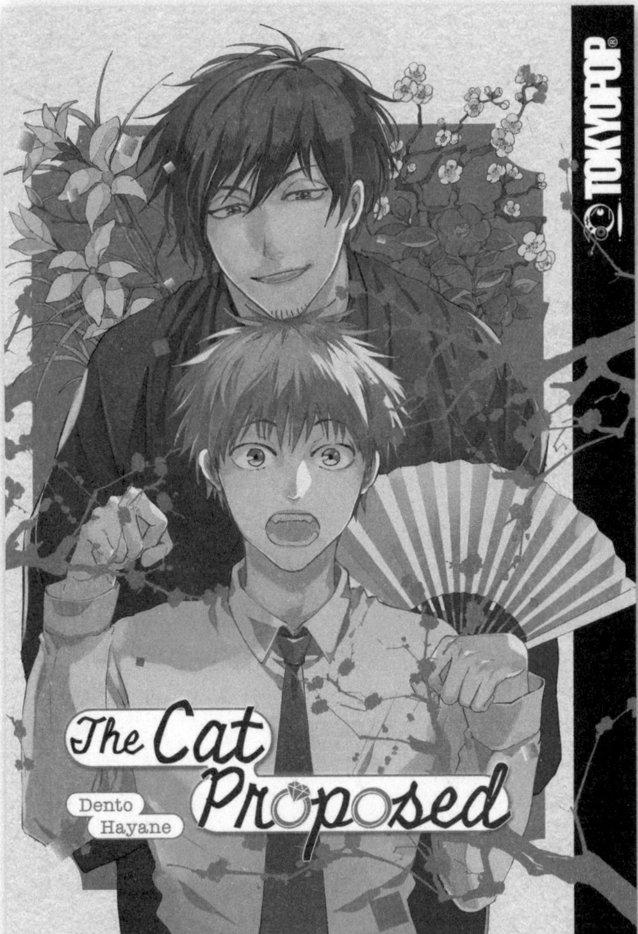
TOKYOPOP
The Cat Proposed
Dento Hayane

LOVE x LOVE

Matoi Souta is an overworked office worker tired of his life. Then, on his way home from a long day of work one day, he decides to watch a traditional Japanese play. But something strange happens. He could have sworn he saw one of the actors has cat ears. It turns out that the man is actually a bakeneko — a shapeshifting cat from Japanese folklore. And then, the cat speaks: "From now on, you will be my mate."

Double, Volume 2
Manga by Ayako Noda

Editor	-	Lena Atanassova
Translator	-	Massiel Gutierrez
Copy Editor	-	Tina Tseng
Quality Check	-	Daichi Nemoto
Proofreader	-	Katie Kimura
Cover & Logo Designer	-	Sol DeLeo
Editorial Associate	-	Janae Young
Retouching and Lettering	-	Vibrraant Publishing Studio
Licensing Specialist	-	Arika Yanaka
Editor-in-Chief & Publisher	-	Stu Levy

A  Manga

TOKYOPOP and 🐸 are trademarks or registered trademarks of TOKYOPOP Inc.

TOKYOPOP Inc.
5200 W. Century Blvd. Suite 705
Los Angeles, 90045

E-mail: info@TOKYOPOP.com
Come visit us online at www.TOKYOPOP.com

f www.facebook.com/TOKYOPOP
▶ www.twitter.com/TOKYOPOP
◉ www.instagram.com/TOKYOPOP

ISBN: 978-1-4278-6909-8
First TOKYOPOP Printing: March 2022
Printed in CANADA

STOP

THIS IS THE BACK OF THE BOOK!

How do you read manga-style? It's simple! Let's practice -- just start in the top right panel and follow the numbers below!

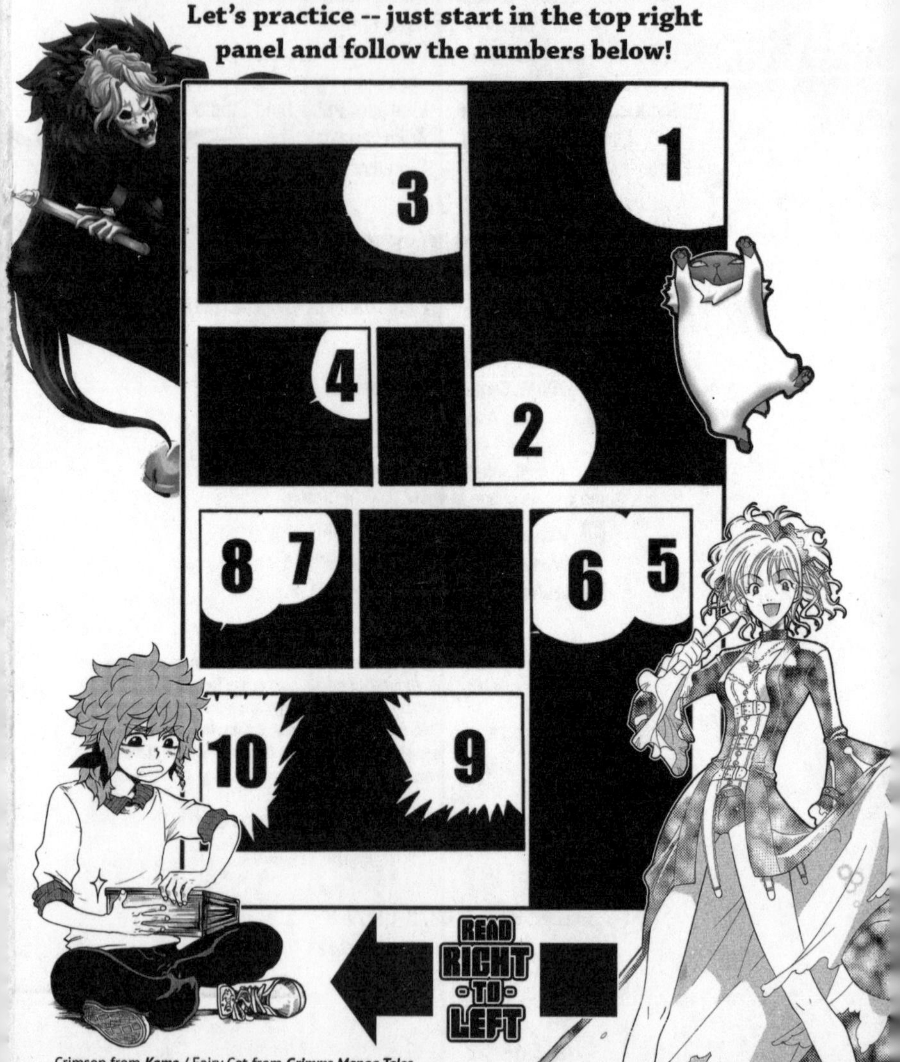
1
2
3
4
5
6
7
8
9
10
READ
RIGHT
-TO-
LEFT

Crimson from ***Kamo*** / Fairy Cat from ***Grimms Manga Tales***
Morrey from ***Goldfisch*** / Princess Ai from ***Princess Ai***